Modern Real Estate Management

William M. Shenkel

Professor of Real Estate
University of Georgia

McGraw-Hill Book Company

New York   St. Louis   San Francisco   Auckland   Bogotá   Hamburg
Johannesburg   London   Madrid   Mexico   Montreal   New Delhi
Panama   Paris   São Paulo   Singapore   Sydney   Tokyo   Toronto

Library of Congress Cataloging in Publication Data

Shenkel, William Monroe,   date
    Modern real estate management.

    Includes index.
    1. Real estate management. I. Title.
HD1394.S53   658'.91'3335   79-14443
ISBN 0-07-056546-5

MODERN REAL ESTATE MANAGEMENT

1 2 3 4 5 6 7 8 9 0 FGFG 7 8 3 2 1 0 9

This book was set in Press Roman by Allen Wayne Technical Corp.
The editor was Donald W. Burden; the cover was designed by Rafael Hernandez;
the production supervisor was Donna Piligra.

Contents

                Occupational Safety   44
                Fair Housing Regulations   48
                Environmental Controls   53
                Energy Legislation   57
                Summary   59

CHAPTER 4 Energy Conservation Techniques   64

                Solar Energy   65
                Building Retrofitting   68
                Energy Conservation Management   75
                Summary   78

2
MANAGEMENT OPERATIONS

CHAPTER 5 Elements of Commercial Leases   87

                The Purpose of Commercial Leases   88
                Common Lease Provisions   93
                Lease Terms for Special Purposes   100
                Summary   104

CHAPTER 6 Rental Terms   109

                Lease Objectives   109
                Rental Adjustments   113
                Summary   120

CHAPTER 7 Property Management Contracts   125

                Elements of the Management Agreement   126
                The Management Survey   138
                Summary   141

CHAPTER 8 Tenant Relations   147

                Common Law Doctrine   148
                Landlord-Tenant Responsibilities   149
                Promoting Tenant Relations   154
                Summary   160

CHAPTER 9 Management Office Organization   165

                Management Organization   166
                Establishing Management Policy   168
                Maintenance Supervision   178
                Management Personnel Policy   183
                Summary   187

3

MANAGEMENT PRACTICE

Preface

This text provides in a single source the technical information required in present-day real estate management. Until now, many of the topics covered have not been conveniently available to real estate managers. The text is organized into three parts—*Management Environment, Management Operations*, and *Management Practice*—and covers the many new topics important to current real estate management.

In Part 1 *Management Environment*, real estate management is reviewed in terms of standards of practice and career opportunities. The introductory chapter is followed by chapters on rental markets, federal legislation, and energy conservation techniques. Familiarity with the material in these four chapters is considered essential to understanding management activities.

Part 2, *Management Operations*, contains a chapter on management office organization. Elements of commercial leases and complex rental terms and contracts are covered in separate chapters, giving managers the proper background for managing a wide variety of properties. Part 2 closes with chapters on tenant relations and an explanation of property records and insurance.

The final part, *Management Practice*, deals with more specific property types. Four chapters are devoted to managing residential property—apartments, condominiums, and low-income housing. And because of their growing importance and special technical complexities, shopping centers are given a two-chapter treatment. Two chapters on office buildings and a final chapter on special purpose properties prepare the reader for managing other common property types.

In preparing this book, the author is indebted to the many individuals and firms who have reviewed portions of the manuscript or submitted illustrative material or examples. Among those who have been especially helpful are Stephen W. Brener, senior vice president, Helmsley-Spear, Inc.; John Kaufman, CPM, of Parker-Kaufman Realtors®; Clifford A. Zoll and George Bailey of Turner, Bailey and Zoll; James O. York, president, R. H. Macy Properties; Randy Wright, CPM, Investment Properties Management, Inc.; Samuel E. Dyer, operating vice president, Federated Department Stores, Inc.; and Kenneth R. Kuhn of Shindler/Cummins Residential, Inc.

Several others have read the manuscript and offered many invaluable suggestions. The author is especially thankful for the contributions of Professors Mark R. Greene, College of Business Administration, University of Georgia; Jack P. Friedman, University of Texas at Arlington; Carroll L. Gentry, Virginia Western Community College; Austin Jaffe, University of Oregon; Karl G. Pearson, University of Michigan; Thomas D. Pearson, North Texas State University; Hans J. Prufer, El Camino Community College; Stanley Salzman, American River Community College; and Donald A. White, Prince George's Community College.

It should be added that the manuscript has been improved by the conscientious work of my personal secretary, Ms. Janice Clark. Although many persons have contributed to this volume, the author assumes final responsibility for possible errors or omissions.

William M. Shenkel

Part One

Management Environment

Chapter 1

Professional Real Estate Management

After studying this chapter, you should be familiar with:
1 The growing importance of real estate management
2 The definition of a real property manager
3 The functions of real estate management
4 How property management offices contrast with owner operation
5 The advantages of professional management
6 Methods of developing professional management expertise from industry sources
7 Career opportunities in real estate management

Today, real estate management is a highly technical specialty. This was not always the case. In the beginning, property managers were not much more than rent collectors. To show how the property manager's role has changed to a more professional status, it is deemed worthwhile to discuss the importance of real estate management and then turn to an explanation of the real property manager's function. A review of management organizations that promote professional real estate management concludes the chapter.

THE IMPORTANCE OF REAL ESTATE MANAGEMENT

Before the Depression of the 1930s there was little need for real property managers. At that time investment properties had been largely under the control of private individuals. These individuals dealt with real estate agents, who collected rent and performed minimal custodial duties as an accommodation to property owners. Indeed, the Institute of Real Estate Management (IREM), an affiliate of the National Association of Realtors ® (NAR), was not organized until 1933. The growing importance of real estate management may be illustrated by tracing the early development of the real estate management field.

Early Developments

Consider the environment affecting property ownership in the early 1930s, before the long-term amortized mortgage. Federal income taxes were not a factor affecting real estate ownership. Recall further that this was the era of the streetcar and the dominant position of the downtown area for shopping, for government offices, for entertaining, and even for dwellings and apartments. There were few large projects—apartment buildings were limited ordinarily to less than 50 units. And since the population was less mobile, there was little need to offset high tenant turnover with a leasing promotion campaign. Many downtown proprietors owned their own land and buildings.

In this environment, professional development of property managers began during the 1930s Depression when banks foreclosed on office buildings, apartment houses, and other income properties. Experienced in banking operations, these institutions had no specialized personnel to handle the management of income properties. For this reason, the Institute of Real Estate Management was organized to educate, train, and qualify persons in real estate management.

Current Trends

Even during the last generation, ownership of real property and its management has been affected by certain institutional changes that have created an even greater need for skilled real estate managers. For example, regional shopping centers, which were originally constructed in open space, are now almost universally being remodeled as air-conditioned, enclosed malls. The newer "super" regional centers are often constructed as multiple-story shopping complexes. Apartment projects that include 500 or more apartment units are quite common. Office buildings of more than 100 stories require supervision of a management staff numbering over 300 persons.

Besides these trends, other changes have affected real estate as an investment. When the Institute of Real Estate Management started, investors did not have to contend with the complex real estate mortgages of today—the wraparound mortgages, leasehold mortgages, secondary financing, equity participation, and many other complex financing arrangements. The present federal income tax forces investors to seek expert advice on the tax consequences of owning and operating income real estate. Others must counsel developers on the environmental effects of new construction.

It should be added that, because of the Energy Conservation Standards for New Buildings Act of 1976, the Department of Energy will enforce energy performance standards for new buildings late in 1979. Accordingly managers must advise property owners on the feasibility of adding energy conservation techniques for existing buildings.

Demographic changes have created a need for the highly informed specialist. Because of the mobility of the population, managers must make special efforts to reduce tenant turnover and to continually recruit new tenants. This mobility is the result of frequent job and residence changes. Buildings have been adapted to serve more single households, which have different needs in apartments and shopping facilities than households with married couples and children.

Truly, real estate management today bears little resemblance to management operations of the early 1930s. Because of more recent institutional changes, real estate managers increasingly require more technical expertise. A brief review of modern management functions supports this point.

THE FUNCTION OF REAL ESTATE MANAGEMENT

Property managers may be defined as *real estate experts who manage real estate for a fee to maximize the benefits of ownership.* The benefits in operating property may lie mainly in their use as a tax shelter. In other instances property is managed to secure the highest capital appreciation. More commonly, management seeks to maximize net income.

Some real estate offices offer property management services as a supplement to brokerage operations. Others concentrate on property management for both the small property owner and the larger projects organized and owned by corporations and limited partnerships. Here brokerage services merely supplement the management business. Their diversified practice ranges over many property types: multiple family projects, duplexes, single-family dwelling rentals, shopping centers, downtown retail space, suburban office parks, industrial parks, mobile home parks, motels and hotels, recreational property, and others. Some managers specialize in operating farms. Those who specialize in farm management and who meet member qualifications may join the American Society of Farm Managers and Rural Appraisers, Inc.

Add to these groups property managers who largely confine their expertise to highly specialized properties. In the larger metropolitan centers will be found offices that have developed reputations for their skill, background, and experience in managing office buildings, apartments, or condominiums. Others concentrate on shopping centers, including their development, management, and sale.

The concept of a property manager should not exclude property managers who work directly for owner-occupants. Many of the larger corporations have established real estate departments to manage buildings operated for their own use, such as telephone companies, utilities, industrial corporations, and government offices like the U.S. Postal Service.

In the broader sense, property managers must have the qualities attributed to the successful real estate broker. Though property managers do not market the fee title, they are responsible for *marketing space,* which requires the skills associated with the sale of real estate. In a more specialized sense, property managers must have a detailed knowledge of leases and of local laws governing land and building use. They must also be successful administrators who are capable of supervising others. An accounting background helps in understanding the management reports that are issued monthly to property owners. Furthermore, the more experienced property manager is fully aware of the tax consequences of real estate ownership. A brief review of the property manager's duties illustrates the many functions of a real estate manager.

Property Manager's Responsibilities

To some extent the responsibilities of the real estate manager overlap those of other specialists, primarily real estate appraisers, real estate brokers, real estate counselors, and even mortgage bankers. Though property managers have the main duty of marketing space and managing property to maximize net income, their job requires other functions to serve the owner properly. Since the property manager acts as an agent of the principal (the owner), much as the real estate broker acts as an agent for the seller (owner), he or she acts in other capacities incidental to management.

The property manager assumes a wide range of responsibilities because of one singular advantage, which is not always shared by other real estate specialists: the real estate manager knows operating details of property under management—details that cover expenses of operation, the current rental market, and the historical operating experience.

Moreover, since the manager specializes in dealing with many rentable properties, more than any other specialist, the property manager has superior knowledge of the market for space, knowledge that is derived from a daily exposure to the market. The property manager will have knowledge not only of a single property but also of numerous other properties, and this scope provides a keener insight into rental opportunities.

Marketing Space   Renting space to give the maximum operating income is the central task facing property managers. If the rent is established at below-market levels, virtually full occupancy will be experienced but at less than market rents and with below average net operating income. On the other hand if the space is overpriced, tenants move to more economical space supplying better services, which increases the vacancy to above-normal rates.

While the marketing function may override other responsibilities, property managers must ensure that services to tenants and the quality of management meet tenant demands. Depending on the locality and tenants served, an apartment house might require operation of a swimming pool, a door operator, cable TV service, and numerous other amenities.

Custodial Responsibilities   The property manager is directly involved in the level of services and their cost and quality. Daily maintenance such as cleaning of public areas, windows, garbage collection, and redecorating of public areas are among the tasks falling under supervision of the property manager. More experienced managers will keep the level of maintenance consistent with high occupancy rates while guarding against overmaintenance and excessive costs. Showing premises to prospective tenants and supervising the timely payment of rent are some other management duties.

Property Records Unlike other businesses, the management office must maintain separate trust accounts, deposits, and records of each managed property. Typically owners are given a monthly statement of receipts and expenditures, which in some instances gives monthly data accompanied by a comparison with the same month of the past year. An annual summary may be prepared for income tax records. Responsibility for records that comply with local, state, and federal tax laws will be assumed by the manager.

Expense Analysis Property owners face a dilemma under inflationary conditions. Property operation requires labor, materials, and utilities, all of which follow unpredictable price increases. Rent receipts tend to lag behind these rising costs—principally because rents are negotiated once a year at most, or over a 3- to 5-year period, or typically for commercial space, over longer terms. Even with adjustment clauses, there is a tendency for expenses to increase more rapidly than rental receipts.

Consequently, and consistent with the agent responsibility, the manager must review personnel practices, expenditures, and the level of services that bear on operating costs. This is particularly critical for utility expenses—an area in which the property manager recommends retrofitting techniques that reduce energy costs.

Counseling Services Technological advance, changes in the local economy, population increases (or decreases), and related events frequently call for land-use change. The luxury apartment constructed 25 years ago may become middle-income housing today. The neighborhood shopping center, originally the highest and best land use, today may be more suitable for high-rise elevator apartments.

Even if no property use change is contemplated, the property manager must recommend the optimum rehabilitation, remodeling, or renovation. In this role, the property manager will show the anticipated rent following from rehabilitation. The property owner will be shown the added investment and anticipated cost and net operating income to be achieved by following property manager recommendations.

Financial Analysis It may be anticipated that certain property owners are more concerned with the after-tax effects of property ownership. Moreover at some point, because of declining income tax deductions over the property life, owners may be advised to sell and reinvest in other real estate assets. Similarly, there may be certain tax advantages in negotiating a tax-deferred exchange.

In these circumstances, the property manager with detailed knowledge of operating results makes complex financial studies that show rates of return under varying finance, income tax, and capital gain tax assumptions. In this latter role the property manager guides the owner to that decision which satisfies investment objectives.

Office Organization

It would be difficult indeed to generalize on the organization of the typical real estate management office. To be sure, in the larger metropolitan areas, property management is highly organized with managers specializing by property types. More often, property management is part of other real estate operations such as real estate brokerage.

Contrast professional property management with owner operations. Without professional management, an apartment owner must keep records and supervise the resident manager and the maintenance staff. With professional management, the owner-principal employs the manager who acts as his or her agent. In serving in this capacity, the manager employs a resident manager to perform daily custodial duties and to enforce management policy. Though property managers supervise operations, they act within the authority granted by their owner-principals. As agent, the property manager must act in the best interest of the principal. These relationships are shown in Figure 1-1.

Though varying by other operations of the firm, property managers organize to supervise four main operations (see Figure 1-2). Starting with the senior property manager, the office staff specializes on sales and leasing, supervision of residential managers, and accounting, with all its recordkeeping and responsibilities for cash and related services. More highly organized offices employ a sales staff whose prime responsibility is to lease vacant space. Some offices pay "space brokers" a commission or a combination of a salary and bonus. They not only negotiate leases but make market surveys that are important to prospective tenants.

The supervision of residential managers incorporates the service function. On behalf of owners the property manager makes expenditures that are necessary for

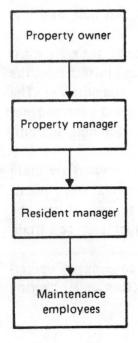

Figure 1-1 Property management relationships.

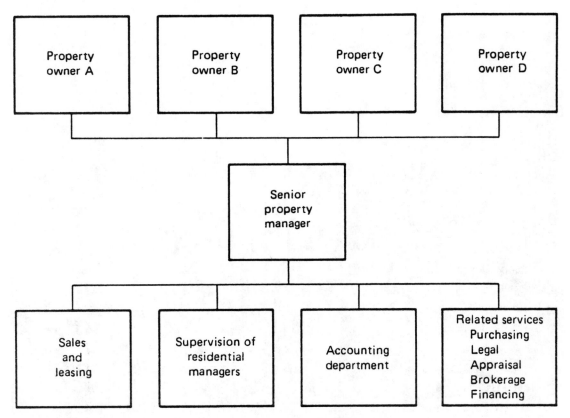

Figure 1-2 An outline of property management organization.

day-to-day operations. Special training programs help residential managers who serve under experienced property managers.

The recordkeeping function falls under the accounting department, which is responsible for all cash deposits and periodic reports to owners. The importance of this function will be appreciated in that each managed property constitutes a separate record which has its own separate deposit, profit and loss, and balance sheet accounting records.

Related services illustrated in Figure 1-2 cover the many arrangements found among property management offices. Their importance depends on the size of the firm and its source of income. In some offices the brokerage operation assumes greater importance and is only supplemented by limited property management. In other companies the property management function assumes greater importance, with real estate brokerage added as a client service. The larger firms will have specialists in purchasing supplies, lawyers to review contracts and leases, and appraisal and financing services.

Managing a Community of Tenants

Few laypersons appreciate the complexity of property management. The management of large-scale shopping centers, apartments, or office buildings calls for supervision of a wide range of skills. These duties are in addition to leasing space and dealing with several hundred or even thousands of tenants and their employees.

Consider for example the Sears Tower Building of downtown Chicago. Shown in the center of Figure 1-3, the 110-story office building of 4½ million gross square feet

Figure 1-3 Completed in 1973, the 110-story Sears Tower in Chicago is the world's largest office building with 4½ million gross square feet. *(Photo furnished courtesy of Sears, Roebuck and Company.)*

requires a 300-person custodial staff. Partly occupied by Sears, the building houses five restaurants and commercial facilities for 16,500 building occupants. The tower includes a bank, a drugstore, a health club, a barber shop, and many other specialty shops. Six automatic unmanned machines clean the exterior walls and windows eight times a year. The staff maintains 103 elevator cabs, 18 escalators, and 6 freight elevators. Since Sears occupies only 2.0 million of the 3.7 million square feet of rentable space, they employ Cushman & Wakefield, Inc. to lease and manage the building.

Advantages of Professional Management

The real estate owner has the option of managing his or her own property, turning the property over to a real estate broker with limited management experience, or delegating management to relatively inexperienced persons. Property managers appeal to informed owners who are attracted to professional management. A brief review of the advantages offered by professional managers helps to explain the management process.

Increased Occupancy Property managers know tenant requirements and they know how to maintain and present the property to gain above-average occupancy. If unusually high vacancies occur, the property manager seeks the cause and works toward its elimination. By employing trained persons to sell occupancy, the owner avoids problems in dealing with unqualified tenants who would be inappropriate for a given neighborhood shopping center, apartment project, and the like.

Reduced Tenant Turnover It is less expensive to renew a lease with an existing tenant than to solicit new tenants. For this reason, property managers operate property to gain the maximum satisfaction from present occupants. The owner benefits from the lower vacancy and the higher rental income resulting from the low tenant turnover that characterizes more professional management.

Expense Analysis Property managers, who closely supervise their maintenance employees, reduce costs by employing only experienced, efficient maintenance personnel. Since they operate more than one property, they gain superior knowledge about performance standards and about the prices of supplies and materials. Expenses are continually monitored both as percentage of gross income and as expenses per square foot to increase operating efficiency.

Property Maintenance Professional managers recommend that a certain allowance of gross income be reinvested for the optimum level of maintenance. While maintenance expenditures reduce current income, the longer-run investment motives are served with maintenance that attracts the new tenants, reduces tenant turnover, and leads to the highest possible rent. Proper maintenance helps to reduce operating expenses.

Improved Tenant Relations Resident managers and others supervised by property managers learn preferred ways of dealing with tenants. A reputation for fair dealing, which is part of professional management, helps to reduce conflicts and tenant abuse. Improved tenant relations lead to the highest possible occupancy.

Property Records Maintenance　Because of computerized property records that have been developed for a series of management contracts, owners gain from numerous monthly, annual and other periodic reports that show the status of their investments. Records maintained for income tax purposes also show the income realized on equity capital. Few individual owners could develop the detailed accounting records of the property manager—records that are essential for local, state, and federal reports.

Management Counseling　The technical and legal aspects of real estate ownership require professional counsel on preferred ways to increase operating income. In some circumstances, because of income tax factors, owners are advised to exchange or sell the property for other investments that give greater after-tax cash flow. The professional manager is in a unique position to offer this added service to the property owner.

Property Specialization　Some property managers specialize in a particular property type. There are those who concentrate on medical/dental buildings and there are those who deal exclusively with shopping centers—their development, sale, and management. Added to this list are the condominium specialists, managers who deal almost exclusively with apartment buildings, and other specialists known for their expertise in office or industrial buildings. Among this group are property managers who operate over a national or even international area and others who dominate a locality or region.

As a result of this specialization, the property owner secures expert advice and management efficiency from managers who are skilled in handling a particular property type. Few owners could duplicate the facilities available from knowledgeable specialists—providing still another reason for employing professional management. A summary of these advantages is illustrated in Figure 1-4.

PROFESSIONAL MANAGEMENT DEVELOPMENT

Property managers may associate with numerous organizations that promote professional management skills. The available organizations range from trade associations and those that provide current information on local, state, and federal regulations affecting property ownership, to others that establish minimum personal qualifications for membership. In both instances management-related organizations publish special studies, annual reports, and monthly journals, and sponsor educational conferences. The Institute of Real Estate Management of the National Association of Realtors ® provides most of these membership functions.

The Institute of Real Estate Management (IREM)

Originating in the Depression before World War II, providing professional management services for foreclosed properties, IREM is one of the affiliates of the National

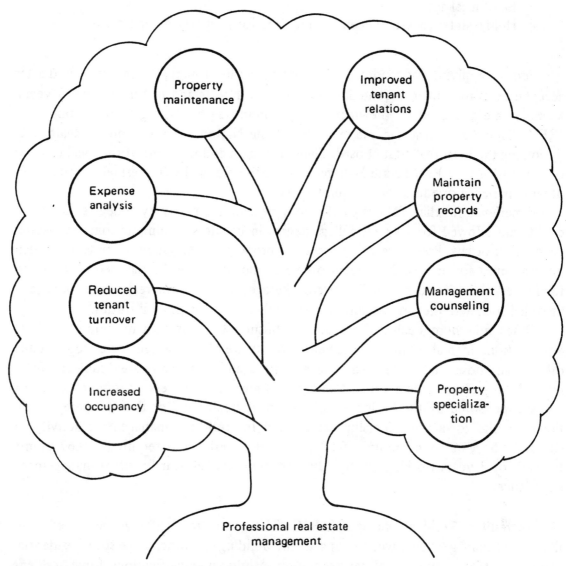

Figure 1-4 The advantages of professional real estate management.

Association of Realtors ®. At the present writing, they supervise a certification program that establishes minimum qualifications of membership. Members may qualify as a Certified Property Manager (CPM) or Accredited Residential Manager (ARM). In the case of management companies, IREM designates qualified management firms as Accredited Management Organizations (AMO).

Certified Property Manager (CPM) IREM conducts an expanding educational service to members; books on property management, *The Journal of Property Management*, and other annual reports and research studies are published for members and the public. Probably IREM is more widely known for qualifying members for the CPM designation. While requirements may change over time, candidates must:

1 Have a high school education or its equivalent
2 Have 1 year of property management experience

3 Be of legal age

4 Hold a state real estate license if required for property management

Persons applying for candidacy must be active in property management and after acceptance must remain a candidate for at least 1 year and not more than 5 years. Members are approved by the membership committee and the governing council of IREM. Candidates must become members of the National Association of Realtors ® by joining the local real estate board. They must gain endorsement of the local chapter of the Institute of Real Estate Management (or the regional vice president) and satisfy other experience or educational requirements.

Experience for the CPM designation may be acquired partly by college education—credits are allowed for a 4-year college degree in business administration, real estate, economics, or law. Points are also granted for property management experience, which must account for at least 25 percent of the applicant's time. Partial credit is awarded for related activities such as real estate brokerage, financing, or real estate appraisal—provided such activities are concurrent with real estate management duties.

Other minimum qualifications are established by passing a minimum of three examinations in real estate management. Credits are also awarded for college credits other than those that pertain to college degrees and business-related subjects, for a master's degree in majors other than real estate and business economics, and for courses sponsored by the National Association of Realtors ® or their affiliates. Additional credits toward membership are granted for full-time management activity in excess of 5 years. A minimum of 50 points of experience is required: 16.67 points for each of 3 years working under a CPM or 10 points per year for other management experience.

Accredited Resident Manager (ARM) The term "resident managers" refers to the on-site managers who work in apartment buildings or other large-scale residential complexes that require local representation. Minimum qualifications for a resident manager include successful completion of a 1-week course on "Successful On-Site Management," which covers such topics as:

human relations
selling
supervisory techniques
maintenance practices
bookkeeping
purchasing
budgeting
insurance

The ARM is awarded by meeting other experience requirements and by supplying suitable references.

Accredited Management Organization (AMO) The Institute of Real Estate Management designates firms that qualify for the AMO designation. Eligible firms must satisfy certain insurance requirements and hold fidelity bonds in favor of depositors. The firm must have been in the management business for at least 3 years and have at least one CPM in the organization who occupies an executive position. The CPM designated must have completed the course called "Managing the Management Office."

The Code of Ethics Like a real estate broker who qualifies as a Realtor ®, the CPM must observe not only the NAR code of ethics but also 11 other articles that apply to IREM members.

Article IV, for example, prohibits a CPM from accepting employment in organizations that do not comply with governmental laws, ordinances, rules, and regulations, and the IREM code of ethics. Adherence to the code requires that CPMs be loyal to their principals and diligent in maintaining and protecting their property.

As also required by agency law, CPMs must not represent conflicting interests or engage in activity that can be reasonably calculated to be contrary to the interests of their principal. Property managers who purchase supplies or services for their clients under this provision are prohibited from accepting fees or other payments that are contrary to the best interest of the property owner. For example, Article VII prohibits CPMs from collecting rebates, fees, commissions, discounts, or other benefits without the knowledge and consent of the client.

The code further requires that CPMs observe the confidential nature of client affairs. CPMs are required to keep clients currently advised in all matters concerning their respective properties or welfare. In addition the CPM "shall cause to be furnished to each client at agreed intervals a complete regular accounting with respect to the operation of that client's property." The code requires that CPMs keep accurate accounting records available for inspections by clients. Members must observe interpretations of the code of ethics by the Ethics and Discipline Committee sponsored by IREM.

Community Associations Institute (CAI)

Organized in 1973, the Community Associations Institute (CAI) assists community associations (also called homeowner associations) in condominiums and planned unit developments to

> ... preserve the quality of life and protect property values by maintaining the common elements, operating shared facilities and delivering community services.

The organization was formed by the Urban Land Institute, the National Association of Homebuilders, with support from the United States League of Savings Association, the Veterans Administration, and the U.S. Department of Housing and Urban Development. The organization serves community associations by:

1 Serving as a clearing house and research center for collecting, testing, and developing new and better techniques of operation and financial management of community associations

2 Providing a national forum for discussing key issues facing condominium associations

3 Focusing national attention on individuals and professionals dealing with community associations

Because more than 24,000 community associations are presently known, local chapters promote local interests by holding monthly meetings and conducting technical workshops. In short, CAI serves as a trade association to further the education and the administrative skills of the condominium manager.

Building Owners and Managers Association International (BOMA)

The Building Owners and Managers Association International (BOMA) deals mostly with office building management. It designates qualified persons as Real Property Administrators (RPAs). To qualify as an RPA the applicant must be a high school graduate or equivalent, must be 21 years of age, and must pass seven examinations. Members receive the annual experience and exchange report for downtown and suburban office buildings and monthly publications of *The Building Owner and Manager*. In addition, BOMA sponsors surveys, a quarterly economic analysis, and a building planning service, which is an ad hoc team of experts assembled for an on-site, comprehensive project study. Some 70 BOMA chapters are organized in metropolitan areas.

The National Apartment Association

Specialists in managing apartment property may earn the Certified Apartment Manager (CAM) designation. This designation is awarded to individuals who have 2 years of full-time, on-site apartment management experience, have received a satisfactory grade in an apartment management course, and have earned certain other optional credits. Ten points each are allowed for the third and fourth years' experience as a full-time on-site manager and 15 points for attendance at a National Apartment Association convention. As a further service to members, the organization sponsors various publications dealing with technical aspects of apartment house operation, maintenance, and management.

Related Organizations

Many other organizations support the management of specialized properties. The Mobile Home Manufacturers Association, the American Hotel Association, and many others promote the special interests of their members. Outstanding among these groups are the International Council of Shopping Centers (ICSC) and the Urban Land Institute (ULI). The ICSC undertakes research on many aspects of shopping centers, holds special conferences on shopping center issues, and undertakes professional-level educational programs. It sponsors case studies of shopping center development, operation, and feasibility, and publishes a variety of publications directed toward shopping center management.

Similarly the Urban Land Institute is a nonprofit institution concentrating on virtually all aspects of land development. Its research studies highlight new developments in apartments, condominiums, shopping centers, recreational land use, and other aspects of urban planning. In short, the specialist in property management has numerous sources from which to learn about the latest developments in the more specialized phases of property management.

CAREER OPPORTUNITIES

It will be appreciated that all income property must be managed. Even property that is held for owner occupancy and use requires the supervisory talent of a property manager. Government agencies—especially local and federal agencies—have significant property management responsibilities. As a result, the prospective property manager has a wide number of sources from which to develop and expand property management skills.

For example, some prospects begin by working as one of the estimated 500,000 resident managers employed by apartment owners. Experience as a resident manager may lead to later certification by an accrediting organization such as the Institute of Real Estate Management. In this respect, IREM maintains and circulates a list of qualified employees and job openings for candidates and CPMs. In short, there is an active market for professional real estate managers.

Corporations that own property incidental to their operations find it prudent to organize real estate management departments. The American Telephone and Telegraph Company and its affiliates operate some 15,000 parcels of real estate, ranging from office buildings to large-scale industrial facilities. The regional telephone companies establish management divisions that contain real estate specialists who manage, negotiate, and undertake site location studies. While most of the property is owner occupied, much of the real estate is under lease, which requires management skills to make rent surveys, lease studies, and site analysis. Other companies with organized real estate departments include J. C. Penney and Company, Sears, R. H. Macy and Company, and the Federated Department Stores, to name only a few.

Special note should be made of government operations in property management. Local governments responsible for low-income housing projects are heavily committed to property management. Management of low-income housing requires expertise not found in other residential projects. As a consequence, many organizations, including IREM and the Department of Housing and Urban Development, have sponsored management training programs for the benefit of local public housing projects.

The U.S. Postal Service, with responsibility for some 40,000 parcels, operates through an office of real estate that administers real estate acquisitions and management. Since many post office sites and buildings are under lease, personnel must be specially trained in property management. The Postal Service, through the Postal Service Training and Development Institute, has organized a training program for property managers and issues several publications that guide management personnel.[1] Figure 1-5 illustrates a form used by postal employees in making a site analysis.

To this list should be added the General Service Administration, which is responsible for space acquisition and management for other federal agencies. Special mention should be made of the important role assumed by the Real Estate Branch, Bureau of Indian Affairs. This agency administers some 55 million acres held under trust for American Indians. Management responsibilities include management services for the Agua Caliente tribe of Palm Springs, California that leases sites for multimillion dollar resorts. Many of their other recreational projects, farm leasing, and urban developments require the combined special training of real estate appraisers, planners, and property managers.

These developments suggest that property management is a growing technical operation requiring much study and opportunity for specialization. The employment and career opportunities are virtually unlimited, ranging from government, corporate, and proprietary employment among large urban centers to smaller communities, which offer a variety of property management services.

SUMMARY

Property managers are defined as real estate experts who manage real estate for a fee to maximize benefits of ownership. Depending on investment objectives, the benefits may lie in tax shelter, in capital appreciation, or in maximizing net income. Property managers work directly for owner-occupants, such as corporations and government agencies, and for real estate management firms that serve the private investor.

Real estate managers specialize in marketing space but because of their detailed knowledge of operating expenses, gross and net incomes, and because of their experience with many properties, including historical experience, their responsibilities overlap other real estate disciplines: namely, real estate appraisers, real estate brokers, real estate counselors, and mortgage bankers.

Besides marketing space—which is their main function—property managers supervise custodial responsibilities, maintain essential property records, undertake expense analysis, and offer both counseling services and financial analysis. To perform these tasks, property management firms organize functionally to serve the sales and leasing responsibility, and at the same time supervise residential managers, provide for property records, and supply related services that are important to management operations.

Because of their specialized training, the advantages realized by professional property managers lie primarily in *increased occupancy* rates. Property managers reduce *tenant turnover* and undertake *expense analysis* leading to more efficient operations. They become experts in *property maintenance*, in itself a factor that reduces operating costs. Property owners benefit from *improved tenant relations* and from *record keeping* that is sufficiently detailed for local, state, and federal reports. Their *management*

---

[1] See, for example, U.S. Postal Service, *Real Estate Training Manual*, Washington, D.C.: Postal Service Training and Development Institute, August 1975, p. 255.

12-2.7498-A Form 7498-A Realty Survey Analysis - Site
a. Facsimile of Form 7498-A

U.S. POSTAL SERVICE REALTY SURVEY ANALYSIS - SITE	ORDER NO. ①	DATE ②

FACILITY ③	CITY ④	COUNTY ⑤	STATE ⑥	ZIP CODE ⑦

NO. OF SITES CONSIDERED ⑧	NO. OF SITES APPROVED FROM SERVICE STANDPOINT ⑨

BASIS FOR SELECTION OF RECOMMENDED SITE ⑩

RECOMMENDED SITE

LOCATION ⑪ — SITE ACQUISITION METHOD ⑫ [ ]OPEN ADVERTISEMENT [ ]UNSOLICITED OFFER [ ]SOLICITED OFFER

OWNER ⑬ — SITE ACQUISITION PURPOSE ⑭ [ ]USPS CONSTRUCTION [ ]LEASE CONSTRUCTION [ ]OTHER

LEGAL DESCRIPTION ATTACHED ⑮ [ ]YES [ ]NO | TITLE INSURANCE BY OWNER ⑯ [ ]YES [ ]NO | OPTION EXPIRES ⑰ | NOTIFICATION BY ⑱

CONTROL DOCUMENTS ATTACHED ⑲ [ ]FORM 7432 [ ]FORM 7428 [ ]FORM 7428-B [ ]FORM 7428-D [ ]FORM 7428-F [ ]FORM 7432 A [ ]FORM 7428-A [ ]FORM 7428-C [ ]FORM 7428-E [ ]FORM 7428-G [ ]OTHER

SIZE AND COST

PARCEL NO. ⑳	DIMENSIONS ㉑	SQUARE FEET AREA ㉒	PRICE PER SQUARE FOOT ㉓	PRICE PER FRONT FOOT ㉔	OPTION PRICE ㉕
1			$	$	$
2			$	$	$
3			$	$	$
4			$	$	$
TOTAL SITE			$	$	$ ⑤

LAND/COST RATIO ㉖	ESTIMATED BUILDING COST $ ㉗	ZONING CLASSIFICATION ㉘	POSTAL USE AUTHORIZED ㉙ [ ]YES [ ]NO

RESTRICTIVE COVENANTS ㉚ [ ]YES [ ]NO (If "Yes," explain on attached sheet.) | RELOCATION REQUIRED ㉛ [ ]YES [ ]NO | NO. OF FAMILIES | ESTIMATED COST

SETBACK REQUIREMENTS ㉜ [ ]NONE | FRONT FT. | SIDE FT. | REAR FT. | BUILDING COVERAGE RESTRICTED TO

PARKING REQUIREMENTS [ ]NONE SPACES REQUIRED ㉝ | EASEMENTS OR ENCROACHMENTS ㉞ [ ]YES [ ]NO (If "Yes," explain on attached sheet.)

UTILITIES AVAILABLE ㉟ [ ]YES [ ]NO (If "No," explain reason and solution on attached sheet.)

CHARACTERISTICS ㊱ [ ]LEVEL [ ]FAVORABLE SLOPE [ ]REVERSE SLOPE [ ]IMPROVED [ ]UNIMPROVED

TOPOGRAPHIC SURVEY AVAILABLE ㊲ [ ]YES [ ]NO | SITE DISABILITIES ㊳ [ ]YES [ ]NO (If "Yes," explain.) | EST. DEMOLITION COST ㊳⑨ $

ANY CONFLICT WITH LOCAL PLANS? ㊵ [ ]YES [ ]NO (If "Yes," explain below.) | MARKET DATA ㊶ PS Forms 7422-D and 7422-E attached with adjusted data for ____ comparable properties

REMARKS (Use additional sheets, as required) ㊷

PS Form 7498-A
Jan. 1975

Figure 1-5 A form for a site analysis used by the Realty Acquisition and Management Staff of the U.S. Postal Service. Circled numbers refer to printed instructions. *(Source: Real Estate Handbook, Series RE-1, Washington, D.C.: U.S. Postal Service, 1976.)*

counseling and *specialization by property types* gives added benefits not realized under owner-management or operations by the inexperienced and untrained.

Because of the growing responsibilities of property management, professional development may take several forms. Individuals may qualify as Certified Property Managers (CPMs), a status designated by the Institute of Real Estate Management on the basis of on-site management experience, successful passing of examinations, and meeting other education requirements. The *Accredited Resident Manager* (*ARM*) designation is issued for others who qualify after passing a 1-week course on on-site management and after satisfying other experience requirements and professional recommendations. The designation *Accredited Management Organization* indicates that the company has met minimum management qualifications as required by the Institute of Real Estate Management. The organization supports a code of ethics that controls the professional practice of members.

The *Community Associations Institute* (*CAI*) specializes in professional development of persons active in condominium associations. Training, publication, and research are supported by this organization.

The *Building Owners and Managers Association International* (*BOMAI*) designates its members as RPAs, Real Property Administrators. Members must meet minimum education and experience standards for this designation. The Building Owners and Managers Association, with 70 local chapters, publishes surveys, a quarterly economic analysis, and *The Building Owner and Manager*, a monthly publication dealing with office operation and management.

The *National Apartment Association* issues the CAM designation, Certified Apartment Manager, for 2 years of on-site apartment management experience, satisfactory completion of a management course, and the meeting of other experience credits. The *Urban Land Institute* (*ULI*), a research and educational organization, and the *International Council of Shopping Centers* (*ICSC*) are other organizations that further professional expertise in real estate management and related areas.

Because of these opportunities for professional development, management careers are available with corporations that own property incidental to their operations and organize real estate management departments. Government agencies, including local government responsible for public housing and agencies such as the U.S. Postal Service, the General Service Administration, and the Bureau of Indian Affairs, among others, are typical of agencies depending on trained and qualified real estate managers.

DISCUSSION QUESTIONS

1 In your own words, define "real estate manager."
2 Explain the main duties of a property manager. Give examples to illustrate your answer.
3 Outline the functional organization of a property management firm.
4 Explain eight advantages of professional real estate management.
5 Explain the methods by which The Institute of Real Estate Management provides for the professional development of its members.
6 What is the purpose of the Community Associations Institute? Explain thoroughly.

7 How do the activities of the Building Owners and Managers Association International promote professional development?

8 What is the function of the National Apartment Association? Explain thoroughly.

9 What career opportunities are available in real estate management?

KEY TERMS AND CONCEPTS

Marketing space   Certified Property Manager
Custodial responsibilities   Accredited Resident Manager
Space broker   Accredited Management Organization
Resident manager   Real Property Administrator
Tenant turnover   Certified Apartment Manager

SELF-QUIZ

Multiple-Choice Questions

_____ 1 Which of the following statements is correct? (a) Property managers only work for owner-occupants; (b) The term "property manager" refers exclusively to members of established real estate departments of large corporations; (c) Property managers are real estate experts who manage real estate for a fee to maximize benefits of ownership; (d) The term "real property managers" refers to government employees.

_____ 2 Property managers enjoy a singular relationship not found among other real estate specialists in that: (a) The property manager is concerned mainly with the gross rentals and expenses; (b) The real estate manager knows operating details of the property managed; (c) The property manager is unconcerned with tax aspects of real estate investment; (d) The property manager delegates the marketing of space to other specialists.

_____ 3 Property managers are organized to supervise: (a) Two main operations: expense analysis and recordkeeping; (b) Three main operations, including recordkeeping, supervision of residential managers, and brokerage; (c) Four main operations: sales and leasing, supervision of residential managers, property development, and personnel supervision; (d) Four main operations: sales and leasing, supervision of residential managers, accounting, and related services.

_____ 4 Which of the following represents an advantage of professional management? (a) Increased occupancy and reduced tenant turnover; (b) Expense analysis and property maintenance; (c) Improved tenant relations, management counseling, and property specialization; (d) All of the above.

_____ 5 The CPM designation is awarded by IREM on the basis of: (a) Educational qualifications; (b) Experience credits; (c) Endorsement by the local chapter of IREM; (d) All of the above.

_____ 6 The Accredited Management Organization (AMO) designation is issued by (a) The Institute of Real Estate Management; (b) The Community Associations Institute; (c) The Building Owners and Managers Association International; (d) The National Apartment Association.

_____ 7 Which of the following organizations specializes in office building management? (a) The Community Associations Institute; (b) The Institute of Real Estate Management; (c) The National Association of Office Building Managers; (d) The Building Owners and Managers Association International.

_____ 8 Under the code of ethics enforced by the Institute of Real Estate Management, members are prohibited from: (a) Representing conflicting interests contrary to the interest of their employers; (b) Exposing the financial affairs of clients; (c) Accepting fees contrary to the interest of the owner; (d) All of the above.

_____ 9 Which of the following would represent a violation of the code of ethics enforced by the Institute of Real Estate Management? (a) Charging a real estate management fee that is more than 6 percent of gross income; (b) Failure to inform property owners of the current market value of their properties; (c) Accepting rebates without knowledge of the owner from contractors performing work on property under a management agreement; (d) None of the above.

_____ 10 Which of the following statements is correct? (a) Property managers are regularly employed by government agencies; (b) Virtually the only employment source for real estate managers is real estate management firms; (c) Corporations that lease property generally do not require real estate management services; (d) Real estate investors may realize few benefits from professional real estate management.

Answer Key

1 (c),   2 (b),   3 (d),   4 (d),   5 (d),   6 (a),   7 (d),   8 (d),   9 (c),   10 (a).

Fill-In Questions

1 Real estate managers may be defined as real estate experts who manage for a fee to maximize the _____ .

2 One advantage held by real estate managers, which is not always shared by other real estate specialists, is that the real estate manager knows _____ _____ of property under management.

3 Property managers are responsible for supervising _____ _____ .

4 Generally it is less expensive to renew a lease with an existing tenant than to solicit _____ .

5 As a result of _____ , property owners secure expert advice in management efficiency from managers who are skilled in handling a particular property type.

6 A designation issued by the Institute of Real Estate Management for meeting minimum qualifications as a property manager is the _____ _____ .

7 On-site managers who work in apartment buildings or other residential complexes that require local representation are _____ .

8 Members of IREM are required by the code of ethics to observe the _____ _____ of client affairs.

9 Members of the _____ are dedicated to maintaining the common elements, operating shared facilities, and delivering community services in condominiums and planned unit developments.

10 The _____ deals mostly with office building management.

Answer Key

1	benefits of ownership	7	resident managers
2	operating details	8	confidential nature
3	resident managers	9	Community Associations Institute (CAI)
4	new tenants	10	Building Owners and Managers Association (BOMA)
5	specialization		
6	Certified Property Manager (CPM)		

SELECTED REFERENCES

The Encyclopedia of Apartment Management, Washington, D.C.: National Apartment Association, 1976, chap. 11.

Hanford, Lloyd D., Sr.: *The Property Management Process*, Chicago: Institute of Real Estate Management, 1972, chap. 13.

Managing a Successful Community Association, 2d ed., Washington, D.C.: Urban Land Institute and Community Associations Institute, 1977, pt. 1.

Realty Acquisition and Management, Washington, D.C.: U.S. Postal Service, n.d., sect. 9.

The Resident Manager, Chicago: Institute of Real Estate Management, 1973, chap. 1.

Chapter 2

Economics of the Rental Market

After studying this chapter, you should be familiar with:
1 Three concepts of rent
2 The principle of comparative advantage
3 The law of diminishing returns
4 Economies of scale
5 The effect of discounting future rents
6 Intensive and extensive land use
7 The filtering process
8 The impact of rent control

In serving as the agent of the owner, a property manager markets space. In performing this function, the property manager appreciates that the market for space—its supply, demand, and price—moves differently from other markets. By understanding the main characteristics of rental markets, property managers may work more effectively with both tenants and owners.

For the present purpose, it seems advisable to review the concept of rent, characteristics of rental markets, and finally, the more important aspects of rent control.

Many accepted management practices have been adapted to the unique characteristics of the rental market.

THE CONCEPT OF RENT

In large measure, relations between landlords and tenants may be explained according to each party's concept of rent. A hostile tenant may labor under the assumption that rent is an unearned income for the landlord. In contrast, an owner negotiating a shopping center lease treats rent as a return on invested capital. Because behavior of both parties may be explained by their differing concepts of rent, it is helpful to review the three most commonly held views of rent: Ricardian rent, rent as unearned income, and rent as a return on investment.

Ricardian Rent

Much of our understanding about rent stems from the classical view of rent developed by David Ricardo (1817). He considered rent a surplus return and not a cost of production. Rent was considered a payment for the "original and indestructible powers of the soil."

Rent Based on Productivity   The doctrine of rent based on productivity followed the assumption that farm prices should be determined by the cost of producing farm products on the least fertile land. Suppose for example that three grades of land produced 30, 20, and 10 units per acre (see Table 2-1).

The analysis starts with 30 units produced on A land. If the price goes up to cover the higher costs on less-fertile B land, B land will be placed in production. C land will be farmed only if the price increases to just cover the cost of production. Therefore since the price is determined by the cost of production on C land, no surplus (or rent) is earned on C land. A and B land both earn rent, which is viewed as a "surplus" return of 20 and 10 units.

In one sense, rent viewed as a surplus parallels the *overage rent*—the amount of rent received above the minimum rent in shopping centers. Overage rent is based on a percentage of gross sales. Hence, certain aspects of Ricardian rent deserve emphasis; the more productive a retail store, the higher the rent. In this illustration retail sites with a higher sales potential are *more productive* and earn more rent.

Explaining rent solely in terms of site productivity excludes the locational advantages. For it may be concluded that market rent measures site productivity and the value of location.

Table 2-1   An Illustration of Ricardian Rent, Emphasizing Productivity

A Land	B Land	C Land
30 units produced (Surplus 20 units)	20 units produced (Surplus 10 units)	10 units produced (No surplus; no rent)

Rent Based on Locational Value One interpretation of rent explains rent in terms of locational advantages. Higher rents are earned for more convenient locations relative to distant locations. These ideas were expressed in early explanations of land rents in the era of horse-drawn vehicles. Farm land near processing centers earned more rent because of the lower cost of transporting products to the market centers.

To some extent, the same reasoning applies to income properties such as retail stores and apartments. In a growth city like Atlanta, Georgia, centrally located apartments near professional offices, commercial centers, and entertainment facilities command higher rents than garden court apartments in the distant suburbs. The lower rental value of the outlying location is explained largely by the higher transportation costs of the more distant site.

Under this view, a rent profile of a city would show a peak in rents at the city center, with rents that decrease in proportion to the distance from the city center. For a particular submarket, such as an apartment, the distance would be so great that land rents would approach zero—the higher transportation costs (and driving time) cause rents to decrease with distance. These relationships are shown in Figure 2-1.

If market rents refer to ground rents, rental values tend to allocate land uses to the most profitable use. In this view the rent profile is a cone-shaped area that peaks around the city center. In Figure 2-1, more expensive ground rents justify high-rise luxury apartments and office buildings. As distance from the high-rent area increases, certain retail uses dominate. At some point less intensive land use results, for example, in garden court apartments. As distance from the city center increases, single-family dwelling subdivisions dominate.

The example emphasizes the location factor. Property managers charge rents, therefore, not only in terms of site productivity, but also in terms of the use value of a particular location. Locational attributes, though varying by property type, deserve critical analysis in property management. Office buildings, shopping centers,

Figure 2-1 Market rent and land use as a function of distance.

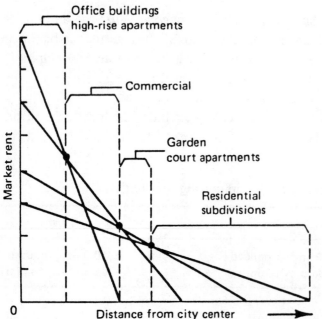

retail stores, and apartments in their many forms warrant location analysis in estimating potential rent.

Rent as Unearned Income

In the view of some observers rent is confused with profit in the sense that profit represents a return to the owner-investor or entrepreneur. Wages, interest, and rent are costs of production made in anticipation of profit earned by the entrepreneur.

The concept of rent as an unearned income represents an extension of the Ricardian view of rent as a surplus return. Henry George, writing in 1879, accepted this view as the basis for the single tax theory. Since rent was viewed as an unearned return, Henry George argued for a single tax that would recoup the unearned return through taxation. Even today, some advocates of rent control imply that rent is "unearned."

Underlying this belief is the implication that property owners enjoy a monopoly that gives owners an advantage over tenants. Observation discloses, however, that each site competes with other sites. While a particular parcel of real estate may have a unique locational advantage, seldom does real estate ownership convey a monopoly right. (A *monopoly* here refers to single control over supply.)

Even if a property owner charges higher rents because of new public improvements, a local population increase, or other external factors, there are many others who gain "unearned" income. Persons with special skills, such as entertainers, inventors, and owners of other resources may benefit from so-called unearned income. Furthermore (and particularly in real estate), the so-called unearned income may be only temporary. New shopping centers, new apartment developments, and new government projects change locational advantages so that present owners often face unpredictable competition with new projects.

Add to this point the fact that rents, which may be unearned in the economic sense, are capitalized in the market. A new owner buys at the market value and earns the going return on the purchase price. Such a buyer would view rent not as an unearned income but as a market rate of return on the investment.

Rent as Return on Investment

The more common view treats rent as an economic return on real estate. Like wages paid for labor or interest paid for money, rent is also determined by market forces; hence owners treat land as other factors of production.

To the owner, real estate is viewed as a capital investment that should earn a return commensurate with the risks and the rate of return earned on competing investments. Commercial tenants view rent as a cost of doing business. The payment of rent gives the tenant control of property for the purpose of earning income. Likewise, households pay rent as a cost of shelter. Rental occupancy substitutes for a housing purchase.

Considering rent to be a rate of return on invested capital opposes the assumption that land has no cost of production. In reality land is more than "a gift of nature"; it must be modified and produced like other factors. Vacant land needs considerable preparation for adaptation to housing—namely, public improvements, access, utilities, land leveling, clearing, and subdividing. With few exceptions, land in its natural state is poorly adapted to urban and, for the most part, agricultural purposes. The possible exceptions relate to grazing, hunting, and recreational land use.

Operation of the Rental Market

Under the competitive ideal, the demand for space would cause tenants to bid for the short supply, thereby raising rents to the point where owners would receive higher rents and increase their rate of return on land and buildings. This normal consequence would cause others to increase the available supply, which would eventually cause rents to decrease because of "overbuilding." Competition among owners would cause rents to reach equilibrium once again. While this result may occur over the long term, rents are unlikely to respond to the ideal competitive market.

For one thing, rents tend to lag behind changes in demand not only because they are negotiated at infrequent intervals, but also because it is often difficult to detect changes in the demand for space. This is particularly true of apartments, retail stores, and office space. Furthermore, even if an increase in demand is noted, the gestation time to increase the supply causes temporary distortions. It may take from 1 year to 18 months to organize, develop, and complete a 200-unit apartment house. By this time the existing demand may not justify another 200 apartment units.

Indeed, rents are slow to move for yet another reason—suppose that 100 tenants in an office building have average leases of 10 years. In any given year, no more than ten leases would be renegotiated. Or, to put it differently, it would take 10 years for all leases to be negotiated in response to new demand and supply conditions—at which time market conditions would have changed. In a multiple-tenant building it is unlikely that all rents would be at the market level at any given time.

It will be appreciated further that tenants often have a limited choice of locations. A jewelry store occupying a preferred location in a shopping center may be unable to duplicate the location elsewhere. The choice is to renegotiate the lease or terminate the business. Because of the premium placed on particular locations, some rents tend to be less influenced by competitive forces. In this case the rent negotiated between landlord and tenant rests on the projected sales in that particular location. Hence, the rent varies not according to the amount of space supplied but according to the profitability of a unique location.

CHARACTERISTICS OF RENTAL MARKETS

Property managers face rental markets that follow certain accepted economic principles. An understanding of these principles helps managers to advise clients about rehabilitation, modernization, and new construction.

Economic Relationships

The more common economic principles governing rental markets concern the principle of comparative advantage, the law of diminishing returns, and economies of scale. In addition, lease negotiations are undertaken with knowledge of the *discounting principle,* that is, the principle that future rents have less value than present rents. A brief explanation of these principles shows how managers apply these concepts in practice.

Principle of Comparative Advantage   Starting with the proposition that land has utility, rent tends to determine property use. Though bound by land-use controls that restrict the legal use of the property, property owners negotiate for the highest possible rent. In practice, a given site may be adapted to become a retail store, an apartment building, or an office building. The final use will tend to be the one that provides the highest income to the land.

Thus the developer of an apartment building must compete for sites that could also be adapted to office space. In general, land tends to be allocated to those uses that earn the highest rent. Or, conversely, land with the least utility earns the lowest rent and is adapted to less urgent uses. This is another way of saying that as land gains utility for more intensive developments, tenants and developers bid rental values upward in competition for scarce land of higher use value.

Real estate tends to be employed in that use in which it has the greatest advantage or the least disadvantage compared with other properties. In the simplest case, suppose that a $100,000 site might be developed for either an apartment or an office building. If the return on the land investment were 10 percent improved with an apartment and 20 percent improved with an office building, the site would have a comparative advantage for an office building. The return earned on land would be after capital recovery and the market rate of return on the building.

Or consider an older apartment building in the downtown fringe area. While the site may have been suitable for an apartment building as originally constructed, it may now have a comparative advantage for an office building. Rehabilitation for a change in use will be dictated by that use for which the site and building have the highest comparative advantage.

Consequently, property managers continually evaluate properties so that the properties tend to be used in the way that provides the highest net return. Because properties frequently have more than one possible use, managers specialize in adapting buildings for the highest net return on invested capital.

Law of Diminishing Returns   By itself, most land is not productive—it requires modification by means of buildings and other improvements. While rental values increase with the addition of labor and capital, the land is subject to the law of diminishing returns. For our purpose, the *law of diminishing returns* may be stated as: *If capital is increased by increments per unit of land, and though the total return will increase, beyond some point the return will become smaller and smaller.*

Although a 10-acre site may have a comparative advantage for a garden court apartment, there are limits to the number of housing units that can be developed for the given land area—even without zoning controls that restrict maximum units per acre. Therefore, in rehabilitating an apartment dwelling or modernizing a shopping center, there is some point where added investment will not increase the rate of return. In an apartment dwelling occupied by moderate income households, it would be pointless to install luxury plumbing or to provide a full-time door operator. For each property under management there is some optimum level of maintenance, repair, and rehabilitation that maximizes income. The law of diminishing returns, however, tends to restrict investments to the point of maximum returns. Thus, property managers must determine the level of operating expenses and capital investment that maximizes net operating income. At some point, additional expenses or investment earn no additional income.

Economies of Scale Probably more than most businesses, real estate operations are affected by substantial economies of scale. These economies are realized (1) in the management organization, and (2) in properties under management.

Management Organization In the first instance there is a clear advantage in having a sufficient volume of business to employ specialists. One firm may benefit by having a manager who specializes solely in shopping centers. Others may concentrate on office building management or apartment houses. By specializing in this way, the firm develops expertise in a narrow specialty that would not be realized with a limited number of clients.

Moreover, technology encourages large-scale operations. Observers have noted, for instance, that the paperwork normally would increase in proportion to the number of apartment buildings managed. Each apartment must have its separate tenant file, wage and hour records, and other forms. Costs of manually processing records increase in proportion to the increase in business.

The growing efficiency of computers, however, has changed these relationships. With computerized records, a new apartment building will not increase clerical costs in proportion to the number of buildings managed. Computer programs for one building may be adapted to many other buildings at a small additional cost. In fact, if the firm has excess computer capacity, additional buildings may be added at a nominal clerical cost.

The objective is to provide for economies to reach the lowest per unit cost of operations. A growing management firm will experience short-run costs that are continually reduced because of economies of scale. The economies are realized by providing for specialized employees and by using more technical equipment, such as computers. The firm would work toward reaching point X as shown in Figure 2-2.

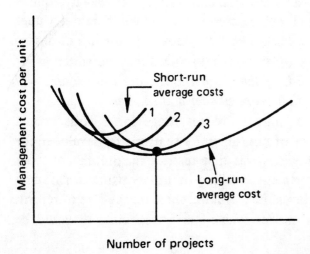

Figure 2-2 Economies of scale realized by a management firm.

In this example, short-run cost curves per unit are shown for separate volumes of business. As the number of units managed increases, per-unit costs go down because of economies of scale. After point X is reached, rising costs may illustrate diseconomies of scale. Diseconomies follow from a firm that does not have the capacity for additional business without additional investment. The cost of supervision of a large firm, for example, may cause long-run costs to increase rather than decrease. At this point the firm becomes more concerned with the efficiency of supervision, control, and coordination.

Properties under Management The same principle applies to income properties. Economies are realized in the management and operation of a 250-unit versus a 10-unit apartment building. The owner of a 10-unit building may not benefit from the on-site management specialization of labor. The owner is unlikely to benefit from more efficient use of equipment and machinery in the larger building. Similar differences in economies of scale are realized between the 2-acre neighborhood shopping center and the 100-acre regional shopping center.

Discounting Future Rents Present dollars are worth more than future dollars. Because of this fact, future rents are discounted. While it is fairly clear that rental income of $5,000 earned over the next year is worth more than $5,000 earned 15 years from now, it is not clear that $5,000 received over the next year is worth more than $20,000 earned 15 years from now. To make this judgment, it is necessary to convert future income to present worth. The final answer depends on the time period and the rate of discount. For instance, an annual rent of $20,000 earned at the end of 15 years has a present value of $1,300 discounted at 20 percent; or $4,780 discounted at 10 percent.

Present Worth The degree to which future rents are discounted at 10 percent and 20 percent discount rates over 25 years is shown in Figure 2-3. This figure is based on the *present worth of one factor* given in compound interest tables. The factor is based on the formula:

$$PW = \frac{1}{(1 + i)^n}$$

where i = discount rate
n = number of years
PW = present worth

To illustrate, $1 postponed for 1 year, discounted at 20 percent, has a present worth of $.83.

$$PW = \frac{\$1.00}{(1 + .20)^1} = .83$$

Under the same formula, $1 a year later discounted at 10 percent would have a present worth of $.91.

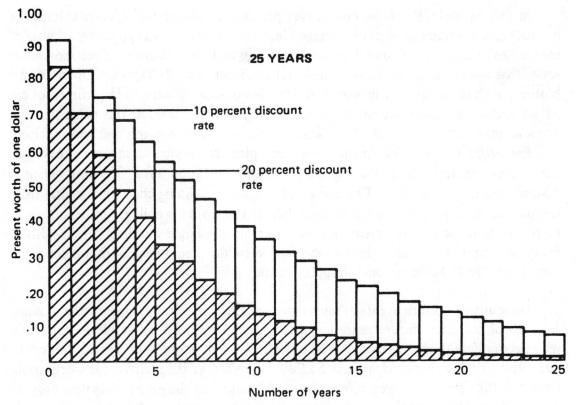

Figure 2-3 Present worth of annual rents discounted at 10 percent and 20 percent.

These relationships stress the importance of maximizing current income. That is, current income is much more valuable than future income. In shopping center leases, overage rent that is expected to be earned in future years is subject to the same discounting principles. Rents that are graduated upward by fixed amounts over a lease term have increasingly less value as they are postponed to later years.

Anticipated Income It is important to realize that investors purchase income properties on the basis not only of the current income, but also of the *anticipated income*. While it is difficult to project real estate earnings with precision, property managers work to earn the going market rent. Since property values follow from capitalizing net operating income, uncertainties over net operating income are accounted for in the discounting process.

Ordinarily the risks of earning future net operating income in a resort motel are greater than the risks encountered in a well-established regional shopping center. The more risky property would be subject to a higher capitalization rate, say 20 percent, because of the uncertainty over net operating income. In contrast, net operating income from the shopping center might be discounted by 10 percent. For any given property there is a rate of return that is appropriate in view of the uncertainty, amount, and duration of the anticipated net operating income.

THE RELATION BETWEEN RENT AND VALUE

In our economic system rent is one of the functional divisions of income. For commercial tenants, rent represents the payment for the use of a durable good. A more formal definition refers to rent as *a price paid for the use of a durable good, which is returned to the owner after a specified time in substantially the same physical condition, less ordinary wear and tear.* For the most part, income property is purchased on the basis of anticipated rental income and possible capital appreciation. In developing real estate, rent is maximized if the developer combines the optimum amount of land and capital in the form of buildings or other land improvements.

Intensive and Extensive Land Use

In planning the optimum combination, investors have the choice of *intensive* or *extensive* land use. Suppose that the local market justifies construction of 360 apartment units. If the 360 apartments of 474,000 square feet were constructed on 4.5 acres, thus providing for a 15-story building, the project would illustrate a highly intensive land use—slightly over 80 apartment units per acre.

Suppose, however, that the project takes the form of a garden court apartment on 16.5 acres of land. Here the development provides for approximately 1 apartment unit per 2,000 square feet, or 21.78 apartments per acre. In the latter case, the land value per acre would be worth less, since that proportion of income allocated to land would be spread over more acres—illustrating an extensive land use.

The issue of intensive versus extensive land use is more commonly encountered in providing parking space. Is it cheaper to acquire additional land for a parking lot expansion? Or is it more advisable to use existing space more intensively and with multiple-deck parking? The answer, given multiple-deck construction costs, would depend on the land value. Multiple-deck parking would employ the same unit of land but would combine additional units of capital, which illustrates the intensive utilization of land.

Therefore as the demand for land increases, developers minimize land costs by making more intensive use of the land, and at some point additional units of capital reach an economic limit. The cost of additional floors for apartments or offices eventually is greater than the revenue earned. At this point, the investor has reached the intensive margin in which additional investment barely yields enough to cover costs. Therefore, while land is limited in supply, managers may consider whether it is advisable to make a more intensive use of space or add units of land, following the principle of extensive land utilization.

The Filtering Process

Filtering is a process in which families move to older dwellings as the price falls. It is presumed that neighborhoods are undergoing a transition; the original occupants tend to move from older dwellings to newer and more costly housing. Since new construction accounts for usually less than 3 percent of the total housing stock, most of the one-out-of-five households that move each year must move into existing apartments or dwellings.

The degree of filtering is partly related to market forces and partly related to management policies. The availability of new construction, combined with population growth, encourages filtering. As neighborhoods and rental or owner-occupied housing competes with new construction, higher-income families seek the more popular neighborhoods and better-quality housing. In these circumstances, filtering is the result of local market forces and is not under management control.

Management affects the degree of filtering by pursuing certain policies that make housing less attractive. An apartment unit that lacks newer facilities, such as a swimming pool or energy conservation construction, or that shows postponed repairs may lack appeal relative to other apartment projects. If the dwelling appeals to tenants whose incomes are rising, managers face added turnover by not meeting tenant needs. As management policy makes units less attractive, the higher-income tenants leave for superior housing. And even if rents are on a rising trend, management may be unable to increase rents on lower-quality units, with the result that new tenants move in at the existing rents. Typically the new tenants earn less income.

As rents of substandard units remain stable in the face of rising costs, maintenance, repairs, and apartment services decline even more. The property continues to deteriorate. With lower-income tenants, higher delinquencies result, repairs and maintenance are deferred, and operating costs increase. Thus, management that does not meet tenant needs increases tenant turnover and encourages postponement of needed repairs and maintenance. The final result increases property depreciation and economic loss.

Therefore, not only is there a relationship between household income and the demand for housing, but the level of maintenance, repair, and services relates directly to gross possible income. Knowing that the filtering process may be evident to varying degrees, management may stimulate demand by appropriate maintenance and rehabilitation schedules. They provide services that are competitive with other housing. An apartment project showing deferred maintenance encourages the higher-income tenants to vacate for superior housing. In sum, as vacancies rise, management may be unable to increase rents; lower-income tenants replace higher-income tenants, which leads to a decrease in gross income and even lower property maintenance.

The Relationship between Vacancy and Gross Income

It is a common misunderstanding that managers must maximize occupancy. While on the surface this would seem to be the ideal, full occupancy suggests that rents are below prevailing levels. To test this proposition, managers try to keep the level of services and rents competitive with the market. Their review of competing projects helps in this determination.

But even if rents are at the market level, it may be demonstrated that it is frequently more profitable to accept a given level of vacancy in order to maximize income. It depends on the slope of the demand curve for rental units.

Consider Example A shown in Figure 2-4. Assuming that 120 units were rented for an average of $240 per month, the project would earn a monthly gross income of $28,800. Now suppose that management were to increase rents to $300 per month. With the assumed slope of the demand curve, 110 units would be rented at $300 per month for a monthly gross income of $33,000. Under these conditions it would be more profitable to accept 10 vacant units with the higher monthly rental.

In Example B of Figure 2-4, 100 percent occupancy is attained when 120 units are rented for $240 per month, producing a monthly gross income of $28,800. With

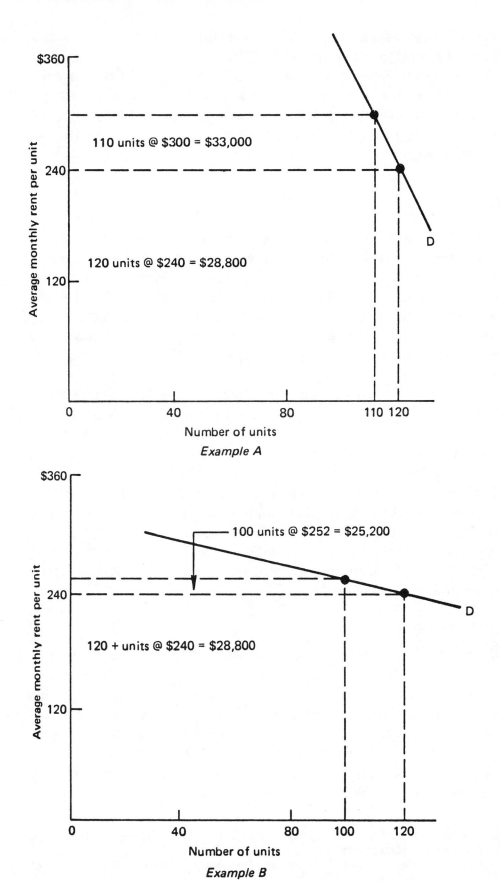

Figure 2-4 The effect of apartment rent increases under varying demand conditions.

the assumed demand curve, raising rents by $12 per month would result in 20 vacant units or a decrease of monthly gross income to $25,200.

Because of the critical importance of the demand factor, managers frequently make small rental changes that test the market. For each project there is a demand curve that provides the maximum gross income given an expected vacancy rate. The main point is that the goal of property management is to *maximize income* and not to maximize the occupancy rate.[1]

RENT CONTROL

Until recent years, rent controls were regarded as temporary war emergency measures. Starting with World War I they were adopted to regulate rents during housing shortages. Similarly the Emergency Price Control Act of 1942 initiated rent controls as part of a system of national wage and price controls. Legislation after World War II permitted states and localities to continue rent control to meet temporary emergency housing conditions. By 1948, 10 states and numerous municipalities had established local rent control—including the State of New York, which largely copied the original 1942 federal law.

The emergency aspect of rent controls is illustrated by New York State's Emergency Housing Rent Control Act of 1950. State laws were authorized by the Federal Housing and Rent Act of 1949. Later, Congress enacted the Economic Stabilization Act of 1970, which allowed the President of the United States to enforce wage, rent, and other price controls.

The current rent controls have been called "second generation rent controls" and are illustrated by those in the state of Massachusetts, where the first state-enabling legislation was passed in 1970. Maine, Alaska, New Jersey, Connecticut, and Maryland are among the states that have adopted a statewide rent control statute. At one time 130 of New Jersey's 567 municipalities adopted rent controls. Likewise, Congress authorized rent controls in Washington, D.C.[2]

Rent Control in Operation

Second generation controls are justified by some people because of claimed emergency housing shortages. The emergency is usually linked to housing shortages among low-income households, among the elderly and welfare recipients who face rising rents with fixed incomes. In this respect, rent controls constitute an exercise of police power as a form of subsidy to certain tenants. Differing from emergency controls, most legislation allows housing owners to earn a "fair net operating income."

In administering these concepts, most formulas to calculate a "fair" net operating income are based on variations of the following:

[1] For a practical illustration of this point, consult Gary Eames, "Rent Pricing for Maximizing Revenue," *Journal of Property Management*, 42 (1): 47–50 (1977).

[2] See Monica R. Lett, "Rent Control: The Potential for Equity," *American Real Estate and Urban Economic Association Journal*, 4 (1): 59 (1976).

1 A value formula that bases fair net operating income on some percentage of the value of the property. The determination of value, however, remains fairly subjective.

2 A gross rent formula that defines fair net operating income as equal to some percentage of total rents.

3 Equity formulas that give the owner a defined percentage rate of return on the actual cash investment. The actual cash investment is subject to various administrative interpretations.

4 A dollar net operating income formula that provides the same net operating income in dollars earned in a stated base year. The dollar income may be adjusted by a price series such as the Consumer Price Index.

While these are the main rent adjustment formulas, others follow complex formulas to shift certain allowable costs above the base rent to tenants.

Long-Term Impact

Serious questions have been raised about the long-term effects of rent control. Some claim that rent controls lead to postponed repairs and maintenance and operate as investment disincentives for new housing. If housing shortages exist, rent controls do not increase the local housing supply. The arguments against rent controls center on four points.

1 *Rent control places the burden of inflation on property owners.* No one will deny that inflation heavily burdens fixed-income groups, and particularly the low-income ones. Yet it is not clear that housing standards should be maintained at the expense of property owners. Operating expenses and other costs rise in sympathy with rents and other prices. Without universal price controls, property owners, in effect, provide private subsidies to tenants.

2 *Rent controls do not increase the supply of available housing.* Housing emergencies arise from shortages of adequate housing at rents within the means of tenants. The central problem is to increase the supply of housing at prices the households can afford. The long-run solution lies in providing added housing or in subsidizing rents. Rent controls are poor substitutes for resolving recognized welfare issues. The central issue is to assist low-income groups in meeting living expenses through increased employment, education, pensions, and other socially oriented programs.

3 *Rent controls discourage new housing construction.* Rent controls increase the cost of compliance; they delay rent increases in response to higher operating expenses and they may even cause lenders to provide mortgages on less favorable terms. The end result decreases the profitability of housing and therefore new housing construction. For the smaller investor, the conversion of owner occupancy housing to rental units would tend to be discouraged. In some extreme cases, marginal buildings have been abandoned in the face of rising costs and controlled rents.

4 *Rent controls lead to the inefficient allocation of housing.* Depending on the type of controls, tenants may continue occupying housing in excess of their needs. Tenants under rent control avoid market forces that relate rent to the cost of occupancy. Tenants may continue to occupy units at lower-than-market rents; they occupy

more housing space than they would ordinarily use under market rents. Tenants are reluctant to move from controlled units and face higher rents in newer, uncontrolled units. Thus, newly married couples and new households migrating to a rent-controlled locality would face higher shortages because housing is less efficiently allocated among tenants.[3]

Rent Control Recommendations

Clearly, rent control is more than a conflict between landlords and tenants. In fact the long-term results of rent control may aggravate the problem that rent control seeks to cure. While on the surface rent control appears to resolve short-term housing shortages, housing economists judge its economic effect according to three questions: (1) Does rent control lead to deferred maintenance, which lowers the quality of local housing? (2) Do rent controls discourage lenders from financing housing modernization, rehabilitation, and new construction? (3) Do rent controls lower property tax revenues as the result of the lower value of housing under rent control?[4]

The real danger is that claimed housing emergencies may continue indefinitely. Preferably, rent controls should provide for automatic, self-liquidating controls that cure the housing emergency by providing investment incentives.

This suggestion was contained in rent control recommendations made by the Urban Land Institute in Washington, D.C. The final recommendations, which followed a case study, were directed to longer-term solutions, and may be summarized in three points.

1 Exempt new construction; shift future operating costs and interest to tenants.
2 Subsidize housing rent and ownership of low- and moderate-income households.
3 With new housing construction, repeal rent controls; enact an excess profit tax on rentals.

The housing subsidy, according to this study, could be financed from the tax surplus gained from new construction. The recommendations concluded with a suggestion for improving "the framework for public policy intervention in the housing market."[5]

SUMMARY

The Ricardian view of rent considers rent to be a surplus return and not a cost of production. Under this theory the price is determined by the cost of production on less productive land, which earns no surplus. The contribution of the Ricardian concept lies in the emphasis on the determination of rent according to site productivity. A complementary view adds locational factors for a more complete explanation of rents.

[3] For additional explanation consult William M. Shenkel, "Rent Control: A Critical Review," *Journal of Property Management,* 39:(3): 101–113 (1974).
[4] Monica R. Lett, op. cit., p. 76.
[5] J. Thomas Black, *Prospects for Rental Housing Production: A Case Study of Washington, D.C.* ULI Research Report 24, Washington, D.C.: Urban Land Institute, 1976, p. 31.

The Ricardian view led to concept of rent as an unearned income. Following this line of reasoning, early writers advocated a single tax equal to land rent and, more recently, justified rent control to offset monopoly (unearned) rents.

The economist views rent as a return on invested capital: land, buildings, and other site improvements. Following this reasoning, economists emphasize operation of the rental market—primarily, the fact that rents lag behind changes in demand, that rents are renegotiated infrequently, that, for some sites, rent varies according to the productivity of the site.

By focusing on economic relationships, it can be found that rents follow the *principle of comparative advantage*. That is, real estate tends to be employed in that use in which it has the greatest advantage or the least disadvantage compared with other property.

The *law of diminishing returns* assumes critical importance because land by itself is ordinarily unproductive—it requires modification. The law states that if capital is increased by increments per unit of land, some point is reached in which the return will become smaller and smaller. *Economies of scale* are realized in properties under management and in the management organization that provides greater specialization. The cost of operation per unit tends to be lower for a 500-unit apartment than for a 20-unit apartment building. When rents are negotiated, future rent is subject to the *discounting principle*. Not only is future rent discounted to estimate present value, but it is the anticipated income, not present income, that is discounted.

Rent is the price paid for the use of durable goods; the goods are returned to the owner after a specified time in substantially the same physical condition, less ordinary wear and tear. In maximizing returns on investment, investors have the option of making an *intensive* or *extensive* land use. Intensive land use refers to the addition of capital to a given site. Extensive land use refers to adding successive units of land.

Filtering refers to the process in which households move to older dwellings as the price falls. The degree of filtering is related partly to market forces and partly to management policies. Market forces refer to original occupants who move to new housing and who are replaced with households of lower income. Management may retard the degree of filtering by rehabilitation and modernization. By meeting the needs of tenants, managers reduce turnover and retain tenants with higher income. Depending on the demand curve, it is also true that income may be maximized with a planned vacancy rate.

Rent control, which was introduced as an emergency wartime measure, is now subject to second-generation legislation. States have defined housing emergencies that justify local rent control. Unlike wartime rent control, the new laws allow for rental adjustments based on one of four formulas. Even with these adjustments, informed observers point out, rent control places the burden of inflation on property owners; it does not increase the supply of available housing; it discourages new housing construction; and it leads to the inefficient allocation of housing. Research has recommended that low-income groups on fixed incomes be provided with some form of housing subsidy. Under this plan, rent control laws should provide for their automatic self-liquidating controls.

DISCUSSION QUESTIONS

1 Explain the contribution of Ricardian rent to current leasing practices.
2 What is the rationale by which rent is viewed as an unearned increment?
3 Discuss rent as a return on investment.
4 Explain the following economic relationships governing the rental market: the principle of comparative advantage, the law of diminishing returns, and economies of scale.
5 What importance does the practice of discounting future rents have in lease negotiations? Explain thoroughly.
6 Contrast intensive and extensive land use.
7 In what way may property owners and managers accelerate or retard the filtering process?
8 Critically evaluate the following: In managing apartments, gross income reaches a maximum with 100 percent occupancy.
9 What is the rationale used to justify rent control?
10 In what way do rent controls aggravate housing shortages? Explain thoroughly.
11 What recommendations would you make on the question of continuing rent controls? Give reasons for your recommendations.

KEY TERMS AND CONCEPTS

Ricardian rent
Surplus return
Locational value
Unearned increment
Return on investment
Principle of comparative advantage
Law of diminishing returns

Economies of scale
Present worth of one factor
Anticipated income
Intensive and extensive land use
Filtering process
Fair net operating income

SELF-QUIZ

Multiple-Choice Questions

_____ 1 Which of the following statements relates to Ricardian rent? (a) Rent is a surplus return and not a cost of production; (b) Rent is payment for the original and indestructible powers of the soil; (c) Price is determined by the cost of production on marginal land; (d) All of the above.

_____ 2 The concept of rent as _____ represents an extension of the Ricardian view of rent: (a) A return on investment; (b) A payment for location advantages; (c) An unearned increment; (d) Payment for land productivity.

_____ 3 According to the principle of comparative advantage: (a) Real estate tends to be employed in that use in which it has the greatest advantage or the least disadvantage; (b) Land tends to be allocated to the most intensive land use; (c) Land with the highest utility earns the lowest rent; (d) Land with the highest utility is adapted to less urgent uses.

_____ 4 Which of the following statements is correct? (a) The law of diminishing returns does not apply to real estate; (b) If capital is increased by increments per unit of land, beyond some point the return will become smaller and smaller; (c) In the absence of land-use controls, the law of diminishing returns will not restrict investments; (d) In the case of real estate, additional land investment earns additional income.

_____ 5 The present worth of one factor applied to future rents means that: (a) Because of inflation, future dollars are worth more than present dollars; (b) Present rents are discounted more than future rents; (c) Rents that are graduated upward by fixed amounts over the life of a lease term have increasingly less value as they are postponed to later years; (d) Income properties are negotiated on the basis of the current income, not anticipated income.

_____ 6 Which of the following represents an intensive land use? (a) The additional purchase of land for a parking lot extension; (b) Adding a parking deck to a 5-acre parking site to double parking capacity; (c) Leasing a site in preference to purchase; (d) None of the above.

_____ 7 Which of the following statements is correct? (a) Owners and managers have no influence on the filtering process; (b) Filtering is related partly to market forces and partly to management policy; (c) Filtering refers to families with higher incomes who move to lower-priced dwellings; (d) Most of the households that move each year move to new apartments or dwellings.

_____ 8 Which of the following statements is correct? (a) Managers maximize gross income by maximizing occupancy; (b) It is frequently more profitable to accept a given level of vacancy to maximize income; (c) It is more important to maximize the occupancy rate than to maximize gross income; (d) Gross incomes are unrelated to the rent level and vacancy rate.

_____ 9 Opponents of rent controls hold that: (a) Rent control places the burden of inflation on property owners; (b) Rent controls do not increase the supply of available housing; (c) Rent controls discourage new housing construction and lead to the inefficient allocation of housing; (d) All of the above.

_____ 10 Preferably, rent controls should: (a) Continue indefinitely; (b) Apply to new construction and existing construction; (c) Provide for automatic, self-liquidating controls that cure the housing emergency by providing investment incentives; (d) Be applied to offset rising rent levels among low-income groups.

Answer Key

1 (d),   2 (c),   3 (a),   4 (b),   5 (c),   6 (b),   7 (b),   8 (b),   9 (d),   10 (c).

Fill-In Questions

1 The Ricardian doctrine followed the assumption that farm prices were determined by the cost of producing farm products on the _____ .

2 The lower rental value of the outlying location is explained by the _____ _____ of the more distant site.

3 The concept of rent as an _____ represents an extension of the Ricardian view of rent as a surplus return.

4 The more common view treats rent as an _____ on real estate.

5 Real estate tends to be employed in that use in which it has the _____ _____ or the _____ compared with other property.

6 The _____ restricts investments to the point at which returns are maximized.

7 Investors purchase income properties on the basis of the _____ .

8 Filtering is a process in which families with _____ move to _____ as the price falls.

9 The goal of the property manager is to _____ and not maximize the _____ .

10 Rent controls constitute an exercise of_____ in the form of a _____ to certain tenants.

Answer Key

1 least fertile land
2 higher transportation cost
3 unearned increment
4 economic return
5 greatest advantage, least disadvantage

6 law of diminishing returns
7 anticipated income
8 low incomes, older dwellings
9 maximize income; occupancy rate
10 police power, subsidy

SELECTED REFERENCES

Barlowe, Raleigh: *Land Resource Economics,* 3d ed., Englewood Cliffs, N.J.: Prentice-Hall, 1978, chap. 5.

Bish, Robert L., and Robert J. Kirk: *Economic Principles and Urban Problems,* Englewood Cliffs, N.J.: Prentice-Hall, 1974, chap. 5.

Emerson, M. Jarvin, and F. Charles Lamphear: *Urban and Regional Economics,* Boston: Allyn and Bacon, 1975.

Keiper, Joseph S., et al.: *Theory and Measurement of Rent,* Philadelphia: Chilton Company, 1961, chap. 8.

Levy, Herbert: "Rent Control in New York City: Another Look," *New York State Bar Journal,* **47**(3): 193–195 (1975).

Chapter 3

Federal Laws Affecting Property Management

After studying this chapter, you should be familiar with:
1 Requirements of the Occupational Safety and Health Act
2 Provisions of the Fair Housing Act
3 The main environmental controls that affect management policy
4 Energy-conservation building standards
5 Federal and state subsidies that encourage energy conservation construction

Among the many federal laws that all managers must observe in common with managers from other businesses, the legislation affecting four topics stands out. In these four groups are laws affecting occupational safety, fair housing, environmental controls, and new energy legislation. Because of new legislation, property managers have the responsibility of operating buildings to take advantage of various subsidies and tax incentives granted for new energy-efficient construction. While this chapter covers recent energy legislation, energy conservation is deemed sufficiently important to warrant separate discussion in Chapter 4.

OCCUPATIONAL SAFETY

Occupational safety falls under the jurisdiction of local, state, and federal agencies. The main federal act of concern to property managers is the Occupational Safety and Health Act of 1970 (OSHA). The act requires all employers in interstate commerce, with minor exceptions, "to provide a workplace free from recognized hazards that can cause death or physical harm to employees."

Coverage of the Act

Employers with less than seven employees are exempt from certain reporting requirements. Employers subject to the act are defined as "persons engaged in a business affecting interstate commerce who have employees." The liberal interpretation of interstate commerce brings most property management operations under the law.

The exemptions are confined to businesses regulated by other federal agencies or by states that have approved job safety and health programs in lieu of the federal program. Under current regulations, professionals, agricultural employers, Indians, non-profit charitable organizations, and domestic household employees are not covered.

Requirements of OSHA

The federal act imposes certain duties on property owners; failure to comply with OSHA regulations subjects the property manager or owner to heavy fines. Building management may create hazards that are in violation of the act. For example, it is the manager's duty to supervise employees' pursuit of safe work rules.

The Occupational Safety and Health Administration, operating under the United States Labor Department, establishes standards for occupational safety and health. These standards are first presented in the Federal Register and adopted for each industry after appropriate hearings. They cover (1) industrial hygiene, (2) machine operations, (3) material handling, (4) medical facilities, (5) personal protection, and (6) plant design and maintenance.

Industrial hygiene refers to maximum levels of radiation, noise, temperature, or pressure. Noise standards, for example, make it unlawful to subject workers to more than 90 decibels of noise. Standards on machine operation refer to the replacement of worn bearings, dull sawblades, and other machine-oriented hazards.

The act requires employers of seven or more persons to maintain records and to make reports on forms that are issued by the Department of Labor. Generally, occupational injuries or illnesses must be reported if they result in (1) fatalities; (2) lost workdays; or (3) injuries that require transfer to another job, termination of employment, or medical treatment. Employers must file Form 200, a log of occupational injuries and illnesses that must be maintained on the premises. The log must remain posted between February 1 and March 1 (see Figure 3-1).

A supplementary record of occupational injuries and illnesses issued by the Occupational Safety and Health Administration (Form 101) must be available for inspection 6 days after an injury, listing details of the injury or illness. The supplementary information gives details of the accident, the name of the employee, and the date of the injury, with the name and address of the hospital and attending physician.

U.S. Department of Labor

Company Name _____   For Calendar Year 19 _____   Page ____ of ____

Form Approved
O.M.B. No. 44R 1453

Establishment Name _____

Establishment Address _____

Extent of and Outcome of INJURY

Fatalities	Nonfatal Injuries				
Injury Related	Injuries With Lost Workdays				Injuries Without Lost Workdays
Enter DATE of death.	Enter a CHECK if injury involves days away from work, or days of restricted work activity, or both.	Enter number of DAYS away from work.	Enter number of DAYS of restricted work activity.		Enter a CHECK if no entry was made in columns 1 or 2 but the injury is recordable as defined above.
Mo./day/yr.					
(1)	(2)	(3)	(4)	(5)	(6)

Type, Extent of, and Outcome of ILLNESS

Type of Illness	Fatalities	Nonfatal Illnesses			
CHECK Only One Column for Each Illness (See other side of form for terminations or permanent transfers.)	Illness Related	Illnesses With Lost Workdays			Illnesses Without Lost Workdays
Occupational skin diseases or disorders (a) / Dust diseases of the lungs (b) / Respiratory conditions due to toxic agents (c) / Poisoning (systemic effects of toxic materials) (d) / Disorders due to physical agents (e) / Disorders associated with repeated trauma (f) / All other occupational illnesses (g)	Enter DATE of death. Mo./day/yr.	Enter a CHECK if illness involves days away from work, or days of restricted work activity, or both.	Enter a CHECK if illness involves days away from work.	Enter number of DAYS away from work.	Enter number of DAYS of restricted work activity.	Enter a CHECK if no entry was made in columns 8 or 9.
(7) (a)(b)(c)(d)(e)(f)(g)	(8)	(9)	(10)	(11)	(12)	(13)

INJURIES

ILLNESSES

Certification of Annual Summary Totals By _____   Title _____   Date _____

OSHA No. 200

POST ONLY THIS PORTION OF THE LAST PAGE NO LATER THAN FEBRUARY 1.

Figure 3-1 OSHA Form 200, which must be posted between February 1 and March 1.

45

An annual summary of occupational injuries and illnesses must be compiled (Form 103) 30 days after the close of the calendar year. Occupational injuries are subdivided into seven categories showing the total number of cases, number of deaths, lost workdays, nonfatal cases without lost workdays, and terminations or permanent transfers. All records must be retained for 5 years.

Employers subject to the act must post official posters provided by OSHA. These posters must:

> ... be posted by the employer in each establishment in a conspicuous place or places where notices to employees are customarily posted. Each employer must take steps to assure that such notices are not altered, defaced or covered by other material.[1]

The required poster is shown in Figure 3-2.

Enforcement

The act requires that employees observe rules and regulations of OSHA. The enforcement of the act is the responsibility of the employer, who is responsible for employees' compliance. Violation of the act subjects the employer to fines of up to $1,000 per day. The civil and criminal penalties imposed against a violating employer are shown in Table 3-1.

Employers are required to grant access to OSHA officials for routine inspections or accident investigation. Enforcement is also provided by the right of employees to file complaints if they have reason to believe that they are unduly exposed to job hazards. The complaining employee has the right of protection against reprisal, retaliation, or other penalties imposed by management.[2]

Safety Administration

The employer has the duty to design, construct, and maintain buildings and equipment according to OSHA standards and regulations. Personal protective devices must be provided as required. If the building is inspected, the OSHA official will be looking for dangerous hazards in the building. To guard against citations and to minimize claims for personal and property liability, some authorities recommend a safety self-audit. A form for this purpose is shown in Table 3-2.

Note that the form lists the physical condition of the building and any housekeeping practices that may result in injury. Misplaced tools; storage of materials and equipment; and even the placement of waste, toxic, and flammable materials are covered. The form further provides for the evaluation of equipment, training, and records.

[1] Walter B. Connolly, Jr., and Donald R. Cromwell II, *A Practical Guide to the Occupational Safety and Health Act*, vol. 1, New York: New York Law Journal Press, 1977, p. 468.
[2] C. Richard Anderson, *OSHA and Accident Control Through Training*, New York: Industrial Press, 1975, p. 16.

job safety and health protection

The Occupational Safety and Health Act of 1970 provides job safety and health protection for workers through the promotion of safe and healthful working conditions throughout the Nation. Requirements of the Act include the following:

Employers: Each employer shall furnish to each of his employees employment and a place of employment free from recognized hazards that are causing or are likely to cause death or serious harm to his employees; and shall comply with occupational safety and health standards issued under the Act.

Employees: Each employee shall comply with all occupational safety and health standards, rules, regulations and orders issued under the Act that apply to his own actions and conduct on the job.

The Occupational Safety and Health Administration (OSHA) of the Department of Labor has the primary responsibility for administering the Act. OSHA issues occupational safety and health standards, and its Compliance Safety and Health Officers conduct jobsite inspections to ensure compliance with the Act.

Inspection: The Act requires that a representative of the employer and a representative authorized by the employees be given an opportunity to accompany the OSHA inspector for the purpose of aiding the inspection.

Where there is no authorized employee representative, the OSHA Compliance Officer must consult with a reasonable number of employees concerning safety and health conditions in the workplace.

Complaint: Employees or their representatives have the right to file a complaint with the nearest OSHA office requesting an inspection if they believe unsafe or unhealthful conditions exist in their workplace. OSHA will withhold, on request, names of employees complaining.

The Act provides that employees may not be discharged or discriminated against in any way for filing safety and health complaints or otherwise exercising their rights under the Act.

An employee who believes he has been discriminated against may file a complaint with the nearest OSHA office within 30 days of the alleged discrimination.

Citation: If upon inspection OSHA believes an employer has violated the Act, a citation alleging such violations will be issued to the employer. Each citation will specify a time period within which the alleged violation must be corrected.

The OSHA citation must be prominently displayed at or near the place of alleged violation for three days, or until it is corrected, whichever is later, to warn employees of dangers that may exist there.

Proposed Penalty: The Act provides for mandatory penalties against employers of up to $1,000 for each serious violation and for optional penalties of up to $1,000 for each nonserious violation. Penalties of up to $1,000 per day may be proposed for failure to correct violations within the proposed time period. Also, any employer who willfully or repeatedly violates the Act may be assessed penalties of up to $10,000 for each such violation.

Criminal penalties are also provided for in the Act. Any willful violation resulting in death of an employee, upon conviction, is punishable by a fine of not more than $10,000 or by imprisonment for not more that six months, or by both. Conviction of an employer after a first conviction doubles these maximum penalties.

Voluntary Activity: While providing penalties for violations, the Act also encourages efforts by labor and management, before an OSHA inspection, to reduce injuries and illnesses arising out of employment.

The Department of Labor encourages employers and employees to reduce workplace hazards voluntarily and to develop and improve safety and health programs in all workplaces and industries.

Such cooperative action would initially focus on the identification and elimination of hazards that could cause death, injury, or illness to employees and supervisors. There are many public and private organizations that can provide information and assistance in this effort, if requested.

More Information: Additional information and copies of the Act, specific OSHA safety and health standards, and other applicable regulations may be obtained from your employer or from the nearest OSHA Regional Office in the following locations:

Atlanta, Georgia
Boston, Massachusetts
Chicago, Illinois
Dallas, Texas
Denver, Colorado
Kansas City, Missouri
New York, New York
Philadelphia, Pennsylvania
San Francisco, California
Seattle, Washington

Telephone numbers for these offices, and additional Area Office locations, are listed in the telephone directory under the United States Department of Labor in the United States Government listing.

Washington, D.C.
1977
OSHA 2203

Ray Marshall
Secretary of Labor

U.S. Department of Labor
Occupational Safety and Health Administration

U.S. GOVERNMENT PRINTING OFFICE

Figure 3-2 Poster required by the Occupational Safety and Health Act of 1970.

Table 3-1 Civil and Criminal Penalties for Violation of the Occupational Safety and Health Act of 1970

Violation	Mandatory	Fine up to	And/or imprisonment up to
Civil penalties			
Imminent danger, willful or repeated	No	$10,000/violation	No
Serious	Yes	$1,000/violation	No
Nonserious (routine)	No	$1,000/violation	No
Failure to correct or abate cited violation	No	$1,000/day	No
Failure to post citation	Yes	$1,000/violation	No
Criminal penalties			
Willful violation resulting in death of employee	Yes	$10,000/conviction	Six months
Second conviction on violation resulting in death of employee	Yes	$20,000/conviction	One year
Falsification of records	Yes	$10,000/conviction	Six months
Unauthorized advance notice of inspection	Yes	$1,000/conviction	Six months
Killing, assaulting, resisting OSHA officers	Yes	$10,000/conviction	Life

Source: C. Richard Anderson, *OSHA and Accident Control Through Training,* New York: Industrial Press, 1975, p. 8.

FAIR HOUSING REGULATIONS

Under fair housing laws, it is illegal to discriminate on the basis of race, color, religion, sex, or national origin in the sale or rental of most housing and vacant land offered for residential construction. Fair housing regulations are enforced under an 1866 law (42 U.S.C., Section 1982) that states ". . . citizens of every race and color . . . shall have the same right, in every state and territory . . . to inherit, purchase, lease, sell, hold, and convey real personal property." The law was held constitutional under the Thirteenth Amendment in *Jones v. Mayer,* 392 U.S. 409 (1968).

The Fair Housing Act

Because the 1866 act did not cover discrimination on grounds of religion or national origin, or cover discrimination in house financing, most complaints are filed under the Fair Housing Act. The act provides for damages and intervention by the Attorney General. Current regulations as provided by the Civil Rights Act of 1968, amended by the Housing Community Development Act of 1974, cover several types of discrimination based on race, color, religion, sex, or national origin:

Table 3-2 Building Safety Self-Audit

Physical condition of facility	Good	Unacceptable
1 Structural soundness		
2 Flooring and roofing		
3 Stairs, treads, and steps		
4 Handrails		
5 Lighting and wiring		
6 Hallways and aisles		
7 Doors and gates		
8 Ventilation and noise		
9 Heating and plumbing		
10 Medical department		
Housekeeping		
1 Placement of equipment and tools		
2 Placement of raw materials		
3 Placement of finished materials		
4 Placement of waste materials		
Equipment		
1 Guards in place		
2 Maintenance of equipment		
3 Personal protection		
4 Proper tools for work		
5 Fire apparatus		
Materials		
1 Hazardous fumes or particles		
2 Substances hazardous to skin		
3 Flammability and ignition sources		
4 Containment and spillage		
Training		
1 Warning signs		
2 Standard Operating Procedure training		
3 Formal classroom training		
4 First aid training		
5 Indoctrination of new workers		
6 Adoption of safety regulations		
7 Enforcement of regulations		
Records		
1 Form numbers 100, 101, and 102 maintained		
2 Medical records of exposure of workers to hazardous substances		

Source: C. Richard Anderson, *OSHA and Accident Control Through Training,* New York: Industrial Press, 1975, pp. 25–26.

1 Refusing to sell or rent to, deal, or negotiate with any person

2 Discriminating in terms or conditions for buying or renting housing

3 Discriminating by advertising that housing is available only to persons of a certain race, color, religion, sex, or national origin

4 Denying that housing is available for inspection, sale, or rent when it really is available

5 "Blockbusting" for profit—persuading owners to sell or rent housing by telling them that minority groups are moving into the neighborhood

6 Denying or making different terms or conditions for home loans by commercial lenders, such as banks, savings and loan associations, and insurance companies

7 Denying to anyone the use of or participation in any real estate services, such as brokers' organizations, multiple listing services, or the facilities related to the selling or renting of housing

Because of the limited exemptions, it is believed that the act applies to 80 percent of residential property. The act covers residential property that is owned by private individuals and listed for sale or rent by real estate brokers. Persons who own more than three houses or within a 2-year period sell more than one house in which the owner was not the most recent resident are covered. Apartments of five or more units are automatically included, while apartments of less than five units are covered if the owner does not reside in one of the units. Minor exclusions are allowed in certain circumstances for dwellings owned by religious organizations and private clubs.

Management Responsibilities

Duties of the property manager under the Fair Housing Act are illustrated in a case brought against a property manager of a 176-unit apartment in Homestead, Florida.[3] In this instance, Captain Ann Jones of the United States Army, a white female and a tenant, was told by the property manager that black persons were not allowed in her apartment. Later, with the approval of the property manager, tenant Jones invited coworkers to a party in the patio area surrounding the project swimming pool. A black couple was denied entry to the party by the property manager who, in the presence of the black couple, told Captain Jones that the two blacks could not attend. The property manager refused to allow the tenant, Jones, to entertain two black guests because of their race or color.

Not only the property manager but also the owner was found guilty of violating the fair housing law. It was ruled that statements made by the property manager created, cultivated, and perpetuated an all-white image. Thus, it was held unlawful to make any statement with respect to the rental of a dwelling that indicates any discrimination, limitation, or preference based on race or color. The court required the defendants to take affirmative steps to correct the effects of the discriminatory conduct and to assure equal housing opportunity in the future. These steps included appropriate instructions to agents and employees with a follow-up inspection by agents of the U.S. government.

[3] *United States of America v. L & H Land Corporation, Inc., et al.,* U.S. District Court, S.D., Florida, Miami Division (1976).

In still another case, the manager was held in violation of the Fair Housing Act after instructing rental agents to discriminate against black persons and members of other minority groups in the rental of 286 apartment units in Palo Alto, California.[4]

Discrimination was practiced by (1) showing black applicants the most expensive apartments, (2) giving them incomplete tours of the complex, and (3) misrepresenting the availability of apartments. In addition, rental agents were instructed to emphasize the security deposit requirements and to inform applicants that 2-week credit checks would be required. Rental agents were told they would not receive a commission for renting to a black or other minority person.

Testimony showed that the credit check was not required of white applicants, who were allowed to move in immediately or within a few days. On the same day in which blacks were told that no apartments were available, white applicants were advised that apartments *were* available. The court ruled that laws prohibiting discrimination in housing because of race prohibit not only overt rejection of applicants but subtle rejection behavior as well. In this instance, the property owner was held responsible for acts of the agent in discriminating against black and other minority groups.

The court permanently enjoined the owner and manager from denying apartment units to any persons on account of race, color, or national origin. The property owner was required to adopt and implement an affirmative program in compliance with provisions of the Fair Housing Act and to report the steps taken to the court. Management was further instructed to display the fair housing poster at its place of business. Detailed reports were required by the court as evidence of compliance.

Persons selling or renting dwellings are required to post and maintain a fair housing poster at the place of business where the dwelling is offered for sale or rental. Failure to display the fair housing poster is deemed prima facie evidence of discriminatory housing practices. The required poster is shown in Figure 3-3.

Affirmative Marketing Plans

The Department of Housing and Urban Development enforces affirmative fair housing marketing regulations. Under these regulations, it is the policy of the Department to administer FHA housing programs affirmatively so that individuals of similar income levels in the same housing market area have a range of housing choices regardless of race, color, religion, or national origin.

The affirmative part of the program requires developers of federally assisted or insured housing to attract "those persons who traditionally would not have been expected to apply for housing, primarily blacks, Spanish-Americans, Orientals, and American Indians." Developers are required to support an equal opportunity hiring policy, display the HUD logo or slogan in advertising material, and post a sign on all FHA projects displaying the HUD equal opportunity statement.

Moreover, developers of FHA housing programs must submit an approved marketing plan as a condition for federal assistance. The plan must indicate the marketing

---

[4] *United States of America v. Youritan Construction Company,* U.S. District Court, N.D., California (1973).

**We Do Business in Accordance With the
Federal Fair Housing Law**

(Title VIII of the Civil Rights Act of 1968, as Amended by
the Housing and Community Development Act of 1974)

**IT IS ILLEGAL TO DISCRIMINATE AGAINST
ANY PERSON BECAUSE OF RACE, COLOR,
RELIGION, SEX, OR NATIONAL ORIGIN**

■ In the sale or rental of housing or residential lots
■ In advertising the sale or rental of housing
■ In the financing of housing
■ In the provision of real estate brokerage services

Blockbusting is also illegal

An aggrieved person may file a complaint of a housing discrimination act with the:

U.S. DEPARTMENT OF HOUSING AND URBAN DEVELOPMENT
Assistant Secretary for Fair Housing and Equal Opportunity
Washington, D.C. 20410

Figure 3-3 Fair housing poster.

activity, the target minority group, and the type of advertising used. Even the sales staff will be reviewed for its experience in marketing to racial and ethnic groups.[5]

Equal Credit Opportunity

In judging prospective tenants, a property manager must observe provisions of the Equal Credit Opportunity Act of October 20, 1975. Under this legislation the Federal Reserve Board enforces Regulation B, which states:

> It shall be unlawful for any creditor to discriminate against any applicant on the basis of sex or marital status with respect to any aspect of a credit transaction.

Under the 1976 amendment, lenders may not practice discrimination on the grounds of race, color, national origin, or age.

Persons approving credit must observe other provisions of Regulation B:

1 Regulation B forbids the use of sex or marital status in judging credit.

2 Creditors are required to provide applicants with reasons for terminating or denying credit.

[5] For additional details, see William M. Shenkel, *The Real Estate Professional*, rev. ed., Homewood, Ill: Dow Jones-Irwin, 1978, pp. 557–561.

3 Lenders may not inquire into birth control practices or into child-bearing capabilities or intentions, or assume, from age, that the applicant may drop out of the labor force because of the possibility of child bearing.

4 Though part-time income may not be discounted, the creditor may examine the probable continuity of the applicant's job. The creditor may ask and consider to what extent an applicant's income is affected by obligations to make alimony, child support, or maintenance payments. Further, creditors may ask to what extent an applicant is relying on alimony, child support, or maintenance payments. Applicants must first be informed that no such disclosures are necessary if the applicant does not rely on such income to obtain credit. Such payments may be considered as income to the extent that they are likely to be made consistently.

5 The credit application, including related correspondence and records, must be maintained for 15 months following the application.

Treating credit applicants less favorably than other applicants on the basis of sex or marital status constitutes discrimination. Persons proving discrimination may sue creditors for actual and punitive damages for up to $10,000.

ENVIRONMENTAL CONTROLS

Managers responsible for property development must deal with environmental controls based on case-by-case regulations. These various regulations, local, state, and federal, supercede the preregulatory land-use controls of zoning ordinances, building codes, and subdivision regulations that control future project development. Under preregulatory controls, property owners could determine how land would be regulated in advance. Case-by-case regulations make final construction approval highly uncertain.

The more important case-by-case regulations fall under the National Environmental Protection Act, The Coastal Zone Management Act, and legislation dealing with air, water, and noise pollution. Some communities have enacted other controls that limit population growth through restrictive development policies.

The Environmental Protection Agency

The National Environmental Policy Act of 1969 established a national policy

> . . . to use all practicable means and measures, including financial and technical assistance, in a manner calculated to foster and promote the general welfare, to create and maintain conditions under which man and nature can exist in productive harmony, and fulfill the social, economic and other requirements of present and future generations of Americans.

In this act, Congress recognized that each person is entitled to a healthful environment and that each person has responsibilities to preserve and enhance the environment.

To implement the act, Congress created the Council on Environmental Quality, which consists of three members appointed by the President with the advice and consent of the Senate. The council's job is to direct and analyze environmental trends and to appraise the environmental programs of the federal government. Under current law, federal agencies must prepare an *environmental impact statement* for federal actions that significantly affect the quality of the human environment. Several states have enacted similar laws requiring statements for private acts that affect the environment. Environmental impact statements must give detailed explanations of:

1 The environmental impact of the proposed action
2 Any adverse environmental effects that cannot be avoided should the proposal be implemented
3 Alternatives to the proposed action
4 The relationship between local short-term uses of man's environment and the maintenance and enhancement of the long-term productivity
5 Any irreversible and irretrievable commitments of resources that should be involved in the proposed action should it be implemented

Accordingly, data measuring the impact must describe the anticipated effect on the local economy. Air pollution, local transportation, change in the quality of housing, neighborhood stability, and even aesthetics have been interpreted as factors that "significantly affect the environment."

Air Pollution The Clean Air Amendments of 1970 make the Environmental Protection Agency responsible for regulating car exhaust emissions and emissions of particulate matter, both controllable and uncontrollable. Uncontrollable emissions refer to wind erosion, forest fires, volcanoes, and pollution from other natural sources. Developers and others must comply with regulations over emission of chemicals, dust, and burning fuels, and even over the location of parking lots that concentrate automobiles.

Some states require a case-by-case review of new developments according to their probable impact on local air pollution. Oregon is one state that has enacted environmental control to supplement federal laws. In this state, noise control and air and water pollution must comply with state regulation. In a 1977 act, the Oregon legislative assembly stated that

the increasing incidence of noise emissions in this state at unreasonable levels is as much a threat to the environmental quality of life in this state and the health, safety and welfare of the people in this state as is pollution of the air and waters of this state.

Accordingly, the statewide Environmental Quality Commission was given authority to adopt "reasonable" statewide standards for noise emissions and to enforce such standards.[6]

Similarly, the State Environmental Quality Commission establishes rules and standards controlling air pollution. The commission may require a permit for allowing air contamination. Under the present law, without a permit, no person may discharge, or

[6] Chapter 467, *Oregon Revised Statutes*, vol. 3, 1977.

admit or allow to be discharged, air contaminants for which the commission requires a permit; nor may a person increase, in volume or strength, discharges or emissions from any air contamination source for which a permit is required.[7] Similar regulations apply to water pollution.

Water Pollution   Property managers have more than a casual interest in legislation that seeks to restore and maintain the chemical, physical, and biological integrity of the nation's waters. These goals are expressed in the Federal Water Pollution Control Act Amendments of 1972. Under this act it is proposed that

1   The discharge of pollutants in the navigable waters be eliminated by 1985
2   Wherever attainable, an interim goal of water quality that provides for the protection and propagation of fish, shellfish, and wildlife and provides for recreation in and on the water be achieved by July 1, 1983
3   The discharge of toxic pollutants in toxic amounts be prohibited
4   Federal financial assistance be provided to construct publicly owned waste treatment works
5   Areawide waste treatment management planning processes be developed and implemented to assure adequate control of sources of pollutants in each state
6   A major research and demonstration effort be made to develop the technology necessary to eliminate the discharge of pollutants into the navigable waters, waters of the contiguous zone, and the oceans

Under this legislation, real estate developers may program new construction if waste treatment facilities comply with water pollution requirements. Under the area-wide waste treatment plan, over 13,000 communities are subject to this regulation. New construction that causes soil erosion is prohibited, as well as water runoff that causes pollution. Earth moving activities—farming, forestry, mining, and even parking lot drainage—come under the areawide waste treatment management plan.

Noise Pollution   The Environmental Protection Agency is required to identify sources of noise under the Noise Pollution and Abatement Act of 1970. To minimize noise pollution, real estate projects such as airports, industrial operations, highways, or transportation equipment or facilities are required to keep noise within specified levels. The Department of Housing and Urban Development is prohibited from providing assistance for dwellings subject to high noise levels.

The Coastal Zone Management Act

The Coastal Zone Management Act of 1972 affects some 30 states. The purpose of the act is to preserve coastal resources, assist the management of coastal zones, and encourage federal agencies to work closely with the state agencies responsible for coastal zone management.

Coastal zones are identified as those areas extending from shorelines to interior land that have a direct and significant impact on coastal waters. States are responsible

[7] Ibid., chap. 468.

for identifying coastal zone boundaries and for organizing authorities to control land and water uses that bear on coastal waters.

Land-Use Restrictions Real estate developments must observe management plans that coordinate local, areawide, and interstate agencies. New populations and economic development of coastal areas must be arranged to protect and preserve marine resources and wildlife. Even the ecological, cultural, historic, and aesthetic values deemed essential to welfare fall under protection of the Coastal Zone Management Act.

Add to these legislative controls the environmental restrictions administered by local agencies: for example, zoning controls that limit further population growth and new construction. Controls that seek to preserve the environment involve zoning ordinances that prohibit construction on flood plains, steep slopes, or potential earthquake and slide areas. Other communities sponsor down zoning—the lowering of available land use from a high-density to a low-density land use, for example, increasing the land area per apartment unit from 1,000 square feet to 5,000 square feet. Zoning for relatively large lots and agricultural zoning that preserves land for agricultural use are other examples of restrictions on population growth. Still others have denied building permits to preserve the water supply or to reduce the load on local waste treatment plants.

State Administration Certain states such as California have enacted more restrictive legislation. The California Coastal Act of 1976 states that

> to promote the public safety, health and welfare, and to protect the public and private property, wildlife, marine fisheries, and other ocean resources, and the natural environment, it is necessary to protect the ecological balance of the coastal zone and prevent its deterioration and destruction.[8]

As defined by statute, the coastal zone extends from Oregon to the Mexican border, from seaward to the state's outer limit of jurisdiction and inland generally 1,000 yards from the mean high-tide line of the sea. In some instances, the coastal zone extends inland to the first major ridge line paralleling the sea or 5 miles from the mean high-tide line of the sea, whichever is less.

Administered by the California Coastal Commission, the zone is divided in six regions; local governments must submit a local general plan for coastal areas not later than July 1, 1980 for certification by December 1, 1980. Since January 1, 1977, new developments in the coastal zone must obtain a coastal development permit.

The issuing agency grants permits only if the proposed development conforms to the certified local coastal program. Permits for subdivisions are granted only where 50 percent of the usable parcels of the area have been developed and the new subdivision lots are no smaller than the average size of surrounding parcels. Public access

[8] Section 30001, California Coastal Act of 1976.

to the shoreline, recreational land use, and preservation of environmentally sensitive habitat areas are protected under the California Coastal Act.

ENERGY LEGISLATION

Recent laws make energy conservation more significant to property managers and their clients. New legislation provides for new construction that meets minimum energy conservation standards. The various states have granted certain energy conservation incentives in the form of tax subsidies for retrofitting older buildings and energy conservation construction for new buildings. More recent federal legislation provides federal income tax incentives for energy conservation construction.

Energy Conservation Standards

The Energy Conservation Standards for New Buildings Act of 1976 encourages reasonable energy conservation features in new commercial and residential buildings. The act provides for performance standards for new residential and commercial buildings to "achieve the maximum practicable improvements in energy efficiency." The act also requires publication of performance standards for new residential buildings in the Federal Register in 1979. Proposed standards will be effective within a period of 6 months to 1 year. After the final performance standards are accepted, no federal assistance will be available for new residential buildings unless the building conforms to performance standards. Enforcement will be through those local governments and state offices that implement building codes and construction codes meeting or exceeding federal performance standards.

Congress enacted the Energy Conservation in Existing Buildings Act of 1976 to retrofit existing dwelling units, nonresidential buildings, and industrial plants. This program encourages state energy conservation plans and provides federal grants for their development and implementation. The act provides for demonstration grants to test the feasibility of installing or implementing improved energy conservation measures in existing dwelling units.

Construction Standards   Solar heating systems in apartment buildings constructed with the financial assistance of the Department of Housing and Urban Development must meet minimum solar heating standards. For example, the Department requires that "the shut-down of the solar heating or domestic hot water system in one unit of a multi-family dwelling shall not interfere with the function of these systems in any other unit."[9] This regulation provides for the repair of solar equipment without interrupting solar heat to other dwelling units connected to the same central system.

Other property standards govern system design. For example, the solar system must have sufficient storage capacity for space and domestic hot water heating of not

[9] HUD, *Intermediate Minimum Property Standards Supplement: 1977 Edition.* Washington, D.C.: Department of Housing and Urban Development, 1977, pp. 6–31.

less than 500 British Thermal Units (BTUs) per square foot of solar collector area. Solar collectors mounted on roofs and walls must conform to wind loads, snow loads, and hail, and must meet other standards governing waterproofing, insulation, and mechanical design. Furthermore, regulations provide that solar energy must be backed up 100 percent with an auxiliary heating system.

State Subsidies   Incentives for constructing energy-efficient buildings are provided by several states. Incentives take the form of income tax deductions and property tax exemptions. California provides that taxpayers building a solar energy system may deduct a maximum of $3,000 from taxable income or 55 percent of the cost of a solar energy system. Condominium owners are given the same credit prorated among the households occupying the condominium project.[10]

Similarly, the Florida legislature declared that "commercial buildings are estimated to use from 20 to 80 percent more energy than would be required if energy-conserving designs were used." The 1974 legislature prohibited state agencies from leasing or constructing buildings without an evaluation of life-cycle costing. Such life-cycle costs are declared to be a primary consideration in the selection of a building design and, furthermore, agencies may lease only if there is a showing that the life-cycle costs are minimal compared to similar available facilities.

Life-cycle costs refer to an analysis of architectural designs and measurement of the efficiency of energy utilization. The analysis includes the expected fuel costs over the life of the building and other energy-consuming equipment cost and operation.[11]

In Arizona, taxpayers are allowed to depreciate solar energy systems over 36 months. The same law provides for an income tax credit to homeowners equal to 25 percent of the cost of energy conservation.[12]

Federal Subsidies

The Energy Tax Act of 1978 (P.L. 95-618) provides a tax credit for expenditures on energy conservation for a taxpayer's principal residence. A 15 percent credit is allowed, up to $2,000 for a maximum credit of $300. Effective April 20, 1977, the credit ends December 31, 1985. Items eligible for the credit allowance include insulation, furnace replacement, automatic furnace emission systems, storm windows, weather stripping, exterior caulking, and the like.

Solar Energy   The same act allows a one-time credit for investment in solar energy on a taxpayer's principal residence up to 30 percent of the first $2,000 investment and 20 percent on the next $8,000 for a maximum credit of $2,200. The tax credit for solar energy was effective April 20, 1977 and ends December 31, 1985.

Business Energy Investment Credit   A 10 percent investment credit is allowed for property used in a trade or business. Investments that qualify for the new 10 percent

---

[10] Section 23, 601, and 17052.5, *Revenue and Taxation Code,* Calif. chaps.
[11] *Florida Laws of 1974,* chaps. 74-187.
[12] Section 42-1312.01, *Arizona Revised Statutes,* as amended.

credit fall into six categories: alternate energy property, solar or wind energy property, specially defined energy property, recycling equipment, shale oil equipment, or equipment for producing natural gas from geopressured brine.

To qualify, the equipment must be new and placed in service after September 30, 1978 and before January 1, 1983. The credit applies to pollution control equipment required by federal, state, and local regulations. The tax credit covers equipment that is specially designed to reduce the amount of energy consumed, such as an automatic energy control system, heat exchanger, or other property as authorized by the Secretary of the Treasury.

SUMMARY

The Occupational Safety and Health Act of 1970 requires employers to provide a workplace that is free from recognized hazards. Property managers, like other employers, must observe standards enforced by OSHA. All occupational injuries or illnesses must be recorded on Form 101, a supplementary record of occupational injuries and illnesses. Employers must post Form 200, a log of occupational injuries and illnesses, between February 1 and March 1. Employers must also file the annual summary of occupational injuries and illnesses 30 days after the close of the calendar year. Failure to observe these rules and regulations and failure to post the OSHA poster subjects the employer to civil and criminal penalties.

Under fair housing laws, it is illegal to discriminate on the basis of race, color, religion, sex, or national origin in the sale or rental of housing. Persons selling or renting dwellings are required to post and maintain a fair housing poster at their place of business. Apartment projects financed with the assistance of the Department of Housing and Urban Development must be marketed under an improved affirmative marketing plan.

Managers are required to observe provisions of the Equal Credit Opportunity Act, which prohibits discrimination in granting credit on grounds of sex, marital status, race, color, national origin, or age.

Environmental controls are administered on a case-by-case basis. Federal actions and in some instances private actions under state law, are permitted only after approval of an environmental impact statement. The statement identifies (1) the environmental impact, (2) adverse environmental effects, (3) alternatives to the proposed action, (4) short- and long-term results, and (5) any irreversible or irretrievable commitments of resources. Concern over air, water, and noise pollution may increase costs of development and, in some instances, prohibit new construction.

In addition, some 30 states are affected by the Coastal Zone Management Act, which limits development in coastal areas. Some states like California have provided for a coastal commission that supervises preparation of local general plans. After certification of the general plan, new developments in coastal zones must obtain a coastal development permit. Permits are withheld if the proposed development does not conform to the local coastal general plan.

Congress has enacted laws setting forth energy conservation standards for new and existing buildings. Even today, apartment buildings constructed with the assistance of the Department of Housing and Urban Development must meet minimum property standards affecting energy. Separate rules have been provided for solar heating systems. Solar heating systems financed with federal assistance must comply with published regulations governing their design and operation. Many states, such as Florida, California, and Arizona, provide subsidies in the form of property tax exemption or income tax credits for investment in energy conservation and solar heating systems.

The Energy Tax Act of 1978 allows homeowners a maximum credit of $300 for energy conservation and up to a $2,200 income tax credit for solar heating systems. Businesses are allowed a 10 percent investment credit for energy-saving investments.

DISCUSSION QUESTIONS

1 What businesses are covered by the Occupational Safety and Health Act of 1970? What persons are exempt from this act?
2 What are the reporting requirements of OSHA?
3 Describe the six main components of a building safety self-audit.
4 What types of discrimination are specifically prohibited by fair housing legislation?
5 What is the purpose of affirmative marketing plans?
6 What main provisions of Regulation B must be observed by persons approving credit?
7 Explain the main components of an environmental impact statement.
8 Explain how a parking lot associated with an elevator apartment could be in violation of the Clean Air Amendments of 1970.
9 Explain how a proposed development could be prohibited because of the concern over water pollution.
10 Explain why the Department of Housing and Urban Development would be unlikely to provide financing assistance for an apartment near an airport.
11 Explain how the Coastal Zone Management Act of 1972 would increase (1) rents, (2) the cost of construction, and (3) land prices.
12 In your view, what effect will building energy standards for new apartments have on older apartments?
13 What subsidies have been granted by various states to encourage energy conservation techniques?
14 What federal income tax incentives encourage new energy conservation techniques?

KEY TERMS AND CONCEPTS

Occupational Health and Safety Act
  of 1970 (OSHA)
Fair housing poster
Affirmative marketing plans

Building safety self-audit
Fair housing law
The Noise Pollution and Abatement
  Act of 1970

Equal Credit Opportunity Act
Environmental impact statement
Clean Air Amendments of 1970
Federal Water Pollution Control Act
   Amendments of 1972

The Coastal Zone Management Act
   of 1972
Energy conservation standards
Minimum property standards
Life-cycle costs

SELF-QUIZ

Multiple-Choice Questions

_____ 1 Employers who are subject to the Occupational Safety and Health Act of 1970 are: (a) Employers with more than seven employees; (b) Businesses that are nonprofit charitable organizations; (c) Persons who are engaged in business affecting interstate commerce and who have employees; (d) Professionals and agricultural employers.

_____ 2 Enforcement of OSHA rules and regulations is the responsibility of: (a) Employees; (b) Subcontractors; (c) Local government officials; (d) Employers.

_____ 3 Which of the following is prohibited by the Civil Rights/Act of 1968 as amended? (a) Refusing to sell or rent to, deal, or negotiate with any person; (b) Denying that an apartment is available for rent when it really is available; (c) Discriminating in terms or conditions for renting apartments; (d) All of the above.

_____ 4 Which of the following is prohibited by the Equal Credit Opportunity Act? (a) Using information about a person's sex or marital status in judging credit; (b) Charging for a credit investigation; (c) Verifying salary or wages from an employer; (d) Verifying bank deposits.

_____ 5 An environmental impact statement includes: (a) The environmental impact and any adverse environmental effects of a proposed action; (b) Alternatives to the proposed action and long- and short-term effects; (c) Any irreversible and irretrievable commitments of resources; (d) All of the above.

_____ 6 New real estate projects may be disapproved because of inadequate sewage treatment under provisions of the: (a) Clean Air Amendments Act of 1970; (b) Federal Water Pollution Control Act Amendments of 1972; (c) National Environmental Policy Act of 1969; (d) California Coastal Act of 1976.

_____ 7 The purpose of the Energy Conservation Standards for New Buildings Act of 1976 is to: (a) Reduce fuel for heating buildings by 50 percent; (b) Initiate solar heating systems in all parts of the country; (c) Achieve the maximum practicable improvements in energy efficiency; (d) Require energy audits for all new buildings.

_____ 8 Which of the following statements is correct? (a) With approval of final performance standards, no federal assistance will be available for new residential buildings unless the building conforms to performance standards; (b) Enforcement of energy performance standards will be through federal government officials; (c) Energy conservation methods are restricted to new buildings; (d) Apartment buildings constructed with the financial assistance of the Department of Housing and Urban Development are exempt from energy conservation requirements.

_____ 9 Solar heating systems in buildings constructed with the financial assistance of the Department of Housing and Urban Development must: (a) Be approved by state officials; (b) Include space heating and domestic hot water heating; (c) Be independently operated without auxiliary heating; (d) Conform to minimum property standards established for solar heating systems.

_____ 10 Under the Energy Tax Act of 1978, (a) An income tax credit of 15 percent is allowed for a maximum of $300; (b) The income tax credit ends December 31, 1985; (c) An income tax credit up to $2,200 is provided for investment in solar energy; (d) All of the above.

Answer Key

1 (c),   2 (d),   3 (d),   4 (a),   5 (d),   6 (b),   7 (c),   8 (a),   9 (d),   10 (d).

Fill-In Questions

1 The _____ seeks to provide a workplace that is free from recognized hazards that can cause death or physical harm to employees.

2 The enforcement of OSHA is the responsibility of the _____.

3 Under fair housing laws, it is illegal to discriminate on the basis of_____ _____.

4 Persons selling or renting dwellings are required to post and maintain a_____ _____ at their place of business.

5 _____ are required to provide applicants with reasons for terminating or denying credit.

6 Under current law, federal agencies must prepare an _____ _____ for federal actions that significantly affect the quality of the human environment.

7 _____ are identified as areas that have a direct significant impact on coastal waters.

8 The_____ provides for performance standards for new residential and commercial buildings.

9 Solar heating systems in buildings constructed with the financial assistance of the Department of Housing and Urban Development must meet _____ _____ required for _____.

10 _____ refers to an analysis of architectural designs and measures of the efficiency of energy utilization.

Answer Key

1 Occupational Safety and Health Act of 1970
2 employer
3 race, color, religion, sex, or national origin
4 fair housing poster
5 Persons approving credit

6 environmental impact statement
7 Coastal zones
8 Energy Conservation Standards for New Buildings Act of 1976
9 minimum property standards, solar heating systems
10 Life-cycle cost

SELECTED REFERENCES

Connolly, Walter B., Jr., and Donald R. Cromwell II: *A Practical Guide to the Occupational Safety and Health Act: Laws, Principles and Practices,* vol. 1, New York: New York Law Journal Press, 1977.

Miller, Ronald H.: "The Economic Impact of Air and Pollution Control," *Urban Land,* 36 (7):10–21 (1977).

National Bar Association: *Title VIII, Legal Procedure Manual,* Washington, D.C.: U.S. Department of Housing and Urban Development, 1977.

Savelson, Donald W.: *Occupational Safety and Health Law 1978,* New York: Practising Law Institute, 1974.

Shenkel, William M.: *The Real Estate Professional,* rev. ed., Homewood, Ill.: Dow Jones-Irwin, 1978, chap. 20.

Chapter 4

Energy Conservation Techniques

After studying this chapter, you should be familiar with:
1 The more common solar energy systems
2 Circumstances favorable to solar heat installations
3 Limitations of solar energy systems
4 Preferred methods of retrofitting buildings for energy conservation
5 Procedures followed in life-cycle costing
6 Recommendations for energy conservation management
7 The purpose of the energy audit

Property managers have fairly limited options in reducing expenses. Minimum wages are largely controlled by law or by union contracts. Property taxes are unaffected by management policies. And while managers may defer maintenance and repairs, the practice is not recommended. However, to reduce energy costs, management today has many new options.

The new options result from rising energy costs. Energy conservation techniques, uneconomic in the past, are now economically feasible. Moreover, under the Revenue

Act of 1978, a 10 percent investment tax credit for investments in energy conservation construction provides an added incentive to conserve energy.

In addition, many states encourage energy conservation by granting subsidies in the form of property tax concessions or income and other tax deductions for energy conservation construction. Consider further the probability of continuing increases in oil prices and the eventual decontrol of natural gas provided under 1978 energy legislation. The importance of these developments recommends a review of solar energy, building retrofitting, and energy conservation management.

SOLAR ENERGY

The feasibility of solar energy depends on the solar energy equipment, geographic region and, in large measure, certain government incentives that encourage solar energy systems. Given these favorable factors, it is fairly clear that solar energy reduces energy costs. Experience has shown that solar energy may lower the annual cost of heating water, building space, and other building operations such as heating swimming pools.

Solar Energy Systems

On analysis, most solar energy systems require a relatively high initial capital investment, which is partly compensated for by low annual operating costs. Thus, the energy savings must be sufficient to justify the initial investment.

System Design Solar systems may be either *passive* or *active*. In the passive system, solar energy is transferred directly to heat without using other energy sources for pumps, blowers, or other transfer devices. For example, a window panel may be designed to store heat from direct rays of the sun and circulate by natural convection and radiation. For commercial buildings, the active solar system seems more efficient. The solar heat is accumulated in collectors, stored, and transferred through pumps or blowers for hot water or space heating. The active system requires the collection, storage, and distribution of heat through pumps or fans.

Figure 4-1 illustrates a combined heating and hot water system. This system converts the radiant energy to heat and stores the heat in an insulated tank. The second function in delivering heat for domestic hot water heating or space heating is provided by a system of valves, pumps, and auxiliary heat. Such a solar system turns on the key component, the collector.

The collector traps the sun's heat, typically by heating water which is then pumped to a storage tank. In some climates, the collector plates may reach 200° F. The collector is insulated and typically passes water through insulated tubes to the storage tank. The tank stores heat that may be withdrawn on demand. In this system, the heat exchanger, made up of coils or metal tubing like an automobile radiator, allows the system to provide building and hot water heat.

If the temperature in the storage tank falls below the minimum required temperature, the auxiliary heating unit provides the needed energy. Hence the keys to

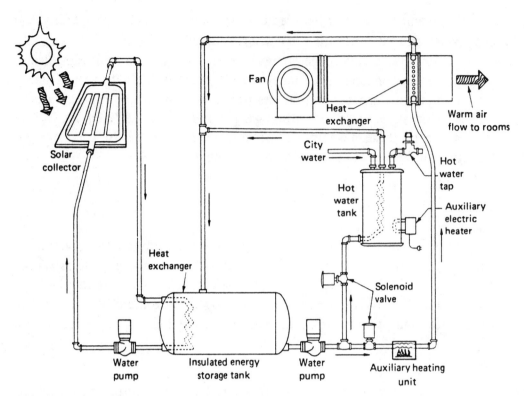

Figure 4-1   Diagram of a solar heating and hot water system.

feasible operation are the placement of collectors and storage tanks, the ideal building orientation, available space, and the roof angle. A commercial office building with solar collectors mounted on the roof is illustrated in Figure 4-2.

The larger the collector, the greater the solar energy collected. Yet because larger collectors increase initial costs, engineers advise limiting collector size at some point and increasing savings by energy conservation construction, including added insulation and storm windows. Most solar systems are designed to supply between 50 and 80 percent of the annual heating and hot water energy requirement.

Energy Savings   Observers have predicted that solar energy will become increasingly economical because of four factors:

1   Prices of fossil fuel will probably increase more rapidly than the cost of solar equipment.
2   As solar equipment becomes mass produced, its cost per installation will tend to decrease.
3   State and federal subsidies for solar equipment make solar systems more economical.
4   New technology will reduce installation and operating costs.

There is the further point that solar energy tends to be favored where fuel costs are increased by transportation costs. For example, fuel costs more in New York City than in Texas cities, which are closer to natural gas and oil supplies.

Yet in other cases, geography does not favor solar energy. In the Pacific North-

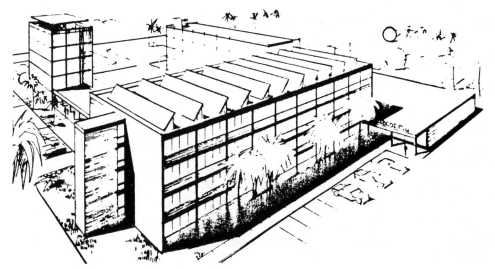

Figure 4-2   Roof-mounted solar collectors for a commercial building.

west, inexpensive hydroelectric power in combination with a relatively large number of overcast days makes the economical feasibility of solar energy doubtful. In contrast, open areas allow for the unimpeded construction of solar collectors. Likewise, the number of cloudless days in New Mexico encourages solar systems.

Limitations of Solar Energy Systems

Solar energy collectors are relatively inefficient. Even on a perfectly clear, windless day, collectors capture only about 60 percent of the sun's energy. Distribution and storage losses reduce the net efficiency to about 30 percent. Yet proponents point out that system losses may be discounted because the fuel or sunshine is costless.

Yet even if the fuel is free, solar equipment and its maintenance tend to be quite costly. The benefits realized from solar heating systems, then, depend partly on the estimated life of the equipment and the capitalization rate used to discount the future benefits. Benefits of solar heating are therefore offset by high initial investment and maintenance costs.

There is the added problem of the effect of solar systems on peak energy demands. At present, electric and utility plants are planned for peak demands, which usually occur in the summer when the air conditioners are operating at full capacity, or on cold days, when most heating systems are operating.

With the universal adoption of solar heating systems, peak loads could be adversely affected. Suppose that 90 percent of utility customers were to use solar energy. After several cold, overcast days, solar storage tanks would eventually cool and automatically turn to auxiliary electrical heating. This could cause an unusual high peak demand for electricity, which, in turn, would cause utilities to construct more generating capacity financed through rate increases. To meet an unusually large peak demand, the electrical system would have idle capacity during nonpeak periods. The end result could increase electrical utility and heating costs.

There is the added difficulty of metering solar energy insulations in multiple-tenant buildings. Because solar energy installations are indivisible, the cost of allocating the system operation to each tenant would be prohibitively high. Yet without individual metering, much of the efficiency of a solar system would be lost under wasteful practices common to master billing.

BUILDING RETROFITTING

As a result of new design and legislation favoring energy conservation construction, older buildings will be unable to compete with new construction without retrofitting. And since buildings constructed before 1973 were built during periods of low energy costs, they are all subject to economies of retrofitting. While in part energy conservation includes techniques that help tenants to conserve energy, savings realized by retrofitting tend to encourage energy conservation construction.

Retrofitting Construction

Retrofitting saves the energy necessary to building operations such as heating, ventilating, and hot water heating, in addition to water and electricity for lighting and other operations. Even with retrofitting, much depends on building management that reduces energy loss. Given the preferred management techniques, retrofitting focuses mainly on reducing the cost of heating and ventilating.

Sources of Heat Loss Heat losses arise mainly from:

1 Exterior walls exposed to the outside air and below grade
2 Partitions separating spaces that are at different temperatures
3 Windows and doors
4 Ceilings below spaces that are at lower temperatures
5 Floors above spaces that are at lower temperatures or in contact with the ground

The feasibility of insulating exterior walls for old buildings is difficult to assess, particularly for exterior walls of wood frame and brick veneer. Experience has shown that adding insulation to the 3 to 4 inches between the exterior and interior walls may reduce heat losses by as much as two-thirds. Preferred practice is to pump urea-formaldehyde foam into the air space. The problem of providing water vapor barriers and the settling or shrinkage of insulation materials over time reduce the effectiveness of providing insulation in exterior walls.

Adding insulation to the attic, walls, and floors, as well as wrapping exposed ducts and adding storm windows and doors, are all feasible depending on the local climate. As the number of degree days increases, benefits from energy conservation techniques increase. The heating degree day is based on the principle that the heat used per day is proportional to the number of degrees the average outside temperature falls below 65° F. For a specific day the number of degree days is equal to 65° F, less the daily mean temperature for that date. The sum of degree days gives the number of degree days per year.

Table 4-1 lists the air-conditioning degree days for selected cities. For most areas of the United States, a minimum of 6 inches of attic insulation, 3½ inches of wall

Table 4-1   The Number of Air-Conditioning Degree Days for Selected Cities, Listed by States

City	Degree days	City	Degree days
Alabama, Birmingham	2,820	Missouri, St. Louis	4,699
Alaska, Anchorage	10,789	Montana, Helena	8,250
Arizona, Flagstaff	7,525	Nebraska, Lincoln	6,104
Phoenix	1,698	Nevada, Las Vegas	2,425
Arkansas, Little Rock	2,982	Reno	6,036
California, Los Angeles	2,015	New Hampshire, Concord	7,612
Sacramento	2,822	New Jersey, Trenton	5,252
San Francisco	3,421	New Mexico, Albuquerque	4,389
Colorado, Denver	6,132	New York, New York City	4,989
Connecticut, Hartford	6,139	North Carolina, Raleigh	3,369
Delaware, Wilmington	4,910	North Dakota, Bismarck	9,033
District of Columbia, Washington	4,333	Ohio, Columbus	5,615
Florida, Miami	178	Oklahoma, Oklahoma City	3,644
Jacksonville	1,243	Oregon, Salem	4,574
Georgia, Atlanta	2,826	Pennsylvania, Philadelphia	4,866
Idaho, Boise	5,890	Rhode Island, Providence	6,125
Illinois, Chicago	6,310	South Carolina, Columbia	2,435
Indiana, Indianapolis	5,611	South Dakota, Rapid City	7,535
Iowa, Des Moines	6,446	Tennessee, Nashville	3,513
Kansas, Topeka	5,209	Texas, San Antonio	1,579
Kentucky, Louisville	4,439	Utah, Salt Lake City	5,866
Louisiana, New Orleans	1,317	Vermont, Burlington	7,865
Maine, Portland	7,681	Virginia, Richmond	3,955
Maryland, Baltimore	4,611	Washington, Seattle	5,275
Massachusetts, Boston	5,711	West Virginia, Charleston	4,417
Michigan, Detroit	6,404	Wisconsin, Madison	7,417
Minnesota, Minneapolis	7,853	Wyoming, Casper	7,638
Mississippi, Jackson	2,202		

Source: Clifford Strock, *Handbook of Air Conditioning, Heating and Ventilating.* New York: The Industrial Press, 1959, pp. A-36–A-44.

insulation, foil insulators in the floor, and storm windows have the greatest potential dollar return. As energy prices increase, additional insulation is justified.[1]

One study showed that adding 3 inches of ceiling insulation over the existing 3 inches at a cost of $3,456 resulted in a first-year savings of $1,143.[2] The main steps taken in retrofitting apartment buildings were to reduce heating and cooling expenses, hot water heating, and electricity for lighting. The recommendations were:

Heating and Cooling
1   Correct for overheating.
2   Limit temperature.

[1]*Retrofitting Existing Houses for Energy Conservation: An Economic Analysis*, Building Science Series 64, Washington, D.C.: U.S. Department of Commerce, 1974, p. 6.
[2]*Energy Cost Reduction for Apartment Owners and Managers*, Chicago: Institute of Real Estate Management, 1977, p. 47.

3 Set back temperatures.
4 Improve and maintain boiler efficiency.
5 Install storm windows.
6 Insulate pipes, tanks, and ducts.
7 Add roof insulation.

Hot Water Expenses
1 Replace shower heads and sink aerators.
2 Reduce hot water temperature.
3 Install timers on hot water circulating pump.

Lighting Expenses
1 Relamp apartments.
2 Relamp public areas.

Heating costs may be reduced by wrapping ducts, uninsulated steam pipes, and hot water lines. Boiler efficiencies are gained by having qualified technicians adjust burners for their most efficient combustion. Regular cleaning and inspection every 6 months are recommended as part of the retrofitting program. Installation of temperature-limiting thermostats and the concealment of thermostats are among other ways to limit temperatures and guard against overheating. Apartment managers recommend replacing thermostats with units that have upper limits for heating and lower limits for air conditioning.

Low-flow shower heads, while not affecting the quality of the shower, typically reduce flow rates from 5 gallons per minute to 2.3 gallons per minute. Similar savings are experienced by installing aerators on water faucets, which cost little, but which help reduce water expenses and water heating cost. Some managers reduce the hot water temperature in off-peak hours such as from midnight to 5 a.m.

Reducing Lighting Expenses An example of reducing lighting expenses in public areas is shown in Table 4-2. In this case 186 60-watt incandescent fixtures were replaced with 8-watt fluorescent fixtures. The table shows the annual electricity cost of $4,888.08 reduced to $651.74. In addition, the longer life of fluorescent fixtures reduced the cost of lamp replacement with the result that relamping resulted in an annual cost saving of $6,129.34. With a cost per fixture of $23.95, the annual savings substantially exceeded the initial investment. If the annual cost savings of $6,129.34 are capitalized at 10 percent, this one step would increase property value by $61,293.40.

Conversion from Master to Individual Meters Master billing was popular in times of relatively cheap electricity. The Institute of Real Estate Management reports that in 1973, 84.2 percent of elevator apartments included heat in the rent. Another 71.9 percent in the same year supplied electricity as part of building services. Originally, master billing reduced accounting costs of public utilities and gave the building the benefit of lower block rates as a volume customer. However, there is common agreement on this point: master billing wastes energy. Tenants have minimum incentive to end the wasteful consumption of heating fuel, electricity, or other supplied utilities.

Table 4-2 Feasibility Analysis of Apartment Relamping

		Existing incandescent lighting	Proposed fluorescent lighting
A.	Number of fixtures	186	186
B.	Kilowatts per fixture (watts ÷ 1,000)	.060	.008
C.	Burning hours per year	8,760	8,760
D.	Electrical utility rate per kilowatt hour	$ .05	$ .05
E.	Power cost per year (A × B × C × D)	4,888.08	651.74
F.	Rated lamp life in hours	1,000	12,000
G.	Lamp changes out per year (A × C ÷ F)	1,629	136
H.	Cost of lamps, @ $ .40 each (× G)	651.60	
I.	Cost of lamps, @ $1.85 each (× G)		251.60
J.	Labor to change lamps, @ $1.00 each (× G)	1,629.00	136.00
K.	Relamping cost per year (H + J)	2,280.60	(I + J) 387.60
	Total Operating Cost (E + K) (L)	7,168.68	(M) 1,039.34
N.	Description of existing fixture:	*60-watt incandescent*	
O.	Description of proposed fixture:	*8-watt fluorescent*	
P.	Cost per proposed fixture	$ 23.95	
Q.	Total cost of replacement fixtures (A × P)	4,454.70	
R.	Annual cost savings: (L − M)	6,129.34	
S.	Monthly savings: (R ÷ 12)	510.78	
T.	Payback period: (Q ÷ S)	8.72 months	
U.	Increased property valuation (R ÷ 10% capitalization rate)	$61,293.40	

Source: Data furnished by United States Lighting Corporation, Westminster (Orange County), Calif.

Observers have noted that converting to individual meters reduces energy consumption by 30 to 35 percent. Moreover, individual meters reduce energy costs to condominium owners. By metering, each owner individually gains by lower consumption. A recent meter conversion of 113 townhouses and 159 garden-type apartments cost individual condominium owners $240. As a result, unit townhouse and apartment owners decreased their annual power consumption by 19 and 27 percent. During the first year after conversion, condominium owners saved $32,823.[3]

Master billing tends to be uneconomical since the cost of electric consumption is included in the rent. Under master billing, rent increases from rising utility costs are deferred until the end of the year and are averaged over all apartments. Thus, master billing shields tenants from market forces that would penalize high-volume users. Since tenants under master billing do not know how much electricity they use—nor its cost—they have no economic incentive to practice energy conservation. In terms of 1975 dollars, individual meters in new apartments have an estimated cost of $200 per unit; it costs about $500 per unit to rewire existing master-metered buildings to individual meters.[4]

[3]W. H. Rhoten, "Converting from Master to Individual Electric Meters: A Case Study," *Journal of Property Management,* 43 (3):119–121 (1978).

[4]Burke D. Grandjean and Patricia A. Taylor, "Public Policy and Renters' Electric Bills," *Social Science Quarterly,* 57 (2):439 (1976).

Life-Cycle Costing

In brief, life-cycle costing is a method of evaluating all costs associated with operations over equipment life. The results provide a basis for decisions about alternative methods of reducing energy costs. The evaluation is based on four components:

1 The capital investment
2 Annual operating and maintenance costs
3 Annual repairs and replacement costs
4 Salvage value

Since the method depends on long-term projections, the value of future costs is reduced to present value, that is, the present worth of a future sum. For example, assume that an investment in relamping, insulation, or storm windows provides benefits of $1,000, $1,500 and $2,000 over 3 years. The present value of these benefits must be discounted. Using the present worth of one factor at 10 percent produces a *present worth* of savings equal to $3,651.30.

Year	Present value factor (10%)		Annual benefit		Present value
1	.9091	X	$1,000	=	$ 909.10
2	.8264	X	1,500	=	1,239.60
3	.7513	X	2,000	=	1,502.60
		Total	$4,500		$3,651.30

Note that the total benefits of $4,500 are realized over the 3 years, which, after discounting, have a present value of $3,651.30. Normally discounting would be over the economic life of the investment. For example, it is common to estimate the economic life of equipment such as an air conditioner, with a remote air cool condenser, as 10 years; boilers over 20 to 25 years; or oil-fired furnaces as 10 years. Similarly, heat pumps have an estimated life of 10 years in the view of recognized authorities. Lists have been prepared by engineers to guide estimates of economic life.[5]

Engineers who calculate operating costs that include repairs and maintenance may introduce a "differential cost escalation factor." The factor refers to the "compound amount of one" to compensate for expected increases in energy costs. For instance, informed observers have predicted that fuel prices will increase by at least the prevailing inflation rate. To complete the analysis, salvage values would be minimal or even negative, especially if the cost of equipment removal exceeds the salvage value. Given the benefits realized from energy conservation investments, certain other measures are important to decisions about energy conservation.

[5] See, for example, Reynolds, Smith, and Hills, *Life Cycle Costing Emphasizing Energy Conservation: Guidelines for Investment Analysis,* rev. ed., Washington, D.C.: Energy Research and Development Administration, May 1977, pp. B-1–B-4.

Savings/Investment Ratio (SIR) The savings/investment ratio relates the net present value of expected savings to the investment cost. Ratios of greater than one indicate a feasible energy investment. Consider, for example, the investment in relamping illustrated in Table 4-2. Again, assume no change in energy costs and an annual saving of $6,129.34 for relamping. If a 10 percent discount is assumed and the new lamps have a 10-year economic life, the savings and investment ratio would be 8.45:

$$\text{Savings/investment ratio} = \frac{\text{net present value of savings}}{\text{investment cost}}$$

$$= \frac{\$6,129.34 \times 6.145}{\$4,454.70}$$

$$= \frac{\$37,664.79}{\$4,454.70}$$

$$= 8.46$$

In this example, the present value of annual savings, $6,129.34, is realized each year for 10 years. The present worth of $1 received at the end of each year for 10 years is equal to $6.145 (the present worth of one per-period factor, 10 percent). Therefore, it follows that the present worth of $6,129.34 realized over 10 years has a present value of $37,664.79, discounted at 10 percent. Since the relamping costs $4,454.70, the savings/investment ratio is 8.46. If it is anticipated that energy prices will increase, the SIR would be greater than this example indicates.

The Payback Period In the present context, the payback period is the length of time required for annual cumulative savings to equal the initial investment. Suppose, for example, that recommended insulation will cost $2,600 and that the present value of annual savings over 7 years is equal to the data of Table 4-3. Recall that the savings represent the discounted savings, that is, the present value of savings realized each year for seven years. Under these assumptions the example shows a payback period of 5.33 years.

**Table 4-3   Discounted Payback Period:
$2,600 Investment**

Year	Present value of savings	Investment amount outstanding
1	$533	$2,067
2	518	1,549
3	502	1,047
4	421	626
5	474	152
6	460	(308)
7	447	

5 and 152/460 years = 5.33 years to payback.

Though this example is based upon the discounted value of anticipated savings, it does not consider the saving benefits after the project has paid out. For this reason, the savings/investment ratio is more widely used.

BTU Savings per Investment Dollar   For this calculation, an engineer must calculate the number of British Thermal Units (BTUs) saved annually from energy conservation. A BTU is the amount of heat required to heat 1 pound of water 1° F. The resulting value is divided by the average annual present value of the investment. The value investment in turn is divided by its economic life in years. While the analysis requires a more detailed study of actual BTUs saved, it is a useful figure when used with other calculations.

For instance, these data are often compared with the *base line*, which is the present condition against which new energy conservation investments are measured. Another term employed in energy conservation decisions is the reference to *incremental costs*. These costs refer to the difference in costs between two energy conservation alternatives.

Insulation Materials   In judging the feasibility of added insulation, engineers refer to insulation "R values." R values measure thermal resistance in terms of fahrenheit degrees per hour. The higher the R value, the better the insulation. The Owens-Corning Fiber Glass Company recommends minimum insulation in terms of R values according to regions of the United States. A generalized view of recommended R values for six geographic zones is shown in Figure 4-3. Note that minimum R values recommended for ceilings and walls range from 19 and 11 in Region 6 (the West Coast) to 38 and 19 in the Northern Midwestern states.

Figure 4-3 Minimum recommended insulation R values by regional areas. (*Source: Energy Conservation Supplement,* Chicago: U.S. League of Savings Associations, 1977.)

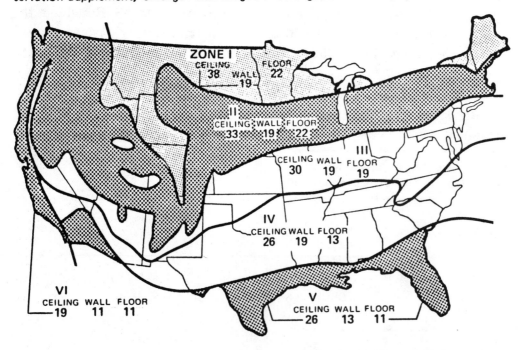

**Table 4-4   Insulation R Values for Selected Insulation
Materials: Ceiling Insulation**

R value	Insulation material
R 19	7½–9 in. mineral fiber loose fill 5 in. cellulose loose fill 6 in. mineral wool batt
R 26	8¼ in. mineral wool batt 2 layers 3½ in. extra-dense mineral wool batts 12 in. mineral fiber loose fill 7 in. cellulose loose fill
R 30	9 in. mineral wool batt 5½ in. mineral wool batt + 3½ in. mineral wool batt 11½–13¾ in. mineral fiber loose fill 8 in. cellulose loose fill
R 33	5½ in. mineral wool batt + 5½ in. mineral fiber loose fill 12½–15 in. mineral fiber loose fill 9 in. cellulose loose fill
R 38	2 layers 5½ in. mineral wool batts 14½–17½ in. mineral fiber loose fill 10 in. cellulose loose fill

R values for different types of ceiling insulation are shown in Table 4-4. For example, an R 38 value may be gained from 12 inches of mineral wool batts or 10 inches of cellulose loose fill. It will be realized that minimum recommended R values will increase if future fuel prices increase more than the costs of insulation.

ENERGY CONSERVATION MANAGEMENT

It will be remembered that most buildings were constructed during periods of relatively low energy prices. As a consequence, management may contribute to energy conservation by introducing certain operating efficiencies. These efficiencies, which made little impact on operating costs before the oil embargo, today produce substantial savings.

Office Buildings

J. P. Basie, who is responsible for managing the 32-story First Federal Savings and Loan Association Building in downtown Miami, reports several operating practices that reduced electricity costs. Like many other office buildings, every night this building glowed from dozens of 1,000-watt floodlights around the building perimeter. Today, exterior light is confined to the rooftop sign.

In the same building, the life of some 1,410 decorative incandescent 10-watt light bulbs was increased by three times by reducing the dimmer control to a 7-watt setting. And though leases require air conditioning 24 hours a day, 7 days a week, not all tenants occupy space for this interval. Therefore, during off business hours, un-occupied space was not air conditioned unless specifically requested by the tenant.

Buildings monitored by automated control systems may take advantage of lower "demand" rates. Demand rates refer to charges based upon the peak electric power demanded during the year. Systems are available to turn off selected air conditioning units or certain lights for 15 minutes when the peak load is exceeded. By reducing the peak load to a minimum, the building secures the advantage of lower demand rates.

Similarly, some public utilities grant reduced rates for interruptible power. In the First Federal Building of Miami, it was determined that the peak demand of 3,700 kilowatts per hour could be temporarily reduced to 1,400 kilowatts for 1 to 5 hours by turning off certain lights and certain equipment. As a result, the public utility reduced monthly power rates by $2,300 a month.[6]

Barbara Kamanitz, President of the Investment Management Group, Inc., Hartford, Connecticut, gains tenant cooperation by sending tenants a letter that reads in part:

... much of the energy crisis depends upon consumer cooperation. We need your help. For you, as a resident and for us, as the managing agent, we have a mutual incentive in stabilizing costs. Please take the time to read and to follow these suggestions. We not only need your understanding in these measures of conservation but your complete cooperation in observing them.[7]

Among the common-sense suggestions, tenants are advised to

1 Set thermostats to 70 or 68° F and wear warm clothing. Research shows that for every degree setting above 68° F, heating bills increase by 3 percent.
2 Lower thermostats for long periods of absence (55° F).
3 Lower thermostats at night.
4 Close rooms not being used.
5 Turn off lights in unoccupied space.

In apartment buildings, managers are advised to reduce the temperature in public areas. This step is usually permissible because people move through hallways in a relatively short time. While the suggestion includes the lowering of thermostats for heating purposes, changing thermostats applies equally to air conditioning: 78° F is believed comfortable for most people during the summer.

In other instances, energy savings are realized by installing equipment and appliances specially adapted for reduced energy consumption. Managers may purchase automatic washing machines that provide for partial loads or rinsing in cold water or that permit the reuse of warm water from the first loading. Likewise, automatic dishwashers that allow for the turning off of the hot-air drying cycle help to reduce energy costs.

[6] J. P. Basie, "Saving Energy and Money in Office Building Management," *Real Estate Appraiser*, 42(4):5-9 (1976).
[7] Barbara Kamanitz, "Communicating an Energy Conservation Program: Part I," *Journal of Property Management*, 41(4):157 (1976).

Apartment refrigerators with more insulation than is common to pre-1975 equipment represent another case in point.

Other recommended management techniques include a high level of maintenance and repair that makes equipment more efficient, that is, replacing filters in heating and air conditioning equipment. In apartment houses, heat and air conditioning may be reduced for vacant units. Prompt repair of water leaks or a preventive maintenance program that reduces losses from this source are other cost-saving steps.

The Energy Audit

A recent survey of 44 office buildings in New York City revealed that only 10 percent of the owners and managers monitor energy consumption and compare their usage with other buildings. Operating experience of these buildings for 2 years before the 1973 oil embargo compared to 1974 and 1975 revealed a 12 percent saving in energy consumption. The 12 percent saving was believed to be the result of lowering building operating heating temperatures and raising air conditioning temperatures, as well as more efficient lighting practices. Apart from this finding, owners and office building managers are found to have little knowledge of building energy consumption patterns.

For this reason, the energy audit is strongly advised. It is an extension of conventional cost accounting and it measures the net amount of nonrenewal natural resources consumed in building operation.[8] The energy audit is particularly appropriate for newer buildings. In the case of office buildings, for example, surveys have shown that older office buildings consume less than the mean average of 112,000 BTUs per square foot per year common to New York City. For example, older office buildings usually have heating, cooling, and lighting under local control. Therefore, when no one is in the office, air conditioning or lighting may be turned off in unoccupied space. Hence the individual controls, in contrast to central controls of new buildings, tend to reduce energy consumption.

The second point making older buildings more energy efficient is the fact that air conditioning units have relatively lower tonnage capacity and buildings have lower lighting levels. The newer office buildings have higher lighting standards and air conditioning tonnage to reduce building temperatures.

The purpose of the energy audit is to inventory the physical characteristics of the building to measure its thermal efficiency. Accordingly, it should be undertaken by specially trained persons. A computer analysis of check sheets filled in by building owners has proved ineffective. Apparently, there is no workable substitute for a visual inspection of a building by a trained observer.[9]

The energy audit reveals retrofitting projects that prove economically feasible. For example, the Federal Energy Administration recommends that the energy audit concentrate on five retrofitting measures dealing with:

[8] Victor John Yannacone, Jr. "Ecology and Real Estate," *National Real Estate Investor,* 30 (1):24 (1978).

[9] Hans R. Isaakson and Deena D. Kushner, *Making the Most of Energy in Real Estate,* Athens, Georgia: Department of Real Estate and Urban Development, University of Georgia, 1978, p. 504.

heating and ventilation
lighting
cooling
water heating
miscellaneous

The recommendations tend to vary according to temperature zones. Zone 4 (communities under 3,000 degree days), delineated by a line extending from central California, east through Northern Texas to North Carolina, suggests the series of retrofitting options illustrated in Figure 4-4. Note that the recommended list covers management practices in addition to retrofitting procedures. Under cooling and ventilation, the suggestions include closing off unoccupied areas. Similarly, under the last two items, energy reduction recommends controlling elevators and reducing power load factors.

SUMMARY

Solar energy systems are either passive or active. In the passive system, solar energy is transferred directly to heat, not relying on pumps, blowers, or other methods of distribution. In the active solar system, heat is collected, stored, and distributed by pumps or blowers for hot water or space heating. Solar systems, used separately for hot water, space heating, or both, depend on auxiliary heat when solar energy falls below minimum daily requirements. Rising fuel prices, volume production, state and federal subsidies, and new technology will make solar energy more popular.

Advantages of solar energy are offset by the high initial cost and the danger of overloading conventional energy sources when solar energy users must turn to alternate sources of heat. For multiple-tenant buildings, there is the added problem of allocating solar energy operating costs to individual tenants.

Retrofitting refers to new construction that minimizes heat loss from (1) exterior walls, (2) partitions exposed to outside air, (3) windows and doors, (4) ceilings, and (5) floors. Insulating feasibility partly turns on the local number of degree days. The *degree day* refers to the number of degrees the average outside temperature falls below 65° F. *Degree days* refer to the annual sum of individual degree days. Generally, the higher the degree day, the more investment in added insulation is justified.

The more common methods of retrofitting buildings such as an apartment are directed toward reducing heating and cooling costs, and decreasing hot water and lighting expenses. Besides adding insulation, managers provide thermostats with set limits and improve heating efficiency by periodic equipment inspection and adjustment. Hot water expenses are reduced by lowering temperatures during off-peak hours, reducing hot water temperatures, and replacing shower heads and faucet aerators. Lighting expenses are reduced by relamping with lower-power-consuming fixtures.

Life-cycle costing is a method of evaluating energy investment based on four components: (1) the capital investment, (2) annual operating and maintenance costs, (3) annual repairs and replacement costs, and (4) salvage value. Under this procedure, benefits expected over the economic life of an investment are discounted by the

ZONE 4 RETROFIT OPTION NUMBERS AND TITLES			POTENTIAL OPTIONS BY BUILDING TYPE				
			Office	Hospital	Research and development	Multifamily housing	Warehouses
Cooling and ventilation	C-1	Replace Inefficient Air Conditioners	✓	✓	✓	✓	
	C-2	Install Time Clocks for Air Conditioners	✓	✓	✓		
	C-3	Install Temperature Controller and Sensor	✓	✓	✓	✓	
	C-4	Control Solar Heat Gain	✓	✓	✓	✓	
	V-1	Install Economizer Cycle	✓	✓	✓		
	V-2	Shut Down Air Distribution System	✓	✓	✓		✓
	V-3	Reduce Air Volume	✓	✓	✓		
	V-4	Install Automatic Thermostats	✓	✓	✓		✓
	V-5	Close Off Unoccupied Areas	✓	✓	✓	✓	✓
	V-6	Install Energy Recovery Equipment	✓	✓	✓		
	V-7	Prevent Air Stratification					✓
Lighting	L-1	Use Energy Conserving Fluorescent Lamps	✓	✓	✓	✓	✓
	L-2	Remove Lamps or Fixtures	✓	✓	✓	✓	✓
	L-3	Install Switching	✓	✓	✓		✓
	L-4	Replace Incandescent Lighting					✓
	L-5	Use More Efficient Lighting Sources	✓	✓	✓		✓
	L-6	Design Lighting for Specific Task	✓		✓		
	L-7	Lower Height of Lighting Fixtures					✓
	L-8	Remove Lights Over Stacks					✓
	L-9	Control Exterior Lighting	✓	✓	✓	✓	✓
Heating	H-1	Insulate Hot Bare Heating Pipes	✓	✓	✓	✓	✓
	H-3	Preheat Combustion Air	✓	✓	✓	✓	✓
	H-4	Replace Worn Boiler Controls	✓	✓	✓	✓	✓
	H-5	Insulate Steam Lines	✓	✓	✓	✓	✓
	H-6	Install and/or Replace Steam Traps	✓	✓	✓	✓	✓
	H-7	Return Steam Condensate to Boiler	✓	✓	✓	✓	✓
Water heating	W-1	Install Decentralized Water Heating		✓		✓	
	W-2	Install Water Flow Restrictors		✓		✓	
	W-3	Use Waste Heat for Water Heating		✓		✓	
	W-4	Insulate Hot Bare Domestic Water Pipes	✓	✓	✓	✓	✓
Misc.	M-1	Control Elevator Operation	✓	✓	✓	✓	
	M-2	Correct Poor Power Factor	✓	✓	✓	✓	✓

Figure 4-4 A guide for energy audits for building retrofitting: zone 4. *(Source: FEA, "Identifying Retrofit Projects for Buildings," Office of Energy Conservation and Environment (September 1976), p. 15.)*

present worth of one factor. The estimated economic life and the capitalization rate assumed for discounting are critical to the final result. To these figures, some engineers recommend a "differential escalation factor." This factor, based upon compound interest, compensates for expected increases in energy costs.

Energy investments are judged according to several ratios. The savings/investment ratio (SIR) is based on the net present value of expected savings divided by the investment cost. Others judge energy investments according to the payback period—the length of time required for annual cumulative savings to equal the initial investment. The more technical analysis of engineers bases BTU savings on the investment dollar. BTU savings are then converted to dollars according to the local price of energy per BTU. In these estimates, energy experts compare results with the base line—the present condition against which new energy conservation investments are measured—and incremental costs, which refer to the differences in cost between two energy conservation alternatives.

Insulation materials are judged according to the R value—the higher the R value the better the insulation. Recommended R value minimums vary by geographic zones. Generally, colder temperatures require investment in higher R value insulation.

Managing buildings to reduce energy costs covers a wide range of procedures. In some office buildings, managers have terminated flood lighting of building exteriors. Relamping and reducing wattage consumption by dimmer controls are other common energy-saving steps. Some buildings are controlled to automatically reduce peak energy demands to gain more favorable rate schedules.

Tenant cooperation is solicited to encourage setting thermostats lower for heat and higher for air conditioning. It is recommended to tenants that they leave vacant rooms unlighted and unheated with no air conditioning. Unused rooms are closed from heated or ventilated space. Managers take long-run steps to reduce energy requirements by providing appliances that are more energy efficient. And increasingly higher energy costs encourage more of the preventive maintenance that make building systems more efficient.

Because most building owners and managers are unacquainted with energy operating efficiencies or retrofitting procedures, an energy audit is usually advised. The energy audit concentrates on five retrofitting measures: heating and ventilating, lighting, cooling, water heating, and miscellaneous steps such as reducing the energy demand factor and controlling elevator operation for reduced energy consumption.

DISCUSSION QUESTIONS

1 Explain the difference between passive and active solar systems.
2 What are the main components of a solar energy system?
3 What factors are expected to make solar energy increasingly economical?
4 Discuss the main limitations of solar energy systems.
5 What are the main sources of building heat losses?
6 Explain the concept of a degree day; how does the number of degree days affect retrofitting feasibility?
7 Discuss the main ways to retrofit an apartment building.

8 Why are individual meters preferred to master billing?

9 What four components are critical to life-cycle costing?

10 Give an example showing how you would calculate the savings/investment ratio.

11 What is the significance of the "payback period"?

12 What type of BTU analysis indicates the feasibility of energy conservation?

13 What is the significance of insulation "R values"?

14 Explain how you would reduce energy consumption of an office building.

15 What recommendations would you give tenants in an apartment building to reduce energy costs?

16 What is the function of an energy audit; what does the energy audit cover?

KEY TERMS AND CONCEPTS

Passive solar energy systems
Active solar energy systems
Building retrofitting
Energy conservation management
Solar collectors
Peak energy demands
Degree days
Relamping
Master billing
Life-cycle costing

Present worth of one factor
Differential escalation factor
Savings/investment ratio
Payback period
BTU savings per investment dollar
R values
Base line
Incremental costs
Interruptible power
Energy audit

SELF-QUIZ

Multiple-Choice Questions

_____ 1 In general, which of the following statements applies to solar energy systems? Solar energy is associated with: (a) High operating expenses and low investment costs; (b) High initial investment costs and low operating costs; (c) Low initial investment and low operating costs; (d) High investment cost and high operating costs.

_____ 2 An active solar system: (a) Transfers solar energy directly to heat; (b) Uses window panels to store heat from direct rays of the sun and circulates heat by natural convection and radiation; (c) Is less efficient than a passive system; (d) Requires the collection, storage, and distribution of heat through pumps or fans.

_____ 3 Solar energy systems will tend to become more economical as: (a) Prices of fossil fuel increase; (b) State and federal subsidies become available for solar equipment investment; (c) Mass production and new technology decreases investment and operating costs; (d) All of the above.

_____ 4 Which of the following statements is correct? (a) As the number of degree days decreases, benefits from energy conservation techniques increase; (b) Energy conservation techniques are unrelated to the number of degree days; (c) As the number of degree days increases, benefits from energy conservation techniques increase; (d) As the number of degree days increases, benefits from energy conservation techniques decrease.

_____ 5 Typically, relamping an apartment building: (a) Lowers the quality of lighting; (b) Reduces annual electrical and lighting maintenance costs; (c) Is usually too expensive for existing buildings; (d) None of the above.

_____ 6 Observers have noted that converting from master billing to individual meters: (a) Reduces energy consumption by 30 to 50 percent; (b) Benefits property owners and not tenants; (c) Has a nominal effect on tenant energy consumption; (d) Benefits apartment building owners but not owners of condominium units.

_____ 7 Life-cycle costing is a method of: (a) Judging building profitability; (b) Estimating the building equipment life; (c) Evaluating all costs associated with operations over the equipment life; (d) Evaluating management operating efficiency.

_____ 8 In life-cycle costing, the differential cost escalation factor: (a) Compensates for expected increases in energy costs; (b) Is based on property management efficiencies; (c) Reflects anticipated labor cost increases; (d) Adjusts for potential rent increases.

_____ 9 The savings/investment ratio: (a) Refers to the length of time required for annual cumulative savings to equal the initial investment; (b) Depends on the estimate of British Thermal Units saved annually from the energy conservation; (c) Compares energy conservation investment to the base line; (d) Relates the net present value of expected savings to the investment cost.

_____ 10 Which of the following are common management techniques to reduce energy costs; (a) Replace incandescent lighting with low-power-consuming fluorescent fixtures; (b) Install temperature limiting thermostats; (c) Provide for the regular repair and adjustment of heating systems; (d) All of the above.

Answer Key

1 (b),   2 (d),   3 (d),   4 (c),   5 (b),   6 (a),   7 (c),   8 (a),   9 (d),   10 (d).

Fill-In Questions

1 A solar system that converts radiant energy to heat, stores the heat, and distributes the heat for hot water or space heating is termed an _____.

2 Rising_____ prices will make solar systems more economical.

3 The heating degree day is based on the principle that the heat used per day is proportional to the number of degrees the average outside temperature falls below _____.

4   Retrofitting apartment buildings focuses on reducing the cost of heating and cooling, heating hot water, and _____.

5   Apartment managers recommend replacing thermostats with units that have _____ for heating and _____ for air conditioning.

6   Under _____, tenants do not know how much electricity they use or its cost. Therefore they have no _____ to practice energy conservation.

7   _____ refer to the difference in cost between two energy conservation alternatives.

8   In general, minimum recommended insulation _____ would _____ if future fuel prices increase more than the cost of insulation.

9   Electric _____ refer to charges based upon the peak electric power _____ during the year.

10 The purpose of the _____ is to inventory the physical characteristics of the building to measure its thermal efficiency.

Answer Key

1	active system	6	master billing, economic incentive
2	fuel	7	Incremental costs
3	65 degrees	8	R values, increase
4	lighting	9	demand rates; demanded
5	upper limits, lower limits	10	energy audit

SELECTED REFERENCES

Anderson, Dwight C., Jay Q. Butler, and John R. Cesta: "Solar Energy Perspectives: 1977 to 1987," *Real Estate Today,* **10**(10):48–53 (1977).

Economics of Solar Home Heating, A Study for the Joint Economic Committee Congress of the United States, Washington, D.C.: Government Printing Office, 1977.

"How to Conserve Energy," *Realtors Review,* **1**(5):4–8 (1977).

Load Calculation, 4th ed. Arlington, Va.: National Environmental Systems Contractors Association, 1975.

Solar Energy . . . Proceed with Caution, Washington, D.C.: National Association of Home Builders, 1976.

Stevens, Thomas H.: "The Economics of Solar Heating Systems for the Southwest Region," *Journal of Energy Development,* **2**(2):279–291 (1977).

Part Two

Management
Operations

Chapter 5

Elements of Commercial Leases

After studying this chapter, you should be familiar with:
1 The general purposes of commercial leases
2 Advantages of leases to owners and tenants
3 Five categories of common lease provisions
4 Lease terms for special purposes: apartments, shopping centers, offices, and industrial property

If you were responsible for finding a site for a clothing store, would you favor a location next to a real estate office or next to a family shoe store? Other things being equal, managers would generally prefer the location near the family shoe store on the grounds that the two stores are mutually attractive—customers of one store are likely to be customers of the adjoining store. To a large degree the same situation applies to property managers in leasing office buildings, shopping centers, downtown space, and even apartments. In fact, the selection of mutually attractive tenants increases project profitability; incompatible tenants tend to decrease income and therefore property values.

By selecting appropriate tenants, the property manager may increase net operating income and significantly affect property value. In large measure, profitable projects turn on selecting the right tenant and, for each tenant, negotiating fair lease terms. Not only the local real estate market but the skill of the manager determines project feasibility. To gain the highest degree of competence, managers must know the main elements of commercial leases.

For the present purpose, an explanation of different types of leases precedes a discussion of specific lease provisions. The last part of the chapter covers preferred leasing practices for specific properties.

THE PURPOSE OF COMMERCIAL LEASES

For commercial property, do not reason the way homeowners do when they say that it is better to buy than to rent; for it is often advantageous for developers, industry, and other businesses to lease rather than to buy. By the same token, the owner may maximize economic interest by leasing rather than selling. To explain these points it is relevant to identify types of leases common for commercial purposes.

Types of Leases

Leases convey the exclusive right to use property according to lease terms for a specific time. That is, leases create a new estate commonly recognized as a *less than a freehold estate,* which may take one of four forms.

Estate for Years An estate for years is for a stated period of time. The time may range from a few days to a year or more. In some states, an estate for years must be in writing; in most states, a lease for a period for more than 1 year must be in writing.

Estates from Year to Year Also known as periodic tenancies, year-to-year estates may be created by agreement or by operation of law. The estate continues for successive periods until the owner or tenant gives notice of termination. Such an estate may include tenancies by the month or by the year which, however, continue for an indefinite number of months of years.

Tenancy at Will Created with the consent of the owner, tenancies at will may be terminated by either party with proper notice. Here the term of the tenancy is uncertain and indefinite, with the tenant holding possession with knowledge and permission of the owner.

Tenancy by Sufferance In a sense tenancy by sufferance is a misnomer, because these tenants have no estate or rights except temporary possession and they hold possession without owner consent.

The last of these leases is created if the tenant, unlawfully and without permission of the owner, holds over under an expired lease. The possession continues because the owner fails to exercise the right to repossess or fails to insist on continuing the tenancy under previous terms. Until the owner grants permission, the tenant remains a tenant by sufferance.

In the main, property managers negotiate leases that create estates for years. In this regard it is important to note that the lease creates two estates: the leased fee and the leasehold interest. These estates are shown in Figure 5-1, which identifies the owner as the *lessor* and the tenant as the *lessee,* who together hold the two estates: the *leased fee* and the *leasehold interest.*

For the present purpose, these estates may be further divided. Under some circumstances, the tenant or lessee may create still other estates or subleaseholds. The original lessee may become the sublessor with respect to the sublessee. This arrangement is common in shopping centers where the master lease provides construction of the shopping center on land leased for a fairly long term, say 99 years. The developer is the lessee with respect to the owner of the land (the lessor). The lessee builds the shopping center on leased land and subleases space over shorter terms (1 year to 20 years) to shopping center tenants. In these circumstances, the original lessee remains responsible to the lessor under terms of the master lease (see Figure 5-2).

The alternative allows the owner of the leasehold interest, usually with permission of the lessor, to assign his or her interest to a third party. Developers of shopping centers, for example, after negotiating subleases, may assign their interest to an investor. In this case, no new estate is created; the assignors merely transfer their interest to the assignee who assumes all the rights and liabilities of the original lessee. This arrangement is illustrated in Figure 5-3. The right to sublease or assign the lease gives the lessee certain financial advantages unique to leased estates.

Long-Term Leases "Long-term lease" is a relative term: an apartment lease of more than 3 years would be unusually long; but in shopping centers, probably leases of more than 5 years (and seldom going beyond 20 years) would be regarded as long-term leases. Net ground leases would qualify as long term if the lease goes beyond 25 years or so.

The main point is that the long-term lease helps to stabilize the value of estates under lease. The owner with a ground lease of 55 years, with appropriate adjustment clauses and secured by a financially strong tenant, helps establish the maximum value for the leased fee estate.

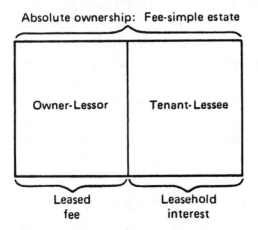

Absolute ownership: Fee-simple estate

Owner-Lessor   Tenant-Lessee

Leased   Leasehold
fee   interest

Figure 5-1 Creation of the leasehold estate and leased fee.

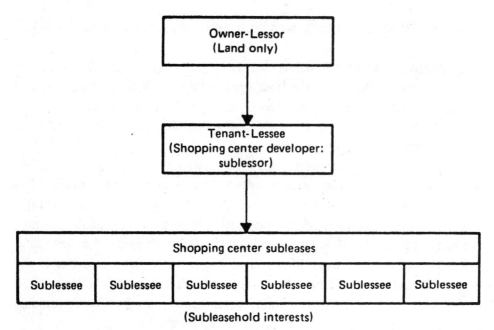

Figure 5-2 Creation of subleasehold interests.

By the same token a tenant with 25 years remaining on a lease, a situation that favors the tenant, may assign the leasehold estate to others for a considerable sum. Mortgage lenders secured by the leased fee or leasehold estate usually require long-term leases.

Net Ground Leases Net ground leases may be preferred by both the landowner and tenant. The tenant benefits from the income tax deductibility of land rent. The owner, by leasing land, defers capital gain taxes and pays net income taxes on the annual rent, less allowable deductions. In one sense, net ground leases constitute 100 percent financing; that is, the tenant gains possession in return for rental payments in contrast to a purchase, which would ordinarily be financed with less than a 100 percent mortgage.

Sale-Leasebacks Like the net ground lease, the sale-leaseback represents a financing arrangement. To illustrate, suppose that a building is sold and leased back by the seller. The seller gains cash and in turn becomes the lessee or tenant; the purchaser then becomes the lessor and owns a leased fee interest. The sale-leaseback may be financed with the assistance of a lender. In other words the purchaser makes an investment earning a return on capital (rent payments), which is partly financed by a first mortgage (see Figure 5-4).

It will be noted that the seller gains cash for the property and still retains possession under a long-term lease. Typically this arrangement is used if the seller has depleted depreciation allowances for income tax purposes and needs additional capital.

Lease Advantages to Owners

In some instances, parties have no alternative to leasing. If tenants desire a particular site, they may be forced to lease since the owner prefers leasing to selling. Furthermore,

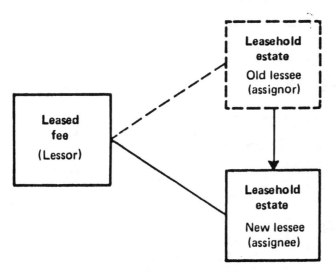

Figure 5-3 Assignment of a leasehold interest.

some companies follow a policy of acquiring possession by leasing land and buildings in preference to buying. Add to this list other owners, who for institutional reasons are restricted in their right to sell. American Indians, who have approximately 55 million acres held under trust by the Bureau of Indian Affairs, are restricted in the right to sell land held in trust status. Consequently, much of Indian-owned land in Palm Springs, California, and in the farming and recreational areas of Washington, Idaho, Montana, and Nevada is under lease.

Other companies that hold land incidental to their main activity, such as public utilities and timber companies, lease land for multiple-purpose, mainly recreational uses. Besides these restraints, owners have certain financing incentives to lease land and buildings.

Leasing Defers Capital Gain Taxes If sold, highly valuable land may be subject to maximum long-term capital gain taxes. Because of the large sums involved, owners may defer capital gain taxes by leasing. Though the rental income is subject to annual income taxes, the tax advantages may recommend long-term lease. Under a lease, benefits of ownership are realized in the form of annual income and not in immediate capital appreciation.

Leases Create Incomes Comparable to an Annuity Ideally, the owner or leasing agent selects tenants who pay rent that is certain and predictable over the lease term. A building leased under a long-term lease to the U.S. Postal Service or an office building leased by the local telephone company is much like a secure annuity with a high certainty of annual payments. The quality of income and its duration and amount are in large measure under control of the owner or the owner's agent.

Owners Benefit from Tenant Improvements Tenants who agree to construct buildings on leased land or remodel leased buildings increase the capital value of leased property. In this sense, the investment of the tenant, which eventually benefits the owner, is taxable only with increased rent when the lease expires, or with capital appreciation if the property is sold.

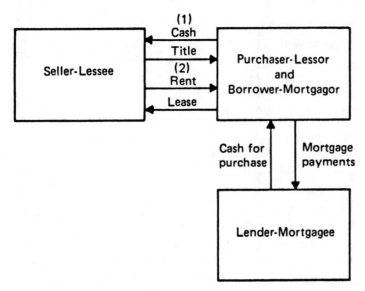

Figure 5-4 Sale-leaseback financing.

This advantage appeals to land owners who lack capital or skill in developing the land for a higher use such as a shopping center or industrial park. Under these arrangements, owners directly benefit from tenant improvements to leased property.

Superior Tenants Add Value to the Leased Fee   Suppose an owner has the option of leasing (1) to a financially strong national corporation, or (2) to a local business with few assets and an uncertain future. Assume further that both tenants agree to pay an annual rent of $10,000. Most owners would select the tenant with the higher credit rating. This is another way of saying that property leased to a financially strong tenant is more marketable than property leased to tenants with questionable credit.

Advantages to Tenants

Besides providing preferred sites that cannot be duplicated by purchase, leases create certain financial advantages to the tenant: some economic and some arising from income tax factors.

Leases Provide Maximum Financing   It is difficult to finance land purchases and, if financing is available, the loan ordinarily would not cover the total land value. The alternative of leasing gives the tenant virtually the same rights of possession with no capital outlay.

Moreover, if the tenant constructs a building on leased land and certain legal requirements are met, the tenant depreciates the building for income tax purposes over the lease term. Under the best circumstances, with a first mortgage on buildings and a long-term net ground lease, the tenant finances 100 percent of the land and building value.

Rent Is Income Tax Deductible   If a business purchases a building and land for commercial purposes, the maximum income tax deduction depends on the allowable building depreciation. No income tax deduction applies to the land. Therefore, for property in which the land value represents a substantial value, tenants are encouraged to lease—the rent on both building and land is income tax deductible. The incentive to lease land increases as the proportion of land to building value increases.

Leasing Reduces Tenant Capital Requirements Buyers gain possession in perpetuity in return for the purchase price. Under a lease, tenants gain possession for a specific time and in return for rental payments. Thus, rather than purchase rights in perpetuity with a large capital outlay, tenants save capital by agreeing to make annual rental payments over a lease term that is succifiently long for business purposes. Capital required for a land or building purchase may be used for other businesses purposes.

It should be added that to the degree market rent increases above contract rent, tenants benefit by the increase in the capital value of the leasehold interest. If market rent rises above contract rent, tenants acquire a valuable leasehold interest that may be sold and mortgaged (subject to terms of the lease) like other property interests. Therefore, leases give tenants opportunities for capital appreciation.

COMMON LEASE PROVISIONS

The outstanding feature of leases is their diversity. There is no standard form that is universally approved. Though printed lease forms are available from numerous sources, typically standard terms must be varied to meet new legal requirements, specially negotiated terms, and the peculiarities of leased property. Though property managers do not write leases, they must be familiar with general lease provisions (1) to guide lease negotiations and (2) to recognize agreements that require legal counsel. Their complexity is suggested by an office lease index (see Table 5-1) which precedes 14 pages of finely printed lease terms.

Though a detailed explanation of commercial lease terms is not relevant for the present purpose, it is believed helpful to explain the main lease provisions, understanding that a lease will not necessarily follow a functional or any other set order. With these qualifications, lease terms are presented in five categories: (1) introductory terms, (2) financial terms, (3) building improvements, (4) insurance, and (5) other legal aspects. Before covering these points in more detail it is worthwhile to review the requirements of an enforceable lease.

In most states, leases for more than 1 year must be in writing and, like other real estate instruments, enforceable leases must meet certain minimum requirements:

1 A beginning and ending date
2 Identification of the owner and tenant
3 A legal description of the property leased
4 Rental terms, including the time and place of payment
5 Signatures of the parties to the lease

It is further presumed that an enforceable lease will be for a legal purpose; it will be executed by competent parties; and it will be signed, witnessed and acknowledged

Table 5-1   An Office Lease Index*

*Furnished by courtesy of the late Vernon Murphy, former counsel, New York State Teachers' Retirement System.

according to state law. In short, the lease as in other contracts must have elements necessary to a legal, valid, and enforceable contract.

Introductory Terms

It will be noted that in Table 5-1 the lease begins with a description of the leased premises. Early in the lease, terms of the lease, the beginning and ending date, provision for lease renewal, and the minimum rent will be specified. Because of the technical nature of leases, the first part may cite definitions employed throughout the agreement.

To avoid misunderstanding, a net ground lease covering residential developments (the Salishan project in Gleneden Beach, Oregon) defines certain technical words covered in an 11-page lease:

> ... *common areas* shall mean all areas within Salishan devoted by Salishan, Inc. to the common use of Salishan tenants and shall include the private ways referred to in Section V, the community house, the swimming pool, and the tennis courts. ... the *primary rental* shall mean the rental provided in Section II.1. ... the *maintenance rental* shall mean the rental provided in Section 2.2 as the same may be increased as provided in Section 2.3 or decreased as provided in Section 2.4.

The lease continues with definitions of other technical terms appearing throughout the agreement. Similar material is provided in industrial and commercial leases that use special legal and technical terms common to special purpose properties.

Financial Rights

Critical to the lease are specific terms covering the rent payment with detailed provisions for (1) place and time of payment, and (2) the amount and its calculation. Recall that leases frequently extend over more than one generation. Consequently, special attention is given to financial terms that will be subject to interpretation by others not party to the original agreement.

Percentage Rent Definitions   The manner of calculating percentage rents for retail tenants requires careful explanation. Since rents are partly based on annual gross sales, it is necessary to define gross sales with respect to bad debts, merchandise returns, sales or excise taxes, and other business receipts.

The shopping center lease developed by Federated Department Stores excludes four items from the definition of gross sales:

sales taxes
exchanges of goods between company stores
purchase returns
sales of stores fixtures

These exclusions from gross sales define sales to retail customers, which serve as the base to calculate percentage rents.

While gross receipts are defined to include all income, the four exclusions define normal sales to retail customers.

In other leases that require tenants to construct building improvements on leased land, the owner may also require percentage rents. In a net ground lease on 20 acres leased for a new hotel and apartment construction in a resort area, the minimum rent was graduated from $5,000 for the first year to $44,000 for the fifth and succeeding years. The 65-year lease, however, required the tenant to construct building improvements with a value of at least $2,000,000 by the end of the fifth year. The lease further provided percentage rents of 5 percent of hotel and apartment rentals.

Lease Assignments Besides percentage rent provisions, where applicable, some provision must be made for tenants to transfer their interest. In still other instances, tenants may wish to sublease portions of the premises. However, these rights are generally granted only with approval of the lessor.

Presumably the lessor initially selects the tenant with the financial means and competency to maximize income. This is especially true if the lease provides for percentage rents. In multiple-tenant occupancy, moreover, the owner must make certain that succeeding tenants and their land-use practices are compatible with other tenants.

Some office leases, however, prohibit assignment and subletting. For instance:

> The lessee shall not (a) assign or convey this lease or any interest under it; (b) allow any transfer hereof or any lien upon the lessee's interest by operation of law; (c) sublet the premises or any part thereof, or (d) permit the use or occupancy of the premises or any part thereof by any other than the lessee.

While appropriate for relatively short-term office leases, longer-term leases common to net ground leases usually provide assignment with lessor approval.

> Lessee shall not encumber, assign or otherwise transfer this Lease, or any right or interest herein, or in or to any of the buildings and improvements on the leased premises, nor shall sublet said premises or any part thereof for a term longer than nine (9) months in any consecutive twelve (12) months period, without the written consent and approval of the Lessor.

Failure to observe these terms places the lessee in default, allowing the lessor to terminate the lease at its option.

The right of assignment may further protect the tenant from unreasonable delay.

> Lessor agrees that it will not unreasonably withhold its consent to any assignment or transfer requiring its prior approval hereunder. . . .

In other long-term leases, terms may allow the lessee to assign the lease without approval or consent provided the lessee remain responsible to the lessor unless the lessor consents in writing to such an assignment.

No such assignment shall release the assignor from further liability hereunder unless Lessor shall consent in writing to such assignment, and Lessor will not require payment of any money except said service charge for such consent nor withhold such consent unreasonably or because of the assignee's national origin, race, color or creed.

Usually long-term leases requiring mortgage financing will exempt the mortgagee or lender from restrictions on assignments.

Building Improvements

These provisions relate primarily to tenant construction. In net ground leases, for shopping centers, apartments, condominiums, or industrial property, the owner has a vested interest in the type of building, its construction, maintenance, and repair. Initially, the building should conform to the highest and best use. And to ensure conformity with owner objectives, tenants must submit architectural plans for owner approval. This provision, while restrictive, ensures that property will be developed to its maximum potential—benefiting the owner and tenant. A typical provision would read as follows:

The lessee shall submit the general plan and architect's design for the complete development for the entire leased premises. The lessor shall either approve or state reasons for disapproval of plans and specifications within thirty (30) days after their submission.

In a similar manner, it is in the interest of the owner to provide proper property maintenance. These minimum building provisions are accompanied by lease terms giving the final date of completion and placing the tenant in default if these restrictions are not observed.

In leases that require construction of buildings on leased land, it is not unusual for owners to require security guaranteeing completion of the building and payment of all construction costs. A corporate surety bond, equal to the cost of the building, satisfies this requirement. Alternatively, tenants may be permitted to deposit cash or securities in escrow sufficient to pay the cost of proposed buildings. It is not unusual for 15 percent of escrow funds to be withheld until time expires for filing of mechanics' or material liens.

Insurance Requirements

Leases include terms that protect the owner from liabilities or damages rising from acts of the tenant. In part the usual lease reads:

Tenant shall not do or permit any act or thing upon the demised premises which may subject the landlord to any liability or responsibility, damages to persons or damages to property or to any liability by reason of any violation of law or of any legal requirement of public authority. . . .

And further,

> ... tenants shall indemnify and hold harmless landlord from and against any and all liability, fines, suits, claims, demands and actions in cause and expense of any kind. ...

As further protection tenants may be required to purchase public liability insurance acceptable to the owner. Current practice recommends a minimum limit of $300,000 on account of bodily injuries to or death of one person and $1,000,000 on account of bodily injuries to or death or more than one person as result of any accident or disaster, and $50,000 on account of damages to property.

In the case of a net ground lease, provisions will be added to protect the tenant from fire and other disasters. If the premises are destroyed, the lease will provide for reconstruction especially during the early years of the lease. During the final years of the lease, which will be specifically stated under total destruction, the tenant may be given the option to cancel the lease or require the lessor to rebuild with insurance proceeds. In illustration a net ground lease would typically require:

> Lessee shall, during the construction of said building and of pertinent structures on the leased premises and at all times thereafter during the term hereof, keep the same insured against all or damage by fire, with extended coverage indorsements, and vandalism jointly in the name of lessee, lessor, the landlord and any approved encumbrancer, and in an amount equal to the full insurable value of the buildings insured.

Usually total destruction or 75 percent or more of the total value of buildings and improvements would give the lessee the option to repair or not to repair buildings and improvements. If the tenant does not reconstruct improvements, the lease will generally require the tenant to remove the remaining structures and pay insurance proceeds to the owner.

Other Legal Aspects

Since the lease commits both parties to long-term commitments, the lease must explicitly define rights and duties of both parties. A brief review of the more critical provisions illustrates the complex legal issues that require legal representation.

Security Deposits The laws of some states require that security deposits be deposited in separate escrow accounts. To comply with state law, many leases must document the security deposit by stating the amount, the date of payment, and the date the security deposit will be returned to the tenant, less any amount applied to damages sustained by tenant breach of lease terms.

The agreement may add further that if the property is sold the security will be repaid to the buyer, making the sale subject to the lease and relieving the owner of further liability with respect to the tenant security deposit.

Eminent Domain   Leases consistently specify rights of parties under eminent domain actions. For instance, some leases state that if the building is taken by eminent domain, the tenant has no right to share in the award, though the tenant will usually have the right to cancel the lease if a substantial portion of the premises is taken. In other instances just compensation is paid to the lessor and lessee "as their interests appear." The terms of the lease may state that no money or other considerations shall be payable by the lessor to the lessee for the right of cancellation.

Tenant Duties   Among the tenant duties are requirements that the tenant "shall commit no act of waste and shall take good care of the premises, fixtures; and appurtenances." In addition, the use and the occupancy of the premises shall conform to all laws, orders and regulations of federal, state and municipal governments. Furthermore, the tenant shall not without owner consent:

> (a) make any alterations, additions or improvements to or about the premises; (b) do or suffer anything to be done on the premises which will increase the rate of fire insurance on the building; or (c) permit the premises to become vacant or deserted.

And further,

> ... tenant shall observe and comply with the rules and regulations hereinafter set forth, which are made part hereof, and with such further reasonable rules and regulations as landlord may prescribe, on written notice to tenant, for the safety, care, and cleanliness of the building and the comfort, quiet and convenience of other occupants of the building.

In the usual case, tenants are prohibited from making any assignments of the property for benefit of creditors and in further illustration, if the tenant defaults in payment of rent, and:

> If the default shall continue 5 days after the owner gives tenant a written notice specifying default and if the default is not remedied within specified number of days [typically 15 days], the owner shall give tenant written notice specifying the time and require that if the tenant does not correct the default within an additional term the owner has the right to terminate the lease according to terms of the lease and state law.

Particular attention will be given to use of the premises by tenants. The tenant's proposed use will be stated and other uses will be restricted: "The lessee shall occupy and use premises during the term for the purposes above specified and none other." Residential leases of multiple-family projects not only control use but the manner of use; namely, no storage in hallways or public areas. Outside antennas may be prohibited, and even outside balcony use may be restricted if the use results in an unsightly appearance.

Owner Duties   The owner will covenant and agree to protect the tenant's right to peaceably and quietly have, hold, and enjoy the leased premises. Depending on the type of lease, the lease will cover specific services to be supplied by the landlord—such items as elevator service, provision for needed heat and air conditioning, cleaning services, and window cleaning, among others.

In some instances the owner may add special provisions on security protection: guards, special locks, alarms, and protection systems.

LEASE TERMS FOR SPECIAL PURPOSES

It is not possible to adapt standard lease forms for all commercial and industrial properties. Leases must satisfy special objectives of tenants and owners, which vary widely by property type. Consequently, leases are subject to almost infinite variation. With this qualification, it will be observed, however, that leases for the more common properties cover points of common interest to owners and tenants.

Apartment Leases

Apartment tenants ordinarily make security deposits which are returned if the premises show no damage at the end of the lease. As a result special attention will be given to the rights of the parties with respect to damages and waste. A clause commonly found in these leases states:

> The lessee accepts said premises in their present condition and agrees to keep said premises in a good clean condition; to make no alterations or additions to the same; to commit no waste thereon; to obey all laws and ordinances affecting said premises; to replace all glass broken or cracked; to repay the lessor the cost of all repairs made necessary by the negligent or careless use of said premises.

Because of the effect on building operations, the tenant is usually prohibited from sharing the premises; keeping roomers or boarders; or assigning, subletting, or transferring premises without owner consent. In signing the lease the tenant agrees to observe all rules and regulations. Finally, the tenant agrees to "peacefully surrender and deliver up the whole of the premises together with all improvements upon expiration of the lease term."

Tenants who hold over beyond the lease term will not be granted an automatic renewal. But with permission of the owner, a holdover tenant will have only a month-to-month occupancy. The lease will specify services agreed to by the owner in furnishing heat, elevator service, and operation of household equipment, hot and cold water, and other services. The lease will state rights of the owner in dealing with tenants in default for not observing other covenants of the lease.

Shopping Center Leases

Shopping center leases are considerably more technical. They are complicated because tenants make their own alterations and, in some cases, pay their own utilities. They are part of a shopping center enterprise and must operate their businesses in a manner that is compatible with other shopping center tenants. The International Council of Shopping Centers provides a checklist to summarize the financial aspects of a shopping center lease (see Table 5-2).

Table 5-2 summarizes the source of income to the owner and identifies the cost of operation assumed by owner and tenant. The form not only summarizes the rental

Table 5-2 Shopping Center Lease Checklist: Financial Terms

Store (tenant) _____

Tenant's address _____

Square foot area _____

Starting date of lease _____

Term of lease _____

Renewal privilege _____

Rental per annum _____

Minimum rental per square feet _____

Percentage clause

_____ % on sales over $ _____

_____ % on sales over $ _____

_____ % on sales over $ _____

Maintenance of leased premises

	Lessor	Lessee
Exterior maintenance	_____	_____
Parking lot	_____	_____
Interior maintenance	_____	_____
Plate glass	_____	_____
Air conditioner	_____	_____
Heating	_____	_____
Plumbing (inside)	_____	_____
Plumbing (outside)	_____	_____

Ownership

	Lessor	Lessee
Light fixtures	_____	_____
Water fountain	_____	_____
Heating	_____	_____
Air conditioner	_____	_____
Store fixtures	_____	_____
Other	_____	_____

Merchants' association required _____

Amount of monthly charge _____

Destruction of premises % _____

Eminent domain % _____

Taxes _____

Exclusive clause _____

Indemnification by landlord _____

Sublet privilege _____

Remarks _____

_____

Source: Adapted from *Lease Abstract Form-Developer*, New York: International Council of Shopping Centers, 1977.

terms but the maintenance of leased premises assumed by the lessor or lessee. Since the tenant may invest considerable sums in alterations, the owner and tenant responsibility for construction is specifically stated. Membership in a merchant's association, tenant charges, the right of the tenant to conduct business and sublet are other significant financial terms.

To be sure, the shopping center lease covers many other rights and duties. The items summarized in Table 5-1 identify only financial terms that are common to shopping center leases.

Office Leases

While office leases are more fully explained in Chapter 18, it should be pointed out here that office leases particularly deal with:

use of premises
the electrical load
owner services

Clauses limiting tenant use of the premises may be quite detailed or simply state that "tenants shall use and occupy the premises for office purposes and for no other purpose." Legal counsel may advise further that an illegal use gives owners grounds to terminate the lease:

It is understood and agreed that in the event that the premises are used at any time during the term for any other, or for an illegal purpose, the landlord shall have the option of terminating this lease.

With the popularity of electronic office equipment and computers, owners must guard against electrical overloads. Office leases cover this point by stating that the tenant shall not use electrical equipment that will overload the wiring, insulation, or interfere with safe and reasonable use by the owner or other building tenants. Agreement on alterations and the responsibility for paying for special construction required by each tenant are made part of the lease agreement.

The financing of office buildings usually requires a subordination clause that makes the leased premises subject to a first mortgage or deed of trust. It will be agreed that the lease is subordinate to any mortgage or deed of trust on the leased premises. Foreclosure on the first mortgage typically provides that the lease continue in full force and effect.

Office leases provide for the right of the owner to show premises to prospective purchasers and tenants during business hours and upon reasonable notice to the tenant. Related statements give the owner the right to inspect and enter premises at reasonable times on reasonable notice for the purpose of making repairs, replacements, and additions.

Industrial Leases

Industrial leases represent a special case. Like office buildings, industrial tenants must adapt the building to their needs. In addition, especially in industrial parks that have other nearby tenants, the property use must be rigidly controlled. Some leases would prohibit outside storage, truck parking in front of the building, and controls that provide landscape and architectural approval. An industrial lease in the Salem Industrial Center of Salem, Massachusetts leased to an apparel company restricts use to "manufacturing, warehousing, fabrication and sale of plastic, rubber, paper and textile products and all other products allied thereto."

Because of this special purpose use, lease clauses that state "the lessee will not make any structural alterations or additions" are often supplemented by a rider that covers repairs and alterations. In illustration:

> The lessee shall accept demised premises in their existing condition and state of repair, except that the lessor will at personal expense do all repair and alteration such as
> (a) spray paint the demised premises with one coat of paint,
> (b) construct a door opening at the west side of the demised premises sufficient to handle trucking of the lessee.

Because of the high-speed textile machinery, the lease may provide for temperature and humidity control (to prevent thread breakage). For example:

> The lessor at personal expense will furnish heat sufficient to maintain the temperature of 68° F on the first floor of the demised premises from 8:00 a.m. to 6:00 p.m. on weekdays during each period from September 1 to April 30, inclusive. Heat during other hours to be furnished at expense of the lessee in the form of additional rent.

In other instances, depending on the condition of the building, lease terms may provide that:

> The lessee agrees to make the following improvements at personal expense: repair roof, replace glass, repair walls, repair doors, clean floor, recondition electric heat and install heat radiators to suit tenant needs, repair plumbing, restore offices, and repair the sewage system.

If the lease is executed for a national tenant, the owner usually will be required to accept the lease agreement used by the leasing company. A lease published by the Westinghouse Corporation requires that the lessor "shall perform any and all maintenance, repairs, and replacements which may be necessary to maintain the leased premises in good and tenantable condition." In this case the lessee reserves the right to assign the lease or sublet the premises without consent of the lessor, provided that the assignment or subletting does not relieve the lessee of duties to perform under the lease.

SUMMARY

Property managers deal mostly with leases identified as an *estate for years*—a lease for a stated period. The periodic tenancies, which continue for successive periods or until the owner or tenant give notice of termination, are *estates from year to year.* The two other estates, *tenancy at will* (terminated by either party with proper notice) and *tenancy at sufferance* (tenants who hold possession without permission), though legally significant, are less important to management operation.

In dealing with estates under lease, authorities differentiate between subleasing and lease assignments. Starting with the proposition that the lease creates two estates: the leased fee (held by the owner-lessor) and the leasehold estate (held by the tenant-lessee), tenants may exercise either of two options—assign the lease (no new estate is created) or sublease, creating a new estate. In this latter instance, the original lessee remains responsible to the owner.

Property managers deal with *long-term leases,* extending up to 99 years, and *net ground leases,* which may be more economical because of income tax factors and minimum capital requirements. *Sale-leasebacks* are another means of financing in which the seller simultaneously "leases back" the premises. The rent to the new purchaser will be viewed as a return on invested capital.

These arrangements give certain advantages to *owners;* they defer capital gain taxes, they create incomes comparable to an annuity, they give benefits from tenant improvements, and they often result in capital appreciation.

By the same token *tenants* enjoy certain unique benefits from a lease; it provides maximum financing, it allows income tax deductions for rent, and it reduces capital requirements. Furthermore, under favorable trends, tenants benefit from capital appreciation.

For the present purpose lease terms have been discussed under five categories: introductory terms, financial terms, building improvements, insurance, and other legal aspects. The introductory terms include definitions important to the lease, the legal description, rental terms, and the beginning and ending date of the lease.

Financial rights not only detail rent and its payment but carefully define the calculation of percentage rent. Provision for lease assignments and subleasing will be reviewed in lengthy and detailed terms.

Building improvements called for by the lease would normally require architectural approval, a limited time for construction, and terms that guarantee completion of the building and payment of all construction costs.

Insurance terms protect the owner from liability or damages arising from the acts of the tenant. Public liability insurance and fire insurance describe rights of the parties in the event of personal injuries or damages to property.

Other legal aspects, while covering numerous requirements of state and contract law, usually define rights of the parties with respect to security deposits, eminent domain, and special duties assumed by the tenant and owner.

Of special importance in *apartment leases* are terms that define property use and the responsibility of the tenant with respect to damages and waste. The tenant is required to observe all rules and regulations and will be governed by the terms of the lease with respect to holding over beyond the lease term.

Similarly *shopping center leases* are considerably more technical. The financial aspects of a lease recommend a checklist covering the source of income to the owner and certain costs of operation variously assumed by owner and tenant. Shopping center leases differ in the way in which tenants pay for alterations, participate in the merchants' association, conduct business, and sublet.

Office leases deal specifically with tenant use of the premises, the maximum electrical load, and other owner services supplied to tenants. Tenant alterations, their approval, financing, and disposition at the end of the lease, will be the result of individual negotiations.

There are others who specialize in *industrial leases* for special property uses. Because industrial users have specialized needs, leases will frequently provide for building alterations and terms covering their cost, planning, and construction, which become part of the lease agreement. Particular attention will be given to the use of the property for industrial purposes, especially in industrial parks that must control industrial use for benefit of other industrial occupants.

DISCUSSION QUESTIONS

1 Explain differences between four types of estates created by leases.
2 Show how the lessee may (a) transfer a leasehold interest without creating a new estate and (b) create a new estate. Give examples in support of your answer.
3 Give an example showing that an owner would be advised to execute a net ground lease.
4 When would you recommend a sale-leaseback? Explain thoroughly.
5 Explain four leading advantages of leases to the lessor.
6 Explain three advantages of a lease to prospective lessees.
7 Give examples of common agreements included in the introductory terms to a lease.
8 What financial rights would be emphasized in the lease?
9 What are some of the common lease provisions with respect to new buildings?
10 What are minimum insurance requirements?
11 Explain certain other legal aspects covered by leases. Include typical duties of the tenant and owner.
12 What special lease terms seem common to apartment leases?
13 What special provisions are found in most shopping center leases?
14 How do office leases vary from other commercial leases?
15 What special provisions must be considered in leasing industrial property?

KEY TERMS AND CONCEPTS

Less than freehold estate	Sublessor
Estate for years	Sublessee

Estates from year to year	Lease assignment
Tenancy at will	Assignor
Tenancy by sufferance	Assignee
Lessor	Net ground leases
Lessee	Sale-leasebacks
Leased fee	Enforceable leases
Leasehold interest	Public liability insurance
Long-term leases	Security deposits
Subleaseholds	Holdover tenants

SELF-QUIZ

Multiple-Choice Questions

_____ 1 An estate for years may be defined as: (a) A periodic tenancy; (b) An estate created with the consent of the owner that may be terminated by either party with proper notice; (c) A lease for a stated period of time; (d) An estate with temporary possession held without owner consent.

_____ 2 A tenant who subleases becomes a _____ with respect to the subtenant: (a) Sublessor; (b) Sublessee; (c) Assignor; (d) Assignee.

_____ 3 Which of the following describes a sale-leaseback? (a) The purchaser becomes the lessee or tenant; (b) The purchaser holds a leasehold interest; (c) The seller gains cash and in turn becomes the lessee or tenant; (d) The purchaser gains cash and remains in possession under a long-term lease.

_____ 4 Which of the following represents lease advantages to owners? (a) Leasing defers capital gain taxes; (b) Leases create incomes comparable to an annuity; (c) Owners benefit from tenant improvements and superior tenants add value to the leased fee; (d) All of the above.

_____ 5 Which of the following is _not_ a lease advantage enjoyed by tenants? (a) Tenants may not depreciate rented buildings; (b) Leases provide maximum financing; (c) Rent is income tax deductible; (d) Leasing reduces tenant capital requirements.

_____ 6 Enforceable leases will be: (a) Executed by competent parties; (b) Signed, witnessed, and acknowledged according to state law; (c) For a legal purpose; (d) All of the above.

_____ 7 Which of the following would be included in gross sales to calculate percentage rents in a shopping center lease? (a) Merchandise returns; (b) Bad debts and sales taxes; (c) Sale fixtures; (d) Budget sales to customers.

_____ 8 Tenants are protected from unreasonable delay on the part of the lessor by terms that state: Lessor agrees that it will not unreasonably withhold its consent to any _____ or transfer requiring its prior approval: (a) Condemnation action; (b) Assignment; (c) Mortgage financing; (d) None of the above.

_____ 9 Lease agreements usually provide that the tenant shall commit no act of _____: (a) Hostility; (b) Passion; (c) Waste; (d) Criminal intent.

_____ 10 Financial terms common to shopping center leases include: (a) Rental terms including renewal privileges; (b) Maintenance of leased premises; (c) Ownership of fixtures, heating, and air conditioning equipment; (d) All of the above.

Answer Key

1 (c), 2 (a), 3 (c), 4 (d), 5 (a), 6 (d), 7 (d), 8 (b), 9 (c), 10 (d).

Fill-In Questions

1 Leases create a new estate commonly recognized as a _____ _____ .

2 Ground leases are attractive to tenants since land rent is _____ .

3 The incentive to lease land increases as the proportion of _____ _____ .

4 Leases generally restrict the right of the lessee to _____ her or his interest.

5 Tenants are usually required to purchase _____ insurance acceptable to the owner.

6 Most leases state that if the building is taken by _____ , the tenant has no right to share in the reward.

7 _____ covenant and agree to protect the _____ _____ to peaceably and quietly have, hold, and enjoy the leased premises.

8 Leases frequently provide that an _____ use gives owners grounds to terminate the lease.

9 Office building leases usually include a _____ that makes leased premises subject to a first mortgage or deed of trust.

10 _____ commonly prohibit outside storage and truck parking in front of the building, and provide for owner landscape and architectural approval.

Answer Key

1 less than freehold estate
2 income tax deductible
3 land to building value increases
4 assign or sublet
5 public liability

6 eminent domain
7 Owners, tenant's right
8 illegal
9 subordination clause
10 Industrial leases

SELECTED REFERENCES

Friedman, Milton R.: *Friedman on Leases*, New York: Practicing Law Institute, 1974, chap. 7.

Kratovil, Robert, and Raymond J. Werner: *Real Estate Law*, 7th ed., Englewood Cliffs, N.J.: Prentice-Hall, 1979, chap. 37.

Lusk, Harold F., and William B. French: *Law of the Real Estate Business*, 3rd ed., Homewood, Ill.: Irwin, 1975, chap. 15.

Chapter 6

Rental Terms

After studying this chapter, you should be familiar with:
1 The impact of inflation on lease objectives
2 Rental adjustment techniques
3 Percentage rents for net ground leases
4 Escalator clauses for long-term leases

Rental terms conform generally to lease objectives. One of the first objectives is to negotiate the market rent, which usually represents the going rate of return on invested capital. But because of rising property values and inflation, methods of adjusting rent during the lease assume equal importance. Accordingly, the first part of the chapter starts with an explanation of lease objectives showing the effect of anticipated inflation on final negotiated rental terms. Methods of adjusting rent over the lease term, including escalator clauses, complete the chapter.

LEASE OBJECTIVES

First consider owners and tenants negotiating under a high degree of uncertainty. The owner may approve only a month-to-month tenancy or at the most a 1-year lease if local conditions are expected to increase rental values. Pending downtown projects, new construction, proposed zoning changes, and new public improvements are among the many conditions that create uncertainty. Next consider tenants who may be unwilling to negotiate leases that are longer than 1 year (or even less) because of uncertainties over business profits. In these circumstances, the *short-term* lease meets objectives of owners and tenants.

Apart from these basic considerations are owner-tenant long-term projections. Tenants with favorable expectations of business profits like long-term leases. If, in contrast, downtown retailers anticipate more competition from shopping centers, they would favor relatively short-term leases. In negotiating leases, owners adopt the opposite strategy. Here optimistic projections favor short-term leases. If, on the contrary, rents, gross sales, and business profits are expected to decline, owners generally favor the longest possible lease.

Long-term leases, however, may be required for certain projects. Tenants and owners alike may invest heavily in land and in buildings that must earn a return over their relatively long economic lives. Such investments are not made without long-term revenue commitments. Moreover, lenders often require long-term leases, which for the present purpose, are considered to be 10 years or longer. If a building is to be financed on leased ground, some lenders require leases that extend beyond the mortgage term; others require minimum lease terms such as 55 years. State-regulated lenders may be prohibited from lending on leaseholds that do not have a lease term of 75 or even 99 years.

Hence, for legal and financial reasons, long-term leases are frequently necessary. The main objective, therefore, is to negotiate a satisfactory method of adjusting rent over the lease term. A review of inflationary trends illustrates the critical importance of rental adjustments.

The Impact of Anticipated Inflation

The index lease (which partly ties rent to changes in prices) and escalator clauses (which increase rent in accordance with changes in selected expenses such as property taxes, insurance, and utility costs) are popular means of adapting long-term leases to continued inflation. The acceptability of these and other measures, which vary rents over the lease term, depends partly on expected price changes over the term of the lease. A review of past price changes illustrates these issues.

The Consumer Price Index   The Consumer Price Index is not a complete measure of the declining value of the dollar. Historically, the Consumer Price Index has measured the average change in prices of goods and services purchased by highly select groups, namely, city wage earners and clerical-worker families. To construct the index, the Bureau of Labor Statistics has based earlier data on some 400 goods and services currently priced in 56 metropolitan areas. The intent was to measure the quantity, quality, and price of commodities and services in the "market basket" purchased by urban workers.[1]

---

[1] Beginning January 1, 1978, a newer version of the Consumer Price Index has been published by the Bureau of Labor Statistics. The newer Consumer Price Index (CPI_w) refers to a broader group of workers. The older Consumer Price Index (CPI_u) is still confined to the prices paid by clerical and blue collar workers in selected metropolitan areas. During 1978, the differences between these indexes were quite nominal.

**Table 6-1 The Consumer Price Index,
Showing the Purchasing Power of the
Dollar, 1967–1978**

(1967 = 100)

Year	Consumer Price Index	Purchasing power (percent)
1967	100.0	100.0
1968	104.2	96.0
1969	109.8	91.1
1970	116.3	86.0
1971	121.3	82.4
1972	125.3	79.8
1973	133.1	75.1
1974	147.7	67.7
1975	161.2	62.0
1976	170.5	58.7
1977	181.5	55.1
1978	195.4	51.2

Table 6-1 indicates that the index has increased to 195.4 at the end of 1978 from the base year of 1967. If this index is used to measure the price level, the purchasing power of the dollar, in terms of 1967 prices, has decreased to $0.51. In other words, an annual rental of $1,000 negotiated in 1967 purchases goods and services today worth $512, in terms of 1978 dollars.

The Wholesale Price Index The Wholesale Price Index is based on prices of 2,700 commodities. Reported monthly, this index tends to show greater variation and slightly larger price increases compared to the Consumer Price Index. Like the Consumer Price Index, it is not necessarily related to changes in local real estate values, rents, or net operating income.

Table 6-2 indicates that from the base year of 1967 to the end of 1978 wholesale prices increased by 209.3 percent. If the purchasing power of the dollar is measured by this index, a dollar in 1978 purchased $0.48 worth of goods and services compared to $1.00 of purchases made in 1967.

The Implicit Price Deflator The implicit price deflator, which is reported in the monthly *Survey of Current Business* published by the Department of Commerce, converts Gross National Product (GNP) from current dollars to constant dollars. Since the GNP represents the annual market value of all goods and services, conversion to constant dollars shows absolute changes in the physical production of goods and services. In other words, the implicit price deflator indicates the GNP undistorted by price inflation or deflation.

In this sense, the implicit price deflator is more comprehensive than the Consumer or Wholesale Price Index. It is drawn from prices of all commodities and services and it

**Table 6-2 The Wholesale Price Index,
Showing the Purchasing Power of the Dollar,
1967–1978**

(1967 = 100)

Year	Wholesale Price Index	Purchasing power (percent)
1967	100.0	100.0
1968	102.5	97.6
1969	106.5	93.9
1970	110.4	90.6
1971	114.0	87.7
1972	119.1	84.0
1973	134.7	74.2
1974	160.1	62.5
1975	174.9	57.2
1976	183.0	54.6
1977	194.2	51.5
1978	209.3	48.0

is weighted by the relative importance of investment, consumption, government purchases, and net foreign investments. Economists prefer this measure to estimate the general price level, since it is taken from all components of national production. Changes in the implicit price deflator are shown in Table 6-3.

In this instance, the series begins with the base year 1972. To provide a comparison with other indexes, purchasing power is shown as a relative change from 1967. The implicit price deflator indicates a decline in the purchasing power of the dollar from 100.0 in 1967 to 51.9 in 1978. The declining purchasing power of the dollar, according to three price indexes, is shown in Figure 6-1.

Rents adjusted according to changes in a selected index ensure that the tenant and owner neither gain nor lose from price inflation. In this respect the index lease stabilizes rent in terms of other prices. Theoretically, neither tenant nor owner gain or lose. Presumably, a lease adjusted for changes in the price level maintains the status quo between owner and tenant.

Price Index Limitations

However, it is not always clear that real estate values and their corresponding rents move according to changes in other prices. First, expenses of operation (primarily property taxes, utilities, and labor costs, which in the service trades are highly unionized) may move upward more rapidly than the general price level. Local construction costs (in an industry that is also highly unionized) and land values may be expected to increase at a more rapid rate than prices in general. When this occurs, the price index will lag behind changes in real estate values and operating costs faced by owner-lessors.

Table 6-3 Implicit Price Deflators for Gross
National Product, 1967-1978

(1972 = 100)

Year	Implicit price deflator	Purchasing power (percent)* (1967 = 100)
1967	79.0	100.0
1968	82.6	95.6
1969	86.7	91.1
1970	91.4	86.4
1971	96.0	82.3
1972	100.0	79.0
1973	105.9	74.6
1974	116.4	67.9
1975	127.2	62.1
1976	133.9	59.0
1977	141.1	56.0
1978	152.1	51.9

*For comparison purposes, purchasing power has been expressed as a percentage change from 1967.

Second, real estate values and rents are highly localized. In growth communities, costs and values may be expected to move upward more rapidly than general prices. Similarly, in declining economic areas or in relatively declining neighborhoods, the converse may be true.

Prospects for continuing inflation are indicative of the declining purchasing power of the dollar, which directs attention to rental terms over the life of the lease. Rental adjustments to meet lessor-lessee objectives and to offset inflation are readily at hand.

RENTAL ADJUSTMENTS

Before considering the variation in rental terms, it is worthwhile to review the interest of the owner and tenant. Consider first the owner, who typically requires the market return on invested capital. When opportunities for capital gains and tax shelters are significant, the owner usually negotiates for the maximum rent.

Assume that over the term of the lease, market rent increases with other prices, values, and construction costs. Under these circumstances, owners are likely to conclude that the higher market rent arises primarily because of site advantages. Owners therefore feel that they should benefit from the higher productivity of the site.

The tenant directly opposes this position, and views the higher market rent as a consequence of tenant capital and prudent operating practices. Thus, the increased market rent is believed to be directly assignable to tenant operations. In these circumstances it would be difficult to negotiate rent unless both parties compromised.

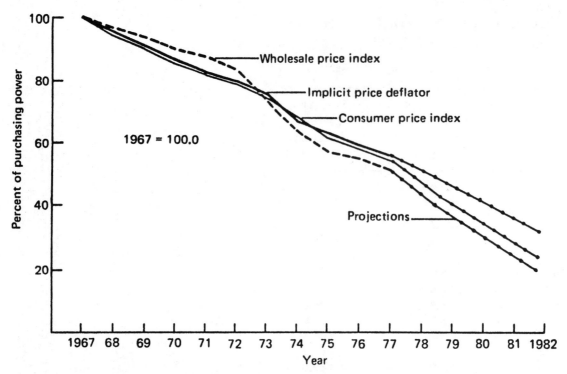

Figure 6-1 Declining purchasing power as indicated by selected price indexes.

Probably there is some truth in both positions. Consequently the real estate manager encourages owners and tenants to compromise on rental clauses that satisfy both parties.

Fixed Rents

If it is assumed that inflation is permanent and that present rates of inflation will remain uncontrolled, then fixed rents are poorly adapted to long-term leases. As a result leases are at present largely confined to short-term, month-to-month tenancies, or limited to 3-to-5 years. In the past, fixed rents were rationalized under stable prices. That is, an investor leasing land worth $100,000, and agreeable to a 10 percent net return on invested capital, might reasonably commit the land to a 25-year lease providing for an annual net rent of $10,000. Indeed, lenders have often insisted on fixed rents so as not to endanger the mortgage security. A fixed and determinable rent establishes with fair certainty the leasehold value and, in the event of foreclosure, the lender knows the limits of the rental liability.

Today, fixed rents under short-term leases are a means of providing market rents. Rents negotiated at the end of each year, for example a 1-year apartment lease, allow the tenant and owner to annually negotiate the market rent. However, for properties involving substantial investments for both owner and tenant, the short-term occupancy is not always satisfactory. Both parties make substantial commitments that require longer-term agreements. For this reason managers rely on other rental terms.

Graduated Rents

Graduated rents, also called step-rate rents, require a schedule of varying fixed rents over the term of the lease. For example, under a long-term lease, the rent schedule might provide:

First 5 years	$ 5,000
Next 5 years	10,000
Remaining years of the lease (15 years)	20,000

These step-rate increases presume that market rents increase closely in correspondence to the negotiated rents. Their use is particularly common in long-term net ground leases in which the tenant constructs buildings on leased land subject to a leasehold mortgage.

Graduated rents, in effect, represent a subsidy to the tenant during the initial years. It is presumed that during the initial years the tenant has not realized the full potential of the investment. A shopping center, for example, may not realize the projected sales volume for 5 years—a period in which population expands to meet investment objectives.

On analysis, the graduated rent is risky. There is no assurance that capital values and market rents move precisely as anticipated in the graduated rent schedules. If the rents are underestimated, the owner receives less than the market rent with a consequent decline in the owner's interest—the leased fee. The tenant, faced with graduated rents above the market rent, may default on rent payments, forcing the owner to terminate the lease. An owner with a nonproductive property faces the same operating loss assumed by the tenant.

Consequently the graduated rent has limited usefulness. It is largely confined to step-rate increases that accommodate the tenant over the initial and less productive years of new projects. After the initial developmental period expires, say in 2 or 3 years, the normal practice is to convert rent to the market level.

Certain precautions should be taken in estimating the value of future graduated rents. The owner's interest—the leased fee—is determined largely by the present value of the net rent. To illustrate, consider two leases with the graduated schedules shown under Lease A and Lease B.

Lease A

Annual Rent	Total Rent	Present Worth*
First 10 years, $10,000	$100,000	$ 61,446
Next 10 years, 15,000	150,000	49,229
Total	$250,000	$110,675

Lease B

Annual Rent	Total Rent	Present Worth*
First 10 years, $ 1,000	$ 10,000	$ 6,145
Next 10 years, 25,000	250,000	82,049
Total	$260,000	$88,194

*Discounted at a 10 percent rate.

Note that in Lease B the total rent of $260,000 is greater than the rent of Lease A ($150,000). However, because the rents of Lease A provide for higher rents in the initial years, the present worth of the Lease A rent, $110,675, is more than the present worth of Lease B rent—$88,194. The fact that the higher rents of Lease B are postponed to the 10th to 20th years reduces their present worth. Therefore, in negotiating graduated rents, greater importance is attached to rent earned over the early years of the lease. Or, to put it differently, the *present worth* of the rental income should be considered—not merely the total rent.

Percentage Rents

Percentage rents, in part, base the rent on a specified percentage of tenant sales. Accordingly, they are restricted to tenants who sell products and who maintain adequate records. For this reason, percentage rents have little application to tenants who provide services, such as lawyers, accountants, and barbers. These rents are poorly adapted to the smaller merchant where enforcement of percentage provisions would be difficult.

Retail Leases Generally, percentage rents are accompanied by minimum rent. Minimum rents give the developer-owner a required rate of return to justify the initial investment. In most cases, minimum rent would be sufficient to pay expenses and to service debt. The percentage rent, which is also referred to as overage rent, usually applies after a minimum sales volume is reached. Percentage rents vary according to sales mark-up and inventory turnover. For example, as reported by the Urban Land Institute, 39 super drugs renting space in regional shopping centers paid a median percentage rent of *3 percent* of sales with an average median sales per square foot of $98.43. In contrast, jewelry stores in the same centers paid an average median percentage rent of *6 percent* of sales; their median sales per square foot was $190. These data on percentage rents prevailing in shopping centers are surveyed every 3 years by the Urban Land Institute.

The wide variations common to percentage rents are illustrated in the latest survey of 63 super regional shopping centers made by the Urban Land Institute. In this survey it was found that leading tenants such as department stores and supermarkets reported relatively low percentage rents, typically between 2.2 and 1.5 percent. The smaller specialty stores typically showed considerably higher percentage rents; for example, Candy and Nuts, 10.0 percent, and Pretzel Shops, also 10.0 percent. In these latter cases, stores have relatively small square foot floor areas (750 square feet or less).

It should be pointed out that the total rent per square foot is usually calculated according to (1) minimum rent, (2) percentage rent over a given sales volume, and (3) common area charges levied against each tenant for parking space, public relations, and other functions.

The percentage rent appeals to tenants and owners alike. The owner benefits since, as the property becomes more productive (which is indicated by increased sales), percentage rents increase. The tenant, in turn, is willing to pay percentage rents since the rent increases only with higher dollar sales. Thus under percentage rents there is a high correlation between price inflation, sales volume, and annual rent.

Net Ground Leases Net ground leases typically are arranged for relatively long terms. Because local land values change independently of other prices, and because parties dislike reappraisal leases, rental adjustment clauses may rely on percentage rents. Consider for example 530 acres committed to a 70-year net ground lease in Palm Springs, California. The 530 acres were appraised for $2,370,000. The minimum rent schedule was based on the following schedule of annual rents:

First 2 years	$ 41,475
Third year	46,375
Next 2 years	59,625
Next 3 years	119,350
Remaining years	159,000

The 70-year lease includes the requirement that the tenant construct buildings that cost at least $4,000,000 during the first 10 years. The proposed buildings included apartments, restaurants, hotels, and residential buildings constructed on subdivided and leased land. Percentage leases earned on subleases provide additional payments to the owner.

Property type	Percentage of sublease rents
Hotel room rentals	5.0
Apartment rents	5.0
Residential lot rents	30.0
Golf course, green fees	10.0
Beverage sales	2.5
Restaurant food sales	2.0
Golf Pro Shop	3.0

Because of the percentage rents, the capitalized value of rent after 8 years (discounted at 8 percent) increased the leased fee value—the value of the owner's estate—to $3,352,522, an increase of almost $1 million over the original value of leased land ($982,522). In this case, percentage leases provided for additional rental incomes from subleases arranged by the original tenant.

Reappraisal Leases

Long-term leases (over 15 years, and up to 99 years) may require periodic reappraisals to establish the fair market rent. Some lenders approve reappraisal leases only if the reappraisal occurs after mortgage payments have been completed. Typically the owner and lessor select qualified appraisers, with a third appraiser selected by the two appointed appraisers. The rent is usually based on a stated percentage of the appraised value.

For example, an industrial lease of 30 years calling for reappraisal every 5 years provides in part that the lessor and the lessees (the lessees acting as one party) shall each select an appraiser and give notice thereof to the other party. In the event of failure on the part of either the lessor or the lessees to select an appraiser . . . the party who has named an appraiser shall have the right to apply to the superior court requesting selection and appointment of an appraiser to represent the party so failing to appoint an appraiser. The two appraisers thus appointed shall select and appoint a third appraiser and give notice thereof to the lessor and lessees.

Failure of the two appraisers to appoint a third appraiser gives either party the right to request the superior court to appoint a third appraiser.

In another example, the rental on a 65-year lease is subject to adjustment after the 25th year. "[The rental] shall be adjusted to a sum equal to eight percent of the fair market value of the leased land at the end of the said 25th year." Failure of the lessor and lessee to agree on the fair rental requires the appointment of an arbitrator by each party with a third arbitrator appointed by the superior court. The majority of the three arbitrators shall determine the fair market value of the leased land.

It is common for leases to require that appraisers must "be recognized real estate appraisers and shall also be members of the local real estate board and/or the American Institute of Real Estate Appraisers, the Society of Real Estate Appraisers or successor organizations." It is not uncommon for the lease to require selection of three new appraisers in the event that two of the three appraisers do not agree on the fair market value.

While reappraisal leases theoretically seem fair, practice reveals that appraisers selected by either owner or tenant may be biased in favor of their clients. And since the reappraisal is undertaken at infrequent intervals, the rent changes are usually substantial. As a consequence, agreement may not be reached on the final appraisal for rental adjustment. Observers have noted that reappraisal leases frequently encourage expensive court litigation.

Index Leases

With the assumption that the declining value of the dollar is indicated by a selected price index, leases may call for the adjustment of rents according to changes in a selected price index. Suppose for example that the Consumer Price Index had been selected to adjust leases at the end of each calendar year. For this purpose the rental adjustment would be based on the Consumer Price Index at the beginning of the year, termed *the base year*. Thus, if the lease began January 1, 1974, the base index would be 147.7, the Consumer Price Index for that year. This figure would be the denominator divided into the price index of the adjustment year. If the lease required an adjustment at the end of 1977 according to the 1977 index, the 1974 rent would be increased by multiplying the base year rent by 122.9 percent (181.5/147.7). The presumption is that the declining value of the dollar would move according to the selected price index.

Alternatively, index leases may specify the formula for a Consumer Price Index (CPI) lease as follows:

1 CPI current year minus CPI base year = absolute CPI increase

2 CPI increase divided by CPI base year = percentage increase in CPI (if 2 percent or more compute additional rent)

3 Minimum fixed rent multiplied by CPI percentage increase = current adjusted rent

In this calculation the percentage increase in the Consumer Price Index applies only if the increase is 2 percent or more.

The rental adjustment clause tied to an index suffers from one common cause: the declining value of the dollar may not correlate with a decrease in net operating income. For the owner is faced not only with the declining value of the dollar but rising expenses. For this reason some owners prefer to base the initial rent on the competitive market, which ordinarily would provide for the market rate of return on invested capital. To protect against expenses that increase more rapidly than gross rents, owners and tenants have agreed to escalation clauses.

Escalation Clauses

Escalation clauses variously cover such items as real estate taxes, which move unpredictably; utility expenses, and certain other costs. While escalator clauses may take many forms, a clause adapted for this purpose is illustrated by the lease of a Chicago office building (2 North Riverside Plaza):

> The tenant shall pay to the landlord as additional rent for the current tax, calen-, dar, or fiscal year (as the case might be) during the term of this lease the sum of:
>
> (a) the tenant's proportionate share of any increase in:
>
>   (1) the lienable charges against the real property subject to this lease for any tax year over and above the lienable charges in the base year as hereafter defined and/or;
>
>   (2) the cost of operating the premises for any calendar or fiscal year over and above such cost in the base year and/or;
>
> (b) an amount computed to reflect an increase of 2% or more in the annual average Consumer Price Index All Items (CPI) over the index as it exists in the base year, such increase being applied to the Minimum Fixed Rent as set forth in paragraph 4 of this lease, annualized to reflect the rent for the current year;

Note that the rent is adjusted according to either the changes in the real property taxes or operating expenses, or an increase of 2 percent or more in the annual Consumer Price Index. The tenant's proportionate share for this purpose is defined as:

> *Tenant's Proportionate Share (TPS)* is expressed as a percentage computed by dividing the space demised or used by the Tenant by the total rentable space of the building of which the demised space is a part;
>
> *Base Year* is the calendar year in which the lease is executed except that in new construction, the base year shall be the calendar year in which the land and building is fully assessed and at least partially occupied for the first time;

Formula (1): *Increase of Lienable Charges*
   Current Taxes minus taxes for base year multiplied by TPS = Current Rent
Formula (2): *Increase of Operating Costs*
   Current Costs minus costs in base year multiplied by TPS = Current Rent

In short, the tenant's proportionate share of rent will be increased according to annual changes in operating costs or lienable charges. Though this formula does not adjust for changes in the purchasing power of the dollar, it protects the owner from disproportionate increases in operating costs.

As explained by George R. Bailey of Turner, Bailey and Zoll of Chicago, Illinois, the escalation clause should maintain the ratio of net operating income to expenses as of the date of the lease. This approach is preferred since certain expenses are highly variable; for example, utility costs may hinge on variations in the weather, while wages and the cost of supplies may show unpredictable changes. In one 2-year period, for example, heating fuels increased from 8 cents a gallon to 32 cents a gallon. In light of these unpredictable expenses of operation, some owners prefer escalation clauses. Given the base year, an escalation clause that preserves the ratio of net operating income and expenses would state:

The rent for each leasehold year after the first leasehold year shall be increased by a percentage of the original rent equal to the percentage of said excess in operating expenses for the fiscal year ending immediately prior to the commencement of such leasehold year, over the amount of operating expenses for any fiscal year exceeding operating expenses for the base year by 1 percent, then the rent for the following leasehold year shall be increased by 1 percent.

The escalation clause defines operating expenses to include:

payroll costs
personal property and real estate taxes
special assessments

The lease states the number of employees by category for purposes of calculating changes in the payroll.

SUMMARY

Rental terms serve mutual objectives of owners and tenants. Under conditions of uncertainty, they generally favor short-term leases that require virtually no rental adjustment, since rents are periodically negotiated as leases are renewed.

In practice, long-term leases may be required for certain projects. The heavy investment in major projects recommends long-term revenue commitments. And since lenders often require long-term leases for mortgage security, parties to a lease must accept long-term rents with provisions for adjusting rent over the lease.

Rent adjustments for long-term leases are favored because of anticipated inflation. The trends in the Consumer Price Index, the Wholesale Price Index, and the implicit price deflator suggest continued and permanent inflation. In this respect, owners anticipating a long-term lease face the problem of offsetting the expected decline in purchasing power and the expected decrease in net income because operating expenses increase in the face of fixed rents. Variations in rental terms provide for these adjustments.

Fixed rents are poorly adapted to long-term leases. Consequently they are largely confined to short-term, month-to-month tenancies or leases, which at the most are limited to 3-to-5 years.

Graduated rents schedule changes in rent over the term of the lease. The danger is that rents negotiated upward over the life of the lease may be above or below the market rent. If graduated rents depart from the market rent, either the owner or tenant suffers economic loss.

Percentage rents, which apply mostly to responsible tenants who keep adequate records and who engage in retailing, seem acceptable to both owner and tenant. Experience has shown that percentage rents above a minimum rent vary largely according to characteristics of gross sales. The low mark-up, high volume, and high turnover retailer typically pays the lower percentage rent, that is, supermarkets and discount drug stores. The specialty shop with high mark-ups and low turnover is at the other end of the scale, with relatively high percentage rents. For net ground leases that provide income from subleases, percentage rents allow the owner to share in the rental income of the sublessor.

In other instances, the *reappraisal lease* provides for periodic readjustment of the rent according to a percentage return on the appraised value. Though discouraged because of the high probability of disagreement over the appraised value, for some types of leases owners and tenants have virtually no alternative. Reappraisal leases are a form of rent determination by compulsory arbitration.

Index leases, though subject to the charge that a national price index is a poor measure of local rental and property values, maintain the purchasing power of the original rent. Index leases may be unrelated to local market rent and they do not adjust for expenses that increase more rapidly than general prices.

Escalation clauses protect net operating income. They do not necessarily correct for the declining value of the dollar but they compensate for unusual increases in the main operating expenses such as property taxes, insurance, utilities, and even labor costs. Escalation clauses increase rent by the amount that expenses exceed expenses of the base or beginning year of the lease. Though rental adjustment clauses are imperfect, they are a preferred alternative to short-term leases, which are unacceptable for certain projects.

DISCUSSION QUESTIONS

1 Under what circumstances would the tenant negotiate for short-term leases? Under what circumstances would the owner negotiate for short-term leases?
2 Give reasons why you would not recommend the Consumer Price Index as a means of adjusting long-term rents. Explain thoroughly.
3 Explain the meaning of the implicit price deflator; give arguments in favor of using this index for adjusting rents in long-term leases.

4 Under what circumstances would you recommend negotiation for fixed rents?

5 Give an example of a lease providing for graduated rents.

6 What are characteristics of percentage rent?

7 What are the main arguments against reappraisal leases?

8 Show by example how rent would be adjusted according to changes in a selected price index.

9 Explain escalation clauses. Give an example in illustration of your answer.

KEY TERMS AND CONCEPTS

Short-term leases	Percentage rents
Long-term leases	Net ground leases
Consumer Price Index	Reappraisal leases
Wholesale Price Index	Index leases
Implicit price deflator	Base year
Fixed rents	Escalation clauses
Graduated rents	Tenant's proportionate share
Step-rate rents	Lienable charges

SELF-QUIZ

Multiple Choice Questions

_____ 1 Owners tend to approve only short term leases if they expect: (a) Higher market rents; (b) Lower business profits; (c) Favorable business profits; (d) Lower operating expenses.

_____ 2 Which of the following statements is correct? (a) The Consumer Price Index accurately measures the declining value of the dollar; (b) The Wholesale Price Index reveals lower price increases compared to the Consumer Price Index; (c) The implicit price deflator is more comprehensive than the Consumer or Wholesale Price Index; (d) The implicit price deflator distorts Gross National Product because of price inflation.

_____ 3 Rents adjusted according to changes in a selected index: (a) Protect the owner from future increases in operating expenses; (b) Ensure that the tenant and owner neither gain nor lose from price inflation; (c) Tend to benefit tenants more than owners; (d) Tend to benefit owners more than tenants.

_____ 4 Which of the following statements is correct? (a) It is not always clear that real estate values and rents move according to changes in other prices; (b) Real estate values and rents are highly localized; (c) In growth communities, cost and values may be expected to move upward more rapidly than general prices; (d) All of the above.

_____ 5 Fixed rents are: (a) Ideally adapted to long-term leases; (b) Largely confined to month-to-month tenancies or relatively short-term leases; (c) A means of providing market rents under long-term leases; (d) Not favored by long-term lenders.

_____ 6 Graduated rents: (a) Correspond closely to market rents over the lease term; (b) Are used when greater importance is attached to rent earned over the later years of the lease; (c) Are largely confined to step-rate increases that subsidize the tenant over the initial years of a new project; (d) None of the above.

_____ 7 Percentage rents: (a) Base rents on a specified percentage of tenant sales; (b) Are restricted to tenants who sell products and maintain adequate records; (c) Have little application to tenants who provide services; (d) All of the above.

_____ 8 Which of the following statements is _incorrect_? (a) Percentage rents usually apply after a minimum sales volume is reached; (b) Percentage rents vary according to sales mark-up and inventory turnover; (c) Percentage rents are not adapted to net ground leases; (d) Percentage rents are not adapted to the smaller merchant with poor accounting records.

_____ 9 The main limitation of reappraisal leases is that (a) Reappraisals are undertaken at too-infrequent intervals; (b) Agreement may not be reached on the appraisal for rental purposes; (c) Reappraisal leases are expensive to administer; (d) Reappraisals always favor the tenant.

_____ 10 The purpose of escalation clauses is to adjust rents according to the: (a) Market value of leased property; (b) Current market rent; (c) Increased construction costs; (d) Increase in annual operating costs.

Answer Key

1 (a), 2 (c), 3 (b), 4 (d), 5 (b), 6 (c), 7 (d), 8 (c), 9 (b), 10 (d).

Fill-In Questions

1 Because of uncertainties over business profits, tenants tend to negotiate for _____ leases.

2 The Consumer Price Index is not a complete measure of the _____ .

3 The _____ tends to show greater variation and slightly larger price increases than the Consumer Price Index.

4 The _____ is weighted by the relative importance of investment, consumption, government purchases, and net foreign investments.

5 _____ tend to view higher market rents as a consequence of tenant capital and prudent operating practices.

6 _____ are likely to assume that higher market rents arise primarily because of site advantages.

7 In practice, _____ represent a subsidy to the tenant during the initial years.

8 Percentage rents for _____ are based on a percentage of sublease rents.

9   Index leases provide rent adjustments by dividing the_____ into the current index.

10 _____ provide that the tenant's proportionate share of rent will be increased according to annual changes in operating costs or lienable charges.

Answer Key

1 short-term
2 declining value of the dollar
3 Wholesale Price Index
4 implicit price deflator
5 Tenants

6 Owners
7 graduated rents
8 net ground leases
9 base index
10 Escalation clauses

SELECTED REFERENCES

Dollars and Cents of Shopping Centers, 1978, Washington, D.C.: Urban Land Institute, 1978.

Kratovil, Robert, and Raymond J. Werner: *Real Estate Law,* 7th ed., Englewood Cliffs, N.J.: Prentice-Hall, 1979, chap. 37.

McMahan, John: *Property Development,* New York: McGraw-Hill, 1976, pp. 354–370.

Statistical Abastracts of the United States, Washington, D.C.: U.S. Department of Commerce, annual issues.

Survey of Current Business, Washington, D.C.: U.S. Department of Commerce, monthly issues.

Chapter 7

Property Management Contracts

After studying this chapter, you should be familiar with:
1 General terms common to the management agreement
2 Terms of management agreements for specialized properties
3 Methods of determining management fees
4 The purpose of the management survey
5 The six main divisions of the management survey

The two main contracts of special importance to real property managers include the *property management agreement* and agreements for the *management survey*. The management agreement serves the property manager as the listing agreement serves the real estate broker. It defines terms of employment and outlines the duties and responsibilities of the agent (property manager) and the principal (the property owner). The contract for a management survey provides for a consulting report in which property managers may recommend modernization, rehabilitation, or conversion and changes in management policy, with the main objective of increasing net income. To some extent, the management survey serves the manager as the appraisal report serves the appraiser.

ELEMENTS OF THE MANAGEMENT AGREEMENT

To be sure, management agreements conform to local, state, and federal laws. Consequently, they require preparation by legal counsel. Therefore, in explaining the management agreement, it is not implied that there is a standard management agreement form that applies equally in all jurisdictions. However, there are certain common features that define the relationship between the management, tenants, and owners.

General Terms

As enforceable real estate contracts, management agreements will be dated and will identify parties to the contract. The term of the management agreement, the beginning and ending dates, the consideration or management fee, and the legal description of the property managed conform to usual requirements of an enforceable contract.

The purpose of the management agreement is to appoint a management firm as the exclusive agent and representative of the owner to manage a designated property. According to the management agreement, the agent "shall do everything reasonably necessary for the management of property."

Management Duties

Some contracts list general management duties to include periodic inspections, supervision of maintenance, and completion of such improvements, alterations, and repairs as may be required. While these are fairly general terms, management contracts frequently list more specific duties:

1 The managing agent will take all reasonable steps to collect rent and other charges due owner from tenants.

2 From gross rent collections, the agent will pay loans, operating expenses, and other authorized liabilities.

3 The agent will take all reasonable steps for the proper management of the property. No single improvement, alteration, or repair must be more than $_____ without owner's prior written authorization. The owner gives the agent the authority to make emergency repairs or alterations as necessary to preserve property values and rights.

4 The owner grants to the agent the exclusive right to negotiate leases, tenancies, and terms as approved by owner. The agent hires, supervises, and terminates the employment of independent contractors and staff who are employees of the owner, not the agent.

5 The managing agent will maintain accurate records of all receipts and disbursements, which are available for inspection by owner at all reasonable times.

6 The agent agrees to remit to the owner the net amount of rent, less expenses and less reserves, on a monthly and annual basis, with supporting vouchers.

7 The management agreement provides that the agent shall manage residential property in full compliance with requirements of the Fair Housing Act of 1968. (State and local law may require this clause to comply with state fair housing laws, local housing ordinances, and affirmative action programs.)

While these duties outline the main agent responsibilities, other clauses of the management agreement cover detailed financial terms. For instance, management agreements include the "hold harmless" clauses that typically state "owner shall indemnify and save agent harmless from any and all costs, expenses, attorney's fees, suits, liabilities, judgments, and damages from or connected with the management of the property by agent." On residential property it is common to specify that the owner carry public liability insurance including bodily injury, property damage, and personal injury at limits of not less than $500,000 combined single limit coverage or split limits of $500,000 per person and $500,000 per occurrence of bodily injury and personal injury and $500,000 property damage.

The management contract administered by the Coldwell Banker Property Management Company gives the owner the right to designate an insurance broker or designate an affiliate company to act as insurance broker:

Coldwell Banker Insurance Brokerage Company is designated as Owner's insurance broker and as such shall survey, recommend and, upon the approval of Owner, will place insurance coverage for the subject property. Coldwell Banker Insurance Brokerage Company will be responsible for offering Owner insurance coverage normally available for the property, with reliable companies, but not including legal counsel.

An engineering inspection for the safety and protection of the property shall be arranged wherever possible with the insurance carrier at no cost to Owner. Owner agrees to consider the recommendations resulting from such inspection to minimize the cost of insurance, possibility of bodily injury, personal injury, property damage and loss of rental income.

In addition to the insurance clause, agreement will be reached on payment of property taxes and mortgages; some contracts allow for a tax reserve providing for monthly deductions for property taxes.

Responsibilities of the Owner

Property owners must give the managing agent certain information necessary for property management. Because of the financial responsibility assumed by the agent, the owner, by contract, usually agrees to accept certain responsibilities:

1 Owner agrees to promptly furnish agent will all documents and records required for property management.

2 The owner agrees to maintain sufficient funds in the trust account to pay obligations. The owner agrees to pay lease commissions provided in a schedule attached to the lease.

The first point requires that all leases, correspondence, mortgage information, payment instructions, service contracts, and insurance policies be given to the manager. Furthermore, it is important to specify that if funds are not sufficient to pay operating expenses, the owner is required to promptly provide the agent with the necessary funds. These agreements specify that the agent is not required to advance funds for the owner's account.

On management compensation, agreements provide that the owner agrees to pay a specified management fee stated either as dollars per month or as a percentage of total collections. In defining commissions on leases, usually the agent agrees to accept one half of the commission schedule for lease renewals. The exercise of a renewal option does not normally result in an additional lease commission, though practice varies widely.

While these are typical terms included in the management contract, it is necessary to vary these terms according to the type of property management. Selected examples show how management agreement varies for specialized properties.

Specialized Management Agreements

To show how management agreements may be adapted to specific properties, a few selected examples of management agreements common to shopping centers, condominiums, vacation homes, motels, and management consulting show how these contracts tend to be highly specialized.

Shopping Centers Here financial terms of the management agreement are more specific—probably because of the larger sums involved. For instance, the shopping center management agreement recommended by the International Council of Shopping Centers requires management to give a detailed monthly statement of receipts, expenses, and charges. Each monthly statement must be accompanied by receipted vouchers covering all expenses and disbursements paid during the month.

And while required by law in some states, the agreement requires the agent to make deposits in a trust account that is separate from the agent's personal account, in a bank approved by the owner. Moreover, in this instance the property manager must furnish the owner with a surety-company fidelity bond. Furthermore, the agent is instructed to participate in the merchants' association in accordance with the written instructions of the owner.

For making rent collections, this agreement instructs the agent to keep records of gross sales for each tenant and compute percentage rents. The agent may sue in the name of the owner to recover rents and other sums due, and to evict tenants with the consent of the owner. The agent is restricted to making contracts for terms that are longer than 1 year and, except in the case of bankruptcy by either party, the owner may terminate the agreement with 60 days' written notice, provided the owner agrees to pay a stated sum for the liquidated damages for each remaining month of the agreement. In the case of bankruptcy, the agreement may be terminated immediately.

By written agreement, the owner provides the management agent with a rent-free office in the shopping center. It is important to add further that the management agreement covers only duties of shopping center management. Leasing services are covered by a separate agreement between the owner and agent. See Figure 7-1 for an example of a shopping center management agreement.

SHOPPING CENTER MANAGEMENT AGREEMENT

Parties

This Agreement entered into this _____ day of _____, 19 _____, between

_____(hereinafter called the "Owner") and

_____(hereinafter called the "Agent").

𝔚𝔦𝔱𝔫𝔢𝔰𝔰𝔢𝔱𝔥:

Shopping Center

The Owner is the sole owner of the following shopping center (hereinafter called "Shopping Center"):

Name:

Location:

The Owner and the Agent agree as follows:

Agency

1. The Owner hereby employs the Agent for the purpose of operating and managing the Shopping Center upon the terms hereinafter set forth.

Compensation

2. The Owner shall pay the Agent for management services rendered hereunder the sum of $_____ per month.

Duties: Management

3. The Agent accepts the employment and agrees:

a. To use due diligence in the exercise of the powers and duties conferred and assumed in paragraph 4 hereof and in the operation, management and maintenance of the Shopping Center for the period and upon the terms herein provided and to furnish the service of its organization for such purposes.

Monthly Statements, Payrolls, Audits

b. To render, on or before the fifteenth day of each month, detailed monthly statements of receipts, expenses (including the Agent's management fee), and charges for the preceding month and to remit to Owner with such monthly statement all receipts less disbursements and the management fees provided for in paragraph 2. Each such monthly statement shall be accompanied by proper receipted vouchers covering all expenses and disbursements paid during the month, and by an itemized list of all arrears of rentals and the payroll list showing (with the exception of the person acting on behalf of the Agent as its manager on the premises) the occupation of and wages paid to all employees hired by Agent for the purpose of performing its duties under this Agreement. The Agent shall keep full and detailed records covering the management of the Shopping Center, and the Owner shall at all times have access to such records as well as to all other books and records of the Agent in connection with the operation, maintenance and management of the Shopping Center, and Owner's accountants shall have the right to audit such books and records.

Separate Bank Account

c. To deposit promptly all funds collected from the operation of the Shopping Center or in any way incidental thereto in a trust account, separate from Agent's personal account, in a bank approved by Owner. The Agent may endorse any and all checks drawn to the order of Owner for deposit in such bank account.

Fidelity Bond

d. To procure and furnish Owner with a surety company fidelity bond in an amount sufficient to protect Owner, and conditioned upon the faithful performance of Agent's duties and the due accounting for all funds received or collected by Agent. Such bond shall be in an amount, and in form and substance satisfactory to the Owner.

Legal Documents

e. To advise Owner promptly, with confirmation in writing, of the service upon Agent of any summons, subpoena, or other like legal document including any notices, letters, or other communications setting out or claiming an actual or alleged potential liability of the Owner or the Shopping Center.

Agent's Powers

4. The Owner hereby grants and delegates to the Agent the following authority, powers and duties and agrees to assume and pay any expenses in connection therewith and Agent agrees to exercise and perform the following powers and duties:

Collect Rent

a. To collect rents, including percentage rents, from tenants of the Shopping Center as and when the same shall become due and payable and give receipts therefor, and in connection with the collection of percentage rents to keep records of gross sales reports of tenants and compute percentage rents; to terminate tenancies, upon consent of Owner, and to sign and serve in the name of the Owner such notices as are deemed needful by the Agent; to institute and prosecute actions with the written consent of the Owner; to evict tenants, upon consent of Owner, and to recover possession of premises occupied by them; to sue for in the name of the Owner, upon consent of Owner, and recover rents and other sums due; and when expedient and upon written approval of Owner to settle, compromise, and release such actions or suits or reinstate such tenancies.

Notices Litigation

Repairs

b. To maintain or cause to be maintained the Shopping Center and common areas thereof including sidewalks, signs, parking lots and landscaping; to make or cause to be made and supervise minor repairs and minor alterations required for the installation of tenants; to purchase supplies required for the operation and maintenance of the Shopping Center, and pay all bills therefor, and to report promptly to Owner, with written confirmation thereof, any conditions in the Shopping Center requiring the attention of Owner. The

Approval of Large Expenses

Agent agrees to secure the approval of the Owner on all expenditures in excess of $_____ for any one item, except monthly or recurring operating charges and/or emergency repairs in excess of the maximum, if in the opinion of the Agent such repairs are necessary to protect the property from damage or to maintain services to the tenants as called for by their tenancy. The Agent shall notify the Owner promptly whenever emergency repairs have been ordered. All expenses incurred by the Agent shall be charged by the Agent at net cost and the Owner shall receive credit for all rebates, commissions, discounts and allowances.

Employees

c. To select, employ at reasonable wages, supervise, direct and discharge all employees in such reasonable numbers as shall be required for the operation and maintenance of the Shopping Center and to use reasonable care in the selection of such employees. All persons employed to perform maintenance services shall be deemed employees of the Owner and not the Agent.

Service Contracts

d. To make contracts for terms no longer than one year for electricity, gas, fuel, water, telephone, window cleaning, ash or rubbish hauling and other services or such of them as the Agent shall deem advisable. The Owner shall assume the obligation of any contract so entered into at the termination of this Agreement.

Mortgage and Tax Payments

e. To pay or cause to be paid mortgage indebtedness, property or employee taxes or special assessments and to place public liability, fire, steam boiler, pressure vessel or any other insurance, if so instructed in writing by Owner and out of funds designated by or made available by Owner.

Figure 7-1 Shopping center management agreement.

Merchant's Association   **f.** To participate, in accordance with any written instructions of the Owner, with the Merchant's Association of the Shopping Center in promotional events of the Shopping Center, or in the event there is no Merchant's Association to conduct or cause to be conducted, in accordance with Owner's instructions and at Owner's expense, such promotional events and in this connection to solicit help of the tenants.

Any powers not heretofore expressly granted to the Agent are reserved by the Owner.

Indemnity   **5.** Owner shall indemnify Agent and save it harmless from and against all claims, losses and liabilities arising out of damage to property, or injury to, or death of persons (including the property and persons of the parties hereto, and their agents, subcontractors and employees) occasioned by or in connection with acts or omissions of Owner or Owner's agents (other than the Agent, or the Agent's agents, employees or subcontractors), employees and subcontractors, and all costs, fees and attorneys' expenses in connection therewith. The Agent shall indemnify the Owner and save it harmless from and against all claims, losses and liabilities arising out of damage to property, or injury to, or death of persons (including the property and persons of the parties hereto, and their agents, subcontractors, and employees) occasioned by or in connection with acts or omissions of Agent or Agent's agents, employees and subcontractors, and all costs, fees and attorneys' expenses in connection therewith.

Term   **6. a.** The Term of this Agreement shall be for the period of one year beginning on the _____ day of _____ 19_____ and ending on the _____ day of _____ 19_____ and continuing thereafter from year to year, unless on or before sixty (60) days prior to the date last above mentioned or thirty (30) days prior to the expiration of any renewal term, either party hereto shall notify the other in writing of an intention to terminate this Agreement in which case this Agreement shall terminate on the last mentioned date or the respective anniversary date thereof.

Termination by Owner   **b.** The Owner may terminate this Agreement during its original term by giving the Agent at least sixty (60) days written notice of termination, in which event this Agreement shall terminate on the date fixed for termination. If such termination is not due to the breach of this Agreement by the Agent, or in connection with the bona

Liquidated Damages   fide sale of the Shopping Center, or destruction materially affecting the operation of the Shopping Center, or for any cause specified in subparagraph 6c or 6d, the Owner agrees to pay the Agent the sum of $_____ per month as and for liquidated damages for each remaining month of the original term of this Agreement. During any renewal term hereof, this Agreement may be terminated by either party, without further obligation, upon giving the other party at least sixty (60) days written notice of termination.

Agent's Default   **c.** The Owner may terminate this Agreement immediately upon giving written notice to the Agent in the event of gross negligence by the Agent in the performance of this Agreement, or in the event of Agent's deliberate or willful default under this Agreement. All the obligations of the Owner to the Agent shall terminate immediately except for the payment by the Owner to the Agent of all fees earned to the date of such notice.

Bankruptcy   **d.** In the event a petition in bankruptcy is filed by or against either Owner or Agent, or in the event that either shall make an assignment for the benefit of creditors or take advantage of any insolvency act, either party hereto may forthwith terminate this Agreement immediately upon giving notice to the other party.

Government Authority   **7.** In the event that any governmental agency, authority or department should order the repair, alteration or removal of any structure or matter in the Shopping Center, and if after written notice of the same to the Owner by such body or by Agent, the Owner fails to authorize the Agent or others to make such repairs, alterations or removal, the Agent shall be released from any responsibility in connection therewith, and Owner shall be answerable to such body for any and all penalties and fines whatsoever imposed because of such failure on Owner's part.

Office   **8.** Owner shall provide Agent with a rent-free office in the Shopping Center in which Agent shall maintain its office, and which shall be known as of the office of the Agent and of the Shopping Center.

9. This Agreement shall be binding upon the parties hereto, their legal representatives, successors and permitted assigns, and cannot be assigned by the Agent without the prior written consent of the Owner.

In Witness Whereof the parties hereto have affixed or caused to be affixed their respective signatures as of the date first above written.

_____
(Owner)

_____
(Agent)

By: _____

By: _____

Note: This agreement is confined to shopping center management. Where managing agent also performs leasing services, separate agreement between owner and agent should be prepared.

SHOPPING CENTER MANAGEMENT AGREEMENT

between

Owner _____

and

Agent _____

Name of Center _____

for

Location _____

Beginning _____ 19___

Ending _____ 19___

Figure 7-1 *(continued)*

Condominium Management Agreement The legal entity of a condominium with its separate ownership of individual units requires special terms not found in other management agreements. In this case, the management agreement establishes a legal relationship between the management agent and the board of directors, who act on behalf of all owners. The condominium management agreement recommended by the Institute of Real Estate Management starts with a recital stating that the declaration and bylaws delegate authority to manage the condominium to an elected board of directors, who in turn employ an agent to manage the condominium.

(1) Primary Duties In this case, the agreement details 10 services provided by the management agent:

1 Collects monthly and other assessments for operation of the condominium (provided that the agent assumes no responsibility for collection of delinquent assessments or other charges)

2 Maintains records showing receipts and expenditures, summarized in a monthly statement that is provided to the board every month

3 Prepares a recommended budget for each year

4 Prepares an annual summary of all receipts and expenditures

5 Maintains common elements according to "appropriate standards of maintenance"

6 Hires, pays, negotiates, supervises, and discharges personnel required to maintain and operate

7 Files all tax returns and related documents required of the board as an employer

8 Negotiates contracts for water, electricity, gas, telephone, and other services as may be necessary

9 Pays from funds of the board all taxes, building and elevator inspection fees, water rates, and other government charges and obligations

10 Maintains appropriate records of all insurance coverage carried by the board

In return for these services, the board agrees to pay management a monthly fee. The agreement provides further that the cost of circulating notices, preparing newsletters, and handling general correspondence is made at the expense of the board.

(2) Special Condominium Relationships Note that, unlike apartment house management, the agent does not act in a legal capacity to collect delinquent charges. While the manager may send notices of delinquency, the board has the sole responsibility for enforcing collection of delinquent assessments through board committees or through proper legal procedures. Management agents should be careful not to practice law.

Besides detailing services of the agent, the agreement covering condominium management must cover certain other unique relationships found in condominiums. For example, it is agreed that agents have no responsibility for maintenance or repairs to individual condominium units. In some instances the board of directors has responsibility for maintenance repairs not only to common elements but also to the exterior of individual condominium units. Maintenance services provided by the agent to unit owners are ordinarily handled under separate contracts on an individual basis.

In appointing a site manager, the board must pay special hourly compensation for attendance at board meetings. The site manager serves as custodian of records of the board but is not required to keep minutes of the meeting. Neither the site manager nor agent accepts instructions from anyone except a designated single individual board member who is typically the elected president.

Attention is specially directed to legal responsibilities of the agent. As in other management agreements, the board agrees to indemnify, defend, and save the agent harmless against adverse claims. The board assumes legal responsibility for compliance with state or federal labor laws. While the agreement may be cancelled before the termination date with a stated number of days' notice, the usual agreement calls for a cancellation fee equal to a percentage of the management fee that would accrue over the remainder of the agreement term.

Vacation Home Management Agreement The employment contract developed by the Parker-Kaufman Realtors and Insurors of Jekyll Island, Georgia illustrates special terms common to the management of short-term rentals of vacation homes. The agreement covers owners who purchase vacation homes in resort areas for investment or a combination of owner occupancy and investment. Because owners are usually absentee owners, duties of the agent are more inclusive. The authority granted by the owner is illustrated in Figure 7-2.

(1) Grant of Authority Note the broad grant of authority; the agent must advertise the rental and is given the authority to sign, renew, and cancel tenancies in the name of the owner. Besides responsibility for repairs and alterations to a stated amount, the agent initiates contracts for electricity, gas, fuel, water, window cleaning, rubbish hauling, and other services. Clearly these special provisions are adapted to the management of single units owned by absentee owners.

Besides the hold-harmless clause common to management agreements, the agreement developed by Parker-Kaufman, Realtors and Insurors, requires that the owner advise the agent in writing if the agent must assume responsibility for paying mortgages, property or employee taxes, special assessments, or insurance premiums.

In this instance, the agent is given the exclusive right to sell the property during the agreement and 60 days after the agreement terminates. In return for management services, this company charges a management fee of 15 percent of gross rents on rentals of less than 90 days. A 10 percent fee applies for rentals of 90 days or more. Expenditures for upkeep and maintenance are provided at cost plus a 10 percent supervision fee.

(2) Rental Advice Vacation homeowners benefit from the marketing knowledge of the agent. Since managing agents deal with numerous properties and rents over the vacation season, they are aware of competitive forces and costs that affect the rental market. Usually vacation homes provide rents that are competitive with motel rates. In preparing advertising material, the management agent must establish recommended rents several months in advance. For vacation homes that are in high demand over the winter season, the Parker-Kaufman firm sends owners the form letter illustrated in Figure 7-3.

3. The Owner hereby gives to the Agent the following authority and powers and Owner agrees to assume the expenses in connection therewith:

a) To advertise the availability for rental of the herein described premises or any part thereof, and to display signs thereon; to sign, renew and/or cancel tenancy at will agreements for the premises or any part thereof; to collect rents due or to become due and give receipts therefor; to terminate tenancies and to sign and serve in the name of the Owner such notices as are deemed needful by Agent; to institute and prosecute actions, to evict tenants and to recover possession of said premises; to sue for in the name of the Owner and recover rents and other sums due; and when expedient to settle, compromise, and release such actions or suits or reinstate such tenancies.

b) To make or cause to be made and supervise repairs and alterations, and to do decorating on said premises, to purchase supplies and pay all bills. The Agent agrees to secure the approval of the Owner on all expenditures in excess of $ for any one item, except monthly or recurring operating charges and/or emergency repairs in excess of the maximum, if in the opinion of the Agent such repairs are necessary to protect the property from damage or to maintain services to the tenants as called for by their tenancy.

c) To hire, discharge and supervise all labor and employees required for the operation and maintenance of the premises; it being agreed that all employees shall be deemed employees of the Owner and not the Agent, and that the Agent may perform any of its duties through its attorneys, agents, or employees and shall not be responsible for their acts, defaults or negligence if reasonable care has been exercised in their appointment and retention. The Agent shall not be liable for any error of judgment or for any mistake of fact of law, or for anything which it may do or refrain from doing hereafter, except in cases of willful misconduct or gross negligence.

d) To make contracts for electricity, gas, fuel, water, window cleaning, ash or rubbish hauling and other services or such of them as the Agent shall deem advisable, the Owner to assume the obligation of any contract so entered into at the termination of this agreement.

Figure 7-2 Owner delegation of authority under a management agreement covering vacation home rentals. *(Source: John C. Kaufman, CPM, Parker-Kaufman Realtors® and Insurors, Jekyll Island, Ga.)*

This form gives management information on new furniture or new construction that accommodates a larger number of persons. In addition, the form allows the manager to plan for occupancy by the owner over stated periods. While the management suggests rental rates, the final determination of the rent rests with the owner, who is asked to return the form shown in Figure 7-3.

Motel Management Agreements Specialists in motel management must be prepared to cover virtually every facet of motor hotel operation. To serve this function, Helmsley-Spear, Inc. (New York City), appoints a regional director who monitors daily motel activity.

(1) The Range of Management Services Indeed, the range of management services requires a detailed management agreement, which according to Stephen W. Brener, senior vice president, covers six main functions:

Parker-Kaufman
REALTORS & INSURORS

──────────── 4 LOCATIONS IN GLYNN COUNTY, GEORGIA ────────────

JEKYLL SHOPPING CENTER • P.O. BOX 3126 • JEKYLL ISLAND, GEORGIA 31520 • 912-635-2512

Dear Owner:

It is already time to start preparing for our winter season, and to establish our rates for next year's brochure.

Last winter's occupancy rate was excellent and we are looking for an even
better winter this year. We realize that the extremely cold weather took
its toll in the form of heating bills. We are considering this strongly
in establishing this winter's rental rates.

1. You will find below the weekly summer rental rate which
    we will be quoting in next summer's brochure. In the
    event that you do not agree with this proposed rate,
    please let us know what rate you wish us to use. Please
    bear in mind that we are trying to remain competitive
    with motel prices.
2. If you plan on making furniture or accommodation changes,
    please complete question #2 below.
3. Please answer question #3 indicating what periods you wish
    to reserve for your own use for this coming year.

Please return this information to us by September 1, 1978. Just tear
along the dotted line and return the lower portion of this form to us. In
the event we have not heard from you by September 1, we will assume that
you are in agreement with the rate we have set and you will make your
plans around our bookings.

Thank you for your kind cooperation.
----

1. In 1978 the _____ Cottage rented for _____ per
    week.
    a. I agree with the new 1979 rate of _____ per week. _____
    b. I do not agree with the new rate and wish the rate set as
        _____ per week.
2. I am planning furniture changes as follows _____
    _____, and my cottage will accommodate _____.
3. I wish to reserve the following times for my own use in the coming
    78-79 season.

Sept 78	Oct 78	Nov 78	Dec 78	Jan 79	Feb 79
Mar 79	Apr 79	May 79	Jun 79	Jul 79	Aug 79

PARKER-KAUFMAN, Realtors & Insurors   If more space
P.O. Box 3126   is needed
Jekyll Island, GA   31520   use reverse
                                             side.

Figure 7-3 Vacation home rental advisory letter.

1 Accounting
2 Systems administration
3 Engineering and maintenance
4 Food and beverage management
5 Marketing
6 Purchasing

In serving these functions, account executives work with the owner under supervision of central management. The account executive negotiates management contracts, assists in the annual budget plan, and reviews financial operational reports.

The range of duties under each of these six functions suggests why a more complex management agreement is required. For instance, the *accounting department* prepares a monthly detailed profit-loss statement and balance sheet showing a comparison with the same period last year. A monthly analysis is also made of accounts payable, monthly journal entries, payrolls, and taxes.

Systems administrators inspect accounting records and control systems on a recurring basis. They are responsible for the training and supervision of bookkeeping personnel and continually revise and improve records, procedures, and control systems.

The company maintains a professional staff of *engineers* to coordinate architecture, design, and construction services. They also supervise training of maintenance personnel for in-house repairs. They help lower operating costs and improve plant efficiency.

In assuming responsibility for *food and beverages,* the management supervises relations with local health, sanitation, and license boards. Personnel are experienced in managing limited menu coffee shops and gourmet dining rooms with respect to purchasing, cost control, preparation, and service.

In assuming a new management project, a *market analysis* aids in pricing the market, defines the potential market, and works toward more effective ways to attract and retain customers. Management emphasizes selling motel facilities with a specially prepared marketing and sales program. Personnel specializing in this function attend trade and travel shows and business meetings to help in packaging facilities for groups, conventions, and commercial businesses. Finally a manager passes savings resulting from *quantity purchases* to the owners.

(2) The Annual Plan   The detail associated with motel management may be appreciated by the annual plan submitted to owners within 90 to 120 days after the effective date of a management contract. For existing agreements, the same report is provided 30 days before the end of the year. The annual plan covers:

1 An annual inspection report
2 A proposed marketing program for rooms, food, and beverage facilities
3 An analysis of operations, including suggestions for converting space for other uses as indicated
4 A proposed budget of expenses, major repairs, and improvement, including recommended projects

In return for these services, the management fee is based on a minimum monthly management fee or a percentage of gross room, food, and beverage sales—whichever is greater. In this case the management fee does not include the cost of payroll preparation, travel expenses, and temporary personnel loaned from the company who occasionally work on premises. The company charges 150 percent of personnel compensation for these services.

The management contract provides that the management may terminate the management agreement if:

(a) the owner shall fail to keep, observe or perform any material covenant, agreement, term or provision of this Agreement and such default shall continue for 90 days after notice by Hospitality Division to the owner.

(b) the owner shall apply or consent to the appointment of a receiver, trustee or liquidator of the owner or take advantage of any insolvency laws.

(c) the licenses for the sale of alcoholic beverages in the motel are suspended, terminated or revoked without the fault of the Hospitality Division and such suspension, termination or revocation shall continue in effect for a specified period.

Both parties have the right to assign the management agreement as a result of a merger, consolidation, or reorganization without the express permission of the other party.

Managing Consulting Agreements According to William D. Sally, CPM of Baird & Warner of Chicago, "more and more opportunities are arising among professional management people who act as consultants for real estate investment trusts, banks, insurance companies and pension funds." As a result of the demand for management consulting, Sally developed a consulting agreement calling for a two-phase study that precedes the negotiation of a management agreement.

The *first phase* consists of a rent analysis. The property manager in this phase defines the upper and lower limits of the rental structure—for example, the maximum rental achieved without encouraging unusually high tenant turnover. In this phase, technical personnel reexamine architectural and engineering details that affect physical maintenance and consequently future operating expenses. If the consulting agreement applies to a proposed project, the analysis of the rental structure includes a recommended marketing plan.

The *second phase* reviews daily operations dealing with staff organization, office procedures, records, leasing policies, forms, and reports. The consultant recommends staff and their qualifications for interior and exterior maintenance and estimates the cost of recommended repairs. For new projects, the consultant estimates operating expenses encountered in property management: electric utilities, water, advertising, office expenses, legal expenses, and contract services such as elevators, scavenger costs and security. For a new project, the best operating organization will be suggested from a review of blueprints and the site plan.

Special attention is given to recreational facilities with respect to their expected competitive impact on rents and sales. Again, for new projects a company will work with attorneys and architects in developing appropriate graphics, media advertising, and the ideal model apartment.

The final recommendation suggests a 3-year management agreement with the management fee related to a percentage of the gross income. If the management agreement is approved, the client is given a 75 percent credit for the consulting fee. Additional travel or consulting at the end of the agreement is charged at $50 per hour.

Management Fees

Traditionally, management fees have been based on a percentage of gross income. The practice is defended by the fact that the manager tends to be rewarded for maximizing occupancy and gross income.

Percentage of Gross Income To some extent, the percentage of gross income varies by type of property. To be competitive in the market, management firms may agree to manage high-income luxury apartments for a relatively low fee, say 4 percent. Not only are the luxury units less costly to manage on a per unit basis, but the higher rents convert to greater dollar income. In contrast, the management of low-income property requires greater attention to tenant relations, maintenance, repairs, delinquent rent collections, and perhaps compliance with several government agencies. A rental fee of 10 percent of gross incomes would not be unusual for the management of these properties.

The Cost of Management There is a relation between the cost of management and the fee collected. William D. Sally, a CPM writing in the *Journal of Property Management*, recommends fees based on the cost of management. Compensation for property management services, in his view, should cover typical management costs, namely, inspections, site visits, capital improvement supervision, owner-meetings, travel time, office hours spent on behalf of the owner, and office supplies. Certain executive services, such as market surveys, budget preparation, accounting, and clerical services add to management costs.

With these costs, which include direct costs and office overhead, management is advised to calculate the per unit costs for each management project. Assume for example that direct and overhead expenses total $960,000 and that the management organization has the capacity to service 10,000 apartment units, resulting in an average annual cost per unit of $96 ($96,000/10,000). Adding 20 percent results in an average annual per unit fee of $115.20.[1]

These average costs are adjusted to a particular project to account for economies of scale. The larger the building, the less it costs per unit to manage. In his analysis, it is recommended that apartments with over 300 units be managed for an annual fee of $90 per unit, while a project with 25 or less units should be charged an annual management fee of $120 per unit. Leasing commissions and other unusual services not included in the management agreement would be subject to separate negotiation.

[1] William D. Sally, "Pricing Residential Property Management Fees . . . Fairly and Accurately," *Journal of Property Management,* 41 (5) 234 (1976).

Compensation on Net Operating Income An alternative method bases management compensation on net operating income. It is argued that the owner, concerned with after-tax cash flow, the taxable income, and tax shelter, looks to net operating income to maximize these benefits. To the extent that the owner capitalizes *net income*, not gross income, it is believed that managers should be rewarded according to the net operating income.[2]

The counterargument rests on practical grounds. Net operating income may vary widely by policies with respect to reserves for replacements, the level of maintenance, and services rendered renters. The gross income, on the other hand, is readily definable and not subject to variations in expenses of operation.

THE MANAGEMENT SURVEY

It seems that virtually every real estate specialist issues a consulting report; appraisers prepare appraisal reports, members of the American Society of Real Estate Counselors issue formally written counseling reports, mortgage bankers submit complex loan applications, and, similarly, property managers make management surveys. Sometimes referred to as the management plan, its preparation follows a format recommended by the Institute of Real Estate Management.

Management Survey Objectives

The management survey is directed to numerous objectives. In making a survey of a 50-year-old, 10-story brick apartment building of 75 units, the owner may need a management program to develop the highest net income at the lowest capital expenditure. Alternatively, in working with a 30-unit walk-up apartment building, the management survey may recommend the market rent developed under the best management program.

In brief, the *management survey* may be defined as a comprehensive economic analysis of income property.[3] Under this definition, the management survey may not necessarily lead to higher net operating income. There are instances where recommendations of the manager may preserve the property and effectively reverse declining net income.

In still other instances, recommendations center on increasing the cash flow—the amount of net operating income remaining after net income taxes. These various purposes are served by a management survey organized under six topics: (1) physical real property inventory, (2) neighborhood analysis, (3) market analysis, (4) gross income analysis, (5) operating expense analysis, and (6) an economic analysis of alternative plans. Final recommendations conclude the management survey.

Physical Real Property Inventory

For the more complex properties, such as high-rise apartment buildings and office buildings, many managers employ checklists covering the physical condition of prop-

[2] Austin J. Jaffe, "Management Fee Assessment Revisited," *Journal of Property Management*, 42(4):181-184 (1977).
[3] William M. Shenkel, *The Real Estate Professional*, rev. ed., Homewood, Ill.: Dow Jones-Irwin, 1978, p. 460.

erty. Others organize the report to describe exterior building features—the condition of the walls, roof, windows, gutters, and downspouts. The interior will be analyzed with respect to the condition of the public areas, primarily the lobby and corridors. The condition of the floor covering, walls, and ceilings will be judged with respect to their effect on the potential rent and operating expenses. If the equipment is complex, consulting engineers may render judgments on the present condition of electrical equipment, elevators, plumbing, heating, and air conditioning. For furnished residential units, the property manager will examine the furniture, kitchen equipment, and machinery.

In this part of the report, detail will be offered on the degree of observed deferred maintenance and obsolescence. For apartment units, some obsolescence may be remedied by installing more modern kitchen equipment such as compactors, sink disposal units, and the like. The physical inspection will close with data on building compliance with local codes and ordinances governing property use and occupancy.

Neighborhood Analysis

For property management purposes, neighborhoods are analyzed according to their physical and social characteristics. First, the manager identifies neighborhood boundaries that may be delineated by streams, rivers, topography, railroads, and similar features. Next the manager studies surrounding buildings, their general appearance, and the condition and quality of public improvements like streets, sidewalks, playgrounds, parks, and other features important to the property under review. It would be difficult to make broad generalizations on the review of physical characteristics, since items emphasized vary by type of property and location.

The social characteristics, especially for apartment buildings, refer to the type of tenants, their occupation, education, and typical income. Judgments will be rendered on the stage of neighborhood growth—rising, stable, or declining. Reasons will be given for estimates of future social trends.

Market Analysis

Market analysis for the management survey turns on (1) a review of present leases, and (2) an economic analysis. Each lease is identified according to its term, renewal options, and rent per square foot. Gross rent is analyzed in terms of bad debts, vacancies, and tenant turnover, that is, the percentage of tenants who renew at lease termination.

The economic analysis covers competitive rents, vacancies experienced by like properties, and economic trends that bear on future rentals. Changes in transportation, highway access, new public or private construction, and employment opportunities are relevant to the market analysis. With these studies in hand, the next two sections of the management survey review income and expense analysis.

Income Analysis

For properties undergoing a management survey, rental income is shown in per unit values such as square foot, per room or per apartment. These data are compared to competitive properties adjusted for differences in location and levels of service. At this point, the manager develops a *stabilized* gross income, which is documented with rents on similar properties.

Operating Expense Analysis

In like manner, current expenses are reviewed according to their percentage of gross possible income, and on a per unit basis—square foot, per room or per apartment. The *stabilized* expenses represent current expenses adjusted for probable short-run changes and appropriate annual allowances for replacing carpets, hot water heaters, and other equipment. The manager reviews the maintenance and repair budget to make adequate allowance for repainting, floor finishing, and other allowances such as the replacement of venetian blinds and furniture.

The purpose of stabilizing income and expenses is to calculate a realistic net operating income. Thus the net operating income represents the best estimate in the light of current information. This estimate serves as the basis for analyzing alternatives to increase income.

Economics of Alternatives

At this point in the analysis, it is likely that the manager will recommend certain capital improvements. For these recommendations, the manager selects one of three alternatives:

Rehabilitation Rehabilitation involves capital improvements that result in no changes in design; the building is restored to like-new condition.

Modernization Modernization provides for no change in property use; replacement of the heating system, lighting fixtures, plumbing, and refurbishing the lobby and public hallways are steps that extend the useful life of the building while maintaining or increasing net operating income.

Conversions Conversion recommendations suggest a change in design or use. Conversion is advised if the current use is less profitable than the proposed conversion, that is, apartment conversion to condominiums or converting a shopping center to an enclosed, air-conditioned mall. Likewise, industrial property in the downtown fringe area may be renovated for retail or warehouse use.

The capital improvement recommendations correct for physical and functional depreciation. Suggestions will be made in the light of the tax consequences faced by the property owner. For instance, *cash flow*—the amount of net income remaining after tax payments—might be increased by leasing operating equipment rather than purchasing.

Alternatives considered cover general leasing policies, tenant relations, employee relations, maintenance and inspection policies, and the level of services provided to renters.

The six steps of the management survey end with the final recommendation. For instance, in a survey of a 204-unit apartment building, 6 years old, which underwent foreclosure, management recommended:

1 Capital improvements: installation of security locks on all apartment doors
2 Replacement of hallway and lobby carpets
3 Repainting of public areas
4 Permanent installation of drapery and curtain rods in all apartments
5 Installation of storm windows
6 Repair of the asphalt parking area
7 Installation of electric meters for each apartment

The management survey recommended competitive bids to refurbish vacated apartment units. This reduced the maintenance staff from twelve persons to four. This step lowered the cost of redecorating vacated units and reduced vacancies while units awaited redecorating by the in-house maintenance staff. Rental policies recommended an increase in rents of approximately $30 a month. The relatively low rents experienced in the project attracted tenants with less secure income. By upgrading the property, higher rents could be charged, attracting tenants who would have more stable and higher incomes. These tenants would result in a lower rate of delinquencies and a lower tenant turnover.

SUMMARY

Management agreements, to be enforceable, must observe requirements of legal contracts. While they must be prepared with the advice of legal counsel, the management agreement appoints a management firm as an exclusive managing agent in representing the owner of a designated property.

In performing this task, management takes reasonable steps to collect rent and other charges due owners from renters. They supervise daily operations and are authorized to pay expenses up to a stated maximum without gaining the owner's written permission. Generally speaking, in negotiating leases, final lease terms are approved by the owner. The agent hires, supervises, and terminates independent contractors and employees.

Moreover, management maintains accurate records of receipts and disbursements and makes monthly reports and prepares annual budgets. For apartments, managers, by contract, agree to manage residential property in compliance with the Fair Housing Act of 1968.

Particular attention should be given to the insurance terms that hold management harmless from suits, liabilities, judgments, and damages connected with management of the property by the agent. Responsibilities of the owner covered in the management agreement require that the owner furnish the agent with all documents and records required for property management. Owners must maintain sufficient funds in a trust account to pay obligations.

Management agreements adapt to specialized property. In *shopping centers,* terms tend to be more specific, requiring detailed monthly statements of receipts, expenses, and charges. Management contracts may be terminated on 60 days' notice by either party, provided the manager is paid a specified amount for liquidated damages.

Condominium management agreements establish a legal relationship between the management agent and the board of directors who act on behalf of unit owners. While the management agreement details a minimum of ten services, the more important services relate to collection of monthly assessments, maintenance of records, preparation of annual budgets, and maintenance of common elements according to "appropriate standards of maintenance." The agent has the added task of preparing tax returns and related documents associated with condominium ownership. Unlike apartment properties, the managing agent assumes no responsibility for delinquent charges or assessments. Usually the management agreement directs a single person to supervise management operations.

Vacation-home management agreements constitute a unique contract of employment. They adapt to the short-term rentals of vacation homes. Accordingly, agents have a much broader grant of authority compared to the usual management agreement. The agent advertises for rentals and is given authority to sign new leases and cancel tenancies. Agents have responsibility for repairs and alterations to a stated amount, and pay utility and other operating expenses. Because managers of vacation homes usually deal with absentee owners, they advise owners of the recommended competitive seasonal rent. While the owner reserves the right to approve the recommended rent, the management agent suggests rents that are competitive with motel rates. In this operation, the manager must solicit information on new furniture, recent alterations, and owner plans to occupy the unit for the forthcoming season.

Specialists in *motel management* prepare management agreements that cover virtually every facet of motel operation. The range of services include accounting, systems administration, engineering and maintenance, food and beverage management, marketing, and purchasing. In assuming management of a new unit, managers prepare an annual plan within 90 to 120 days after the effective date of a management contract. Management agreements call for an annual report 30 days before the end of the year, which covers an inspection, a proposed marketing program, operation analysis, and a proposed budget of expenses. Annual recommendations may also cover major repairs and improvements.

Add to the list of management agreements *consulting agreements* which, according to one authority, cover two phases: the first phase is a rent analysis that reports the upper and lower limitations of the rental structure. For new projects the study of rental structure includes a marketing plan. The second phase reviews daily operations, staff organization, office procedures, records, leasing policies, forms, and reports.

Management fees ordinarily are based on a percentage of gross income. Fees for managing the larger projects, because of economies of scale, are lower than fees for smaller projects that require more management time per unit. Low-income units, because they require more management effort, may have management fees of 10 percent of gross rents. While management fees tend to be competitive, there is an attempt to base management fees on costs of management operations adjusted for economies of scale for individual projects. Some authorities recommend management fees based on a percentage of net income rather than gross income.

The *management survey*, which is defined as a comprehensive economic analysis of income property, recommends the best means of increasing net operating income.

To be sure, there are other instances in which recommendations of the manager preserve the property and reverse declining net income. Other management surveys are directed to increasing cash flow—the amount of net operating income remaining after net income taxes.

Covering a six-part survey, the management survey deals first with the *physical property inventory.* The second part of the management survey, *neighborhood analysis,* analyzes the physical and social characteristics that affect the rent potential. The third part of the report—*market analysis*—reviews present leases and deals with competitive rents, vacancies, and economic trends that bear on future rentals. This part of the report leads to the last three sections of the report—*gross income analysis, operating expense analysis,* and *economics of alternatives.* The latter point considers *rehabilitation,* restoring the building to like new condition; *modernization,* with no change in property use; or *conversion,* which results in a change in property design or use. With this six-part analysis, the property manager makes final recommendations for maximization of net operating income.

DISCUSSION QUESTIONS

1 What is the main purpose of the management agreement?
2 Discuss three main management duties and explain how a property manager would implement these duties in managing an apartment complex.
3 Explain three responsibilities of the owner to the management agent.
4 In what ways are management agreements for shopping centers specialized? Explain fully.
5 What differences may be cited in condominium management agreements in comparison to agreements for apartment building managment? Explain fully.
6 What are the most common features of a management agreement covering vacation homes?
7 What special duties face the manager of a motel? Describe fully.
8 What are the two phases common to a management consulting agreement? Explain thoroughly.
9 How are management fees commonly determined?
10 Describe the data covered in the six-part management survey. Give examples in illustration of your answer.

KEY TERMS AND CONCEPTS

Property management agreement	Economics of alternatives
Management survey	Rehabilitation
Hold harmless clauses	Modernization
Systems administration	Conversion
The annual plan	Stabilized income
Managing consulting agreements	Stabilized expenses

SELF-QUIZ

Multiple Choice Questions

_____ 1 The purpose of the management agreement is to: (a) Increase rents; (b) Improve tenant relations; (c) Decrease operating expenses; (d) Appoint a management firm as an exclusive agent and representative of the owner to manage a designated property.

_____ 2 Which of the following is _not_ included among management duties required by a management agreement? (a) Make periodic inspections; (b) Estimate market value; (c) Supervise maintenance; (d) Arrange for such improvements, alterations, and repairs as may be required.

_____ 3 Responsibilities of the owner outlined in the management agreement include the duty to: (a) Furnish agent with all documents and records required for property management; (b) Maintain sufficient funds in the trust account to meet all obligations; (c) Pay lease commissions based on an agreed lease commission schedule; (d) All of the above.

_____ 4 Which of the following would not be common to a management agreement covering shopping centers? (a) The agent keeps records of gross sales and computes percentage rents; (b) The agent is not responsible for collecting delinquent rents; (c) The agent advertises rentals and is given authority to sign, renew, and cancel tenancies in the name of the owner; (d) The management supervises relations with local health, sanitation, and license agencies.

_____ 5 Which of the following would not be common to a management agreement covering shopping centers? (a) The agent keeps records of gross sales and computes percentage rents: (b) The agent is not responsible for collecting delinquent rents; (c) The agent advertises rentals and is A monthly analysis is made of accounts payable, monthly journal entries, payrolls, and taxes; (d) The agent makes a two-phase study consisting of a rent analysis and a review of daily operations.

_____ 6 In managing motels, management agreements provide for: (a) Account executives who work with the owner under supervision of central management; (b) Systems administrators who inspect accounting records and control systems on a recurring basis; (c) A professional staff of engineers who coordinate architectural designs and construction; (d) All of the above.

_____ 7 Prevailing practice is to base management fees on: (a) Net operating income; (b) Gross possible income, assuming 100 percent occupancy; (c) A percentage of gross income; (d) Fifteen percent of actual rents collected.

_____ 8 Management fees: (a) Vary by type of property; (b) Should cover typical management costs; (c) For managing vacation homes are typically based on 10 to 15 percent of rentals received; (d) All of the above.

_____ 9 The management survey: (a) Is prepared for income tax and property tax purposes; (b) Is directed to a single objective; (c) May be defined as a comprehensive economic analysis of income property; (d) Represents an engineering analysis of building equipment.

_____ 10 The market analysis for a management survey: (a) Turns on a review of present leases and an economic analysis; (b) Concentrates on tenant purchasing power; (c) Describes the physical features of the building under review; (d) Covers a detailed analysis of gross incomes and operating expenses.

Answer Key

1 (d),   2 (b),   3 (d),   4 (b),   5 (b),   6 (a),   7 (c),   8 (d),   9 (c),   10 (a).

Fill-In Questions

1 The _____ serves the property manager as the listing agreement serves the real estate broker.

2 The management agreement provides that the _____ must take all reasonable steps for the proper management of the property.

3 Management agreements require that owners agree to maintain sufficient funds in a _____ to pay obligations.

4 A common provision of the management agreement grants the agent the _____ _____ if the property is offered for sale during the agreement.

5 For management agreements on shopping centers, the agent is instructed to participate in the _____ in accordance with written instructions of the owner.

6 Management agreements on condominiums do not make management responsible for enforcing collection of _____.

7 In managing vacation homes, managers are aware of _____ and _____ that affect the rental market.

8 The management survey includes a neighborhood analysis of _____ and _____ characteristics.

9 In the management survey, managers develop an estimate of _____ _____ and _____.

10 _____ provides for no change in property use.

Answer Key

1 management agreement	5 merchants association
2 agent	6 delinquent assessments
3 trust account	7 competitive forces; costs
4 exclusive right to sell	8 physical; social

9 stabilized gross income; stabilized   10 Modernization
   expenses

SELECTED REFERENCES

Downs, James C., Jr.: *Principles of Real Estate Management,* Chicago: Institute of
    Real Estate Management, 1975, pp. 388–390.
Harris, Ronald A.: "Resort Condominium Management: What's It All About?" *Journal
    of Property Management,* 42 (1): 5–10 (1977).
Sally, William D.: "Pricing Residential Property Management Fees . . . Fairly and
    Accurately," *Journal of Property Management,* 41 (5): 233–238 (1976).
Walters, David W.: "Negotiating the Property Management Agreement," *Journal of
    Property Management,* 42 (6): 291–297 (1977).

Chapter 8

Tenant Relations

After studying this chapter, you should be familiar with:
1 The difference between leases treated as conveyance instruments and those treated as contracts
2 Principal responsibilities of a landlord
3 Principal responsibilities of a tenant
4 Methods of promoting tenant relations

Current tenant-landlord relations have considerably changed from the former common-law doctrine, which considered a lease as a conveyance instrument like a deed. Consequently, the tenant accepted the premises in an "as is" condition. Furthermore, under early common law, landlords had no duty to remedy defects in leased property—defects such as a leaky roof in an apartment.

Current practice treats a lease as a contract. This means that the landlord has the duty to perform a series of enforceable requirements. One of the requirements is the "implied" warranty of habitability. Courts, in considering the lease as a contract with this implied warranty, would require landlords to repair a leaky roof. Besides the changed interpretation of leases, owners and tenants are subject to state landlord-tenant legislation, and stricter municipal housing and building codes.

It should be added that the terms *tenant* and *landlord* have a strict legal connotation. They correspond to *lessee* (tenant) and *lessor* (landlord). In communications with tenants, property managers prefer "resident" to these legal expressions. Even the term "renter" is avoided in the interest of better public relations. Therefore while the term "tenant-landlord" is used in the present context, it is only for clarity of expression and it is not meant to imply that property managers use legal terms in public communications.

COMMON LAW DOCTRINE

Originally under common law the only duty of the landlord was to warrant the tenant's right to quiet enjoyment. This refers to the right to peaceably occupy the premises without interference from the landlord or others. In short, the ideal landlord would grant possession warranting quiet enjoyment over the lease term; the ideal tenant would pay rent on time and would not demand more than possession; for example, the lease served merely to convey a leasehold interest.

Leases as Conveyance Instruments

Under early property law, landlords leased the agricultural land that tenants used to produce crops. Therefore any structures on the land were incidental to the main purpose. Under this system, tenants gained possession under the rule of caveat emptor; there was (1) no implied duty of the landlord to deliver suitable premises nor to maintain premises during the lease, and (2) lease covenants were mutually independent.

The rule of caveat emptor meant that tenants who neglected to inspect the premises before signing the lease were not protected by a warranty of fitness from the lessor. An inspection implied that tenants legally accepted premises in their existing state. Moreover, the landlord had no duty to maintain the premises or make needed repairs during the lease term. In fact, in the absence of an express agreement, the tenant was obliged to maintain the premises under the duty not to commit waste.

And, finally, in that covenants of the lease were mutually independent, a breach by the landlord of any lease covenant did not invalidate other lease terms—terms, for example, that required the tenant to pay rent. That is, tenants could not refuse to pay rent because of the landlord's default. Only if the tenant could prove "constructive eviction" could the tenant refuse to pay rent.

To prove constructive eviction, tenants had to show that the property was vacated because there was substantial interference with the tenant's right of quiet enjoyment. The burden was placed on the tenant to prove substantial interference with the right of quiet enjoyment. In the absence of acceptable proof, tenants remained obligated to pay rent.

The Lease as a Contract

These early agrarian concepts were unworkable for urban property, particularly for apartments. Today the primary interest is not in leasing productive land but in acquiring suitable shelter in rented housing or apartments. In a modern apartment, for example, the tenant's ability to correct defects has markedly declined with the complexity of modern apartment house construction and its built-in equipment.

As a consequence, the various states have enacted landlord-tenant laws that have changed common-law rules. The change is justified on grounds that urban tenants are in a poor position to bargain for minimum conditions of habitation. Critical shortages in low- and moderate-income housing have been cited as another reason for new legislation that revises common-law rules. State and local housing codes and new court decisions represent a further reaction to common-law doctrines.

LANDLORD-TENANT RESPONSIBILITIES

The landlord-tenant legislation and court rulings have revised traditional relations between landlord and tenant. Under these new laws, both the landlord and the tenant have added responsibilities which, if not stated in the lease, are legally implied.

Landlord Responsibilities

Four basic practices have been revised by dealing with leases as contract documents. Most courts, local and state law provide (1) warranty of habitability, (2) in certain circumstances, tenants are given the right to repair and deduct expenses from rent payable, (3) prohibition of retaliatory eviction, and (4) more strict administration of security deposits.

The Warranty of Habitability The landlord's obligations toward the tenant are illustrated under the Ohio Landlord Law (Section 5321.04), which provides that landlords must:

1 Comply with all building and housing codes
2 Make all repairs and keep the premises in habitable condition
3 Keep the common areas in safe and sanitary condition
4 Maintain all electrical, plumbing, heating and ventilating facilities in good and safe condition
5 Provide trash containers and remove trash (only applies to four or more dwelling units in the same structure)
6 Supply water and heat, except where these utilities are under control of the tenant
7 Not abuse the tenant rights of access
8 Give reasonable notice of intent to enter the premises (24 hours is presumed reasonable notice, in the absence of contrary evidence).

These provisions represent a clear reversal of landlord-tenant law. For example, the Boston Rental Housing Association reports that in 1946 a tenant leased 1,900 square feet on the second floor of an apartment building. After the building burned down, the landlord demanded the rent check on the first of the month. When the tenant refused to pay, the local court decided that the tenant's real interest was the exclusive right to occupy a certain fixed area and, since the tenant still had this right, he was still obligated to pay rent.[1]

Recall that under common law a tenant could not legally withold rent until a landlord made repairs. If the provisions of a model residential landlord-tenant code are followed, the owner must observe state or local housing codes and landlord-tenant legislation. Under the Uniform Residential Landlord-Tenant Code, the landlord shall at all times during the tenant occupancy:

1 Comply with all applicable provisions of any state or local statute, code, regulation, or ordinance governing the maintenance, construction, use, or appearance of the dwelling unit and the property of which it is a part

2 Keep all areas of the building, grounds, facilities, and appurtenances in a clean and sanitary condition

3 Make all repairs and arrangements necessary to keep the dwelling unit and the appurtenances thereto in as good condition as they were, or by law or agreement had been at the commencement of tenancy

4 Maintain all electrical, plumbing, and other facilities supplied in good working order

5 Except in the case of a single-family residence, provide and maintain appropriate receptacles and conveniences for the removal of ashes, rubbish, and garbage, and arrange for the frequent removal of such wastes

6 Except in the case of a single-family residence, or where the building is equipped for other purposes, supply water and hot water as reasonably required by the tenant and supply adequate heat between October 1 and May 1

If the lease must comply with local building or housing codes, the landlord must observe certain other minimum requirements. For example, in the city of Chicago, landlords must provide minimum temperatures between September 15 and June 1 according to the following schedule:

60° F at 6:30 a.m.
65° F at 7:30 a.m.
68° F from 8:30 a.m. to 10:30 p.m.
55° F from 10:30 p.m. to 6:30 a.m.

Similarly, in the city of Philadelphia buildings of two or more apartments must have heat at a temperature of 68° F for each apartment from October 1 to April 30 and during May and September when the outside temperature falls below 60° F. Other provisions of local codes typically provide minimum square foot areas, lighting, ventilation, and similar requirements.

Repair and Deduct Provisions The legislatures of some states have granted tenants limited rights to repair premises and deduct the cost from their monthly rent.

---

[1] Philip S. Lapatin and Herbert S. Lerman, *Residential Landlord-Tenant Law: A Modern Massachusetts Guide,* Boston: Rental Housing Association, A Division of the Greater Boston Real Estate Board, 1977, p. 1.

For instance, in the state of Hawaii tenants may deduct not more than one month's rent from actual expenses incurred to correct an objectionable condition, provided the tenant submits to the landlord, at least 30 days before the repair work begins, a signed estimate from two qualified workers. If the repair work costs more than $100, the tenant is required to obtain a written statement from the department of health that the objectionable condition, in fact, constitutes a violation of a health law or regulation.[2]

While state laws on this point vary, these terms are indicative of the change in landlord-tenant law. Currently, landlords have the duty to maintain premises in a habitable condition. Yet, rent-deduct statutes, according to most authorities, have been ineffective because tenants are required to waive rights by lease provisions and because the amount of the expenditures authorized is usually limited to an insignificant sum.[3]

Retaliatory Eviction   Under landlord-tenant laws that follow the model residential landlord-tenant code, landlords are barred from evicting tenants after tenants have filed notices or complaints of housing violations or other regulations under local or state law. Moreover, owners are barred from increasing the rent or decreasing services, provided tenants continue to pay rent.

According to section 5.101 of the model code, landlords may not act against tenants within 1 year after a tenant has complained of code violations affecting the tenant's dwelling unit to an enforcement agency.[4] Tenants are also free from adverse actions of the landlord if the local agency has filed a notice or complaint of such a violation or if the tenant has requested necessary repairs. Recall that under common law, owners were relatively free to convey an unrestricted nonfreehold interest. In most areas, eviction is not permitted as retaliation against adverse complaints or reports of landlord violations.

Security Deposits   Laws regulating security deposits usually limit the amount of security and detail conditions under which a landlord may retain security deposits. Some states, such as Georgia, require security deposits to be held in a special escrow account. In Arizona, according to the *Residential Landlord-Tenant Act*, security deposits must not exceed 1½ months rent. Security may include anything of value. Arizona, like some other states, requires that landlords give tenants an itemized list of deductions from security deposits. The remaining balance of the security deposit must be paid within 14 days after a tenant vacates and applies for return of the deposit.

Under these regulations, typically the landlord may deduct the cost of repairing damages beyond normal wear and tear. Landlords subject to this legislation must be

---

[2] *Hawaii Landlord Tenant Manual*, Honolulu: Hawaii Association of Real Estate Boards, pp. 29–30.

[3] Jerome G. Rose, *Landlords & Tenants*, New Brunswick, N.J.: Transactions Books, 1973, p. 11.

[4] See *Uniform Residential Landlord and Tenant Act.* Chicago: National Conference of Commissioners on Uniform State Laws, 1972.

prepared to prove (1) that damage exists, (2) that it was caused during the tenant's period of possession, (3) that the damage is beyond normal wear and tear, and (4) that the cost of repair equals the claim for damage payments. Most management organizations provide an inventory and a signed statement of conditions of the premises before and after the tenancy.

In Hawaii, for example, landlords may not charge more than 1 month's rent as security. Compensation for damages caused by the tenant would be paid only if the tenant were notified in writing and given written evidence of the cost of tenant default, such as the actual cost of cleaning, or receipts for supplies and equipment. In the event of disagreement, landlord and tenant take their dispute to the small claims division of the court.

Tenant Responsibilities

While new legislation requires landlords to make repairs and maintain habitable premises, tenant duties are also affected by the "contract interpretation" of leases. In Ohio, the law (Section 5321.05) requires that tenants:

1 Keep the premises safe and sanitary
2 Dispose of all trash
3 Keep plumbing fixtures as clean as conditions permit
4 Use all electrical and plumbing fixtures in the proper manner
5 Not destroy or damage, nor permit invitees to destroy or damage the premises
6 Comply with housing, health, and safety codes
7 Maintain appliances in good order if the tenant is required to maintain them under a written rental agreement
8 Not disturb the neighbors

Most leases give the landlord the right to inspect the premises upon reasonable notice and during reasonable times. The standard lease form in Boston permits owners to make entry at reasonable times, in case of emergency or on reasonable notice and during reasonable hours to inspect, to make repairs, or to show the apartment.

Generally speaking, if tenants are not good housekeepers, they violate lease covenants. Alterations of the premises require written approval; residential leases often restrict other tenant privileges such as installation of water beds. Here the landlord's chief concern is whether the weight of the water bed exceeds floor load capacity and whether damage will result from accidental leakage. Tenants must be good neighbors by observing house rules and regulations.

The Chicago Building Department advises tenants that by law all tenants are prohibited from leaving open garbage in hallways, stairways, back porches, or basements. Further, unless supplied by the owner, tenants must hang and remove all screens required for each apartment. In Chicago, tenants are prohibited from using public space for storage: hallways; under stairs; on stairs; in lobbies, vestibules, or exitways. Local law prohibits tenants from storing material that will cause a fire hazard or endanger health or safety. Occupancy by four persons requires a minimum floor area of 450 square feet. For each additional occupant there must be at least another 75 square feet of floor area. Two people are prohibited from occupying less than 250 square feet of rental space.

General Landlord and Tenant Responsibilities

Laws and ordinances deal with specific lease terms. Besides meeting these regulatory requirements, it is worthwhile to focus on the general responsibilities inherent in the lease contract. In this respect, there is common agreement on general rights and duties of landlords and tenants.

Landlords Generally speaking, owners may devote property to uses permitted by law and local ordinances. The fee owner may sell or rent the property and may set conditions under which the property will be used by another party. Provided fair housing rules are observed, the owner may decide who can live in the building, their tenure and, within limits, under what conditions. Owners decide on the amount of rent and may request references from the tenant's previous landlords.

With minor qualifications, the owner has the right to enter leased property to inspect premises, and to make necessary or agreed-on repairs, alterations, or improvements. Access to leased property will be allowed to supply building services or to show the unit to prospective tenants, purchasers, lenders, workers, or contractors. The right of access must not unreasonably be withheld by the tenant, and the landlord in turn must seek entry only at reasonable hours, at the convenience of the renter, and with reasonable notice.

The lease must comply with local and state laws that affect occupant health and safety. Landlords must make repairs, keep the premises in habitable condition, and maintain common areas of the premises in clean and safe condition. All plumbing, electrical, and sanitary equipment; and heating, ventilating, air-conditioning, and other facilities are required to be maintained in good, safe working order. Landlords must arrange for garbage collection, running water in reasonable amounts with hot water, and reasonable heat according to agreement and the law.

Tenants Tenants, in turn, must observe lease provisions that control use of the premises. Tenants are required to keep the premises safe and clean and dispose of waste material in a clean and safe manner. Plumbing fixtures and appliances must be used in a reasonable manner and tenants are prohibited from deliberately or negligently destroying or defacing, impairing, or removing any part of the premises. Tenants are required to conduct themselves in a manner that will not disturb their neighbors' enjoyment of the premises. Tenants must make certain that family pets do not abuse the property rights of other tenants. In observing good tenant relations, tenants are advised to report problems as they occur to the management in writing and promptly pay rent when due.

Though the tenant is granted the right of peaceful possession and quiet enjoyment, the owner has the right to the rent payable on a certain day each month or each week. If tenants are delinquent in paying rent, with proper notice the owner has the right to eviction. Furthermore, if the tenant violates other terms of the lease, the landlord generally may seek eviction.

Landlord and Tenant Remedies

Some jurisdictions have established special arbitration boards to administer local landlord-tenant regulations. In Los Angeles, for example, a landlord-tenant mediation board has been formed by the Los Angeles City Council and consists of a five-member staff and a fifteen-member board formed to resolve landlord and tenant grievances, to promote harmony and understanding, and to make recommendations to the council on legislation for solving landlord-tenant problems.

The 15 members are divided into 5 groups of 3-member neighborhood boards to mediate disputes over rent and other tenant-landlord relationships. Early experience shows that landlords' complaints involve owners who are seeking rent and tenant eviction; tenants seem to complain about substandard or unrepaired conditions that make premises uninhabitable. Over 20,000 cases were heard during the first year and only about one quarter of the cases filed went to trial.

Similar legislation in Washington, D.C. provides for the Landlord and Tenant Court. Only landlords can file complaints, and during 1977 they filed 110,461 complaints against more than 30,000 people. The superior court of the District of Columbia also provides space for members of the Department of Human Resources, which acts as a consultant to the court.

The record of housing courts has led at least one management authority to recommend county housing courts. On this point it is argued:

> In the interest of owners and managers, good tenants, neighborhood groups, and city officials, a county housing court should have judicial powers to issue search warrants to health and public safety authorities in order to examine units where owners and tenants will not provide access; to hear cases that pertain to codes dealing with regulations for the construction of new buildings; to judge on the use, occupancy, maintenance, rehabilitation, and demolition of existing structures; and hand down decisions on electrical, plumbing, and environmental standards.[5]

According to this source, housing courts should be empowered to hear cases on the improper disposal of trash, intentional damage to property by tenants, zoning, consumer protection, and discrimination. In this respect, the court is viewed as a forum for housing justice. It is further recommended that judges should understand that while unemployed tenants need places to stay, so must the apartment house they occupy be maintained in a habitable condition. This source believes that judges should realize that each apartment tenant must pay his or her share of utilities, maintenance, taxes, mortgage payments, and proper building maintenance.

PROMOTING TENANT RELATIONS

Favorable tenant relations reduce collection costs and lower the rate of tenant turnover. To this end, steps undertaken by professional managers cover a broad range of activities.

[5] Joe L. Mattox, "Guest Editorial: Housing Court's Answer to Problem Tenants," *Journal of Property Management*, 41 (1) 29 (1976).

Tenant Public Relations

Some property managers prepare a resident handbook for new tenants, with a map and description of the apartment community and surrounding neighborhood. The handbook emphasizes important sections of the apartment lease. Other measures to improve tenant relations include:

1 Preparation of change-of-address kits
2 Publication of a newsletter with tips on apartment living and notices of coming events. Newsletters are preferably distributed in the middle of the month so they are not lost with other bills and monthly publications
3 A suggestion box placed in the lobby or clubhouse
4 Bulletin boards in an entrance lobby used to announce local activities and items for sale
5 Returning tenant calls promptly (within 24 hours).

Other managers promote the landlord-tenant relationship by concentrating on two-way communications. The communications start with the initial assumption of management duties. At this time a memorandum is sent to each tenant explaining plans for the building. The memorandum will list new management policies, including anticipated remodeling, new security measures, renovation of lobbies and other common areas, or updated laundry facilities or other services.

The memorandum is distributed on a monthly or bimonthly basis, informing tenants of problem areas. A memorandum may remind tenants of a policy affecting pets or of the improper use of passenger elevators for freight or security. In the monthly communication, management may promote activities by announcing bridge clubs, guest speakers, and other programs encouraging tenants to develop their own recreational program.

The importance of communication is indicated by Leon D. Laffal, a Certified Property Manager, who states:

> We're sold on communication with our residents. All letters are answered promptly and in detail. If we can use a resident's suggestion, we do so and thank him in writing. If we must deny a request, we go into detail to explain why.[6]

According to this source, improved communications decreased tenant turnover and increased resident cooperation.

Tenant Associations

Opinion is strongly divided on tenant associations. There is the view that tenant associations should be strongly discouraged, that management should not attend tenant organization meetings, and that management should not respond in any way to tenant associations. They are viewed as an interference to "the orderly and efficient operation of real estate." According to one expert, "because they do not understand—

[6]"Full Communication Key to Happy Residents," *Journal of Property Management*, 41(1): 45 (1976).

and often have no need to understand—the need for good business practices, they make decisions on grounds of emotion and pressure."[7]

In reality, militant tenant associations generally form because of legitimate complaints—a development that management should never permit. Confronted with committee residents, management is advised to seek solutions to legitimate problems as they would if dealing with a single resident.[8]

Some of the larger housing developments have formed tenant associations that meet regularly to discuss common concerns, for example, rental policies, security, and project maintenance. If the premises are well maintained and tenants are courteously treated, these associations turn into social organizations. Associations are often effective in managing parking, traffic, and security problems that affect the apartment community.

If tenant organizations are actively supported, tenants become a part of operations rather than objects of management; management looks to the tenant organization for support of management policies, house rules, and regulations. More specific reasons offered in support of tenant organizations include the following:

1 Problems are solved more easily.
2 Management policies become more realistic.
3 Social programming is more effective.
4 Tenants' self-help skills are increased.
5 A sense of community is developed.
6 A power base is established for dealing with political pressures.

In short, problems are solved more easily, since tenants may voice complaints to the tenant organization that works directly with management. When a solution to the problem is reached jointly, management can execute the suggested remedy, knowing that the new policy will gain tenant support.[9] Figure 8-1 illustrates a statement circulated among tenants that explains management's attitude toward tenants and encourages participation in the tenant organization.

Organized tenant associations are most effective in dealing with certain decisions that are difficult for management to enforce. For example, tenant associations are effective in improving relationships between maintenance personnel and tenants; they help police illegal adult activities and they reduce antisocial behavior among tenants. Experience shows further that tenant associations are highly effective in reducing vandalism and property destruction. On a longer-term basis, tenant organizations help tenants to understand the importance of paying rent promptly and the management problems in meeting payrolls, utility costs, and morgage expenses.[10]

[7] Edward N. Kelley, *Practical Apartment Management*, Chicago: Institute of Real Estate Management, 1976, p. 89.

[8] See Sidney Glassman, *A Guide to Resident Management*, 2d rev., Washington, D.C.: National Association of Homebuilders, 1978, p. 41.

[9] See *Tenant Councils: Preparing the Climate*, Urbana-Champaign, Ill.: Housing Research and Development, University of Illinois, no date, p. 3.

[10] Ibid., pp. 22–28.

```
                        TENANT ASSOCIATION

To All Tenants

     Allow us to share with you the following brief statement
of our view of you:

A Tenant . . . is the most important person in our business.

A Tenant . . . is the life-blood of our business.

A Tenant . . . is a person who brings us his wants--it is our
                job to try to fill those wants.

A Tenant . . . is a person who makes it possible for us to
                receive our "Pay to the Order of" each month.

A Tenant . . . is not dependent on us--we are dependent on him.

A Tenant . . . is not a lease number--he is a human being with
                feelings and emotions like our own.

A Tenant . . . is not an interruption of our work--he is the
                purpose of it.

A Tenant . . . is not an outsider--he is an essential part of
                our operations.

A Tenant . . . is not someone to argue or match wits with--he is
                one whose respect and confidence we want to gain.

A Tenant . . . IS, THEREFORE, DESERVING OF THE MOST COURTEOUS,
                THE MOST SYMPATHETIC, AND THE MOST ATTENTIVE
                TREATMENT WE CAN GIVE HIM AT ALL TIMES.

     In keeping with the views expressed in this "creed," we are
urging all tenants to become involved with the tenant councils in
their various projects.  The tenant council is YOUR organization.
The management has no control over its formation or its activities,
except in an advisory capacity whenever desired.

     We look forward to its continued progress because the views
and suggestions offered by a strong, active tenant council composed
of concerned residents provide us with a source of information con-
cerning your needs.  We also anticipate the formation of the Execu-
tive Council with members elected from each tenant council to work
together toward improving conditions and services in projects at large.

     The establishment of tenant councils has proved tremendously
beneficial to apartment resident.  We have no doubt that you can
and will experience like success.

     Your tenant council will be holding an organization meeting
at _____ on _____, _____, 197_ at _____.  We hope that
every tenant will attend this meeting with a view toward actively
participating in future council activities.
```

Figure 8-1 A management statement promoting tenant associations. *(Source: Tenant Councils: Preparing the Climate, Urbana-Champaign, Ill.: Housing Research and Development, University of Illinois, no date, p. 35.)*

The formation of tenant associations may follow an informal social organization or develop from a formal constitution. The constitution of the organization would include the following articles:

Article I.	The organization name
Article II.	Purpose of the organization
Article III.	Duties and terms of officers
Artical IV.	Membership requirements
Artical V.	Meetings
Artical VII.	Amendment of constitution
Artical VIII.	Tenure of operation
Artical IX.	Standing committees

Following this more formal organization, the tenant association would require bylaws to govern the nomination of officers and their election, to define membership requirements, to remove officers, to govern meetings, to state order of business, and to make provision for amending bylaws.

Management Responsibilities

If tenant turnover is high and a large number of tenants seem continually dissatisfied, management is probably at fault. Questions that help evaluate the effectiveness of management include:

1 How sensitive is management to tenant needs and concerns?

2 To what extent are responsibilities for tenant relations delegated to the project manager?

3 What qualifications does the on-site manager have with respect to understanding human behavior and community relations?

4 Has the management staff received training and exhibited understanding in developing skills for working with tenants?

5 Do tenants have a clear understanding of extra charges for services?

6 Does the management staff call upon delinquent tenants to discuss their problems?

7 Are tenants invited to come to the manager to discuss their delinquency problems?

8 Does management publish and distribute a tenant handbook describing responsibilities and services of landlord and tenant?

9 Has management worked effectively in forming a tenant association?

To be sure, management is directed toward earning the greatest possible net return over remaining building life. And certainly the property must be maintained in an acceptable condition. But more than that, these questions focus on interpersonal relations: supervising the staff and building good employee and tenant relations. In this respect, the manager provides the residents with numerous services that increase the social acceptability of the rental project.

Problem Tenants While management may work toward increasing efficiency, there is the alternative view that problem tenants are the most critical part of the housing problem. This conclusion follows from two facts: (1) Higher trade association standards and new federal, state, and local laws on health, safety, equal opportunity, and tenants' rights result in good quality housing; and (2) legal aid and tenant organizations have largely eliminated the unscrupulous owners and housing managers.

In the case of problem tenants, housing owners and managers should take prompt court action. Problem tenants are defined as tenants who do not pay the rent, deliberately destroy property, steal from neighbors, and move frequently from place to place. Typically such an individual does not maintain a clean unit and largely ignores apartment rules promoting group safety, such as locking doors and not giving keys to friends. Problem tenants include parents who are unwilling or unable to discipline children and who allow children to wantonly abuse and destroy property. The family that wastes electricity, gas, water, and heat and causes unusually high repair bills also represent problem tenants.

Tenant Guidebooks In directing attention to this problem, the United States Department of Housing and Urban Development has published a guide for tenants that advises:

> rules are usually instituted to promote the common interest of all renters. Rules can encourage peace, quiet, privacy, and some of the other qualities that make a house a home. It is entirely up to you to determine in advance if these particular rules are compatible with your living patterns. If you feel you can not live with them, don't move in! You may find it more comfortable to continue looking for another unit. Be sure to consider all these things before you sign your name to the rental arrangement.[11]

The pamphlet advises prospective tenants that the most common rules and restrictions for apartments concern:

house parties, noise, hi-fi's, TV's, or musical instruments
mounting pictures on the walls
painting or papering walls
parking space for tenant and guests
pets
recreation and common-use facilities
special furniture and appliances, such as water beds or hot plates
unsolicited salespeople
use of grounds for such outdoor activities as games, gardening, bicycles, and loitering
use of laundry facilities and public accommodations
use of unvented oil and gas heaters

[11] *Wise Rental Practices*, Washington, D.C.: U.S. Department of Housing and Urban Development, 1977, p. 18.

Other managers suggest that the tenant guidebook include certain practical information for new tenants. The practical information would include such items as:

utility companies: name, address, and telephone number
nearby churches and synagogues
nearby schools, both public and private
nearest public library
available public transportation
the closest shopping district
the nearest post office
a list of emergency telephone numbers
voting precinct number
the names and locations of city and county officials[12]

Management steps to improve tenant relations strongly emphasize tenant services. This point was illustrated by a real estate manager who required management and maintenance personnel to wear a 6-inch round button reading "We care." Not only did the "We care" motto motivate people to do a better job, but it impressed tenants with the sincerity of management in serving their needs.

SUMMARY

Property managers have responded to the new legal relationships between landlord and tenant. The earlier view treated leases as a conveyance instrument in which the tenant accepted the premises in an "as is" condition and, in absence of agreement, leases in which the landlord had no duty to remedy defects in leased property.

Under the concept of the lease as a contract, landlords must conform to the *warranty of habitability*, which requires that the premises be kept in a habitable condition. In certain jurisdictions, tenants are given the limited right to *repair and deduct* repair expenses from rent. The laws of most states prohibit *retaliatory eviction*, defined as eviction as a consequence of tenant notices or complaints of a housing violation. *Security deposits* are yet another area covered by landlord-tenant legislation. Where deposits are under regulation, both the maximum amount and procedures for deducting the cost of repairing damages must follow legally established procedures.

While these provisions relate to landlord responsibilities, it is equally clear that tenants have the duty to keep premises in a safe and sanitary condition, avoid waste, and pay rent on time.

The critical importance of administering landlord-tenant responsibility has led to housing courts that are administered by specially appointed courts or landlord-tenant commissions. Some authorities have recommended universal county housing courts to deal with problem tenants.

In like manner, tenant associations have an important bearing on management policy. While some tenant associations are strictly social, the militant tenant associa-

---

[12] See Edward N. Kelley, op. cit., p. 79.

tion arises because of management inadequacies—which should not be allowed to occur. While some managers deny that tenant organizations represent a constructive step, others recommend them as a way to help discipline problem tenants. For the problem properties, tenant associations help to solve problems, develop a sense of community, and are a means of communicating management policies to tenants.

In sum, management works toward improving services and, above all, improving communication. Communication includes, among other items, publication of a tenant newsletter that promotes management policy and specifically warns tenants of violations that cause nuisances to others.

DISCUSSION QUESTIONS

1 What landlord-tenant rights are implied in viewing the lease as a conveyance instrument? Explain fully.
2 What landlord-tenant rights are implied in treating the lease as a contract? Explain fully.
3 Explain and give examples of four basic practices revised by treating leases as contract documents.
4 Discuss main tenant responsibilities prevailing under the view of a lease as a contract.
5 What are the advantages of housing courts in dealing with landlord-tenant relations?
6 Critically evaluate tenant associations as a means of improving landlord-tenant relations.
7 Explain how management may effectively promote good tenant relations.

KEY TERMS AND CONCEPTS

Common-law doctrine
Caveat emptor
Warranty of habitability
Repair and deduct provisions
Housing courts

Mutually independent covenants
Constructive eviction
Retaliatory eviction
Uniform Residential Landlord-Tenant
  Code

SELF-QUIZ

Multiple-Choice Questions

_____ 1 Which of the following does *not* follow the common-law doctrine? (a) Tenant accepts premises in an "as is" condition; (b) Landlords have no duty to remedy defects in leased property; (c) Lease covenants are mutually independent; (d) The landlord is subject to an implied warranty of habitability.

_____ 2 Which of the following statements is correct? (a) Under constructive eviction, tenants had to show that the property was vacated because there was substantial interference with the right of quiet enjoyment;

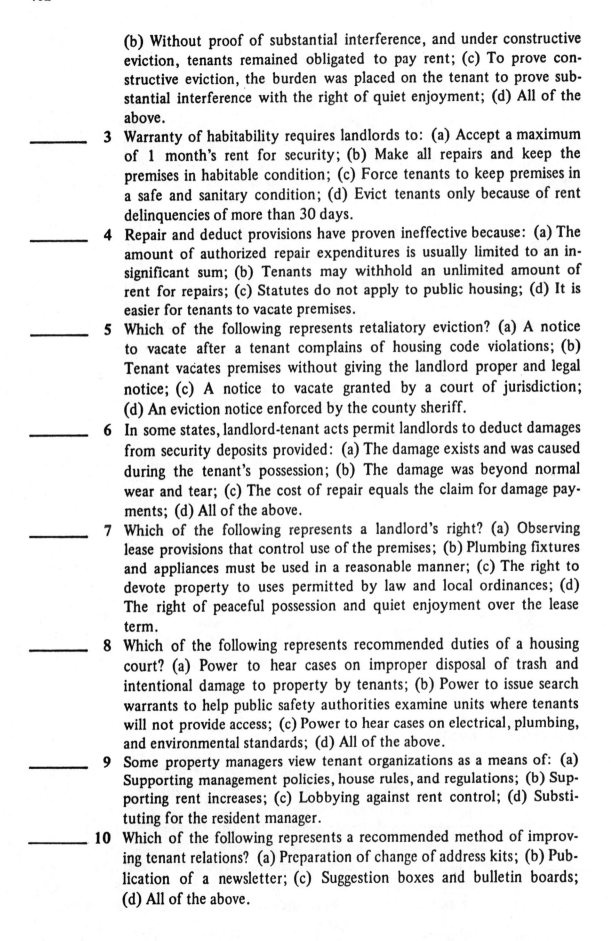

(b) Without proof of substantial interference, and under constructive eviction, tenants remained obligated to pay rent; (c) To prove constructive eviction, the burden was placed on the tenant to prove substantial interference with the right of quiet enjoyment; (d) All of the above.

3 Warranty of habitability requires landlords to: (a) Accept a maximum of 1 month's rent for security; (b) Make all repairs and keep the premises in habitable condition; (c) Force tenants to keep premises in a safe and sanitary condition; (d) Evict tenants only because of rent delinquencies of more than 30 days.

4 Repair and deduct provisions have proven ineffective because: (a) The amount of authorized repair expenditures is usually limited to an insignificant sum; (b) Tenants may withhold an unlimited amount of rent for repairs; (c) Statutes do not apply to public housing; (d) It is easier for tenants to vacate premises.

5 Which of the following represents retaliatory eviction? (a) A notice to vacate after a tenant complains of housing code violations; (b) Tenant vacates premises without giving the landlord proper and legal notice; (c) A notice to vacate granted by a court of jurisdiction; (d) An eviction notice enforced by the county sheriff.

6 In some states, landlord-tenant acts permit landlords to deduct damages from security deposits provided: (a) The damage exists and was caused during the tenant's possession; (b) The damage was beyond normal wear and tear; (c) The cost of repair equals the claim for damage payments; (d) All of the above.

7 Which of the following represents a landlord's right? (a) Observing lease provisions that control use of the premises; (b) Plumbing fixtures and appliances must be used in a reasonable manner; (c) The right to devote property to uses permitted by law and local ordinances; (d) The right of peaceful possession and quiet enjoyment over the lease term.

8 Which of the following represents recommended duties of a housing court? (a) Power to hear cases on improper disposal of trash and intentional damage to property by tenants; (b) Power to issue search warrants to help public safety authorities examine units where tenants will not provide access; (c) Power to hear cases on electrical, plumbing, and environmental standards; (d) All of the above.

9 Some property managers view tenant organizations as a means of: (a) Supporting management policies, house rules, and regulations; (b) Supporting rent increases; (c) Lobbying against rent control; (d) Substituting for the resident manager.

10 Which of the following represents a recommended method of improving tenant relations? (a) Preparation of change of address kits; (b) Publication of a newsletter; (c) Suggestion boxes and bulletin boards; (d) All of the above.

Answer Key

1 (d), **2** (d), **3** (b), **4** (a), **5** (a), **6** (d), **7** (c), **8** (d), **9** (a), **10** (d).

Fill-in Questions

1 Under common law, tenants gain possession under the rule of

_____ .

2 In dealing with leases as contracts, landlords are subject to an

_____ .

3 Covenants of a lease that are _____ means
that a breach by the landlord of any lease covenant does not invalidate other
lease terms.

4 Under _____ , a tenant could not legally withhold rent
until a lardlord made repairs.

5 Under landlord-tenant laws, landlords have the duty to maintain the premises in a

_____ .

6 _____ have the duty not to destroy or damage nor to permit
their invitees to destroy or damage the premises.

7 Generally, _____ are required to keep the premises safe and
clean and dispose of waste material in a clean and safe manner.

8 _____ reduce collection costs and lower
the rate of tenant turnover.

9 Management steps to improve tenant relations strongly emphasize

_____ .

10 According to one view, _____ help to solve problems,
develop a sense of community, and are a means of communicating management
policies to tenants.

Answer Key

1 caveat emptor
2 implied warranty of habitability
3 mutually independent
4 common law
5 habitable condition

6 Tenants
7 tenants
8 Favorable tenant relations
9 tenant services
10 tenant associations

SELECTED REFERENCES

Gerwin, Leslie E.: "A Study of the Evolution and Potential of Landlord Tenant Law
and Judicial Dispute Settlement Mechanism in the District of Columbia," *Catholic
University Law Review*, Spring 1977, pp. 457–512; Summer 1977, pp. 641–
755.

Glassman, Sidney: *A Guide to Residential Management*, 3d ed., Washington, D.C.: National Association of Homebuilders, 1978.

Residential Landlord-Tenant Law, Boston: Rental Housing Association, 1977.

Rose, Jerome G.: *Landlords & Tenants*, New Brunswick, N.J.: Transaction Books, 1973, pp. 288.

Chapter 9

Management Office Organization

After studying this chapter, you should be familiar with:
1 Management operations
2 Functions of the resident manager
3 Routine maintenance procedures
4 Responsive maintenance procedures
5 The importance of the management policy book
6 Management personnel administration, including recruiting, job training, and establishing job performance standards

Management offices are quite diverse and follow many functional plans. Accordingly, their operations vary depending on the organization, the type of properties managed, and the services offered.

Though organizations vary, the dominant form of organization is embodied in the firm that is paid a management fee by building owners. Management companies specializing in this work employ real estate managers who are responsible for several types of buildings, including hotels, office buildings, apartment houses, condominiums, shopping centers, and even industrial property. The management company formed on this plan follows the organization represented in Figure 9-1.

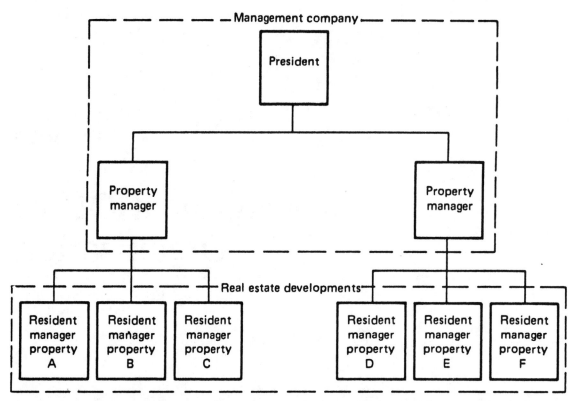

Figure 9-1 Property management office organization. *(Source: Adapted from Administrative and Accounting Guide, Washington, D.C.: National Center for Housing Management, 1974, pp. 1-2.)*

MANAGEMENT ORGANIZATION

In the highly specialized management firm, the president of the company reviews performance of the property managers as part of the normal duties of a business executive. Supervisory duties of the property manager vary widely, according to the project. A high-rise office building, apartment house, or regional shopping center may require the full-time attention of a single property manager. In other cases, property managers may devote time to numerous buildings owned by relatively small investors.

A variation of this plan treats property management as a division of a real estate brokerage office. Some of the larger real estate brokerage offices manage property as a supplementary service to listing and selling real estate. In other cases, licensed real estate brokers give time to both real estate sales and property management. In this latter instance, real estate sales are closely integrated with real estate management; frequently the property to be managed is sold by the same agency. Similarly, prospects who buy investment buildings turn management over to the selling agent.

Other real estate managers work directly as employees of property-holding institutions. Corporations require managers to operate their own buildings; government agencies must provide management services for federal, state, and local offices. Examples include the telephone company, retailing chains, real estate investment companies, the post office, churches, and charitable organizations. Though property managers who are employees of the property-holding institution do not work for a commission as agents, they have equal concern for efficient building operation and must follow an established management policy.

In the management firm, property managers represent the management company, which acts as an agent of the owner. Resident managers report directly to the property manager, who has overall responsibility for assigned projects. The manager must assume responsibility for personnel in each project, including their selection, training, and supervision. All policies and procedures are established by the manager. Time must be spent "on-site" and in the management company to complete the administrative work, to answer resident manager inquiries, to deal with new prospects, and to complete correspondence.

Management Operations

The detailed duties facing property managers are summarized in Figure 9-2. Some of the duties are fairly general, such as continually reviewing the rental market and recommending new rent schedules. These duties stem from the agency relationship—the manager must act in the best interest of his or her principal, the property owner. More specific duties on behalf of the owner deserve added explanation.

Budget Preparation

Property managers prepare an annual budget for each building. In this task they critically review projected operating expenses, including maintenance, utilities, taxes, and costs of material and labor. It is the manager's further duty to plan for the impact of inflation on each expense item. Expenses are individually reviewed; operating expenses are compared with expenses of similar buildings, and the best estimate is

Figure 9-2 Duties of a property manager serving as managing agent to a property owner.

1 Continually review current rental markets.
2 Analyze the investment potential of property under management.
3 Supervise resident managers and other personnel serving management functions.
4 Recommend a rental schedule that maximizes income.
5 Market rentable space.
6 Assume responsibility for cash collections and disbursements, including operating expenses, mortgage payments, taxes, insurance, and utilities.
7 Keep appropriate records and accounts.
8 Recommend repair and maintenance schedules; recommend rehabilitation, remodeling, or renovation.
9 Establish overall operating policies and procedures affecting management decisions.
10 Make monthly and annual reports to owners on all funds received and disbursed.

prepared from the manager's knowledge of property—overall expenses are not projected by percentage factors. For the larger projects, budget preparation involves consultation with project engineers, maintenance staff, and the resident manager.

In preparing the annual budget, property managers will compare the proposed rent schedule to current rents of competitive buildings. Once approved, the budget is reviewed on a periodic basis—quarterly or at least semiannually. Deviations from the budget must be investigated and justified. Frequently the manager must recommend operating changes to increase income or reduce expenses.

Recordkeeping

The management office is responsible for preparation of records, accounts, and operating statements. The larger firms will have specialists to process records. The operating statement is issued monthly and compared with the same month of the preceding year. By reviewing payrolls by functions, the property manager may constantly judge operating efficiencies for supervisory purposes. Indeed, the importance of recordkeeping justifies a more complete discussion in Chapter 10.

ESTABLISHING MANAGEMENT POLICY

Under owner direction, the manager establishes operating policies and procedures. Not only must managers supervise staff, but they are responsible for the appearance of the building, its maintenance, all advertising, and the rent schedule. Supervisory tasks call for training new personnel and maintaining control of income and expenditures.

The critical importance of management policy is indicated by surveys that show how management policies and procedures significantly affect operating income. Though related to residential property, findings can be summarized in three points.

1 Management expenses tend to be lower if residents are aware of house rules and regulations.

2 Operating expenses tend to be relatively high if management is more lenient about late rent payments.

3 Properties in which management makes timely repairs in response to tenant complaints show relatively low rent delinquencies.[1]

The central task of a manager is to organize, direct, and coordinate operations of several specialists to meet owner objectives. The policies include dealing with both tenants and employees. Property managers assume final responsibility for the quality of service, collections, employee relations, and the efficiency of operations. To gain operating efficiencies, the manager must establish performance standards, especially for maintenance and repairs; determine causes of unsatisfactory performance; and take remedial action. Central to the administration of management policies are duties undertaken by the resident manager.

---

[1] Morton Isler, Robert Sadacca, and Margaret Drury, *Keys to Successful Housing Management*, Washington, D.C.: The Urban Institute, 1974, pp. 61–65.

Resident Manager Duties

The resident manager works as the link between the manager and the development with all its tenants. The main areas of responsibility in this role center around three functions:

1 Marketing space
2 Rent collection
3 On-site supervision

While management policies are established by the property manager, their on-site implementation must be executed by the local resident manager under close supervision.

Marketing Space The marketing program starts with good public relations, such as management policies that create favorable images and reputations in the neighborhood and among project residents. Since the resident manager speaks for the building owner, the acts and attitude of the resident manager largely determine the project image.

And while the resident manager may not be directly responsible for advertising programs, frequently the on-site manager is the first point of contact with prospects who come to the property after encountering newspaper ads, billboards, or other advertising. Because of this relationship, resident managers must acquire interpersonal communication skills and learn how to present property much as a salesperson presents a house to prospective buyers.

But here the task is more complex. For, in leasing space, the tenant acquires certain management services. In an apartment, for example, residents will be shown a model unit but will be equally concerned with recreational facilities, operating hours, and other management policies as expressed in house rules. It is difficult to implement a successful marketing program without detailed knowledge of the neighborhood, competitive buildings, and building details.

(1) The Neighborhood Tenants will make inquiries about neighborhood services; they will be primarily concerned with shopping convenience, community organizations, recreational facilities, and, depending on the type of project, local schools and their reputation. Local transportation will be judged by travelling time to employment, by the cost and availability of public transportation, and by driving time to freeways.

To help in this analysis, some managers prepare a checklist itemizing the neighborhood details. A neighborhood analysis form for this purpose is shown in Figure 9-3. This form may be varied according to the type of project; detail included should outline local information relevant to prospective residents. Information appropriate for a high-rise luxury unit in Fort Lauderdale, Florida, differs from information relevant to renting a suburban apartment house project in Atlanta, Georgia.

(2) Competitive Buildings Resident managers are in a unique position to judge competitive advantages of comparable apartments. Details of special concern to resident managers are the vacancies in competing buildings; the number of units available by bedrooms; the rent schedule; and services included, such as utilities, appliances,

THE COMMUNITY

Schools

Elementary:_____

Location_____ Transportation_____

Principal_____ Phone_____

High School:_____

Location_____ Transportation_____

Principal_____ Phone_____

Expansion Plans_____

New Schools Planned_____

Private Elementary:_____

Location_____ Transportation_____

Principal_____ Phone_____

Private High School:_____

Location_____ Transportation_____

Principal_____ Phone_____

Other Schools Nearby:_____

_____

_____

Public Playgrounds:_____

_____

Library:_____

Figure 9-3 Neighborhood analysis worksheet. (*Source: On-Site Apartment Procedures Manual, Washington, D.C.: National Apartment Association, 1970, pp. 33-35.*)

YMCA & Other Civic Facilities:_____

_____

Fire and Police Departments:_____

_____

Hospitals:_____

_____

_____

Shopping Needs:_____

　　Super Markets_____

_____

　　Department Stores_____

_____

　　Drug Stores_____

_____

　　Hardware Stores_____

_____

　　Liquor Stores_____

_____

　　Dry Cleaners_____

_____

Adult Recreation:_____

　　Bowling_____

_____

Figure 9-3 *(continued)*

Airport _____

Post Office _____

Banks _____

_____

Employers in Area: _____

_____

_____

Medical -- Dental — Emergency Ambulance Service: _____

_____

_____

_____

Baby-Sitting Services: _____

_____

Federal — State — County and City Offices: _____

_____

_____

Utility Companies: _____

_____

_____

Churches — List nearest of every faith with pastor's name: _____

_____

_____

_____

Figure 9-3 *(continued)*

Golf _____

_____

Movies _____

_____

Fishing _____

_____

Boating _____

_____

Skating _____

_____

Night Clubs _____

_____

Restaurants _____

_____

Tennis _____

_____

Transportation: _____

Bus Service _____

_____

Taxi Service _____

_____

Driving Time To: _____

Downtown _____

Figure 9-3 *(continued)*

carpet and drapes. Information on location characteristics and competitive building condition help the resident manager market space. Resident managers must develop an acquaintance with resident managers of competing buildings. In short, resident managers review rental rates so that management may compare rental rates by rooms; by square foot area adjusted for competitive differences in appliances; and by security, parking, utilities, carpeting, and other features, such as added closets, swimming pools, patios, and the location. Clearly the competitive market evaluation depends heavily on facts secured by resident managers working on-site.

Figure 9-4 illustrates the kind of detail that allows management to make comparisons with competing projects. Note that the apartment features section covers physical aspects of the apartment, in addition to project amenities listed at the end of the form. Space is available to record basic impressions of competitive buildings.

(3) Building Details As part of their job assignment, resident managers of office buildings, shopping centers, residential projects, and the like are expected to know utility systems, square foot areas, management policies, and rules and regulations governing tenants.

In the case of residential property, a resident manager must be ready to explain who lives in the development. Residential requirements must be known to establish eligibility for low-income groups, the elderly, single residents, and families with children. The resident manager must be familiar with particular requirements of each group and prove that present tenants are satisfied with building services.

By comparing the features under management with those of competitive buildings, the resident manager becomes better equipped to overcome prospect objections. The talent of the resident manager is quite significant on this point, since management may have expended much time and money in advertising to secure prospective residents. To the extent that resident managers are the first point of contact, project management requires a thorough knowledge of the neighborhood; competitive available units; and present building characteristics, including the amenities, services, and management policy. Competence in this area helps turn tenant prospects into satisfied residents.

Rent Collection Some property managers provide self-addressed envelopes so that tenants can mail the rent check to the central office. In other projects, rent payments are made to the resident manager. In each instance resident managers must follow established collection procedures. Ordinarily the resident manager delivers late rent notices, collection letters, and notices of eviction. If a company requires that the resident manager talk to delinquent residents, the resident manager must be instructed to make polite but firm inquiries. The resident manager must instruct tenants that company policy requires payment of rent on the due date and that the resident manager has no authority to change policy. The required delinquent rent notices must follow management policy and local legal requirements.

On-Site Supervision On-site supervision incorporates certain administrative and operational responsibilities. Tenant records, maintenance files, personnel records, and numerous other details must be maintained by the resident manager. Even in the case of computerized record systems, the resident manager provides the source data.

GENERAL

Report by _____

Development name: _____ Builder: _____ Date: _____
Location: _____ Total acres: _____
Number of units planned: _____, Under construction: _____, Completed: _____
Number of buildings: _____ Rented: _____
Number of units per building: _____ Number of stories: _____ Vacant: _____
Density (Acres ÷ no. of units): _____ Design style: _____ Vacancy rate: _____
Rentals started: _____ Approximate rental (leases)—per week average: _____
Rating: Luxury _____ Semi-luxury _____ Middle income _____ Moderate _____ Low income _____

TERMS

Rent only: 1st mo _____ 1st & last mo _____ Other _____
Lease only: 3 mo _____ 6 mo _____ 9 mo _____ 1 yr _____ 1–2 yr _____ 2 yr + _____
Clean up deposit amount: $ _____
Security deposit amount: $ _____
Other deposit amount: $ _____
Any special monthly fees _____
Any special concessions offered: _____ $ _____
Children: Yes _____ No _____ Comments: _____

	Utilities	Incl.	Tenant Pays
	Water:		
	Gas:		
	Electric:		

APARTMENT FEATURES

Plan number and/or name							
Number of bedrooms (efficiency, 1, 2, 3, 4)							
Number of full baths							
Number of ½ baths							
Number of ¼ baths or powder rooms							
Monthly rental—lease amount (furnished)							
Monthly rental—lease amount (unfurnished)							
Apartment square footage							
Rent value ratio (unfurnished mo. rental ÷ sq. ft.)							
Living room Dimensions							
Dining room or area: No _____ Yes _____							
Bedroom sizes: Master Dimensions							
no. 2 "							
no. 3 "							
no. 4 "							
Kitchen Dimensions							
Kitchen counter: T (tile) or L (laminate)							
Kitchen appliances: G (gas) or E (electric)							
Kitchen cabinets: A (adequate), NA (not adequate)							
Kitchen cabinets: P (paint grade), S (stain grade)							
L (laminated, formica)							
Private entry (foyer): Yes/No							
Heating: 1. Gas							
2. Electrical							
Closets: 1. Walk-ins							
2. Not walk-ins							
Bath 1: T (tub), TS (tub-shower), S (shower)							
Bath 2: " " "							
Inventory: 1. No. built to date							
2. No. rented to date							
3. No. unrented to date							
4. Vacancy rate							

Figure 9-4 Apartment competitive evaluation. *(Source: Richard F. Russell, How to Rent and Lease Apartments, Newport Beach, Calif.: Russell and Associates, 1972, pp. 23-24.)*

BASIC ITEMS

A. APARTMENT	None (√)	Included (√)	Optional (yes–no)	Cost/ Month	Description

1. Carpets
    a. living room
    b. master bedroom
    c. all
2. Drapes
3. Dishwasher
4. Disposer
5. Range					

6. Oven
    a. standard
    b. self-cleaning
7. Air conditioning
    a. central
    b. window type
8. Paneling
9. Wallpaper
10. Refrigerator					

11. Fluorescent kitchen
      lighting
12. Balconies
13. Patios
14. Bulk storage area
15. Insulation:
    C   (ceiling)
    CW (ceiling & walls)
16. Fireplace					

B. PROJECT AMENITIES					
1. Club house (est. value $_____) 2. Tennis courts (no._____) 3. Putting green 4. Tot lot playground					
5. Swimming pool (size_____) 6. Outdoor barbeque 7. Jacuzzi 8. Party room					

9. Laundry room (coin)
10. Guard
    a. 24 hours
    b. night only
11. Doorman
12. Switchboard					

13. Maid service
14. Elevator
15. Parking:
    G (garage)
    CP (carport)
16. Other					

BASIC PROJECT IMPRESSIONS	Excellent	Good	Poor	Comments
Condition of exterior building Condition of landscaping Condition of sales office				
Condition of interior building Condition of models Ability of salesman				

Figure 9-4 *(continued)*

Operational responsibilities represent more than maintenance and repair. The resident manager undertakes scheduled inspections and works to keep the property attractive. While property managers must know residents and competitive buildings, collect rents, and keep records, they must also operate the property to please tenants. The object is to reduce tenant turnover, decrease vacancies, and lower operating costs. Many of the procedures described in this chapter and in other parts of the book relate to technical operating duties assumed by the resident manager.

While these duties describe overall responsibilities, resident managers also have important administrative responsibilities in collecting rents, keeping records, and administering to tenant needs and daily requirements. Other related responsibilities cover supervision of maintenance and repair—by staff or by contract— and regular inspections of building components. The resident manager is responsible for minimizing tenant turnover and placing vacated units back in service in the least possible time.

Resident Manager Training

The National Corporation for Housing Partnerships recommends that resident managers acquire knowledge in four major areas: (1) housing in the community, (2) management of physical facilities, (3) the administrative process, and (4) human relations. This process has been described as a "housing proficiency cycle" as illustrated in Figure 9-5. Special training courses have been formed especially for resident managers.

Figure 9-5 The housing management proficiency cycle. *(Source: Needed: Strategy for Housing Management Training, Washington, D.C.: National Center for Housing Management, 1971.)*

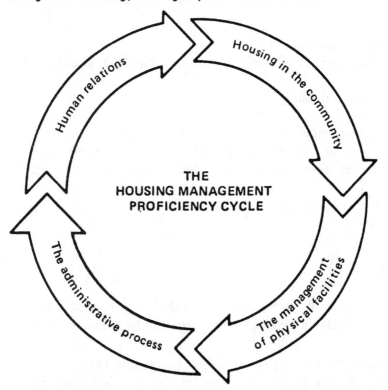

At least one organization, the Institute of Real Estate Management, sponsors a formally organized course specifically for resident managers. The course concentrates on specific duties required of resident managers. Early in the course students learn that "apartment management is more than providing mere housing to the public: it is a totally 'people oriented' business designed to serve one of the most basic of human needs—shelter."[2]

A summary of topics recommended for training is shown in four groups in Table 9-1. While related largely to public housing, the first group of 15 topics includes a study of mortgages, legal and development issues, federal laws, and social needs and services.

Considerable attention is given to the management of physical facilities, which includes 14 topics. An additional 24 subjects on the administrative process and human and family relations deal mostly with communication and interpersonal relationships.

Some companies sponsor in-house training. Charles E. Smith Management, Inc., Washington, D.C., instructs resident managers in showing vacant apartments; in screening prospective residents; and in reporting on vacate notices, rentals, and vacancies. In that resident managers are responsible for maintenance of building and grounds and for all redecorating and cleaning of apartments, they provide special instructions on physical building operation such as:

1 Boiler rooms
2 General outline of some physical principles involved in the operation of major building equipment
3 Seasonal changeovers
4 Importance of preventive maintenance
5 Oil deliveries
6 OSHA coding
7 Filter change and water treatment
8 Scheduled maintenance programs, such as fan coil cleaning and flushing condensate lines
9 Cooling tower—operating and maintenance
10 Utility conservation
11 Handling routine and emergency maintenance procedures
12 Role of building engineer and maintenance workers, including work tickets, follow-up procedures, building logs (boilers, elevators, A/C units, compactors, etc.), ordering supplies, and coding
13 Role of mechanical property manager
14 Role of property manager[3]

MAINTENANCE SUPERVISION

Regardless of the property, maintenance work can be divided into two categories: either (1) *routine maintenance*, which includes all tasks that may be prescheduled, or

[2] *The Resident Manager*, Chicago: The Institute of Real Estate Management, 1973, p. 11.
[3] See Sidney Glassman, *A Guide to Residential Management*, 3d ed., Washington, D.C.: National Association of Homebuilders, 1978, p. 17.

Table 9-1 Suggested Resident Manager Training Program

Housing in the community	Management of physical facilities	The administrative process*	Human and family relations
1 The problem-solving approach to the role of management in the housing system	1 Building structure and design	1 Principles of organization	1 Understanding human behavior
2 The impact of good and bad housing on the urban situation	2 Lighting and color	2 Functions of housing management	2 Human adjustment A focus on housing cliental characteristics
3 Social needs and services	3 Grounds maintenance	3 Budgeting accounting	3 Group dynamics
4 Problems in community development	4 Building exterior maintenance	4 Occupancy procedures	4 Motivation
5 Equal opportunity	5 Building interior maintenance	5 Turnover, repossession, eviction	5 Attitudes
6 Federal subsidy programs for housing	6 Recreation facility maintenance	6 Purchasing	6 Leadership
7 Urban renewal	7 Elevator maintenance	7 Insurance	7 Concepts of authority
8 Metropolitan development	8 Heating, refrigeration, air conditioning	8 Forms management	8 Management of change
9 Model cities	9 Water and sewer system plumbing maintenance	9 Service contracts	9 Participation programs
10 Turnkey housing	10 Electrical equipment and services	10 Supervisory skills	10 Communications
11 State and local housing	11 Trash disposal systems	11 Manpower analysis	11 Personal skills
12 Real estate transfer and economics	12 Pest control	12 Grievance management	12 Careers in housing management
13 Mortgages	13 Buildings and grounds safety		
14 The legal picture	14 Buildings and grounds security		
15 Planning and developing a housing complex			

*Emphasis on (1) Preoccupancy counselling and (2) Future home ownership opportunities.

Source: Needed: Strategy for Housing Management Training, Washington, D.C.: National Center for Housing Management, 1971.

(2) *responsive maintenance*, which refers to maintenance performed in response to tenant requests for repairs.

To plan for both types of maintenance, operating managers set maintenance goals, which are written instructions guiding maintenance staff. Goals might include requirements that: (1) 90 percent of tenant requests for service should be completed within 24 hours, (2) preventive maintenance programs should reduce tenant requests for repairs to a stated number per month, (3) a maintenance repair budget should not exceed a projected cost per square foot per month, and (4) the staff should provide emergency maintenance on a 24-hour basis. With these goals guiding the maintenance staff, managers concentrate on programs for both routine and responsive maintenance.

Routine Maintenance

Routine maintenance is largely preventive. While in the short run certain preventive measures may be postponed, long-run economic benefits may be realized from a planned program of preventive maintenance. Experience has shown that scheduling a certain portion of the maintenance staff for preventive maintenance reduces the number of tenant requests for repairs, which are especially expensive to satisfy on weekends or holidays, or at night.

Professional managers construct lists of items that need servicing during the year. The list, which is typically quite lengthy, covers mechanical equipment, building exterior, building interior, and grounds maintenance. For an apartment house, the list would include such appliances as range tops, ovens, refrigerators, dishwashers, sink disposals, water softeners, components of the building heating and air-conditioning system, the security system, the sprinkler system, and numerous other items. Oiling and lubricating pumps, fans, and motors leads the list of items requiring regular attention.

For each item listed, the manager notes the service required, its cost, and recommended preventive measures. By listing the brand name and the name of the supplier, the manager may arrange for replacements quickly.

The next step is the preparation of an annual maintenance schedule. The maintenance service work is scheduled over a period of 52 weeks, so that the staff divides its time between preventive maintenance and tenant requests.

Closely related to the routine maintenance program is the programming of typical janitorial tasks such as cleaning public areas, policing grounds, and washing windows, interiors, and the like. These operations are coordinated with certain inspections that should also be routinely performed on schedule, daily in some cases, to determine the adequacy of janitorial and other kinds of maintenance. Some managers use checklists to ensure the review of fire protection equipment and building appearance and landscaping. The inspection is closely related to preventive maintenance on a pre-scheduled basis to check building service systems.

Responsive Maintenance

Maintenance in the responsive category is inevitable. Machinery breakdowns, accidents, and worn-out parts require that on-site managers provide for:

faulty plumbing
broken windows
broken appliances
plumbing leaks
defective electrical equipment

This list does not include breakdowns in major systems such as elevators, heating, and air conditioning, which usually constitute emergencies and require advanced procedures to accommodate emergency maintenance. Service requests are monitored to judge preventive maintenance programs. Managers review the source of tenant service requests to indicate whether requests are caused by the lack of preventive maintenance or by resident negligence. For example, requests to replace faucet washers, which expire between 6 and 12 months, could be avoided by regular replacement of all faucet washers over a planned cycle of several months. Waiting for resident calls and replacement on an individual basis waste time and money.

Tenant Requests To minimize delays in responding to tenant requests, managers should maintain an inventory of replaceable parts. For a 50-unit apartment project, approximately 500 square feet are required for a workshop and storeroom. Projects of over 50 units require another 10 square feet of storeroom space for each additional unit; a 200-unit property would normally have 2,000 square feet of workshop and storage space.

To prepare for breakdowns, apartment managers maintain an inventory of spare items: for example, a spare refrigerator, range, basin, sink, toilet, light fixtures, switches, plugs, and plumbing parts. The inventory would include thermostats, timers, knobs, and an assortment of cleaning and groundkeeping supplies.[4]

Emergency Services Emergencies are inevitable. Since they occur at unpredictable times, tenants should be furnished with an emergency telephone number. Tenants should recognize only true emergencies, a point particularly important for apartment residents, but when true emergencies exist tenants should be encouraged to report them immediately. For apartments, emergencies may be identified as:

1 Water damage resulting from defective plumbing
2 Failure of heating and air-conditioning equipment
3 Damage caused by inclement weather: snow, ice, wind, and rainstorms
4 Faulty electrical equipment
5 Violence, burglary, or vandalism

Instructions to the tenant would include steps to take in each of these emergencies. If tenants have been given a guidebook, they should be encouraged to report each of these emergencies, since property damage and personal injury may result. If

[4] Roland D. Freeman, *The Encyclopedia of Apartment Management*, Washington, D.C.: National Apartment Association, 1976, pp. IV–VI.

extensive damages result, property managers are responsible for securing the premises to protect any remaining undamaged property.

The record shows that sound maintenance leads to resident satisfaction, fewer vacancies, lower turnover, and more profitable operation. The converse holds for poor maintenance as suggested by Figure 9-6. In sum, good service minimizes the conflict with residents and helps create a good image.

Management Policy Book

Management firms that administer numerous projects prepare a policy book to guide supervisors and resident managers. The written document covers standards that apply to employees with respect to administrative and management operations.

Figure 9-6 Results of sound and poor maintenance service. (*Source: The Housing Manager's Resource Book, National Center for Housing Management, 1976, p. 165.*)

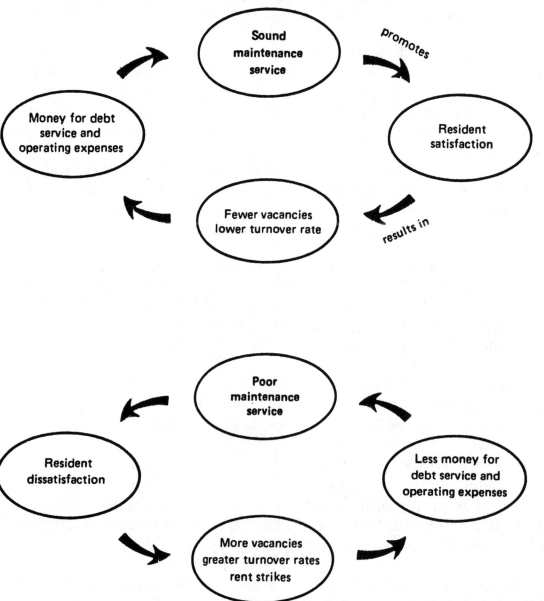

That portion covering employees details management policy on working hours, duties, vacations, and relations among supervisors, maintenance personnel, contractor services, and tenants. Standards of conduct are specified for employees working for the management firm.

Another part of the policy statement covers day-to-day operations. The policy book may be organized into the following categories:

1 Tenant selection
2 Policies followed in leasing new space
3 Administration of rent collection and security deposits
4 Procedures followed in vacating premises
5 Processing rent collection
6 Procedures followed in paying operating expenses
7 Recordkeeping procedures

While policy books differ among organizations, procedures will include examples of forms and records that must be maintained on a daily, weekly, or monthly basis. More significantly, management policy with respect to satisfying resident complaints, accepting responsibility for repairs, and handling emergencies would be described in the policy book.

The importance of the policy book can be shown by the amount of detail needed to describe procedures for selecting tenants and leasing new apartments. The policy book explains policies toward keeping pets, accepting children, establishing credit worthiness, securing tenant references and security deposits, setting lease terms, and the like. Sample forms will be included with an explanation of how they are to be completed.

In apartment house management, resident managers will be provided with a check-sheet outlining steps to follow in the move-in procedure. For example, no keys are given to new tenants unless the unit has been cleaned, painted, and placed in the best habitable condition. Keys are provided not more than two days before move-in, but only after the new resident pays security deposits and the first month's rent.

Resident managers orient new tenants by explaining the content of the "tenant guide," which describes the development, community services, transportation, and house rules and regulations. The resident manager will explain the rights and duties of the tenant and the services available.

Depending on the record system, the resident manager will be instructed on how to update the rental ledger and make other record changes showing the change in occupancy. Each resident will have a file that includes the application, the credit verification letter, the lease, and the apartment condition checklist. In short, the policy guidebook instructs staff on the records necessary for the move-in.

MANAGEMENT PERSONNEL POLICY

It is abundantly clear that the property manager is dependent on a team of specialists. Skills employed vary from those of contractors, who supply highly technical services such as elevator maintenance, to janitorial and cleaning services. For housing projects subsidized by the Department of Housing and Urban Development, the recommended management staff varies from two members for less than 50 units to at least eight members for a 400-unit project (see Table 9-2).

Because of the large numbers of persons employed in building management, personnel policy must be such that employees know their job descriptions, performance standards, and employee selection criteria. The organization's compensation plan, with incentive rewards and promotion policy, should be well understood. The larger firms will have a written personnel policy that outlines procedures ensuring equal treatment to all employees and conforming to legally required personnel actions. More importantly, employees should be advised of opportunities for growth within the organization.

Recruiting Personnel

Property owners are highly sensitive to the quality of management employees. Employees handle cash, keep confidential records, and to an important degree, their dealings with tenants affect turnover and vacancy rates. Like other aspects of the management process, recruiting may be undertaken systematically. Particular attention is given to job descriptions, sources of new employees, and reference checks. By matching the job description with applicant qualifications, recruiting not only meets management objectives but complies with federal, state, and local regulations.

Job Descriptions A job description serves multiple purposes. If the job description is conscientiously prepared, it guides employees in understanding their responsibilities. Furthermore, knowing the job description helps managers assign qualified persons to specific tasks. A study of job descriptions in large measure results in a fair, logical salary structure.

The job description contains a statement that distinguishes between major and minor duties. Following this statement, the amount of training, experience, and special talents needed would be described. The description sets limits to authority and defines

Table 9-2 Recommended Residential Management Staff by Number of Apartments

Recommended staff	Number of Apartments				
	1–49	50–99	100–149	150–249	250–400
Manager	1	1	1	1	1
Maintenance aide	1	1	2	2	2
Janitor/yardworker		1	1	1	2
Clerk/secretary			1	1	1
Assistant manager				1	1
Engineer/maintenance superintendent				1	1
Security guards			As required		

Source: The Housing Manager's Resource Book, Washington, D.C.: The National Center for Housing Management, 1976, p. 323.

responsibilities both in supervising others and in handling materials, equipment, and, in some cases, money and records. The required physical effort and possible physical hazards associated with the job will also be noted.

Sources of New Employees   While real estate managers rely heavily on newspaper advertisements and employment agencies, prospective employees may be reached through numerous other sources, such as educational groups, personal contact, and other types of advertising.

The larger communities support vocational schools and adult training programs in subjects related to property management. Adults attending noncredit courses, though lacking substantial experience, may be expected to be more highly motivated than persons without specialized education courses. Add to this list the courses offered by associations active in real estate management. For example, the Institute of Real Estate Management circulates a list of CPM candidates and members seeking new positions.

Personal contacts of the property manager with community clubs, churches, and social agencies are commonly used to recruit staff. For residential projects, an announcement of available positions for residents may uncover qualified candidates. Announcing the position to present employees encourages employees to seek higher-paid positions with greater responsibilities and leads to referrals of qualified persons from the present employees.

Besides advertising in newspaper help-wanted sections, managers seek career employees through advertisements in professional and trade magazines. Help-wanted signs posted in the management office and even radio and television spot announcements have been used effectively.

Reference Checks   Job applications are carefully verified with respect to previous jobs held and reasons for leaving them. Besides verifying employment references, verifying references from school officials and former instructors is usually advised. A credit investigation is another necessary requirement. Property management, because of the unusual responsibilities, requires applicants who have managed their personal affairs with responsibility. Hiring employees with an irresponsible financial record introduces considerable risk for the supervising manager.

During the initial interview, the job will be described to the applicant, along with the information needed to qualify the applicant for the job. Moreover, the critical trust placed on management employees requires that a police check be made for each job applicant.

Employee Training

Working as part of the management team gives employees opportunities for advancement. Courses sponsored by trade associations, community colleges, and the management organization permit employees to learn new skills, advance to more technical jobs, and assume supervisory positions.

Professional management companies sponsor technical schools for maintenance and engineering personnel. The Charles E. Smith Management Company of Washington,

D.C., arranges for courses in air conditioning, heating, appliance repair, and boiler operation. In addition to this, janitorial supply houses often sponsor clinics for maintenance and janitorial help. In this way employees are encouraged to increase skills so that they may assume better jobs when openings occur.[5] Consequently, training programs are scheduled not only for the property manager, who attends professional conferences, but for employees at all grades and for all skills.

Job Performance Standards

Job descriptions may be used to develop performance standards that measure employee efficiency. While job descriptions state what the worker does, the performance standards describe the amount of work to be performed. For each task in the management operation, work is measured in terms of what is accomplished in a unit of time and the final results expected after each performance.

With established performance standards, managers may evaluate workers by spot-checking their work, tracking the daily work flow, and reviewing complaints from residents or coworkers. Alert managers judge workers' job performance and recommend promotions as a result of outstanding performance. While the employee may be performing his or her present job satisfactorily, performance standards established for other jobs help in deciding whether the employee could be considered for the new opening. Managers judge employees according to how they meet performance standards, as well as their attitude, training, education, and experience.

Personnel administration requires that real estate managers observe certain laws and regulations affecting the management staff:

1 Title VII of the Civil Rights Act of 1964 (Equal Employment Opportunity), which applies to employers with 15 or more employees, makes it unlawful for an employer because of race, color, religion, sex, or national origin to fail or refuse to hire, discharge, or discriminate with respect to compensation and other employment matters.

2 The Age Discrimination and Employment Act of 1967, which must be observed by private employers with 20 or more employees (including government agencies), prohibits age discrimination against anyone 40 to 65 years old in hiring, discharges, promotions, pay, and other benefits.[6]

3 The Occupational Safety and Health Act (OSHA) requires that property managers keep detailed records—and subjects them to a $1,000 fine for each violation. On each apartment property, the managers must post an OSHA poster on the premises, and must record occupational injuries and illnesses on Form 100 within 48 hours. An annual summary of injuries must be posted by the end of January of each year.

Besides these regulations, managers must observe numerous state and local regulations that apply to managed properties.

[5] Sidney Glassman, op. cit., pp. 57–58.
[6] *The Housing Manager's Resource Book*, op. cit., p. 327.

MANAGEMENT OFFICE ORGANIZATION

Employment Contracts

In the managing of apartments, the unusual service requirements of the resident manager call for a written agreement on hours, working conditions, and salary. Moreover, because part of the compensation is represented "in kind" in the form of an apartment, its value for salary purposes must be determined. In this regard, the resident manager's apartment is usually larger than the person would normally rent. Partly this follows because the resident manager's unit doubles as the project office. These items are best written into an employment contract.

The employment agreement for a resident manager used by the Prufer Management Company of Mission Viejo, California, is reproduced in Figure 9-7. The agreement identifies the rental value of the apartment and utilities, for purposes of computing wages. The agreement also provides for a specific rental value per month in addition to the hourly compensation. The working hours each day, which are to be posted, are set forth in the next paragraph. The "inconvenience time" allows for off-hour emergency assignments.

Payroll procedures and provisions for termination of the contract complete the agreement. Note that the employee agrees to surrender the apartment immediately on termination of employment. An action by the employer against the employee to recover possession of premises allows for legal costs and fees to be levied against the employee.

In brief, the real merit of the employment contract is that it provides for stated, posted hours during which the resident manager agrees to show units to prospects. At the same time, the agreement provides for compensation for off-hour emergency work. Misunderstandings over working hours and compensation are minimized by the agreement illustrated in Figure 9-7.

SUMMARY

The real estate management company functions through a president who supervises professional property managers. The professional property managers in turn are assigned to a real estate project, where they work directly through resident managers. The resident manager, acting under the property manager, supervises daily operations of the project.

While management operations cover a broad range of activity, one of the principal duties of a resident manager is to prepare an annual budget for each managed building. Budget preparation requires a critical review of projected operating expenses in light of the expenses for the preceding year and for similar buildings. Once prepared, the budget is reviewed periodically to allow for an investigation of deviations from the planned budget.

To implement the management policy, the property manager works through the resident manager, who concentrates on *marketing space*, *rent collection*, and *on-site supervision*. To help market space, the resident manager learns about the neighborhood, about competitive buildings, and about the building details that are important to prospective tenants. The technical demands made on resident managers have

Employment agreement entered into this ____ day of _____, 19___,
between the PRUFER MANAGEMENT COMPANY, herinafter called the employer,
and _____, herinafter called the employee.
Whereas, the Employer employs the Employee as a Manager for the _____

_____, located at _____

City of _____, State of California.

Now, therefore, it is mutually agreed as follows: The compensation for
such employment shall be an apartment and utilities, all of which have a
market rental value of $_____ per month. However, for the
purposes of computing wages, this facility shall be valued at $_____ .
In addition to the apartment, the employee shall receive cash wages. The
total compensation shall be computed at $_____ per hour.

It is further agreed that the employee and an agent of the employer have
reviewed the tasks to be performed, and that both parties agree that these
tasks can normally be performed during _____ hours each working day. The
employee shall post office hours at the building, which will advise tenants
and visitors to the building of the hours that the Manager will be available to conduct the business of the property, and that these posted hours
shall not exceed the time specified above. The employee agrees to take the
following day off each week: _____. It is recognized that the
Manager may be disturbed for emergencies at hours other than those posted,
and it is mutually agreed that this "inconvenience time" shall be computed
at _____ hours per working day.

The employee further agrees that, if there should be work that cannot be
done in the hours specified above, the employee will notify the employer
in writing, and such work shall not be done until permission is obtained
in writing from the employer.

The employee acknowledges receipt of a copy of the Payroll Procedures of
the employer, and agrees to abide by those Procedures in order that he may
be properly paid.

Employment may be terminated at any time upon written notice by either
party to the other without liability for compensation, except such as may
have been earned at the date of sucn termination, and said apartment will
be vacated and surrendered immediately upon the termination of said employment.

In the event the employer shall bring an action against the employee to
recover possession of the premises under the terms of this agreement,
and the employer wholly or partly prevails in any such action, then in that
event, the employee shall pay the employer, in addition to the costs of
such action, reasonable attorney's costs and fees to be fixed by the court
hearing such action.

It is further agreed that there are no other, or further agreements between the parties not contained in this agreement.

_____   _____
        (Employee)   (Employer)

Figure 9-7 Resident manager employment agreement.

prompted management firms and several organizations to offer special training courses for managers' benefit.

Maintenance supervision may be either *routine maintenance*, which includes all tasks that may be prescheduled, or *responsive maintenance*, which is maintenance performed in response to tenant requests for repairs. Routine maintenance, sometimes called preventive maintenance, includes scheduled inspections of building equipment. Tenant requests are best satisfied by maintaining an inventory of parts so that repairs may be made within 24 hours. Special procedures are developed in advance to handle emergencies.

The *management policy book* guides supervisors and resident managers on standards that apply to employees. The book covers administrative and management operations that deal with employment conditions and relations with supervisors, maintenance personnel, contractor services, and tenants. The policy book provides standards of conduct for employees working for the management firm.

Because of the variety of skills needed in managing real estate, managers would do well to canvass numerous sources in order to attract prospective employees. The development of job descriptions allows property managers to select persons with the proper training and experience for each task. In qualifying job applicants, managers should pay special attention to personal references, including policy checks and credit references.

Employees are exposed to many forms of educational training and programs. The training extends to maintenance personnel and is supplemented by clinics, adult education classes, and classes sponsored either by trade associations or by company-organized training programs.

The manager develops performance standards for specific tasks so that employees may be evaluated and promoted on the basis of job performance, training, and experience. In real estate management, property owners must comply with regulations and local and state law that affects real estate building operation.

DISCUSSION QUESTIONS

1 Explain the relationships among the property owner, the property manager, and the resident manager.
2 What steps are followed in preparing an annual budget?
3 Discuss three factors that explain the critical importance of management policy.
4 Explain the three main areas of responsibility assumed by resident managers.
5 What type of information must a resident manager acquire to market space effectively?
6 What four main topics have been recommended for resident manager training?
7 Explain the difference between routine maintenance and responsive maintenance. Are they interrelated? Explain fully.
8 What is the purpose of the management policy book? Explain thoroughly.
9 What sources would you recommend to recruit management personnel?
10 What is the purpose of writing job descriptions for management tasks?

11 Why is the training program so critical to successful real estate management?

12 What is the purpose of identifying job performance standards?

KEY TERMS AND CONCEPTS

Resident manager
Management policy
Marketing space
Neighborhood analysis worksheet
Competitive buildings
Building details

The housing management proficiency
  cycle
Routine maintenance
Responsive maintenance
Management policy book
Job description
Performance standards

SELF-QUIZ

Multiple-Choice Questions

_____ **1** Which of the following statements is correct? In a management firm: (a) Resident managers represent the owner; (b) Property managers represent the management company, which acts as an agent of the owner; (c) Resident managers act as agents of the management company; (d) Resident managers report directly to the president of the management firm.

_____ **2** In preparing an annual budget, the property manager: (a) Reviews expenses individually and reviews the expenses of similar buildings; (b) Projects overall expenses by percentage factors to account for inflation; (c) Investigates deviations from the budget only at the end of the year; (d) Does not propose a rent schedule as part of the annual budget.

_____ **3** Which of the following statements is correct? (a) Management expenses tend to be lower if residents are aware of house rules and regulations; (b) Operating expenses tend to be relatively high if management is more lenient about late rent payments; (c) Properties in which management makes timely repairs in response to tenant complaints show relatively low rent delinquencies; (d) All of the above.

_____ **4** To market residential apartments, resident managers must acquire information about: (a) Local property taxes, the neighborhood, and utility costs; (b) Competitive buildings, the neighborhood, and local police protection; (c) Building details and operating expenses; (d) The neighborhood, competitive buildings, and building details.

_____ **5** Which of the following is an example of routine maintenance? (a) Repair of a leaky faucet in response to a tenant request; (b) Repair of a window that was broken in a windstorm; (c) Replacement of all faucet washers every 9 months; (d) None of the above.

_____ 6 Which of the following would be common to management maintenance goals? (a) To complete 90 percent of tenant requests for service within 24 hours; (b) To reduce tenant requests for repairs to a stated number per month by preventive maintenance; (c) To provide emergency maintenance on a 24-hour basis and to hold the repair budget to a stated cost per square foot per month; (d) All of the above.

_____ 7 The management policy book: (a) Is given to each tenant; (b) Covers standards that apply to employees with respect to administrative and management operations; (c) Is required by law; (d) Must be available for inspection by tenants.

_____ 8 When a manager is qualifying prospective management employees: (a) References are confined to former employment; (b) References are required only from school officials; (c) References are verified from former employment records, school officials, credit sources, and police records; (d) None of the above.

_____ 9 Management performance standards: (a) State what the worker does and what gets done; (b) Describe the amount of work to be performed; (c) Have no bearing on worker evaluation; (d) Measure the accuracy of job descriptions.

_____ 10 The Occupational Safety and Health Act requires that property managers: (a) Keep detailed records, subject to a $1,000 fine for each violation; (b) Post an OSHA poster on the premises; (c) Record occupation, injuries, and illnesses within 48 hours; (d) All of the above.

Answer Key

1 (b), 2 (a), 3 (d), 4 (d), 5 (c), 6 (d), 7 (b), 8 (c), 9 (b), 10 (d).

Fill-In Questions

1 _____ report directly to the property manager, who has overall responsibility for assigned projects.

2 In the preparation of the annual budget, the proposed rent schedule will be compared to current rents of _____ .

3 Management policies and procedures significantly affect _____ _____ .

4 The _____ works as the link between the property manager and the development.

5 Resident managers concentrate on _____ , _____ _____ , and _____ .

6 All maintenance tasks that may be prescheduled are referred to as _____ _____ .

7 Scheduling routine maintenance reduces the amount of _____ _____ .

8 Preferably, tenant requests for repair service are completed within _____
   _____.

9 _____ measure work in terms of what is accomplished in
   the unit of time and the final results expected.

10 Management firms that employ 15 or more persons must observe the _____
   _____ provisions of the Civil Rights Act of 1964.

Answer Key

1 Resident managers
2 competitive buildings
3 operating income
4 resident manager
5 marketing space, rental collection,
   on-site supervision

6 routine maintenance
7 responsive maintenance
8 24 hours
9 Performance standards
10 Equal Employment Opportunity

SELECTED REFERENCES

Freeman, Roland D.: *The Encyclopedia of Apartment Management*, Washington,
   D. C.: National Apartment Association, 1976.
Glassman, Sidney: *A Guide to Residential Management*, 3d ed., Washington, D. C.:
   National Association of Homebuilders, 1978.
The Housing Manager's Resource Book, Washington, D. C.: National Center for Hous-
   ing Management, 1976.
Kelley, Edward N.: *Practical Apartment Management*, Chicago: Institute of Real
   Estate Management, 1976.
The Resident Manager, Chicago: Institute of Real Estate Management, 1973.

Chapter 10

Property Records and Insurance

After studying this chapter, you should be familiar with:
1 Monthly owner statements and supporting records
2 Property management records for income tax purposes
3 Techniques of asset management
4 Other supporting records
5 Advantages of computer records
6 Available computer systems for property management
7 Planning new computer operations
8 The insurance coverage that is important to property management
9 The importance of workers' compensation records
10 Management responsibilities for insurance administration

A workable system of records is critical to professional management. The record system must satisfy accounting demands, which include monthly statements to the owner, income tax requirements, payroll records, and a system for cash control. It must also satisfy requirements for decision-making data. Increasingly, records are adapted to computer format, making the record system more efficient. The second part of the chapter deals with computer systems for management purposes.

While property managers are not expected to be insurance experts—though some firms have highly qualified insurance departments—they must know the special types of required insurance and the administration associated with property insurance. The last part of the chapter summarizes the minimum insurance requirements for property managers.

PROPERTY MANAGEMENT ACCOUNTING

Leading the list of accounting statements is the monthly owner statement, which summarizes income and expenses and gives supporting data. Equally important are the income tax records that record receivables and accounts payable, and serve as a basis for asset and cash control. Certain other subsidiary records are associated with property management, such as payroll records, tax records, the tenant file, maintenance inspections, and repairs. Managers are responsible for seeing that the data entered on the profit and loss statement and balance sheets are accurate.

Owner Statements

Owner statements serve two purposes: (1) they show the net balance remitted monthly to the owner, and (2) they provide a summary of disbursements and receipts. With monthly statements, most managers supply detail about the rent roll.

Such a monthly summary for an apartment, developed by Randy Wright, CPM, of Investment Properties Management, Inc., of Lubbock, Texas, is shown in Figure 10-1. Termed the "income recap," it shows the total potential rental income as if the property were fully occupied. Income from miscellaneous charges, prepaid rent, and delinquent sums are entered to indicate the current income. Note that this form is manually prepared from subsidiary records.

In this instance the manager gives the owner certain other monthly supporting schedules:

> monthly deposits
> security deposits
> laundry income and expenses
> bank reconciliation
> a statement of income showing the calculation of the management fee (3.75 percent of gross income collected)
> the real estate rental statement, listing each tenant
> monthly balance sheet
> monthly profit and loss statement

The profit and loss statement shows income and expenses for the current month and for the current year, cumulative to the present month. Expenses and income are also shown as a percentage of total income. These computer records give the owner additional information for decision-making and income tax purposes (see Table 10-1).

Investment Properties Management, Inc.

REALTOR

1610 AVENUE R • LUBBOCK, TEXAS 79401 • 744-4505

Real Estate Rental Statement

Income Recap

For Month of ___JUNE___ 19_78_

POTENTIAL RENT INCOME	$	53,844.00
PREPAID PREVIOUS MONTH	-$	—
DELINQUENT PREVIOUS MONTH	+$	—
MISCELLANEOUS CHARGES	+$	461.05
PREPAID CURRENT MONTH	+$	—
DELINQUENT CURRENT MONTH	-$	—
VACANT CHARGES	-$	2 293.28
AMOUNT PAID THIS MONTH	=$	52,011.77

RENT INCOME PERCENT _96.60_ %

Property ___WINWOOD   APTS.___

Figure 10-1 Monthly net income summary for an apartment building.

Table 10-1 Net Operating Income Less Capital Expenditures

Item	Amount	Percentage of total collections	Cumulative amount over the year	Percentage of total collections
Total income	$57,033.78	100.0	$658,695.37	100.0
Operating expense	-24,896.50	-43.6	-203,917.46	-31.0
Capital expenditures				
Principal	$ 1,159.59	2.0	$ 13,346.69	2.0
Interest	23,649.14	41.5	284,358.07	42.9
Insurance	1,266.67	2.2	19,557.54	3.0
Mortgage insurance premium	1,472.30	2.6	17,721.51	2.7
Tax escrow	5,542.34	9.7	69,940.33	10.6
Total capital expenditures	-33,090.04	-58.0	-404,924.14	-61.5
Cash for distribution	-$ 952.76	- 1.7	$ 49,853.77	7.5

196

For the current month, the property shows a net operating expense of 30.8 percent. The cash for distribution is found by deducting principal, interest, property insurance, mortgage insurance premiums, and the monthly tax escrow for annual property taxes. The cash before income taxes totals $49,853.77, or 7.5 percent of gross income.

A monthly summary produced by a computer used by Baird & Warner, Inc. of Chicago lists total collections, expenses, the management fee, and the amount remitted to the owner. The monthly collections are supported by a listing of monthly income from several sources. Baird & Warner provides a computer printout of the status of each apartment, showing date of lease expiration, apartment number, name of the tenant, and details on rent and collection (see Figure 10-2).

Income Tax Records

Property managers provide information for income taxes. While accounting systems vary and some are even fully or partly automated, managers usually keep a record of checks written and monies received. For example, the monthly net income statement would be documented by schedules that identify sources of income:

Deposit forfeits	$ 2,150.00
Beverage income	539.35
Pool table income	63.25
Laundry income	1,269.35
Cleaning income	323.24
Furniture rental income	557.66
Apartment rental income	52,011.77
Total	$56,914.62
Less management fee ($56,914.62 × .0375)	−2,134.29
Total monthly income	$54,780.33

In addition to these itemized amounts, income may be earned from swimming pool rentals and from interest on deposits and the like. For budget and other accounting purposes, a chart of accounts normally groups together common operating expenses. For most properties, property managers develop their own system of accounts for control purposes.

For shopping centers and office buildings, trade associations have developed recommended accounts for specific property types. The Urban Land Institute recommends a system of accounts to standardize accounting for shopping centers. Similarly, the Building Owners and Managers Association International recommends standard accounts for office building management. Their chart of ledger accounts provides for assets, liabilities, and capital accounts. Considerably detailed, the chart lists expenses by main operational categories: administrative expenses, alterations, fixed charges, and financial expenses. The recommended profit and loss statement is illustrated in Table 10-2.

In this instance, note that expenses are reported functionally. For instance, wages are itemized separately for cleaning, electrical, heating, air conditioning, and many

STATEMENT OF RENTS/ASSESSMENTS AND SUNDRY CHARGES

PAGE 3 MONTH OCT 19XX PROPERTY NO. 1-410

TYPE UNIT
A - APARTMENT (NO ROOMS)
C - COOPERATIVE APT
. - CONDOMINIUM APT
M - MISCELLANEOUS
O - OFFICE
P - PARKING
S - STORE

TYPE UNIT	LEASE EXPIRATION (MO DAY YR)	UNIT NO.	SECURITY DEPOSIT	NAME & DESCRIPTION	ACCT. NO.	DUE BEGINNING OF PERIOD C=CREDIT	CURRENT RENT & SUNDRY CHARGES	COLLECTIONS	DATE (MO DAY)	ADJUSTMENT AT C'S CREDIT	DUE END OF PERIOD C=PREPAYMENT
A25	08 31 XX	205	200.00	AIDA REYNO	5110		216.00	216.00	10 10		
A30 A	05 31 XX	206	225.00	RONALD GORDON / SEP RENT	5110 / 5110	242.00 / 242.00	242.00	242.00	10 01 / 9 30		242.00
A25	09 30 XX	207	92.00	ANGLITA PORTEA	5110		208.00	208.00	10 09		
A35	04 30 XX	208	245.00	JAMES JORDAN / PARKING	5110 / 5175		278.00 / 20.00	278.00 / 20.00	9 30 / 9 30		
A35	05 30 XX	209	245.00	JOHN M MOERIDE / PARKING	5110 / 5175		284.00 / 20.00	284.00 / 20.00	10 01 / 10 01		
A50	09 30 XX	210	345.00	A VALENTA & A RAZMA	5110	13.80C	380.00		10 01		366.20
A35	NT IN UN	211		R HORTON & M ANTHONY	5110	10.22C					10.22C
A35	05 31 XX	211	245.00	EUGENE CHIU / PARKING	5110 / 5175		262.00 / 20.00	262.00 / 20.00	10 03 / 10 03		
A35	08 31 XX	212	245.00	ROBERT N HOLLANDER	5110		250.00	250.00	10 03		
A35	03 31 XX	213	225.00	T FLANNIGAN	5110		238.00	238.00	10 03		
A30	06 30 XX	214	200.00	WHENDY S OKAMOTO	5110		240.00	240.00	10 10		
A30	09 30 XX	215	225.00	RAINISH K GUPTA / PARKING	5110 / 5175	5.25C	242.00 / 20.00	242.00 / 14.75	10 03 / 10 03		
A25	04 30 XX	216	200.00	MARY WEIDEMAN	5110		204.00	204.00	10 10		
A35	08 31 XX	217	245.00	EDWARD & L SOLAN / PARKING / DISHWASHER	5110 / 5175 / 5190		280.00 / 20.00 / 10.00	280.00 / 20.00 / 10.00	10 03 / 10 03 / 10 03		

OWNERS COPY

Figure 10-2 A monthly rental list provided to property owners.

Table 10-2 Office Building Profit and Loss Statement

Acct.	Description	Detail	Subtotals	Total
	Rental income			
503	Office rent	XXXX.XX		
504	Store rent	XXXX.XX		
505	Storage area rent	XXX.XX		
506	Rent of special areas	XXXX.XX		
	Total rental income		XXXX.XX	
	Miscellaneous income			
542	Total net service income	XX.XX		
547	Interest income	XX.XX		
548	Other	XX.XX		
	Total miscellaneous income		XXX.XX	
	Total rental and misc. income			XXXX.XX
	Operating expenses			
619	Cleaning expense (see schedule)	XXX.XX		
629	Electrical expense (see schedule)	XXX.XX		
639	Heating expense (see schedule)	XXX.XX		
649	Air-conditioning and ventilating expense (see schedule)	XXX.XX		
650	Combined HVAC (see schedule)	XXX.XX		
669	Elevator expense (see schedule)	XXX.XX		
699	General expense—building (see schedule)	XXX.XX		
709	Administrative expense (see schedule)	XXX.XX		
729	Energy expense (see schedule)	XXX.XX		
	Total operating expense		XXXXX.XX	
	Alterations, decorating, and repairs expenses			
749	Alterations—tenants' premises (see schedule)	XXX.XX		
759	Painting or decorating—tenants' premises (see schedule)	XXX.XX		
	Total alterations and decorating		XXXX.XX	
	Fixed charges			
809	Insurance expense (see schedule)	XXX.XX		
829	Operating taxes expense (see schedule)	XXX.XX		
849	Tenant alterations—amortization/expensed	XXX.XX		
	Total fixed charges expense		XXXX.XX	
	Total expenses			XXXX.XX
	Net operating profit			XXXX.XX
939	Ground rent (see schedule)	XXXX.XX		
949	Organization expense (see schedule)	XXX.XX		
959	Interest expense (see schedule)	XX.XX		
979	Corporate taxes (see schedule)	XX.XX		
990	Other financial expense	XX.XX		
	Total financial expense			XXXX.XX
	Final net profit			XXXX.XX

(Subsidiary schedules must be prepared for each expense group
indicated in this condensed statement)

Source: 1978 Downtown and Suburban Office Building Experience Exchange Report, Washington, D.C.: Building Owners and Managers Association International, 1978, p. 153.

other functions necessary to office building operations. With these detailed expense records, managers may compare their operations with those of similar buildings. The detailed chart of expenses provides for the necessary subsidiary accounts for profit and loss statements and income tax purposes.

Asset Management

The tax consequences of real estate ownership make the property manager go beyond determining the costs of the daily operation and physical maintenance of a property. In evaluating several investment alternatives, managers operate real estate as a financial investment. Suppose, for example, that a 106-unit apartment complex requires exterior painting, upgrading of landscaping, and replacement of carpets and drapes. Suppose further that the unit includes 32 furnished bachelor apartments of 550 square feet that need new furniture. With a net operating income of $149,500, capitalized at 8 1/2 percent, the property has an estimated market value of $1,758,800.[1]

Under these conditions, asset management requires an analysis of the costs involved in: (1) continued operation of the property in an "as is" condition, (2) refinancing, (3) selling the property in its present condition, (4) rehabilitating the property at a cost of $56,000, (5) rehabilitating and refinancing, and (6) rehabilitating and selling. By investing $56,000 in rehabilitation, which would provide for an increase in net operating income, the property manager would increase the market value to $2,327,000. In this example as analyzed by Gary Langendoen, a CPM with Gribin Von Dyl, Realtors, of Sherman Oaks, California, refinancing would give the owner tax-free cash proceeds of $707,295.[2]

New market value		$2,327,000
A 75% loan would be		1,745,000
New debt service (9¾%, 30 years)		179,900
Principal payment, first year		10,794
Costs of refinancing:		
Prepayment penalty	$ 18,720	
1.5 points for new loan	26,985	
		45,705
Refinancing proceeds		
New loan amount		$1,745,000
Less		
Payoff of old loan	$936,000	
Cost of refinancing	45,705	
Loan for rehabilitation	56,000	
Total		-1,037,705
Cash proceeds		$ 707,295

In this case, the $56,000 rehabilitation cost is financed with a second trust deed. The $56,000 in rehabilitation expenses was depreciated on a straight line basis over

---

[1] Gary Langendoen, "Growing Field of Asset Management," *Journal of Property Management*, 43(1):47, 1978.

[2] Ibid.

5 years. Assuming an investor in the upper 70 percent income tax bracket, there would be a tax savings of $28,962 and a total return of $62,668. These data are summarized in Table 10-3.

Assuming further that the owner gains a 4 percent return (after taxes) on the cash from refinancing the $707,000 investment, the overall return, including equity build-up and the mortgage, increases to $62,668. This compares to an overall return, calculated on the same basis, of $44,250 before refinancing and rehabilitation. Other alternatives might consider tax-deferred exchanges and different financing.

In short, property managers, along with establishing owner objectives and handling management operations, provide financial advice that is not available from other sources.

Other Supporting Records

Property management is partly a task of administering various record systems. Among the more important are records of maintenance, including service requests; payroll records; and the resident file. Though these records may be prepared by computer, the property manager must ensure that source records are maintained for computer entry.

Table 10-3
Cash Flow and Tax Analysis of
Rehabilitation and Tax Analysis

Cash flow analysis

Net operating income	$174,532
Less new debt service	-179,900
Cash loss	-$ 5,368

Tax analysis

Net operating income		$174,532
Less		
Interest expense (1st T.D.)	$169,106	
Interest expense (2d T.D.)	5,600	
Depreciation (regular)	30,000	
Depreciation (rehabilitation)	11,200	
Total		215,906
Taxable loss		-$ 41,374
Tax savings @ 70%		28,962

After-tax analysis

Cash loss	-$ 5,368
Tax savings	28,962
4% return on $707,000	28,280
Cash return	$ 51,874
Plus equity buildup	10,794
Overall return	$ 62,668

Maintenance Records Most managers recommend a system of recording and follow-up on resident service requests, which are summarized in weekly, monthly, and annual reports.

Payroll Records Managers must review requirements of the Fair Labor Standards Act, which requires that employees be paid the statutory minimum hourly wage and, with minor exceptions, time-and-a-half for work over 40 hours per week. This requires some system for filing time cards and payroll records that lists deductions and cumulative earnings. These records are important for meeting quarterly deposits for workers' compensation and withholding taxes. They require a file and record system for each employee that includes:

1 The application form
2 Job description
3 W-2 form for withholding taxes
4 Time records
5 Pay records showing weekly pay, overtime, bonuses, commissions, and pay increases
6 Vacation and sick day records
7 Social security deductions and accident reports[3]

In addition to these common records, the file would contain records of personnel evaluations, commendations, complaints, or disciplinary action taken against the individual employee. A system of time cards listing the hours worked each day, and filed by the week, supports local, state, and federal requirements, in addition to serving as source data for wage calculations.

The Resident File For apartments, the resident file includes numerous documents. As a minimum, the current resident file would have:

1 The lease application
2 The lease and other supporting documents and riders covering special arrangements for pets, garage rent, escalator clauses, or tenant construction
3 The security deposit agreement
4 The move-in checklist
5 The move-in inventory listing carpets, drapes, appliances, and furniture
6 Copies of delinquent notices, complaints, disciplinary action taken against tenants, and correspondence

Because of fair housing and credit laws, files must be maintained for prospective tenants who have been rejected, and must state reasons for the rejection.

In addition, alphabetical files are maintained for past residents to show (1) the move-out notice, (2) the move-out checklist, (3) the move-out inventory, and (4) the

[3]For further detail consult Edward N. Kelley, *Practical Apartment Management*, Chicago: Institute of Real Estate Management, 1976, pp. 273–274.

disposition of security deposits, including reductions and the net amount returned. Reasons for moving and the rent ledger card are part of the file.

COMPUTER SYSTEMS

Recordkeeping practices vary, from those that rely on a manual system of reporting to those that rely on automation for virtually all management accounting and reports. The smaller firm often prefers the manual system to maintain "the personal contact we have with each property."[4] While attitudes toward computer accounting systems vary, the trend is toward more computer applications. Computer systems tend to be favored because property managers rely on repetitive reports. Thus a computer program may be economically adapted to recurring tasks, thereby eliminating a large portion of manual recordkeeping. The increasing availability of electronic data processing equipment at lower capital and operating costs increases the feasibility of computer systems.

Advantages of Computer Records

Property managers face recurring data problems. They must make frequent financial decisions, they must provide owners with periodic reports of operations, and they face peak working loads in processing monthly rents and expenses. The advantages of computer records lie in their ability to perform these operations at lower costs and with increased efficiency.

Computers Reduce Clerical Expenses In property management, clerical costs increase in direct proportion to the increase in business volume. The management of a 100-unit apartment building requires the maintenance of 100 tenant files, monthly reports to the owner, and other records that duplicate those of all other apartment management projects. Computer routines not only reduce clerical costs for present operations but provide more capacity for added business at relatively low additional costs. For example, in a multiple-tenant building with tax escalation clauses in each lease, computer calculation of property taxes billed to each tenant was completed in 20 minutes compared to several days for manual calculation.[5]

Computers Provide Precise Cash Control Computers allow managers to produce checks with discounts automatically calculated, which helps reduce costs. At the same time computers produce identifying records. And in collections, the system produces bills on a stated date, say the 20th of the month, for payments that are expected by

---

[4] See, for example, Jay D. Couch, "Reporting to Owners of Smaller Properties," *Journal of Property Management*, 42(1):19 (1977). For an opposing view, see Robert Kuhn, "The In-House Automated Management System," *Journal of Property Management*, 41(2):77--81 (1976).

[5] Bennett Rechler, "Developing an In-House Mini-Computer System," *Journal of Property Management*, 43(4):217 (1978).

the 30th. Computer processing of collections and the payment of bills gives managers more precise and more timely control over receipts and disbursements.

Computers Improve Management Services Computers may be programmed to call advance attention automatically to lease expiration dates. The computer system allows managers to initiate renewal negotiations on a regular schedule, and automatically keeps track of other critical actions. With the popularity of tax, utility, and other escalation clauses, current per foot charges may be calculated immediately by computer. Moreover, computer calculations minimize clerical errors. Numerous computer editing routines improve data accuracy for decision making.

Managers benefit by providing owners with a continuously documented series of reports that analyze cash flow and net operating expenses with appropriate ratios. Percentage income and expense comparisons may be made with the current budget, year to date, or last year to date. Such a volume of analytical reports would be uneconomical under manual processing.

The end result of these computer services is that management time shifts from clerical details to more analytical management functions. More time is available for promoting added business and communicating more frequently with owners and tenants.

Available Computer Systems

Advancing technology opens numerous options to management firms. Indeed, some authorities report that the rate of technical advances limits the economic life of a computer to 5 years. Improved equipment and the newer minicomputers with the availability of more complex "software" (computer instructions or programs) make computer adaptations feasible for even the smallest management operation. Property managers generally have three main options in selecting computer services.

Computer Service Bureaus Computer service bureaus operate in most communities. Many have prepared programs immediately available for payroll accounting, for inventory control, and, in some instances, for property management. Service bureaus will write programs for individual clients.

While service bureaus reduce capital costs and avoid the danger of purchasing equipment that might soon become obsolete, their clients must pay user charges. Service bureaus generally make a one-time installation charge to convert the service bureau to an individual customer's procedures. In addition they usually charge a fixed set-up charge per process and charge for each transaction processed by the system. The charge is based partly on the number of lines printed.

Time-Sharing Services *Time sharing* refers to computer services that are provided through an office terminal unit connected to a central computer by telephone. The terminal, a printing device or cathode ray tube (CRT) like a television screen, provides a means of entering data into the central computer. Ordinarily the output will be available on the terminal unit or in printed form at the computer center.

While little initial investment is required, prohibitive time-sharing charges may necessitate development of an "in-house" computer system. Time-sharing costs cover the cost of buying or leasing the terminal, storing data, and paying for computer time. Programs may be supplied by the computer center or developed by computer consultants or office staff. Time-sharing advantages are similar to the advantages of service bureaus.

The Lease or Purchase of Computer Equipment While requiring an initial capital investment in equipment and programming services, the minicomputer is believed to be competitive for use by firms managing more than 1,500 apartment units.[6] If the business is expanding, leased or owned equipment allows volume to increase without adding to fixed costs. With some computers, capacity may be increased as needed. Moreover, with in-house equipment, a company has immediate access to computer time. By leasing or buying computers, management has greater control over data and its processing. Yet because of the heavy commitment necessary for in-house computers, management must carefully plan for a computer system.

Planning a Computer System

Planning for a system of computer records requires determining how the firm may maximize computer investments (or operating costs). Managers anticipating new computer services follow a plan divided into a formulation stage and an implementation stage. The steps followed in each stage are outlined in Table 10-4.

The Feasibility Study The formulation stage starts with a feasibility study. In this application, the feasibility study constitutes a systematic evaluation of record and report requirements to determine the best way to arrange for computer services. The feasibility study avoids uneconomical computers that are too large for current needs or too small for anticipated expansion. Often managers have reported delays in business operations because of incomplete programming. Others have reported that a change to a larger computer required the redevelopment of original programs. In brief, the feasibility study identifies inadequacies and redundancies in present paperwork, information flow, and reporting requirements.

Computer Selection Factors to consider in selecting a computer system include equipment, software, and economic factors as illustrated in Figure 10-3. In identifying organization needs, management must see to it that the speed, storage capacity, and expandability features are suitable for the planned system. Reliability in maintenance service avoids delays in meeting payrolls, completing required reports, and handling other management operations. Even with favorable equipment characteristics, software requirements vary from system to system. Some companies offer software packages that are adapted to property management, while others provide programming assistance; some managers prefer to control their own programming with

---

[6] James C. Weinberg, "Minicomputers (Second of a Three-Part Series)," *Journal of Property Management,* 43(5):25 (1978).

Table 10-4 Procedures for Introducing a Computer System*

I   The formulation stage
   A   Conducting the feasibility study
      1   Establishing the feasibility group
      2   Determining computer needs
      3   Analyzing and improving the existing system
      4   Making recommendations
   B   Computer system selection
      1   Service bureau
      2   Time sharing
      3   Purchase or lease: type of equipment recommended
II The implementation stage
   A   Preparing for the computer
      1   Personnel required
      2   Physical space preparation
   B   System design and programming
      1   Systems investigation
      2   Systems design
      3   Programming applications
      4   Implementing applications
   C   Installing equipment
   D   Follow-up and review

*For additional detail consult High J. Watson and Archie B. Carroll, *Computers for Business: A Managerial Emphasis*, Dallas: Business Publications, 1976, p. 282.

in-house equipment. Economic factors are considered in the light of the initial cost, the operating cost, and the return on investment.

Computer Functions Computer functions adapted to property management would fall into a minimum of five subsystems: (1) management operations, (2) accounts payable, (3) payroll accounting, (4) financial reporting, and (5) special reports and file maintenance.[7] For example, management operations would include computer programs to enter new properties, process lease applications, post rent and cash receipts, report delinquencies, and process tenant terminations or lease renewals.

According to a special committee of the Institute of Real Estate Management, the system selected should be flexible and have the capability to retrieve, compare, and analyze specific data on command. The committee identified 10 mandatory capabilities, including the ability to:

    1 Prepare cash flow statements for monthly and annual reports on receipts, disbursements, and vacancies
    2 Calculate vacancy and rent losses
    3 Produce a cash receipt register as required

[7]James C. Weinberg, "Minicomputers" (Third of a three-part series), *Journal of Property Management*, 43(6):333 (1978).

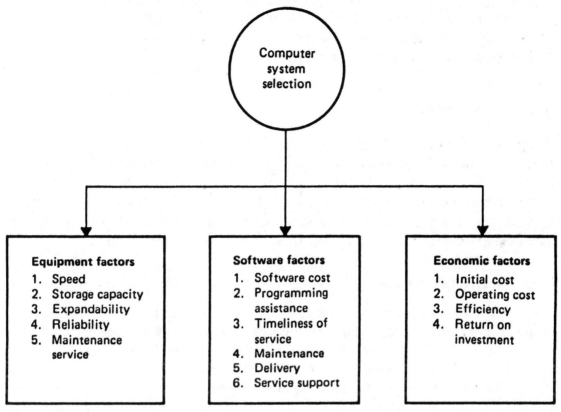

Figure 10-3 Significant factors considered in selecting a computer system. *(Source: Adapted from Hugh J. Watson and Archie B. Carroll, Computers for Business: A Managerial Emphasis, Dallas: Business Publications, 1976, p. 290.)*

4 Record a check register of disbursements by check number, account number, and date

5 Print a security deposit list with relevant details

6 Produce a rent roll with accompanying detail on units, tenants, fixed charges, and lease information

7 Record and list charges such as cleaning and maid service as required

8 Provide an automated system of reporting move-ins and move-outs

9 Adjust accounts for bad debts

10 Handle file maintenance: a simple method to make corrections, additions, and deletions.[8]

The list includes nine other options, such as automatic typing of expense checks and the calculation of income and operating expenses per square foot.

In one instance the computer system for residential property management led to 130 computer programs that produced 110 reports and some 40 inquiry displays on the cathode ray terminal. The computer was able to do the same amount of work that formerly had taken two bookkeeping clerks to accomplish; a third bookkeeping clerk

---

[8] "Computerized Accounting: Recommended System Capabilities," *Journal of Property Management*, 43(1):10 (1978).

was sent to computer school to learn the computer terminal operation. Under this system, owner statements were mailed within 2 days following the end of the month. The managers now respond immediately to tenant inquiries and owner questions, which gives them more time to market services.[9]

INSURANCE COVERAGE

The agent-principal relationship between the property manager and the building owner makes the manager responsible for recommending insurance coverage. Though property managers may not be trained in insurance matters, they must be aware of the more common types of insurance coverage and their main features. In fact, property managers play a key role in administering insurance clauses, in notifying the owner of renewal dates, and in supporting a record system for insurance purposes.

Types of Insurance Coverage

To be sure, recommended coverage varies by type of property and location. In general, the more specialized policies that are important to property management may be grouped under three categories: fire and extended coverage, liability insurance, and certain forms of casualty protection. Contracts covering workers' compensation and fidelity bonds are also of direct concern to property managers.

Fire and Extended Coverage Consider the owner of a 60-unit apartment in downtown Sacramento, California, which was totally destroyed by fire. Because the building manager, William A. Scott, CPM, had arranged for full fire coverage, the insurance company paid for the total loss of approximately $500,000. An adjoining building, which was grossly underinsured, suffered a fire loss of $70,000. In this instance, the owner recovered only $17,500; he was subject to a coinsurance penalty.[10]

(1) Coinsurance Under the coinsurance clause, the property owner bears a portion of losses *only* if the property is underinsured. As a consequence, coinsurance provides an incentive to keep the coverage equal to or above the amount required by the coinsurance clause. Otherwise, the owner must bear a part of the loss.

The coinsurance clause prorates partial losses between the insurance company and the owner in the same proportion that the *actual* insurance carried bears to the *required* insurance. Suppose, for example, that the coinsurance clause for a particular building requires insurance coverage that is equal to at least 80 percent of the building value. Thus, a $100,000 building, insured under an 80 percent coinsurance clause, would require $80,000 insurance coverage. With this coverage, the owner collects in full for partial losses.

Coinsurance provides for recovery according to the coinsurance formula:

[9] James C. Weinberg, op. cit., p. 339.

[10] William A. Scott, "Under-insured? A Deadly Risk," *Journal of Property Management,* 42(6):285–287 (1977).

$$\text{Recovery} = \frac{\text{actual insurance carried}}{\text{required insurance}} \times \text{loss}$$

Suppose that the insurance on the $100,000 building were $40,000 instead of the required $80,000. Under an 80 percent coinsurance clause, a $50,000 loss would result in a recovery of only $25,000.

$$\text{Recovery} = \frac{\$40,000}{\$80,000} \times \$50,000$$
$$= \$25,000$$

Coinsurance results from the fact that most fire losses are partial losses. Therefore it is cheaper to insure under an 80 percent or 90 percent coinsurance clause—and benefit from the lower premium—than pay for coverage on the total building value. However, property managers must guard against being unintentional coinsurers. If building values increase, the property manager must increase the amount of coverage or risk coinsurance penalties.

For larger projects, it is usually advisable to have qualified appraisers periodically review building values to determine the required coverage. In the event of fire, the appraisal also helps to establish the amount of loss.

(2) Insurance Coverage A typical policy covers only the actual cash value at the time of loss. The actual cash value is defined as not more than the cost of repairing or replacing the property with material of like kind and quality. Furthermore, the actual cash settlement may not necessarily be the amount to replace the building, but will be the replacement cost at the time of loss less accrued depreciation.

In other words, fire insurance places the insured in the same financial position with respect to damaged property *after* the loss as *before* the loss. Only in states that have so-called "valued policy laws" will the owner recover for replacement value, and then only if the property is totally destroyed.[11] Policies are also available that insure up to the replacement cost, which eliminates the depreciation deduction.

(3) Exclusions Certain other precautions must be observed by the property manager. If the manager (or owner) deliberately fails to call the fire department until the fire has made a good start, coverage will probably be denied because the loss resulted from the willful neglect of the manager or owner in not using all reasonable means to save the property.

Moreover, it is common to exclude losses from war, rebellion, civil war, and theft of building contents, such as money and securities. Money and securities may be covered by separate policies. The property manager must also determine whether losses exclude damages occurring after the building has been vacant for a stated period, usually 60 consecutive days.

(4) Multiperil Policies Fire insurance may be extended for different perils under multiperil policies. For business properties, owners have the option of insuring against

[11] Mark R. Greene, *Risk and Insurance*, 4th ed., Cincinnati: Southwestern Publishing, 1977, p. 215.

explosions, theft, riots, civil commotion, vandalism, liability, malicious mischief, and damages from aircraft and vehicles. The standard multiperil policy may also provide protection against earthquakes. The main advantage is that all perils are covered under one contract.

Others perils, called allied lines, cover damages from leaking sprinklers, certain types of water damage, and leases on machinery and equipment. Such coverage is also available on personal property, such as lobby furniture and appliances. Special multiperil policies have been adapted to the special protection needs of apartments, offices, and motels. Their advantage lies in lower rates, typically 15 percent less than the rates for various coverages if purchased separately.

Liability Protection   Property managers recognize that there is virtually no limit to liability judgments. Moreover, liability risks seem to be increasing because today the public is more aware of the right to hold responsible persons liable for personal losses. This fact, combined with liberal juries that may make awards on the basis of falsified and exaggerated claims, further increases the liability risk. Continuing inflation is another factor that leads to higher awards for property damage and personal injury.

Under present law, one can be held financially responsible for injury to another's person or property as the result of neglect or carelessness. Claims of negligence may arise if the property manager does not use the degree of care required by law.

Thus, for example, a newly waxed vinyl floor may be dangerously slippery. A tenant or guest who breaks a leg after slipping on the floor may have grounds for a liability judgment. The risk could be reduced if the manager posts a sign warning residents of the floor condition.

Other liabilities are difficult to predict. A tenant who tripped over a crack in a cement slab was awarded a substantial judgment because the tenant's broken leg was later amputated. Another landlord was held liable after a tenant was injured by a loose porch floorboard.[12]

(1) Owners', Landlords' and Tenants' Policy (OL&T)   Owners of rental property are advised to obtain the owners', landlords', and tenants' policy, or the comprehensive general liability (CGL) policy. The former policy protects the owner from liabilities for bodily injury or property damage occurring in an apartment house, shopping center, office building, or other rented premises. The coverage protects against each occurrence "arising out of the ownership, maintenance or use of insured premises and all operations or incidental thereto." The protection also extends to liabilities occurring in elevators. To protect against damage from a falling elevator, elevator collision coverage must be added by endorsement.

Common to other liability insurance contracts, the OL&T policy provides dollar limits for liability damages. Commonly limits might be $100,000 for bodily injury for any one person and $300,000 for each accident. Policies commonly provide property damage limits of $50,000 for each accident. Thus, if three persons are injured in a single accident, the total limitation is $300,000 with $100,000 maximum coverage for each individual.

---

[12] Mark R. Greene, op. cit., p. 297.

The exclusions cover liabilities arising from the ownership, maintenance, operation, use, loading, or unloading of automobiles or aircraft. Other exclusions relate to liabilities resulting from war; liquor; bodily injury to an employee; pollution; and damage to property in the insured's care, custody, or control.

(2) Comprehensive General Liability Policy (CGL) The comprehensive general liability policy covers most business liability exposures in one policy. Owners may insure against several types of liability under the CGL policy:

1 Liability arising out of the use of premises
2 Liability arising out of other business activities of the insured
3 Liability for medical payments
4 Contingent liability for acts of independent contractors
5 Products and completed operations liabilities
6 Contractual liabilities

Some of these exposures may be purchased separately under individual contracts. For instance, the first liability listed is similar to the liability in the OL&T policy. The second type insures against liability arising from contracting operations. For the other perils, the CGL automatically covers newly acquired premises, elevators, or other hazards during the policy term.

The phrasing of the CGL is such that the claims arising from property operations required by the landlord's business are covered. For instance, a contingent liability may arise from independent contractors who engage in hazardous activity, such as handling window-washing equipment that may fall to the ground and injure a tenant.

Likewise the product liability could protect from a poorly repaired heating system that later explodes, causing a shopping center or apartment to be vacated. The liability for the contingent loss in use would be covered by products liability.

CGL also contains the usual exclusions covering liabilities arising from war; workers' compensation claims; and property in the care, custody, or control of the insured. Liabilities arising from responsibilities under the liquor law are excluded (the "dram shop exclusion"). Many of these liabilities may be assumed by separate contract.

Special Insurance Coverage Property managers are advised to review coverage of damages resulting from boiler explosion, since some fire insurance policies exclude damages from explosion. Under *boiler and machinery insurance* coverage, special protection may be extended for explosions and damages to building equipment, such as air-conditioning systems, air tanks, motor generators, transformers, control panels, and stand-by generating systems. These policies may even cover insured property for business interruption.[13]

Boiler and machinery insurance provides a schedule identifying the item insured and the coverage provided. Such insurance may include:

[13] Marshall W. Reavis, "Boiler and Machinery Insurance," *Journal of Property Management*, 43(3):166 (1978).

1 Repairs to the objects and other property that is damaged
2 Coverage for the cost, up to $1,000, to expedite repairs
3 Coverage for damage to property of others for which the insured is liable
4 Coverage for legal defense and other related costs
5 Automatic coverage of new equipment

An added advantage of boiler insurance is that it requires a detailed inspection of the item insured. The inspection leads to recommendations of items to be insured. In some states the insurance inspection satisfies safety inspection requirements.

Property managers who deal with properties in which liquor is distributed, sold, or served may be held liable under laws that regulate alcoholic beverages. Service to a minor or to a person under the influence of alcohol, or acts that cause or contribute to the intoxication of a person may subject owners to the penalties of liquor liability laws. Generally there is no liquor liability exclusion in the CGL policy covering private guests. If liability insurance does not cover liquor liability, the owner may purchase *host liability insurance*. This coverage is not standardized across the country, since policies are tailored to meet local and state laws.

A negligent tenant causing a fire that destroys premises may be sued by the insurer of the building. The landlord suffering losses in rent could hold the tenant liable. Tenants guard against this liability by assuming no responsibility for loss by fire under terms of the lease; or, by contract, the property owner could hold the tenant harmless.

Some policies make the tenant and owner named insurers on the fire policy. However, lenders may object to adding another party to the contract. Another method is for tenants to buy *tenant fire legal liability insurance*.

Sprinkler Leakage Liability The property manager must determine whether damage from rain; snow; or defective windows, doors, skylights, ventilators, and sprinklers is excluded under a water damage exclusion. If liabilities from water damage are not covered, the property manager may recommend *sprinkler leakage insurance* with adequate limits.

An option under the comprehensive general liability policy is the *crime endorsement*. Under this option, coverage is available for employee dishonesty, losses inside buildings, losses outside buildings, counterfeit losses, forgery, and losses of money from burglary or theft. Crime insurance covers many other types of losses beyond common burglary insurance policies. Some agents offer burglary, fidelity, and forgery insurance in a single policy called a comprehensive dishonesty, disappearance, and destruction policy, known as the *C-3D policy*. Federally sponsored crime insurance is also available.

Numerous agreements may be added by endorsement to cover burglary and theft, theft of office equipment, credit card forgery, and dishonesty of officers and employees. Premiums for these coverages are based on actual exposure amounts. For example, premiums might cover loss or theft of money or securities up to a stated amount of $100,000. Higher coverage limits would increase the premiums.

Workers' Compensation

Workers' compensation developed as a means of compensating victims of industrial accidents. As the first type of social insurance adopted in the United States, it represented a merger of private and social insurance. Since the 1972 Report of the National Commission on State Workers' Compensation Laws, states have revised laws governing workers' compensation. Some 48 states provide for compulsory workers' compensation; most states since 1974 have increased benefits.

Depending on the jurisdiction, employers may comply with legal requirements by (1) purchasing a workers' compensation and employers' liability policy from a private commercial insurer, (2) purchasing insurance from a state fund or federal agency provided for this purpose, or (3) providing self-insurance. Every state requires one of these methods.

The standard policy makes all claims required by law where the injury occurred, including occupational disease benefits and penalties, assessable to the employer. A second agreement defends all employee suits against the employer and pays judgments resulting from these suits. The standard basic limit of liability per action is $25,000, which may be increased by endorsement. Because of the agency created by the management agreement, the property manager must determine whether owner-employees are properly covered under state law. Provisions regarding recordkeeping, safety regulations, and payroll deductions, along with their administration, represent other significant tasks falling under management responsibility.

Insurance Administration

Besides advising owners on the type of coverage to be secured in observing renewal dates, property managers advocate certain steps to make certain that losses will be reimbursed promptly. The more significant issues relate to a *notice* of loss and the *proof* of loss.

Notice of Loss Insurance contracts require immediate written notice of loss. Immediate notice gives the insurance company a reasonable opportunity to inspect the loss before the evidence supporting the claim has been lost. In some cases, necessary witnesses may not be identified if notice is delayed. Indeed, if the property manager is negligent in not notifying the owner and insurance company of the loss, the insurance company may invalidate the claim on grounds that it was denied the right to question witnesses, to examine evidence of arson, or in other ways prevented from protecting its interest.

Proof of Loss The burden of proving loss rests on the insured. If personal property has been damaged, the property manager must furnish an inventory and property description of each item lost or damaged. This requirement justifies the inventory file on personal property, appliances, equipment, machinery, and other fixtures. For the building, recommended practice advises a professional appraisal of the building at periodic intervals (1) to make certain that coinsurance limits are met, and (2) to provide proof of loss. The appraisal report and the testimony of the appraiser support damage claims.

SUMMARY

Monthly accounting statements show the net balance remitted to the owner and provide a summary of disbursements and receipts. For income tax purposes, managers provide detail showing sources of income. The summary statement for apartments lists monthly rents by tenant, with other collection and lease details. Trade associations specializing in particular property types have developed recommended charts of accounts for property managers and owners.

Because of the tax consequences of real estate ownership, managers participate in *asset management* by evaluating several investment alternatives. That is, managers operate real estate as a financial investment. Alternative investment plans, that is, refinancing, rehabilitation, sale "as is," and sale after rehabilitation or refinancing are analyzed in the light of tax consequences.

Management organizes a record system to support operations and satisfy various government requirements. Included in this list would be maintenance records, payroll records, and resident files.

Computer systems tend to be favored for property management because property managers rely on repetitive reports. The increasing availability of data processing equipment and the resulting decrease in operating costs further encourage the use of computer systems. Moreover, computers reduce clerical expenses. They provide precise cash control and improved management services.

Planning a computer system with a *service bureau* or with *time-sharing* or *in-house* facilities calls for a carefully planned study. The *feasibility study* helps to determine the best computer system for each situation. In making this study, management reviews how computer functions may be adapted to a particular property management operation. Property management computer systems fall into five subsystems: management operations; accounts payable; payroll accounting; financial reporting; and miscellaneous reports, including file maintenance.

Managers assume responsibility for recommending insurance coverage. They must be familiar with *fire* and *extended coverage, liability insurance*, and certain forms of *casualty protection. Workers' compensation* and *fidelity bonds* are also of direct concern to property managers.

In the case of fire and extended coverage, lower premiums are available for *coinsurance*, but insurers recommend that insurance coverage be purchased for the full value of the building. Insurance of less than this amount subjects the owner to the risk of a coinsurance penalty. A *multiperil policy* is recommended for business properties to cover risk of explosions, riots, civil commotion, vandalism, mischief, and other sources of damage.

Property managers are responsible for using the degree of care required by law to reduce liability claims. Liability policies protect the owner from liabilities for bodily injury or property damage. The *comprehensive general liability policy* provides lower premiums than would separate endorsements purchased individually. The *owners', landlords', and tenants' policy* is a similar coverage that protects property owners against claims arising out of the ownership, maintenance, or use of insured premises. Additional insurance would include boiler and machinery coverage, sprinkler leakage, and crime endorsements. Managers must observe state laws regarding workers' compensation coverage.

In administering insurance, the manager or the owner must notify the insurance company of losses immediately. Failure to observe this requirement may jeopardize recovery. Records, appraisals, and inventories also help to prove losses.

DISCUSSION QUESTIONS

1 What information would be included in the monthly statement that is provided for the owner of an apartment house?
2 What are the main operational categories in office building expense accounts?
3 What is meant by asset management? Explain fully.
4 Describe some of the supporting records organized by property managers.
5 What is generally included in the apartment resident file?
6 What property management records are adaptable to computer processing?
7 Discuss three advantages of computer records.
8 Explain the available computer systems for property management.
9 Critically evaluate three methods of providing computer services.
10 What are the main steps in planning for computer systems?
11 What three significant factors are considered in selecting a computer system?
12 Discuss five operations commonly provided by computer systems for property management.
13 Explain three insurance coverages that are important to property management.
14 What is meant by coinsurance? Give an example in illustration of your answer.
15 Why is liability protection necessary for buildings under management?
16 Describe the general coverage and exclusions of a comprehensive general liability policy.
17 What special insurance coverages are often recommended for property owners?
18 Name two essential requirements to observe in insurance administration.

KEY TERMS AND CONCEPTS

Owner statement	Liability insurance
Profit and loss statement	Casualty protection
Chart of accounts	Workers' compensation
Asset management	Coinsurance
The resident file	Actual cash value
Time sharing	Valued policy laws
Fire and extended coverage	Multiperil policy

Property damage liability   Owners', landlords', and tenants' policy
Personal injury liability   Notice of loss
Comprehensive general liability policy   Proof of loss

SELF-QUIZ

Multiple-Choice Questions

_____ 1 Which of the following statements is correct? (a) In monthly statements, managers show the rental income as if the property were fully occupied; (b) Monthly statements provide a summary of disbursements and receipts; (c) With monthly statements, most managers supply detail on the rent roll; (d) All of the above.

_____ 2 Which of the following is *not* included in the main operational categories of office building expenses? (a) Reserve for replacements; (b) Administrative expenses; (c) Alterations and fixed charges; (d) Financial expenses.

_____ 3 Which of the following defines asset management? (a) Investment decisions recommended according to the before-tax net operating income; (b) After evaluating several investment alternatives, operating real estate as a financial investment; (c) Managing real estate to maximize capital gains; (d) The process of decreasing net operating expenses.

_____ 4 Which of the following is *not* an advantage of computer records? (a) Computers reduce clerical expenses; (b) Computers provide precise cash control; (c) Computers improve management services; (d) Computers reduce the dependence on management judgment.

_____ 5 Which of the following statements is correct? (a) If the business is expanding, leased or owned computer equipment allows volume to increase without adding to fixed cost; (b) With some computers, the capacity may be increased as needed; (c) With in-house equipment, the company has immediate access to computer time; (d) All of the above.

_____ 6 For property management; (a) Computer selection is restricted to service bureaus or time sharing; (b) Computer feasibility studies disregard the existing system; (c) Computer equipment should be installed before system design; (d) None of the above.

_____ 7 According to a special committee of the Institute of Real Estate Management, the computer system selected: (a) Should be flexible and have the capability to retrieve, compare, and analyze specific data on command; (b) Would not be feasible for the management of less than 5,000 apartment units; (c) Should have an operating budget of not more than 20 percent of the total expenses; (d) Should be developed on a time-sharing basis before computer equipment is owned or leased.

_____ 8 Under an 80 percent coinsurance clause: (a) The property owner recovers only 80 percent of partial losses; (b) The property owner bears a portion of the loss only if the property is insured for under 80 percent of value; (c) Insurance premiums pay for 80 percent full coverage; (d) Coverage applies only to total losses.

_____ 9 Typically, fire insurance covers: (a) Only the actual cash value at the time of loss; (b) In the case of partial losses, the current cost of reconstruction with materials of like kind and quality; (c) In the case of total loss, current costs of reconstruction with material of like kind and quality; (d) Losses so that the insured is in a better financial position after the loss than before the loss.

_____ 10 Under liability laws: (a) The property manager is not liable for personal negligence; (b) The property owner assumes all the responsibility for property damage and personal injury; (c) Negligence may arise if the property manager does not use the degree of care required by law; (d) Regardless of negligence, a person becomes liable to another in the event of personal injury or property damage.

Answer Key

1 (d), 2 (a), 3 (b), 4 (d), 5 (d), 6 (d), 7 (a), 8 (b), 9 (a), 10 (c).

Fill-in Questions

1 Owner statements serve two purposes: they show the net balance remitted monthly to the owner and they provide a summary of _____ and _____ .

2 Managers must review requirements of the _____ _____, which requires that all employees be paid the statutory minimum hourly wage.

3 Asset management refers to evaluating several _____ .

4 In property management, clerical costs generally increase in direct proportion to the increase in _____ .

5 Planning for a system of computer records determines how the firm may maximize the return on computer _____ and minimize _____ _____.

6 Selection of a computer system turns on _____ , _____ , and _____ factors.

7 The coinsurance clause prorates partial losses between the insurance company and the owner in the same proportion that the _____ insurance carried bears to the _____ insurance.

8 _____ insure against explosions, riots, civil commotion, vandalism, malicious mischief, and damages from aircraft and vehicles.

9 The _____ policy covers most business liability exposures in one policy.

10 Since some fire insurance policies exclude damages from explosion, property owners are advised to contract for _____ and _____ insurance coverage.

Answer Key

1	disbursements, receipts	**6**	equipment, software, economic
2	Fair Labor Standards Act	**7**	actual, required
3	investment alternatives	**8**	Multiperil policies
4	business volume	**9**	comprehensive general liability
5	investments, operating costs	**10**	boiler, machinery

SELECTED REFERENCES

Gibbs, Thomas E.: "EDP for Property Management: A Procedure for Rational Choice," *Journal of Property Management*, **43**(1):6–9 (1978).

Greene, Mark R.: *Risk and Insurance*, 4th ed., Cincinnati: Southwestern Publishing, 1977.

Grejtak, C. M.: "Minicomputers or Data Processing Services? A Dilemna [sic] for Property Managers," *Journal of Property Management*, **42**(4):208–212 (1977).

Huebner, S. S., Kenneth Back, and Robert S. Cline: *Property and Liability Insurance*, 2d ed., Englewood Cliffs, N.J.: Prentice-Hall, 1976.

The Property Manager's Guide to Forms & Letters, Chicago: Institute of Real Estate Management, 1971.

Part Three

Management Practice

Chapter 11

Apartment Leasing Policy

After studying this chapter, you should be familiar with:
1 The supply and demand for apartments
2 Apartment marketing techniques
3 Apartment leasing procedures
4 Apartment rental policy

Leasing apartments is a process of merchandising space. The final policy adopted in leasing apartments rests on a clear understanding of characteristics of apartments and prospective tenants—the supply and demand for apartments. Given the current market for rental housing, management centers on marketing apartment space, understanding apartment leases, and administering rental policies. A discussion of these policy issues precedes a discussion of apartment financial analysis in Chapter 12.

THE MARKET FOR APARTMENTS

The market for apartments depends on the interaction of available apartments and their demand. Yet there is no single market as there is with other goods and services;

local apartments consist of separate and unique types that form discrete submarkets; that is, the supply of A apartments cannot be substituted for B apartments. The preferences for apartments vary widely among prospective tenants.

The Supply of Apartments

Apartments are classified in numerous ways. To analyze income and expenses, they fall within four well-defined groups:

> elevator buildings
> low-rise buildings: 12 to 24 units
> low-rise buildings: 25 or more units
> garden-type buildings

Within each category, buildings may be either furnished or unfurnished. Real estate managers define high-rise elevator buildings as apartment buildings with four stories or more. The low-rise buildings under 25 units include walk-up buildings and elevator buildings of three stories or less. The same classification holds for low-rise buildings of 25 units or more. Garden-type apartments refer to low-rise apartment buildings on a landscaped site under one management.

In addition to these classifications, it is common to identify apartment buildings as *townhouses*—an apartment unit that has no common area either attached or detached. Planned unit developments of detached single-family dwellings with a common ground area and recreational space would qualify as a townhouse apartment project. In still other instances, apartments may be constructed in combinations of these groups; for example, garden-type apartments and townhouses might be mixed in the same project.

For other purposes, buildings are classified by age, since operating expenses and rent schedules vary for buildings constructed at different times. An apartment building constructed before World War II will show substantial differences in construction, layout, and building services when compared to modern construction.

It is also common to deal with apartments as either central-city oriented or suburban. In still other cases, for insurance purposes, the type of construction is emphasized: brick, concrete block, or frame construction.

The importance of identifying building types is that it relates to management policy on rent and expenses. Typically the high-rise elevator apartment will experience the highest gross income, net operating income, and expenses of operation. In contrast, garden apartments and the low-rise 12- and 24-unit apartment buildings will have lower rents and lower expenses. To be sure, differences in quality within each group may be more significant than comparisons among the different apartment types. Nevertheless, by classifying buildings by structural type, property managers may make more valid comparisons of rent and operating expenses.

Similar differences will be noted for furnished apartments. Although furnished apartments earn more gross rent, they appeal to a more transient tenant population. For example, according to the annual survey of the Institute of Real Estate Management, furnished garden apartments reported an annual turnover rate of 81.1 percent in 1977.

Room Size Apartment managers generally agree on the terminology used to classify apartments. In listing apartments by numbers of rooms, the manager does not count bathrooms, porches, halls, closets, and storage space. The accepted method of counting room size follows recommendations of the Institute of Real Estate Management.[1] The standard system lists the number of rooms and half-rooms.

Dining Room If the dining room is combined with the living room and totals less than 260 square feet, the combination is counted as one room. If the combination is more than 260 square feet, it is listed as one-and-one-half rooms. If a breakfast room is more than 100 square feet, it is counted as a separate room.

Kitchen A separate walk-in kitchen equals one room. A combination dining and kitchen room will be classified according to the square foot area; if the combined dining and kitchen space is 105 square feet or less, it equals one room. If the combined area is over 105 feet and less than 140 square feet, it equals one-and-one-half rooms. If the total area is over 140 square feet, it counts as two rooms. If a kitchen is constructed as part of the living room, it is counted as a half-room.

Expenses, incomes, and vacancies are commonly listed by apartment and by room. More accuracy is gained, however, by reducing expenses and incomes to the annual amount per gross square feet or the net rentable area.

Floor Area The gross square feet in an apartment building includes the basement area, mezzanines, penthouses, corridors, lobbies, stores, offices, and garages within the building, but excludes architectural setbacks or projections. The gross square feet calculation includes each floor for all areas with a minimum clear standing headroom of 6 feet, 6 inches.

The rentable area includes only space rented by tenants—excluding public areas, stairways, elevators, and utility space not under control of individual tenants.

Other Classifications For some purposes, apartments are classified by their adaptation to a certain group of tenants. Housing for the elderly, usually financed under subsidized plans, may have special features, locational characteristics, and construction important to more elderly tenants. Low-income housing, public housing, nursing homes, condominiums, and cooperative housing are other more specialized forms of rental properties. Add to this list the mobile home park, which caters to transient working families and to upper-income households in the Southwestern states and Florida. In each of these groups, specially constructed apartments have features that establish a separate supply and demand.

The Tenant Demand for Apartment Space

The demand for apartment space falls into several tenant groups. Some of the more common groups that have specialized apartment needs are elderly groups, those with mobile occupations, low-income groups, newly married couples, single groups (of all ages), families with children, and tenants who prefer luxury apartments.

[1] These definitions and other details are published in each annual issue of *Income/Expense Analysis: Apartments*, Chicago: Institute of Real Estate Management.

Demand Classified by Tenant Groups Ordinarily an apartment will be constructed and managed to meet the needs of one of these specialized groups. Those specializing in housing for the elderly would incorporate construction features, security measures, and services particular to this market. Others, because of transient work, have difficulty adapting to single-family ownership and prefer the more convenient apartment rentals. This is the case, for example, with highly skilled construction workers. In the same manner, low-income groups have few alternatives. Their cash resources and inability to service mortgages creates a permanent demand for apartment space that offers maximum shelter at the least cost.

Newly married couples with or without children may occupy apartment space temporarily while cash reserves are accumulated for ownership. Frequently the insecurity of their employment necessitates apartment occupancy over the early marriage years. Families with children absorb a considerable share of available apartment space. Though the children create management problems, these families tend to have more responsible attitudes toward rental occupancy than the low-income group.

Members of the single group may be attracted to the apartment that meets their living styles: It is a highly mobile group that creates management problems not found in more stable groups.

Add to these groups professional people who prefer the convenience and maximum services of central high-rise apartment space. The demands on their time are such that they are willing to pay for a premium location near entertainment sources and office employment. Their ability to pay and their life-style creates a market for luxury accommodations not found in alternative housing.

In other respects the apartment market may be dominated by occupational groups. In the college community, students turn to apartment occupancy as a temporary housing measure. Management policies will be adapted to the needs of this highly mobile group with limited resources.

Localized Demand Communities dominated by a military base or federal facility provide space for personnel whose tenure may be unpredictably limited to a few weeks or months. Add to this list the short-term demand created by temporary employment. These conditions are found in the construction of large dams, seaways, canals, and power plants, which may take several months to complete. Such communities need short-term rental space for housing temporary employees and providing specialized services.

The Demand for Individual Units Besides serving a particular market, apartment developers serve the widest possible market by adapting the unit mix to the current demand. The *unit mix* refers to the combination of one-, two-, or three-bedroom units and their variations. For instance, a project of 204 units developed for moderate-income single persons (no children) provided one- and two-bedroom units as follows:

Unit	Number of units	Percentage of total number
1 bedroom	112	55
2 bedroom, 1 bath	32	16
2 bedroom, 2 baths	60	29
Total	204	100

Fifty-five percent of the 204 units (i.e., the one-bedroom units) were rented to single individuals. A 5 percent vacancy rate was reported for the third year for the 112 one-bedroom units. At the same time, vacancies in the two-bedroom, two-bath units, which account for 29 percent of the unit mix, were 20 percent.

The unit mix demanded varies according to the housing market. During periods of unemployment, tenants show a preference for one-bedroom or efficiency apartments. When they are facing lower incomes, tenants prefer an efficiency apartment in a better building to a one- or two-bedroom unit in an older structure with a less desirable location. Moreover, there is a tendency for households to share housing in a tight housing market. Similarly, families with children absorb a greater share of the market for two- and three-bedroom apartments in an economic atmosphere where they are likely to encounter unfavorable mortgage credit. Such families prefer to rent apartments temporarily, pending later decisions to purchase a home. Because of these variations in market demand, apartments usually provide a range of units showing a mix of efficiencies, one bedrooms, and two- and three-bedroom units with one or two baths.

APARTMENT LEASING

To rent apartments, managers must maintain them in a rentable condition. Clean apartments have been called the first golden rule of residential management, and more important than leasing and rent collection procedures: "Cleanliness is as basic as any fundamental rule of management can be."[2]

Therefore, it is assumed that the landscaping, the parking area, the building exterior, and the interior are in the best possible condition. To ensure that apartments are in proper condition, property managers advise a *ready checklist*. The checklist ensures that painting, carpeting, windows, light fixtures, heating and air conditioning, kitchen, and bathrooms are immaculate.

Probably the leading cause of losing prospective tenants is the condition of the apartment. To guide the preparation, checklists must cover several points:

1 Cleaning and debris removal
2 Repainting and redecorating

[2] Dan German, "Golden Rules of Residential Management," *Journal of Property Management*, 43(4):187 (1978).

3 Cleaning of draperies and blinds
4 Maintenance and repairs
5 Checking appliances' operating condition:
  a Repair all appliances
  b Repair electrical equipment
6 Repair of damaged woodwork, glass, or other hardware
7 Cleaning or replacing carpets
8 Cleaning and polishing floors

These steps are undertaken immediately after the apartment has been vacated. The final inspection may correct unsatisfactory work and remove remaining dirt and scratches.

Marketing Promotion

Since many prospects inspect apartments as a result of identification signs, managers provide attractive exterior signs. With new apartments, model apartments and brochures are used to attract tenant-prospects. Most managers rely heavily on display advertising and classified ads that list specific features of the apartment.

Apartment managers may work closely with apartment locator services, housing directors of local corporations, and government agencies. In addition, tenant referrals—recommendations by present residents—provide a possible source of prospective tenants. However, an attractive sign and newspaper ads have been proven more effective in leasing apartment units.

In showing prospects space, managers offer a tour of the apartment complex showing recreational facilities and services provided to tenants, such as the coin laundry and the clubhouse. Apartments are normally scheduled to be shown between fixed hours, such as 10:00 a.m. to 6:30 p.m. on weekdays and Saturdays. On Sunday afternoons, resident managers must be available for showing apartments on request.

Move-In Procedure Assuming that the prospective tenant accepts the space offered, move-in procedures follow well-defined steps. Provided the tenant references have proven satisfactory, the prospect is informed by letter that the apartment is available. Again the apartment is inspected for final occupancy. The inspection must be made with the tenant so that the tenant signs the form showing the condition of the apartment, which will be used later to calculate damage deductions from the security deposit. Keys are not given to the applicant before payment of the security deposit and the first month's rent. See Figure 11-1 for a recommended apartment condition checklist.

On the move-in date, arrangements must be made for staff assistance for moving furniture and personal property. Freight elevators must be made available, or if passenger elevators are used, padded liners must be installed.

The new resident is given an orientation covering the apartment community—namely, services, transportation, rules, and the resident handbook or tenant guidebook. Though the tenant will be given a copy of the house rules, which are normally printed with a copy of the lease, these rules are explained to the tenant. The house

APARTMENT CONDITION CHECK LIST

RESIDENT'S NAME _____

APARTMENT # _____   APARTMENT SIZE _____

DATE IN _____   DATE OUT _____

	LIVING AREA	DINING AREA	HALL	BR (1)	BR (2)	BR (3)		
	IN OUT	IN OUT	IN OUT	IN OUT	IN OUT	IN OUT	IN OUT	IN OUT
BLINDS, DRAPES, SHADES	☐☐	☐☐	☐☐	☐☐	☐☐	☐☐	☐☐	☐☐
CEILINGS								
CLOSETS								
DOORS								
FLOORS, CARPETS								
LIGHT FIXTURES								
PAINT								
SCREENS								
SWITCHES & RECEPTACLES								
TRIM								
WALLS								
WINDOWS								

KITCHEN
CABINETS · CEILING · COUNTER TOPS · DISPOSER · DOORS · EXHAUST FAN · FLOOR · HARDWARE · LIGHT FIXTURES · PAINT · RANGE · RANGE HOOD · REFRIGERATOR · SCREENS · SINK · SWITCHES & RECEPTACLES · TRIM · WALLS · WINDOWS

BATHROOMS (1) (2)
CEILING · COMMODE · DOORS · FAN · FLOOR · HEATER · LAVATORY · LIGHT FIXTURES · MEDICINE CABINET · MIRRORS · PAINT · SCREENS · TOWEL BARS · TUB & SHOWER · VANITY · WALLS · WINDOWS · AIR CONDITIONING · HEATING SYSTEM · WATER HEATER

INSPECTED BY

IN SIGNATURE _____ DATE _____
   TITLE _____
OUT SIGNATURE _____ DATE _____
   TITLE _____

I HAVE INSPECTED THE APARTMENT SPECIFIED ABOVE AND HAVE FOUND IT TO BE IN NORMAL CONDITION EXCEPT AS NOTED. I UNDERSTAND THAT IT IS MY RESPONSIBILITY TO MAINTAIN THE APARTMENT IN A SAFE AND PROPER CONDITION AND TO LEAVE IT AS I FOUND IT EXCEPT FOR NORMAL WEAR.

RESIDENT'S SIGNATURE _____ DATE _____
RESIDENT'S SIGNATURE _____ DATE _____

NCHM FORM 121
6/74

Figure 11-1 Apartment condition checklist. *(Source: The Housing Manager's Resource Book, Washington, D.C.: National Center for Housing Management, 1976, p. 84.)*

rules shown in Figure 11-2 illustrate points common to apartment rules. If the project has a swimming pool, the rules and regulations governing its operation are discussed with new tenants. Final details require resident managers to complete accounting records and other records for processing occupancy.

Qualifying the Tenant Tenants qualify for occupancy on the basis of the probability of their paying rent. The credit application for rentals will identify the place of employment, the type of job, and the length of time on the job. Supplementing this information will be the credit rating indicating whether the applicant has a record of meeting payments and obligations. Tenants who list themselves as self-employed or living with relatives, who state, "I will make the deposit as soon as my home is sold,"

Figure 11-2 Apartment rules and regulations.

These rules are for the mutual benefit of all tenants. Please cooperate. Violations may cause termination of your Lease.

1. No animals without written consent of OWNER (which may be refused or revoked at any time). No animals without leash in any public area of the Building.

2. Passages, public halls, stairways, landings, elevators and elevator vestibules shall not be obstructed or used for any other purpose than for ingress to and egress from the Building or apartments. All personal possessions must be kept in the Apartment or in lockers, if provided.

3. All furniture, goods and packages of every kind shall be delivered through the rear or service entrance, stairway or elevator.

4. Carriages, bicycles, sleds or the like shall not be left unattended in the lobbies, public halls, passageways, courts or elevators of the Building and shall be stored only in places designated for their storage by the OWNER.

5. Washers and dryers cannot be kept in the Apartment.

6. No sign, signal, illumination, advertisement, notice or any other lettering, or equipment shall be exhibited, inscribed, painted, affixed or exposed on or at any window or on any part of the outside of the Apartment or the Building.

7. No awnings or other projections including air conditioners (without OWNER'S consent), television or radio antennas or wiring shall be attached to or extended from the outside walls of the Building.

8. No property shall be placed in the halls, on the staircase landings, nor shall anything be hung or shaken from the windows or balconies or placed upon the outside window sills.

9. No spikes, hooks or nails shall be driven into the walls or woodwork of the Apartment without first obtaining the written consent of the OWNER.

10. There shall be no cooking or baking done in or about the Apartment except in the kitchen. Cooking on a barbecue or other similar equipment on a porch or balcony is expressly forbidden.

11. If TENANT desires TV master antenna hookup, only OWNER'S authorized agent shall install TENANT'S TV set to master antenna and TENANT agrees to pay installation cost and mutual maintenance fee. TENANT agrees to free access to the Apartment by OWNER to disconnect hookup for nonpayment. TENANT agrees to pay $50.00 liquidated damage to OWNER'S authorized agent for each illegal hookup in TENANT'S Apartment.

12. No water beds or other furniture filled with a liquid substance shall be brought in or used in the Apartment.

or who are moving in from out of town may require further inquiries about their credit status. Credit is verified from the local credit bureau and from the owner or manager of the present address; the latter helps to verify character, living habits, and credit history.

Resident managers acquire skills in judging tenant compatibility; for example, families with three or four children may be incompatible with a group of single tenants under 30. Proper interviewing techniques, a knowledge of verbal and nonverbal communication, and questioning probes help the resident manager just as they help real estate salespersons.[3]

Special attention is given to the security deposit, which is often subject to state regulations. Suppose that the minimum deposit would normally be $100. The tenant is asked to sign an inventory that acknowledges the present apartment condition and the equipment's working operation as indicated on the report (see Figure 11-2).

Apartment Leases

Apartment leases, under the more modern interpretation, serve as a contract that outlines rights and duties of landlord and tenant. While apartments may be leased on a month-to-month basis under an oral contract, most jurisdictions require enforceable leases of 1 year or longer to be in written form. Though practices vary among the states, leases have certain common legal requirements.

Legal Requirements The lease is signed by parties to the lease, and they must give their correct names. It is assumed further that the parties signing are legally competent to execute the lease—an issue that affects minors, the mentally incompetent, and individuals acting in behalf of corporations and partnerships. Moreover, the lease must describe the leased premises in definite terms. Addresses alone are unreliable, since street numbers and street names do not always agree with public or other records.

In addition, the lease should state the beginning and ending date of its term. And for enforceability, some states require that the lease must be under seal or have a certain number of witnesses. The lease is not effective until it is delivered to the tenant.

Apartment leases describe the rights of the parties with respect to assignment or subletting of the premises. If the apartment is taken over by a third-party tenant for the remaining term of the lease, there is an assignment. If the third party takes the premises for less than the remaining term of the lease, there is a subletting and the original tenant remains responsible for observing the terms of the lease.

Rental Terms The lease states the amount of rent, when the rent is payable, and where it should be paid. Agreement will be reached on the payment of utilities. Leases will usually state that the holding-over tenant on a 1-year lease automatically converts the tenure to a month-to-month tenancy. State laws may vary on this point. Terms

---

[3]For an explanation of these techniques as applied to real estate, consult William M. Shenkel, *Marketing Real Estate*, Englewood Cliffs, N.J.: Prentice-Hall, 1980.

under which the security deposit may be retained by the landlord for stated damages will be carefully drawn by local attorneys. Rights of the landlord to evict a tenant will be stated if the rent is in default. Again, this right is subject to state and local regulations.

Property Use The lease will state the number of persons by name who will occupy the premises and will set forth the rights and obligations of both parties with respect to maintenance of the premises. The lease will include the covenant of quiet enjoyment—the tenant is granted quiet, peaceful, and exclusive enjoyment—but by the same token, the tenant will be required to use the premises for residential purposes without causing nuisances or disturbances to other tenants.

Other Lease Terms The technical requirements of the lease include other provisions that anticipate events restricting the rights of tenant and landlord. For instance, the list of these additional items covered by the lease would include:

1 Prohibition against nonresidential use of the leased premises
2 The status of the lease if the property is destroyed by fire or other casualty
3 Hold-harmless clauses that relieve the tenant or landlord from liabilities arising from damages or injuries sustained on the leased premises
4 The right of the landlord to reenter the premises under certain circumstances
5 Rights of parties if the landlord or tenant declares bankruptcy and insolvency
6 Rights of the parties if portions of the property are taken by eminent domain

A summary of lease terms is shown in Figure 11-3. The summary lists the table of contents of a lease recommended by William B. Kaplan, CPM, of Romanek-Golub and Company, Chicago, Illinois.

Apartment leases are too complex to arrange without the assistance of an attorney. Because of differences in state law, local ordinances, and federal requirements, leases should be drawn by local counsel. With a standard lease form, resident managers must ensure that the lease is properly filled out, signed, executed, witnessed, acknowledged, and recorded. It is the document that establishes the relationship between landlord and tenant. It should be added that leases, in the case of apartments, usually require the tenant to observe house rules.

In summary, a careful reading of residential leases requires that tenants must (1) maintain the premises in a clean and sanitary condition, (2) report any damages and needed repairs promptly, (3) pay service charges for repairs of any damage not the result of normal wear and tear, and (4) permit the landlord or staff to enter the unit for inspections or repairs.

Normally the lease will require the tenant's agreement *not* to engage in certain other acts without permission: (1) using the premises for purposes other than residential, (2) keeping pets—with permitted exceptions such as birds or goldfish, for example, (3) making major alterations, (4) installing appliances such as dishwashers or air conditioners, (5) wasting utilities, or (6) infringing on the rights of others.

ROMANEK golub
AND COMPANY/REAL ESTATE

Apartment Lease

DATE OF LEASE	TERM OF LEASE		MONTHLY RENT	SECURITY DEPOSIT	APT. NO.	BUILDING
	BEGINNING	ENDING				

Tenant

Signatures TENANT

ROMANEK-GOLUB & COMPANY
as Agent ("Agent") for the beneficial owners
("Owner") of the Building

By _____

Lease Topics

1. Lease of apartment
2. Rent
3. Monthly rent; late payment charge
4. Increase in monthly rent for real estate taxes
5. Security deposit
6. Owner's agreement for maintenance
7. Condition of apartment and building
8. Use of apartment

9. Assignment
10. Alteration, additions, decorating
11. Access to apartment
12. Default
13. Heating, water, and air conditioning
14. Fire and casualty
15. Eminent domain
16. Miscellaneous

Figure 11-3 Lease summary included in an apartment lease. *(Source: Lease form supplied by William B. Kaplan, CPM.)*

In return for agreement on these points, the landlord promises to maintain premises in a habitable condition, to keep equipment in a workable order, and to comply with local ordinances and common law (which is not always in writing).

Move-Out Procedure

It is costly to prepare an apartment unit for a new tenant. To minimize turnover, the alert resident manager keeps a suspension file listing leases that terminate in 90 days. When this time is reached, resident managers interview tenants concerning their intention to renew. If the tenant is dissatisfied, often steps may be taken to remove the source of dissatisfaction and commit the tenant to a new lease. If the resident manager waits until the last month, chances are that the dissatisfied tenant will have already selected a new apartment and the decision is irreversible.

The tenant who has elected not to renew provides an important source of information, hence resident managers try to determine why the tenant is moving. Comments about the main attractions and limitations of the apartment are solicited. With this information the resident manager may correct management deficiencies, for instance, by improving the physical condition of the apartment or by revising management services and policy. Comments of terminating tenants may also suggest the feasibility of alterations or remodeling.

Though managers work to reduce tenant turnover, tenants will move out for unavoidable reasons: changes in income; new jobs; changes in family size, tastes, and life-style. Some move out, with or without notice, and some moves result from eviction. Since there are extra costs in processing an apartment when a tenant moves out, scheduled procedures should be followed to minimize costs of tenant turnover. By anticipating move-outs, managers can schedule move-out procedures more efficiently for clean-up, redecoration, advertising, and presenting. The cycle of move-outs would follow the steps shown in Figure 11-4.

Note that the preliminary inspection is made with the resident. Since good policy and legal requirements necessitate justification of damage deductions from security deposits, such charges must be documented. The tenant is not responsible for normal

Figure 11-4 Move-out procedures. *(Source: The Housing Manager's Resource Book, Washington, D.C.: National Center for Housing Management, 1976, p. 89.)*

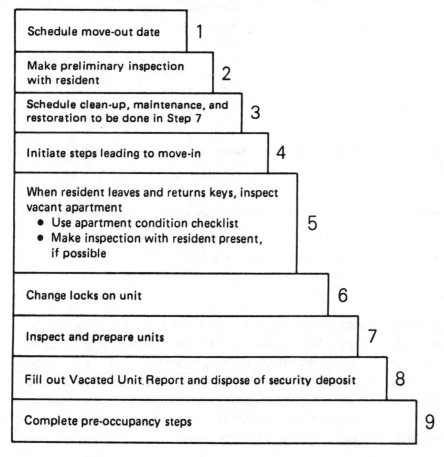

wear and tear. For instance, interior painting ordinarily lasts a minimum of 2 years. For occupancy that is over in less than 2 years, new paint is required to meet standards of occupancy justifying a deduction for repainting.

Some property managers recommend a deduction schedule that is based partly on length of occupancy. For an occupancy of less than 6 months, a deduction for repainting a three-bedroom apartment should cover the total repainting cost. A move-out check form that the tenant signs before occupying the premises documents damages for repairing and cleaning appliances, replacing and cleaning carpets, and the like. The move-out cycle progresses to the move-in procedures, which also require preparatory steps such as changing locks, final inspection, and other preoccupancy steps.

RENTAL POLICY

While other aspects of management provide service and good maintenance leading to tenant satisfaction, special efforts are taken in designing the rental policy to reduce tenant turnover. Assuming a 15-day vacancy between move-out and a move-in, an apartment rented for $240 per month would result in a rental loss of $120. Add to this sum the pre-move-in expenses of redecorating and cleaning, and the administrative cost of preparing for a new tenant—writing new leases, creating new tenant files, and making credit checks. For this reason managers pay particular attention to general procedures followed in administering rent increases and collecting delinquent rent.

Administering Rent Increases

Two problems are encountered in raising rents: (1) convincing the resident manager that property managers must maximize income rather than occupancy and (2) reducing tenant turnover caused by a rent increase.

Resident managers tend to believe that the goal of maximum occupancy prevails over the goal of maximum returns. They believe that their job is to rent 100 percent of the apartments, and they believe that they are judged primarily on this issue. Yet experience reveals that 100 percent occupancy will not always maximize returns. For example, consider a 490-unit garden apartment complex with 100 percent occupancy and an average rent of $250 a month. After announcement of a 7 percent rent increase to an average monthly rental of $267, 98 tenants, or 20 percent, gave notice. On the day of the effective increase, 30 units were vacant.

The before-and-after comparison showed that the resulting 94 percent occupancy increased income as follows:

After the Rent Increase
460 apartments @ $267 average rent   = $122,820
Before the Rent Increase
490 apartments @ $250 average rent   =   −122,500
Increased Monthly Income   = $ 320

Even with a 6 percent vacancy, the 7 percent rental increase resulted in an increase in monthly income of $320. As the 30 vacant units became rented in the space of a few months, occupancy returned to 100 percent and to total monthly collections of $131,000 or $9,000 more per month.[3]

While this explanation may gain the confidence of the resident manager, professional managers must provide tenants with reasons for the increase. The rental increase letter advised by Sidney Glassman of the Charles E. Smith Company, Washington, D.C., begins by stating: "It has been our consistent policy to exercise voluntary restraint in our rent increases. In line with this policy we are limiting your rent increase to a maximum of eight percent."[4]

Roland D. Freeman, writing in *The Encyclopedia of Apartment Management*, illustrates a rental increase letter that begins with the statement:

Yes, this is a rent increase letter.

As you are probably well aware from the media, we are anticipating an 11 percent increase in property taxes this year and over the last two years our utility expense has increased by better than 50 percent. It is indeed painful to ask you to pay more rent with the same services that you are presently receiving, but we see no alternative other than cutting back services which we are sure you will agree is not an acceptable alternative.[5]

Accordingly, property managers are advised not to raise rents more than once a year to avoid making tenants insecure. It is further recommended that residents be given a 60-day notice of a rent increase and that increases be limited to 10 percent, or $25, for moderate-income apartments.

After informing tenants of the rent increase, Roland D. Freeman Associates close by stating, "We like you as our resident, and want you to stay. We hope we have your understanding, if not your enthusiastic support." Managers who receive notice of an intent to move counsel residents to stay. During the move-out interview, resident managers seek reasons for the tenant's proposed move. Resident managers try to understand why the tenant likes the new apartment better than the present unit. If the tenant has not been committed to another apartment, the interviewer, by listening carefully to the tenant's objections and complaints, may succeed in keeping the tenant.

Rent Collection

Strict enforcement of a rent collection policy discourages habitual delinquencies. For instance, during the pre-move-in interview, tenants are informed that rents are due the first of the month and that delinquent notices will be sent on the fifth of the month.

[3] See Edward N. Kelley, "How to Get Your Manager to Raise Rents," *Journal of Property Management,* 40(2):77 (1975).

[4] Sidney Glassman, *A Guide to Residential Management*, 3d ed., Washington, D.C.: National Association of Homebuilders, 1978, p. 139.

[5] Roland D. Freeman, *The Encyclopedia of Apartment Management*, Washington, D.C.: National Apartment Association, 1976, pp. III–16.

Some firms establish late charges for rents not paid by the tenth of the month.[6] A statement of the delinquent sum due would be accompanied by a letter that states:

> I know you value and appreciate the importance of a good credit rating. However, to protect your good credit rating, your account must be paid in full within five (5) days of the above date. If your account is still delinquent after that time, we shall take whatever legal action is necessary to affect collection, and/or terminate your lease.[7]

Other managers advise that if rent is *5* days past due, the resident manager should send a friendly reminder; if the rent is *10* days past due, the resident manager should personally visit the tenant; and, if rent is *15* days past due, the resident manager should send the tenant a written demand.

Some companies require that rent be paid within 3 days or "the lessor will take legal proceedings to recover possession of the premises." On the twentieth of the month (if rent is due on the first) in some jurisdictions, the tenant is sent a legally termed "notice to pay rent or quit." In California, for example, this notice must be given three days before the notice to surrender the premises. Special care must be taken to ensure that delinquent notices conform to local and state laws.

The notice of eviction will be followed by the service of a complaint on the resident. If the eviction is uncontested, the tenant will receive a formal eviction notice from the sheriff. If the eviction is contested, but after a trial the tenant receives a judgment and writ of execution, the sheriff executes the formal eviction notice in most communities.

A typical rent collection schedule would conform to the following timing:

Day	Action
1	Rent is due in full.
3-5	Prepare and deliver Delinquent Rent Notice.
5-7	Visit or telephone the resident personally to find out why the rent has not been paid.
8-9	Prepare and personally deliver a second Delinquent Rent Notice.
10	Personally visit resident to work out a specific agreement to pay. If no agreement is reached, begin eviction proceedings.

It is the responsibility of the resident manager to determine why the rent payment is late. Generally, resident managers have no authority to agree to accept partial rent or a promise of payment at a later date. Most managers recommend a fixed policy of following the recommended schedule for collecting rents. After the first notice, the second delinquent note is more threatening:

---

[6] Delinquent charges are discouraged by some managers on the grounds that tenants view the late charge as the price for the "privilege" of making delinquent rent payments.
[7] Sidney Glassman, op. cit., p. 170.

Our requests for payment of your rent of $300 for Apartment 101 have been ignored. We now find it necessary to advise you that unless you contact our office in 3 days we must begin eviction proceedings. Please send your payment immediately so that we can clear up this delinquent rent situation.

The resident manager makes personal inquiries to determine reasons for the delinquent rent. Every effort is made to work out a payment agreement, since management tries to avoid the time-consuming eviction. Resident managers have no alternative with uncooperative tenants but to pursue the eviction order.

Besides evicting for delinquent rents, managers may initiate eviction notices because of violations of house rules. The most common reasons would be alcoholism or drug addiction, excessive and repeated noise, destruction of property, dangerous or immoral conduct, and unrestrained pets. While the manager pursues alternatives to eviction—that is, making requests that tenants do not abuse property or do not cause other tenants discomfort—failure of the tenants to comply results in eviction notices, which must follow local legal procedures.

One authority recommends personal contact as the principal means of collecting delinquent rents. This recommendation makes sense, since habitually delinquent tenants learn the steps in other rent collection procedures and only respond after receiving the final notice of payment.

In making personal contact, resident managers learn not to accept certain excuses, such as the excuse that rent is being withheld pending completion of requested repairs. On this issue, managers should insist on full rent payment and "not trade repairs for rent." Repairs should be undertaken as a normal tenant request, and the tenant should respond by paying the rent when due.

In other instances, tenants who have no funds may defer rent payments on the promise of money expected later in the month. Here again managers disallow rent delinquencies since, in effect, the property owner is lending the tenant funds. Tenants have access to other credit sources if they are temporarily short of funds. The weight of authority, therefore, advises the strongest possible delinquent rent procedure.[8]

SUMMARY

The supply of apartments is judged in terms of *elevator apartments*, which are high-rise elevator buildings with four stories or more; *low-rise apartments* of 12 to 24 units and 25 units or more, which are walk-up and elevator buildings of three stories or less; and *garden apartments*, which are low-rise apartment buildings on a landscaped site under one management. Apartments may be managed to include *townhouses*, which have no common area either attached or detached, or *planned unit developments* with common areas and recreational space. Within these classifications, income and operating expenses show wide differences.

[8] See Edward N. Kelley, *Practical Apartment Management*, Chicago: Institute of Real Estate Management, 1976, p. 202.

In making comparisons, apartment managers carefully define the number of rooms per apartment and convert operating expenses to an annual amount per *gross square feet* or *rentable area*. The demand for apartment space is generally stratified according to tenant groups that have specialized apartment needs; included in these groups are the elderly, low-income groups, newly married couples, single groups, tenants who prefer luxury apartments, and families with children. Not only do these groups have widely different needs for physical space, but management policy must adapt to different levels of service. Even within an apartment project, apartments of varying size and room numbers appeal to a mixture of tenants. By adapting space to the largest number of tenants, owners reduce risk as the demand for one-, two-, or three-bedroom units changes with variations in the housing market.

In marketing, available apartments are placed in the best possible condition by following checklists that cover apartment preparation for new tenants. Move-in procedures begin with an inspection, with the tenant, to identify the apartment condition and its inventory. New residents are given an orientation covering the apartment community, the available services, and house rules. Tenants qualify for occupancy on the basis of their probable rent-paying ability and their compatibility with other tenants.

Apartment leases must be signed by parties to the lease and must otherwise conform to the requirements of a legally enforceable contract; the lease is not effective until it has been delivered to the tenant. Rental terms deal specifically with payment of utilities, security deposits, and rights of eviction if rent is in default.

Another main part of the lease concerns property use, which is confined to residential purposes; and avoiding nuisances or disturbances to other tenants. Other terms of the apartment lease are common to other leases: the right of assignment, alteration, access, default, eminent domain, and related topics.

Move-out procedures follow a well-defined schedule that requires a preliminary inspection with the resident to determine damage deductions from the deposit. In making clean-up and restoration schedules, managers employ an apartment condition checklist. Changing locks and starting other preoccupancy steps complete the move-out cycle.

Rental policy maximizes income, not occupancy. Because managers hope to avoid turnover costs, rent increases are carefully administered. Depending on the local demand for apartment space, maximum income usually results in a "normal" vacancy factor. While the rent increase may encourage tenant turnover, tenants are less likely to move if (1) they are given adequate advance notice, for example, 60 days; (2) rents are not raised more than once a year; and (3) rents are increased annually by the least possible amount.

The consensus of opinion recommends strict enforcement of rent collection policy to reduce the number of incidents of habitual delinquency; practice recommends a personal visit by the resident manager to remedy delinquencies. Failure to correct a delinquency initiates legal eviction proceedings according to local legislation.

DISCUSSION QUESTIONS

1 Identify four well-defined apartment groups that can be used to analyze income and expenses.
2 What other classifications influence the available supply of apartments?
3 What are the standards for counting apartment rooms?
4 What are the main tenant groups representing a specialized demand for apartment space?
5 Explain how the demand for individual units varies with the housing market.
6 In marketing apartments, why do apartment managers recommend a ready checklist?
7 Which steps are involved in the move-in procedure?
8 How do managers qualify tenants? Explain thoroughly.
9 Explain the main elements of an apartment lease.
10 Which steps are followed in the move-out cycle?
11 As a property manager, how would you administer a rent increase? Explain fully.
12 Explain the preferred method of collecting delinquent rents.
13 Construct your own rent collection schedule.

KEY TERMS AND CONCEPTS

Elevator buildings	Rentable area
Low-rise buildings	Unit mix
Garden apartments	Ready checklist
Townhouses	Move-in procedure
Room size	Move-out procedure
Gross square feet	Rent collection policy

SELF-QUIZ

Multiple-Choice Questions

_____ 1 A three-story elevator building would be classified as: (a) A garden apartment; (b) An attached or detached townhouse; (c) A low-rise apartment building; (d) A high-rise elevator apartment building.

_____ 2 Which of the following statements is correct? (a) In listing apartments by room, the manager does not count bathrooms, porches, halls, closets, and storage space; (b) A dining and living room of less than 260 square feet is counted as one room; (c) A breakfast room of more than 100 square feet is counted as a separate room; (d) All of the above.

_____ 3 The apartment unit mix: (a) Varies according to the housing market; (b) Should consist of a single floor plan; (c) Should be designed for the least cost per square foot; (d) None of the above.

_____ 4 The inspection for final occupancy must be made with the tenant so that: (a) The tenant knows building operations; (b) The tenant signs the form showing condition of the apartment; (c) The tenant demonstrates familiarity with house rules; (d) The tenant may decide on the decorating scheme.

_____ 5 Tenants qualify for occupancy on the basis of: (a) Age and marital status; (b) Number of children; (c) The probability of their paying rent; (d) Their type of employment, such as white collar, managerial, professional, or laborer.

_____ 6 Residential leases require that tenants: (a) Maintain premises in a clean and sanitary condition; (b) Report damages and needed repairs promptly; (c) Pay charges for damages that are not the result of normal wear and tear, and permit the landlord to enter the unit for inspections or repairs; (d) All of the above.

_____ 7 Residential tenants are required by lease not to: (a) Use premises for nonresidential purposes; (b) Install appliances; (c) Infringe on rights of others or make major alterations without permission; (d) All of the above.

_____ 8 Which of the following statements is _not_ correct? (a) Maximum occupancy is more important than earning maximum returns; (b) One hundred percent occupancy will not always maximize returns: (c) After a rent increase, an apartment may show higher vacancy with higher gross income; (d) Resident managers should realize that maximum returns prevail over maximum occupancy.

_____ 9 Strict enforcement of a rental collection policy: (a) Increases vacancies; (b) Increases expenses; (c) Lowers operating expenses; (d) Discourages habitual delinquencies.

_____ 10 Personal contact has been recommended as the principal means of collecting delinquent rents because: (a) It takes less time; (b) It is cheaper than preparing notices; (c) Habitually delinquent tenants learn the rent collection procedures and respond only after receiving the final notice; (d) Personal contact is required by law.

Answer Key

1 (c), 2 (d), 3 (a), 4 (b), 5 (c), 6 (d), 7 (d), 8 (a), 9 (d), 10 (c).

Fill-In Questions

1 The _____ in an apartment building includes the basement area, mezzanines, penthouses, corridors, lobbies, stores, offices, and garages within the building.

2 Apartment developers serve the widest possible market by adapting the _____ to the current demand.

3 To ensure that apartments are in proper condition, property managers advise a
_____ .

4 If a third party takes premises for less than the remaining term of the lease, there
is a _____ .

5 In the case of apartments, leases usually require the tenant to observe _____
_____ .

6 When damages are deducted from security deposits, the tenant is not responsible
for _____ .

7 Some property managers recommend a damage deduction schedule partly based
on _____ .

8 Property managers maximize _____ and not _____ .

9 Generally, _____ have no authority to agree to accept
partial rent or promises of payment at a later date.

10 Besides evicting tenants for delinquent rents, managers may evict tenants because
of _____ violations.

Answer Key

1 gross square feet
2 unit mix
3 ready checklist
4 subletting
5 house rules

6 normal wear and tear
7 length of occupancy
8 income; occupancy
9 resident managers
10 house rules

SELECTED REFERENCES

Campbell, Marjorie: "How to Show and Rent Apartments," in *How to Manage an Apartment House*, Los Angeles: California Real Estate Association, 1974, chap. 6.

Eames, Gary: "Rent Pricing for Maximizing Revenue," *Journal of Property Management*, 42(1):47–50 (1977).

German, Dan: "Golden Rules of Residential Management," *Journal of Property Management*, 43(4):186–189 (1978).

Glassman, Sidney: *A Guide to Residential Management*, 3d ed., Washington, D.C.: National Association of Homebuilders, 1978, pp. 27–31.

Kelley, Edward N.: *Practical Apartment Management*, Chicago: Institute of Real Estate Management, 1976, pp. 185–205.

Tools for Creative Property Management, Chicago: Institute of Real Estate Management, 1974.

Chapter 12

Apartment Financial Analysis

After studying this chapter, you should be familiar with:
1 Methods of analyzing gross operating income
2 Methods of evaluating operating expenses
3 The calculation of cash flow
4 Financial ratios important to apartment investment analysis
5 Procedures followed in converting apartments to condominiums

Why is financial analysis important to apartment management? The answer may be stated in four parts:

1 Because of continuing inflation, special efforts must be taken to keep rents at a competitive market rate. The owner is highly dependent on the expertise of the property manager, with his or her special insight and sources of information.
2 Apartment expense analysis, on a per unit basis, permits property managers to make valid comparisons with apartments of like kind. Management efficiency is judged largely according to how expenses for managed property compare to expenses for similar buildings.
3 The impact of federal income taxes virtually demands that property managers give owners an analysis of the *after-tax returns* on property investment.

4 Property managers increasingly turn to financial ratios that reveal investment performance for decision-making purposes. Financial ratios give greater insight into current and prospective investment returns.

Thus, in the last analysis, property managers are selected not only for their expert knowledge and supervisory abilities but for their ability to analyze apartment operations.

While managers maximize net operating income as their main objective, the objective is subject to certain qualifications. That is, apartment managers consider not the short-run returns but the long-run impact of management policies. Furthermore, they work to preserve property amenities. In still other cases, management works to maximize capital appreciation while operating the property to earn the prevailing rate of return for comparable properties.

Accordingly, managers direct attention to the gross income and to net operating expenses, including provision for replacement of short-lived property such as appliances, lobby furniture, and other equipment. Indeed, the comparative analysis of gross income and operating expenses occupies much of their professional time. With these data at hand, managers calculate cash flow and selected financial ratios that lead to the best management plan. Their management role includes counsel on apartment conversions to condominiums, the topic that closes this chapter.

GROSS INCOME ANALYSIS

To analyze annual gross income, managers use three commonly accepted terms:

Gross Possible Rental Income *Gross possible rental income* includes (1) apartment rents collected as if all units were occupied, including apartments of employees who pay no rent; (2) rental income from garages and parking leases; and (3) rental income from stores and offices, as if they were all rented. (Statistics on gross possible rental income do not include apartment buildings in which office or store occupancy represents more than 20 percent of the total rentable area.)

Gross Possible Total Income The *gross possible total income* equals the gross possible rental income plus miscellaneous income.

Total Actual Collections *Total actual collections* are defined as the gross possible total income *less* vacancies and rental delinquencies.

The larger apartment buildings earn miscellaneous income from maid service, laundry, and other coin machines, and in some instances from gas and electricity sold to tenants on the premises. Other sources of income would be grouped in this category. The sum of gross possible rental income and miscellaneous income gives gross possible total income. From this figure, vacancies and delinquent rents are deducted, which results in total actual collections. This latter figure is equivalent to effective gross income as defined by real estate appraisers. (Some managers substitute gross scheduled income for gross possible rental income.)

Table 12-1 The Analysis of Total Actual Collections*

Annual income data	Dollars per room	Percentage of gross possible total income	Dollars per gross square foot	Dollars per rentable square foot
Rental income				
Apartments	$916.94	94.3	$2.90	$3.97
Garages; parking	21.37	2.2	.07	.09
Retail space	6.80	.7	.02	.03
Office space	11.66	1.2	.04	.05
Gross possible rental income	$956.77	98.4	$3.03	$4.14
Miscellaneous income	15.55	1.6	.05	.07
Gross possible total income	$972.32	100.0	$3.08	$4.21
Less vacancies; delinquent rents	−39.84	−4.1	−.12	−.17
Total actual collections	$931.95	95.9	$2.96	$4.04

*Because of rounding, totals may not add correctly.

Because apartments vary by the number of rooms, the gross square foot area, and the rentable square foot area, the Institute of Real Estate Management recommends that annual gross income be shown per room, per gross square foot area, and per square foot of rentable space. For additional comparison, total actual collections per year are shown as a percentage of gross possible total income per room. An elevator high-rise unfurnished building following this format would be reported in these four categories.

The format of Table 12-1 permits a comparison of total actual collections with data from other like property. For the smaller, low-rise units, miscellaneous sources of income and the rental of nonapartment space typically represents a small proportion of total actual collections. But for the larger properties, certain norms in total collections per unit will be observed. The apartment manager analyzes these data with the data for comparable apartments, adjusted for different property combinations and operating characteristics. The level of services, the age of the building, its location, and its facilities would be considered in comparing a particular property to total actual collections of other apartment buildings.

Apartment Rent Comparisons

There is a limit to the amount by which operating expenses may be reduced. Generally speaking, an apartment showing a low net operating income will experience "below market" rents. Thus, the most critical problem facing managers is to maintain total actual collections. For this reason, apartment managers continually monitor prevailing rents for competitive buildings. In making rent comparisons, it will be found that rents vary according to a few common differences among apartment projects:

1 The prestige of the apartment complex
2 Management's reputation for serving tenants
3 Differences in locational advantages

4 The tenant mix, for example, singles, the elderly, or families with children
5 The attitude of the resident manager
6 Lease terms and house rules
7 The quality of maintenance and repairs

While combinations of these differences make rental comparisons highly complex, forms have been developed to reduce judgmental errors (see Figure 12-1).

Competitive Apartment Evaluation

The form for a *competitive apartment evaluation*, shown in Figure 12-1, itemizes the more important apartment features that affect apartment rents. For example, if a two-bedroom apartment under review rents for $300 a month, and the location of the property managed is more desirable than the location of comparable properties, the monthly rent would be adjusted, say, to $310, for location.

Or alternatively, for each item compared, a quality rating from one to ten could be given. While subjective, such a rating would indicate whether the apartment building managed is rented on a basis that is comparable to those of competitive buildings.

Shoppers are also employed to review management efficiency in merchandising apartment space. To gain the maximum objectivity, property managers employ teams of shoppers to visit a competitive project on the same day in order to establish management patterns. The competitive apartment evaluation form may also be used to test the competition's competence in showing properties (see Figure 12-2).

Rental Market Comparisons

To illustrate competitive rental analysis, consider rentals for the 197-unit Villa apartments shown in Table 12-2. The 197 units produce a monthly rent of $24,670, or approximately $296,000 per year. To verify the market rent, five competitive apartments were compared to the property under management. The type of apartment, the range of monthly rent, and the monthly rent per square foot are shown in this comparison. Monthly rents for comparable properties range from $180 to $335.

Besides these direct rental comparisons, the average monthly rents and the average square foot rent were compared with the Villa apartments. As a result of these studies, management recommended rents based on competitive rents which, after a vacancy allowance of 4 percent, would increase total actual collections to $410,328. These data are summarized in Table 12-2. As a result of the competitive evaluation of similar apartment buildings, the property manager proposed an annual gross income increase of over $100,000. Final recommendations are shown in Table 12-3.

There is one remaining point. In comparing rents, managers must relate their data to average monthly rents. For on analysis, it will be found that a one-bedroom unit on the ground floor will typically rent for less than the same one-bedroom unit on the fifth floor, occupying a corner with a view. Hence, within a building, property managers vary rents according to the desirability of each apartment. A corner location, upper floors with a view, and many other factors are considered in varying rents for

Apartment feature	Rating		
Location	_____	Property shopped _____	
Accessibility	_____	Address _____	
Landscaping	_____	Manager _____	
Design	_____	Phone _____	
Parking	_____	Number	
Amenities	_____	of units Type Size Rent Furn. Vacant	
Reputation	_____	_____	
Resident profile	_____	_____	
Maintenance	_____	_____	
Unit size	_____	_____	
Unit floor plan	_____	_____	
HVAC	_____	Terms of lease _____	
Kitchen size	_____	Security _____	
Bath size	_____	Pets _____ Children _____	
Room size	_____	Parking spaces _____ Covered _____	
Appliances	_____	Pools _____ Tennis courts _____	
Carpeting	_____	Sauna _____ Clubhouse _____	
Draperies	_____	Brochure _____	
Antenna system	_____	Remarks _____	
Security	_____	_____	
Closet space	_____	_____	
Patio/balcony	_____	_____	
Window area	_____	_____	
Washer/dryer connections	_____	Shopper _____	
Lease terms	_____	Date _____	
Total	=====		

Figure 12-1 Competitive apartment evaluation. *(Source: Adapted from Roland D. Freeman, The Encyclopedia of Apartment Management, Washington, D.C.: National Apartment Association, 1976, pp. 111–112.)*

Call (512) 341 9175

ED DENNIS & Associates
1013 N.W. LOOP 410, SAN ANTONIO, TEXAS 78213

EMPLOYEE SHOPPED: DATE SHOPPED: TIME SHOPPED:

PROPERTY SHOPPED: AUTHORIZED BY:

SPECIAL INSTRUCTIONS: SHOPPER CODE:

YES/NO   (Shopper's Explanations on Part D)

A. TELEPHONE TECHNIQUE

1. Was the phone answered promptly? On which ring was it answered?_____ How many attempts were made? _____
2. Was Shopper "sold" on visiting the property? Note Employee's most effective selling phrase. _____
3. Was a DEFINITE/VAGUE (circle one) appointment made to see the property?
4. Did Employee introduce self by own name/title (circle appropriately). Indicate any title used _____
5. Did Employee ask for the name of the Shopper at the beginning/middle/end (circle appropriately) of the conversation.
6. Was an attempt made to obtain Shopper's phone number?
7. Did the Employee qualify the Shopper on the phone? Did Employee ask about children/pets/price/size/location/furniture/ employment (circle).
8. Did Employee have an acceptable phone voice? Did there appear to be a SMILE/FROWN (circle appropriately) in the Employee's voice.
9. Did the Employee project genuine interest in the Shopper? Employee did/did not use Shopper's name in the ensuing conversation.
10. Did the Employee project genuine interest in the property and its uniqueness?
11. Was over-all technique sufficient to motivate Shopper to property? Shopper rates technique as HARSH/WEAK/ROUTINE/PLEASANT/ INVITING.
12. Was it necessary for Shopper to indicate name without being asked? What name (if any) was given Employee?_____

B. APPEARANCE & INITIAL RAPPORT

1. Was Employee neat in appearance (pleasant but "business-like")? Grooming was/was not equal to the property represented (circle one).
2. Was Employee's dress, mannerisms and voice quality reflective of self-confidence, poise and "love" of position with the property?
3. Did Employee invite Shopper to come into the office? Shopper was/was not able to enter office without Employee's notice.
4. Did Employee rise or pause in a conversation to greet Shopper? Indicate greeting. _____
5. Did Employee make a self-introduction? by name? by position? (circle appropriately)
6. Did Employee ask for the Shopper's name. Employee did/did not ask for spelling. Indicate name given. _____
7. Did Employee ask Shopper to sign a guest card or log Shopper's name in traffic sheet (circle which)?
8. Did Employee qualify Shopper before showing property? Did Employee ask about children/pet/location/size/furniture/employment (circle).
9. Did Employee ask why the Shopper was moving? Employee did/did not ask for Shopper's last address and did/did not ask how long lived there.
10. Did Employee ask how many persons would be living in the apartment?
11. Did Employee ask how soon the Shopper could move onto the property?
12. Did Employee indicate that the property was selective in accepting new residents? The Employee did/did not describe residents of the property.
13. Did Employee indicate that there were more than one vacancy on the property (except as needed to rent to the Shopper)?
14. Did Employee ask questions in such a manner as to establish better rapport and encourage the Shopper to disclose information freely?
15. Did Employee listen carefully when the Shopper made comments?
16. Did Employee smoke when talking in office? when on the phone? while showing apartment(s) or amenities? (circle appropriately)
17. Did Employee mention that lease or rental agreement was required? Employee did/did not point out that it was a contract that would be enforced.
18. Did Employee attempt to verify that Shopper's interest in what was being said was sufficient to warrant showing the property?
19. Did Employee create the impression of interest in the Shopper as a prospective resident and would be interested in the Shopper if Shopper leased.
20. Did Employee use Shopper's name a little/a lot during the time spent with Shopper. How many minutes were used in office? _____ showing? _____

C. SHOWING & CLOSING

1. On the way to the apartment to be shown, did Employee point out landscaping/maintenance/management as benefits to the Shopper?
2. Upon entering the apartment/each room (circle) did the Employee make a "stage setting" comment(s) to direct Shopper's attention to a feature.
3. Did the Employee point out the MAIN advantages of EACH room shown? Note in EXPLANATIONS (below) Employee's comments (if any) on (a) living/dining areas; (b) kitchen; (c) baths; (d) bedroom(s); (e) patio/balcony; (f) closets, inside/outside storage; (g) parking provisions.
4. Did the Employee indicate that the apartment was easy to keep up?
5. Did the Employee indicate how the apartment could be decorated or ask the Shopper for suggestions on how the Shopper would decorate it?
6. Did the Employee show only apartments that were ready to be shown? If not, explain below.
7. Did the Employee adapt his/her "selling techniques" to the Shopper by drawing out Shopper's opinion and/or agreement?
8. Was the Employee confident in "product knowledge" about the community, apartment, appliances, amenities, and/or project policy?
9. Did the Employee point out and "sell" the amenities of the property?
10. Did the Employee point out the location of the property in relation to area streets, highways, bus lines, schools, shopping, churches, etc.?
11. Did Employee point out the features of the property in such a manner as to emphasize the direct BENEFITS to the resident?
12. Did the Employee ask when the Shopper could move in?
13. Did the Employee offer any "free rent" or other "give away?"
14. Did the Employee ask the Shopper for a deposit on an apartment?
15. Did the Employee indicate that there were other persons interested in leasing the apartment?
16. Did the Employee "sell" the amenities of the property? Indicate amenities pointed out by Employee in EXPLANATIONS (below).
17. Did the Employee indicate that there were any management/resident organized group activities of the property?
18. Did the Employee invite the Shopper to return to the office after the showings?
19. Did the Employee try for a "close" while in the apartment shown/on the way back to the office/in the office after showing (circle appropriately).
20. Did the Employee again try to obtain a phone number or another method of contacting the Shopper to "follow up" after the Shopper's visit?
21. Did the Employee refrain from suggesting that the Shopper see specific properties or use other services other than those of the property's owner?
22. Did the Employee offer descriptive literature and/or a business card of the property to the Shopper?
23. Did the Employee use "closing" techniques based on what the Shopper had said on the telephone and/or during the visit to the property?
24. Did the Employee frequently refer to the Shopper by the name the Shopper had given?
25. If the Shopper were actually the "prospect portrayed" would that "prospect" have taken the apartment?

Figure 12-2 Apartment shopper's report. *(Source: Roland D. Freeman, The Encyclopedia of Apartment Management, Washington, D.C.: National Apartment Association, 1976, pp. 111-114.)*

Table 12-2 Rental Market Comparison

Apartment project	Square feet	Monthly rent, $	Monthly rent per square foot, $
Dover Cliffs apartments			
Jr. 1-bedroom	480	205–220	.42–.46
1-bedroom	560	225–240	.40–.43
Modern garden apartments			
Studio	425	180	.42
1-bedroom	644	230	.36
2-bedroom	974	290	.30
Cortex apartments			
1-bedroom	622	230	.37
2-bedroom	736	265	.36
Sunroof apartments			
1-bedroom	624	225	.36
2-bedroom, 1-bath	692	250	.36
2-bedroom, 2-bath	841	280	.33
Mona apartments			
1-bedroom	725	260	.36
2-bedroom, 2-bath	900	335	.37
Villa apartments (under management)			
Studio	444–500	135–160	.31–.32
1-bedroom	604–648	225–255	.37–.39
2-bedroom, 1-bath	831	275–290	.33–.35
2-bedroom, 1½-bath	982	225	.23

Source: Data have been supplied by Lloyd Hanford, Jr., CPM, San Francisco, California, and have been rounded.

the same apartment floor plan. Moreover, as tenants change, rents provided in new leases will vary from rents on the same apartment under existing leases. For this reason, in making comparisons managers express rents as an average for each apartment type.

OPERATING EXPENSE ANALYSIS

Unlike some other property types, apartment buildings have no standard set of accounts for recording operating expenses. This is partly because some apartment operators hire staff to perform ordinary maintenance tasks, such as window washing and exterior painting. Others provide for these services by employing outside contractors. Since payrolls are not recorded functionally, one apartment building might have unusually large payroll expenses, while another might show larger expenditures for contract services. Therefore, in interpreting apartment expenses, it should be

Table 12-3 Recommended Competitive Market Rents

	Average monthly rent	Monthly rent	Annual rent
1 Small studio	$145	$ 145	$ 1,740
56 Studio, junior 1-bedroom	155	8,680	104,160
21 Small 1-bedroom	170	3,570	42,840
78 Standard 1-bedroom	180	14,040	168,480
25 2-bedroom, 1-bath	200	5,000	60,000
16 Townhouses, 2-bedroom, 1½-bath	240	3,840	46,080
Gross rental income		$35,275	$423,300
Less vacancy and delinquent rent (4%)		-1,411	-16,932
Subtotal		$33,864	$406,368
Miscellaneous income		330	3,960
Total collections		$34,194	$410,328

realized that individual expenses vary from one apartment building to another, because payrolls in one apartment could cover employees who perform certain duties that are contracted out by competitive apartments.

Functional Operating Expenses

Even though there is no standard set of accounts, there are certain functional operating expenses typical of most apartment buildings. These expenses, which are identified in Figure 12-3, apply mostly to high-rise elevator apartments. For the smaller units, certain expenses such as those for porters, maids, telephone operators, and security personnel would be omitted. It will be appreciated further that the relative importance of expenses varies not only among individual buildings, but among different types of apartment buildings, of different ages and conditions, and in different geographic regions.

Operating Expense Comparisons

For comparison purposes, it is useful to compare the relative importance of expenses by broader groups than by the accounts listed in Figure 12-3. In illustration, the percentage of annual gross possible total income per room by broad categories indicates the general importance of the main expenses of operation. These data are shown in Table 12-4.

This table indicates the importance of certain expenses that managers try to minimize. First, however, it will be realized that net operating income will be sensitive to changes in gross possible total income. If actual rents are less than the prevailing market rent, net operating income will be distorted downward. Similarly, every effort will be made to reduce annual vacancy and delinquent rents.

Given these qualifications, payroll expenses, supplies, decorating, repairs, and maintenance account for 19.3 percent of gross possible total income. The second highest group of expenses includes insurance and taxes, 14.9 percent, of which real estate taxes represent the largest single expense of operation. In this example, utility

Payroll expenses
Administrative
   Resident manager
   Assistant manager
   Clerical
Maintenance
   Engineer
   Maintenance
Custodial
   Porters
   Maids
Telephone operators
Security
Doorman
Garageman
Groundskeeper
Painters
Vacations
Bonuses
Payroll taxes
Group hospitalization
Pension contribution

Administrative expenses
Audit fee
Credit reports
Donations
Dues and subscriptions
Legal expenses
Licenses and permits
Management fee
Miscellaneous administrative
Postage
Stationery and printing

Utilities
Electricity
Fuel
Gas
Telephone
Sewer
Water

Repairs and maintenance
Appliances
Building and building equipment
Electrical
Elevator
Grounds
Heat and air conditioning
Plumbing
TV

Supplies
Electrical
Hardware
Janitor
Miscellaneous
Paper products
Plumbing

Redecoration
Contractor—interior painting
Paint—interior
Painters—interior
Contractor—exterior painting
Paint—exterior
Painters—exterior

Services
Building cleaning
Extermination
Music
Security
Service contracts
Snow removal
Trash removal
Uniforms
Window cleaning

Swimming pool
Contract
Repairs
Supplies

Advertising
Newspaper
Brochures
Other

Miscellaneous operating expenses
Equipment rental
Furniture rental
Miscellaneous
Motor vehicle

Other fixed expenses
Insurance
Real estate taxes
Franchise tax
Personal property tax
Other

Figure 12-3 Functional apartment operating expenses.

**Table 12-4   Median Average Operating Expenses per Room:
Elevator Unfurnished Buildings**

	Percentage of annual gross possible income per room*	
Gross possible rental income	98.9	
Miscellaneous other income	2.6	100.0
Less vacancies and rent loss		-2.6
Total collections		96.0
Less expenses		
Management costs	5.7	
Other administrative	1.5	
Subtotal administrative	(7.2)	
Supplies	.7	
Heating fuel	6.7	
Electricity	9.0	
Water/sewer	1.7	
Gas	1.1	
Building services	.9	
Other operating	.7	
Subtotal operating	(17.8)	
Security	1.1	
Grounds maintenance	.5	
Maintenance, repairs	5.0	
Painting/decorating	1.8	
Subtotal maintenance	(8.3)	
Real estate taxes	11.9	
Other tax/fee/permit	.4	
Insurance	1.7	
Subtotal tax-insurance	(13.9)	
Recreational/amenities	.5	
Other payroll	6.5	
Total all expenses		56.2
Net operating income		40.8

*Detail may not add because individual items represent averages of reporting buildings and because of the method of reporting.

Source: Income/Expense Analysis: Apartments, Chicago: Institute of Real Estate Management, 1978, p. 56.

costs (which vary by type of apartment, construction features, regional location, and type of fuel) absorb 13.9 percent of gross possible total income. With the addition of administrative and management fees of 6.4 percent, operating expenses total 53.5 percent of gross possible total income.

Note, however, that in these data, no allowance has been made for replacement of short-lived assets such as refrigerators, appliances, and lobby furniture. To show the true operating costs of an apartment, an allowance must be made for the replacement of these items on an accrual basis. While not a direct cash outlay each year, there is an annual cost of "using up" refrigerators or other appliances over their economic life.

Replacement Reserves

Replacement reserves refer to an annual allowance for replacing fixtures and other equipment. In listing apartments for sale, real estate brokers often fail to report an annual allowance for replacements, since these sums would not be included on the owner's operating statement. The consequence is to overstate the operating income.

Some authorities recommend reserving 3 percent of gross income for replacements. An older building showing considerable deferred maintenance would require a much higher figure. In contrast, a 2-year-old building would require a lower replacement reserve.

An alternative method estimates the life of the equipment, providing an annual reserve to replace individual items over their estimated life.

For instance, assume that 200 refrigerators cost $250 each or $50,000 total. With a 15 year estimated life, the annual cost would be $3,333.33 ($50,000/15). This procedure is illustrated in Table 12-5 for short-lived items needing periodic replacement. Without suitable estimates for replacement reserves, net operating income would be distorted upward.

Operating Expenses per Unit

While a detailed review of each account would be made in preparing the annual budget, for analytical purposes it is common to analyze operating income and expenses by broad groups reduced to the price per apartment, per square foot, and per room.

The expenses listed in Table 12-6 apply to a 204-unit apartment building developed for low-income occupancy. In this instance the maintenance and repair allowance provides for the replacement of refrigerators, ovens, and range tops over a 5-year cycle. Since the apartment is an all-electric unit, the annual expenses for electricity only cover space heating in the public areas. Total expenses as a percentage of gross possible income, 44.9 percent, closely agree with typical expenses of high-rise elevator unfurnished apartments.

Expenses, reduced to per unit values and shown as a percentage of the gross possible income, allow the property manager to make comparisons between their operating costs and those of like buildings. The main variations will be found in

Table 12-5   The Calculation of Replacement Reserves

Item	Life of item (yrs)	Number of items	Individual cost per item	Annual reserve amount
Stoves	15	200	$250	$ 3,333.33
Refrigerators	15	200	250	3,333.33
Carpets	8	200	600	15,000.00
Drapes	7	200	175	5,000.00
Fixtures	15	for 200 units	100	1,333.33

Source: Daniel G. Carless, "More than Rents and Repairs," *Real Estate Today,* **11**(5):26 (1978).

Table 12-6 Apartment Expense Analysis: Summarized

Expense item	Annual expenses	Annual expenses per room	Expenses per gross square foot	Percentage of gross possible income
Payroll	$ 27,570	$ 48.54	$0.19	10.4
Utilities				
Electricity	9,900	17.43	0.07	3.7
Water	5,000	8.80	0.03	1.9
Management	8,150	14.08	0.05	3.0
Administrative costs	13,120	22.89	0.09	4.9
Painting and decorating	10,430	17.61	0.07	3.8
Maintenance and repairs	20,270	35.70	0.14	7.7
Supplies	1,200	2.11	0.01	0.5
Miscellaneous operating expenses	975	1.72	0.01	0.4
Insurance	2,200	3.87	0.02	0.8
Real estate taxes	20,710	36.46	0.14	7.8
Total	$119,525	$209.21	$0.82	44.9

Source: Data calculated by the author.

payrolls, utilities, and maintenance expenses and repairs. If property taxes are non-conforming to those of like property, the property manager has grounds for appealing the assessment with the local assessor. By comparing costs per unit with those of like properties, the property manager will establish a norm showing the level of services and their costs, to use in management decision making.

Operating Expense Projections

From these detailed per unit figures, management may prepare an operating budget showing the projected net operating income. To show how expense items are derived, Table 12-7 lists expense items projected for an apartment building after owner reports have been analyzed.

With total actual collections projected at $410,328, and after considering miscellaneous income, vacancy, and delinquent rents of 4 percent, the manager projects each expense with an explanation. While these expenses may vary individually over time, the technique of expense estimation deserves added explanation.

In considering utilities, the appraiser referred to the electric utility costs supplied by the local public utility. After reviewing past electric utility expenses, the manager projected the annual budget at $21,600. By referring to public utility records (with the owner's permission), managers may analyze more detailed records. Similarly, the water expenses are taken from the expenses of the preceding year, adjusted for projected rate increases. Telephone answering services and scavenger service are derived from contract rates of local companies. Payroll salaries and employee benefits, totaling $35,454, are based on the following annual allowances:

On-site manager	$12,000
Maintenance worker, $800/mo	9,600
Ground maintenance worker, $4.00/hr	8,320
Assistant manager	2,400
Total	$32,320
Add: vacation pay	1,243
employer salary taxes	1,891
Total	$35,454

The salary expense includes the rental cost of one apartment reserved for the on-site manager. Salary rates are based on the union scale in each category.

In considering repairs and maintenance, this figure covers the elevator maintenance contract and the cost of minor replacement parts; ground maintenance is undertaken by the staff maintenance men. Similarly, painting is based on a 4-year life for apartments and a 3-year life for public areas, which results in an average annual cost of $175 per apartment and $1,800 for repainting public areas. Carpet replacement is based on a 7-year life at an average cost of $350 per apartment and $800 per hallway (carpets of lower quality would justify a lower average life). Apartment cleaning is

Table 12-7
Projected Net Operating Income and Expenses:
A High-Rise Elevator Apartment

Gross possible rental income		$423,300
Add miscellaneous income		+3,960
Gross possible total income		$427,260
Less vacancies and delinquent rents		−16,932
Total actual collections		$410,328
Less expenses:		
Utilities	$21,600	
Water	2,400	
Telephone/answering service	1,500	
Scavenger service	10,680	
Salaries, salary tax, and fringe	35,454	
Repairs and maintenance	5,000	
Painting	10,400	
Carpet replacement	11,450	
Apartment cleaning	1,725	
Landscape maintenance	600	
Supplies and office equipment	1,800	
Pest control	960	
Security patrol	4,800	
Miscellaneous expenses	600	
Advertising	1,500	
Management fee	16,413	
Insurance	1,620	
Property taxes	72,221	
Total expenses		−200,723
Net operating income (as stabilized)		$209,605

based on a 35 percent tenant rate of turnover. Landscape maintenance refers to contract services supplementing the staff grounds worker.

Security control is derived from a bid for patrol services at $2 per unit per month. Advertising of $125 per month was believed reasonable for this particular apartment. Similarly, the management fee of 4 percent and the property tax projections are based on past experience. In sum, the total expense of 40 percent of gross possible income agrees with other projects and experience of the manager in managing like buildings. The final estimate of net operating income provides the basis for investment analysis.

APARTMENT INVESTMENT ANALYSIS

Because property managers have access to current and past operating expenses, they commonly make investment projections. For instance, cash flow projections reveal the after-tax effects of rehabilitating an apartment project. *Cash flow* refers to income remaining after income tax and mortgage payments. Because of the allowable tax deductions on income properties, property owners who pay income tax rates of 40 percent or more are often less concerned with net operating income than with the money remaining after tax and mortgage payments.

Cash Flow Analysis

To illustrate this point, consider a 204-unit apartment building, rehabilitated at a cost of $300,000. This sum was required to replace carpets, repaint public areas, redecorate the lobby and hallways, and add security locks. The rehabilitation included other minor repairs, such as installing new drapery rods and curtains, adding storm windows, and correcting for deferred maintenance of the grounds.

In this instance the property manager projected gross income according to a revised rent schedule that resulted in an annual net operating income (after a 10 percent vacancy allowance) of $141,762. To show the tax flow over the first 10 years of investment, certain assumptions were made:

> Federal personal net income tax rate: 50 percent
> State and net income tax rate: 6 percent
> First mortgage financing: $1,000,000, 9.5%, 25 years
> Depreciation schedule: 125 percent of straight-line rates

The depreciation was based on a 40-year life, a straight-line rate of 2.5 percent, and a 125 percent declining-balance depreciation rate of 3.125 percent (2.5 X 1.25). The depreciation was based on a building depreciable basis of $1,092,574 and a personal property worth of $58,500. Personal property was depreciated straight line over a 5-year term. Given these assumptions, the cash flow over the first 10 years is shown in Table 12-8.

Note that at the end of the first year, cash flow before taxes of $36,918 remains after payment of principal and interest. Re-adding the principal and deducting depreciation results in a taxable income of $1,360, which increases to $23,671 at the end of

Table 12-8 Cash Flow Analysis of a 204-Unit Apartment

					Projected cash flows					
	Year 1	2	3	4	5	6	7	8	9	10
Income after taxes										
Net operating income	$141,762	$141,762	$141,762	$141,762	$141,762	$141,762	$141,762	$141,762	$141,762	$141,762
Debt service first mortgage:										
Principal	10,285	11,306	12,429	13,663	15,020	16,511	18,150	19,952	21,933	24,110
Interest	94,559	93,538	92,415	91,181	89,825	88,333	86,694	84,892	82,911	80,734
Principal and interest	-104,844	-104,844	-104,844	-104,844	-104,845	-104,844	-104,844	-104,844	-104,844	-104,844
Cash flow before taxes	$ 36,918	$ 36,918	$ 36,918	$ 36,918	$ 36,917	$ 36,918	$ 36,918	$ 36,918	$ 36,918	$ 36,918
Principal—first mortgage	10,285	11,306	12,429	13,663	15,020	16,511	18,150	19,952	21,933	24,110
Depreciation—real	- 34,143	- 33,076	- 32,042	- 31,041	- 30,071	- 29,131	- 28,221	- 27,339	- 26,485	- 25,657
Depreciation—personal	- 11,700	- 11,700	- 11,700	- 11,700	- 11,700	- 11,700	- 11,700	- 11,700	- 11,700	- 11,700
Taxable income (or shelter)	$ 1,360	$ 3,448	$ 5,605	$ 7,840	$ 10,166	$ 12,598	$ 15,147	$ 17,831	$ 20,666	$ 23,671
Income tax	-680	-1,724	-2,802	-3,920	-5,083	-6,299	-7,573	-8,915	-10,333	-11,836
State tax	-82	-207	-336	-470	-610	-756	-909	-1,070	-1,240	-1,420
Income after taxes	$ 598	$ 1,517	$ 2,467	$ 3,450	$ 4,473	$ 5,543	$ 6,665	$ 7,846	$ 9,093	$ 10,415
Depreciation—real	34,143	33,076	32,042	31,041	30,071	29,131	28,221	27,339	26,485	25,657
Depreciation—personal	11,700	11,700	11,700	11,700	11,700	11,700	11,700	11,700	11,700	11,700
Principal—first mortgage	-10,285	-11,306	-12,429	-13,663	-15,020	-16,511	-18,150	-19,952	-21,933	-24,110
Cash flow after taxes	$ 36,156	$ 34,987	$ 33,780	$ 32,528	$ 31,224	$ 29,863	$ 28,436	$ 26,933	$ 25,345	$ 23,662
Equity returns										
Equity buildup from original equity of $296,739	$307,024	$318,330	$330,758	$344,422	$359,442	$375,953	$394,103	$414,055	$435,988	$460,098
Taxable income/equity	.44%	1.08%	1.69%	2.28%	2.83%	3.35%	3.84%	4.31%	4.74%	5.14%
Cash flow/equity	11.78%	10.99%	10.21%	9.44%	8.69%	7.94%	7.22%	6.50%	5.81%	5.14%
Return on equity	46.17%	44.53%	42.86%	41.16%	39.44%	37.71%	35.97%	34.24%	32.52%	30.81%

the tenth year. The cash flow or income remaining after taxes and mortgage payments (including depreciation) amounts to $36,156 at the end of the first year. The cash flow decreases to $23,662 at the end of the tenth year. Note further that this example assumes unchanging operating income and expenses.

Based on these assumptions, the investor benefits further from equity build-up resulting from mortgage principal repayments each year. Cash flow expressed as a percentage of the original equity of $296,739 provides an 11.78 percent rate of return for the first year, declining to 5.14 percent by the tenth year. Relating the net operating income of $141,762 to the original equity of $296,739 shows an annual return on equity ranging from 46.16 percent to 30.81 percent.

Financial Ratios

In addition to requiring cash flow analysis that shows the after-tax income, investment analysis depends on a series of financial ratios important to investment decisions. For the property shown in Table 12-8, these ratios may be calculated as follows.

Debt Service Coverage Prudence dictates that net operating income be sufficient to cover mortgage payments in addition to providing a suitable reserve. This is referred to as *debt service coverage* and is calculated as:

$$\text{Debt service coverage} = \frac{\text{net operating income}}{\text{total mortgage payment}}$$

$$= \frac{\$141,762}{\$104,844}$$

$$= 1.35 \text{ or } 135\%$$

The data reveal that net income is 135 percent of the mortgage payment—or 10 percent above the 125 percent minimum industry standard. In other words, income may decline by $36,918 ($141,762 to $104,844) or some 26 percent and still provide enough to make mortgage payments.

Operating Expense Ratio In comparing the expenses with net operating income, the manager compares the projected expenses of the property managed with those of comparable properties. The operating expense ratio shows operating expenses as a percentage of total actual collections:

$$\text{Operating expense ratio} = \frac{\text{operating expenses}}{\text{total actual collections}}$$

$$= \frac{\$224,142}{\$365,904}$$

$$= .61 \text{ or } 61\%$$

If the operating expenses ratio is above the ratios for comparable properties, either the rents are below market, the vacancy rate is unusually high, or operating expenses are excessive. By turning to these variables, the manager may explain unusually high or low operating expense ratios and take corrective measures.

The Break-Even Ratio   There will be a minimum occupancy rate required to meet expenses and mortgage payments. Thus, to break even, the total actual collections must be equal to the sum of the operating expenses and mortgage payments. For the property shown in Table 12-8, the break-even ratio would be equal to:

$$\text{Break-even ratio} = \frac{\text{operating expenses} + \text{mortgage payments}}{\text{gross possible income}}$$

$$= \frac{\$224,142 + \$104,844}{\$406,560}$$

$$= .809 \text{ or } 80.9\%$$

With the given total actual collections and mortgage payments and projected operating expenses, the project must earn at least 80.9 percent of total actual collections to meet expenses and mortgage payments, or a minimum net operating income of $328,986. A vacancy rate of more than 19.1 percent means that the project will not meet operating expenses and mortgage payments.

Property Tax Assessment Ratios   Since property taxes represent the single largest operating expense, managers carefully review the fairness of the property tax. To make valid comparisons, managers reduce property taxes to a series of assessment ratios. They show property taxes per unit, per room, per square foot, and as a percentage of market value and gross income. These ratios are summarized here:

Property tax assessment ratios

Property taxes per unit	$201
Property taxes per room	$ 68
Property taxes per square foot	$ .27
The ratio of property taxes to market value	3.4%
The ratio of property taxes to gross income	10.1%
The total assessed value as a percentage of market value	48.5%
Land assessed value as a percentage of land value	59.3%
Building assessed value as a percentage of building value	43.9%

After converting annual property taxes per apartment, per room, and per square foot, managers may judge the fairness of property taxes by comparing these data with similar ratios for other projects. In making this comparison, it will be realized that property taxes assume a normal relationship based on per unit values. While there will be some variation in property tax ratios, extreme departures from typical values deserve investigation.

For example, if property taxes as a percentage of market value are above the local norm, then either the estimate of market value is unusually low or the property is overassessed. By the same token, if property taxes are normally 20 percent of gross income, and if the same ratio is 30 percent for a particular building, either the assessed value is too high or the gross income is too low. Likewise, assessed values must show a typical ratio to land and building values. In the present case the property tax ratios compare favorably with those of other buildings. Unusual or atypical ratios would constitute grounds for appealing the assessment.

APARTMENT CONVERSIONS TO CONDOMINIUMS

Apartment conversions appeal to investors who face rent control or the prospects of rent control and who hope to realize capital appreciation by the sale of apartment units as condominiums. Tenants purchase apartments converted to condominiums to gain advantages of ownership; namely, income tax deductibility of mortgage interest and property taxes, equity build-up, and the possibility of capital appreciation.

To the condominium sponsor, apartment conversions have certain advantages over the development of new condominiums:

1 The location of existing apartment buildings is frequently superior to available locations for new construction.

2 A substantial proportion of tenants may be expected to purchase their rented apartment; frequently 30 to 40 percent of tenants purchase their rented unit.

3 Income from leases continues until apartments are ready for condominium sale, thus providing a source of income during conversion.

Realization of these advantages depends largely on the selection of apartments adapted to conversion.

Selection of Apartments for Conversion

Condominium units converted from apartments must be readily marketable. While not all apartment units will satisfy conversion requirements, the most successful conversion projects include apartments with certain special characteristics:

1 Preferably a substantial number of tenants will have savings for the down payment and will qualify for mortgage credit.

2 The available financing and the price of the unit should make mortgage payments competitive with the prevailing rent. Mortgage payments after taxes are compared to rent payments.

3 The apartment project should be located in an area with well-maintained buildings.

4 The ideal apartment for conversion will have facilities or space for a swimming pool, clubhouse, and other recreational facilities, such as tennis courts, saunas, cabanas, and parking.

5 The floor plan mix should be dominated by two- and three-bedroom apartment units. While one-bedroom units may be converted, the demand for two- and three-bedroom units dominates the condominium market.

Developers have reported that older-style high-rise buildings constructed in the form of the alphabet letters, that is, H, E, U, have little appeal since their view and ownership amenities are minimized. Because condominium owners desire more amenities than renters do, apartments suited to condominiums should have the extra features found in buildings originally constructed as condominiums.

Conversion Rehabilitation

Conversion to condominiums requires that each apartment be placed in like-new condition and that common areas be similarly treated with the appropriate repairs and maintenance. For instance, consider the conversion of a 545-unit apartment ideally located for schools, employment, shopping, and highway access, with 700 uncovered parking spaces, consisting of the following unit mix:

Unit type	Number of units	Size (ft^2)
Efficiency, 1-bath	5	426
1-bedroom (small), 1-bath	5	552
1-bedroom, 1-bath	131	759
1-bedroom-and-den, 1-bath	13	892
2-bedroom, 1½-bath	206	989
2-bedroom-and-den, 1½-bath	11	1,122
3-bedroom, 2-bath	153	1,161
3-bedroom-and-den, 2-baths	21	1,296
Total	545	

Source: HUD Condominium Cooperative Study, vol. III, Washington, D.C.: Department of Housing and Urban Development, 1975, p. B-31.

As apartments, these units rented from $150 to $300 per month. The conversion operation statement called for $200,000 of improvements to the common area, including $70,000 for landscaping. The conversion was budgeted to

> paint the building exterior
> repaint and seal the swimming pool
> replace the swimming pool filtering system
> repair concrete around the swimming pool
> resurface internal streets and parking areas
> construct two new tennis courts
> paint, repair, and refurnish common buildings
> install an entrance wall and security gate

Rehabilitation of individual units was planned at an average of $3,000 per apartment. The total cost of rehabilitation was projected with an assumed average sales price of $25,000 according to the following estimate:

	Conversion expenses (in thousands)
Purchase price	$ 7,500
Unit renovation	1,000
Common area renovation	200
Interest on interim loan	1,200
Permanent financing fees	300
Reserve buildup	100
Miscellaneous	200
Total conversion expenses	$10,500

To estimate project feasibility, it was necessary to compare a typical mortgage payment with present apartment rents. For this purpose a 20 percent income tax rate was assumed. The example below applies to a two-bedroom, one-and-a-half-bath unit that rented for $220 per month. The purchase price was $25,000 and was financed with a first mortgage requiring $2,500 equity and a closing cost of $500.

Mortgage payment (8% loan)		
Principal	$ 10	
Interest	155	$165
Condominium fee (includes utilities)		65
Real estate taxes and insurance		40
Total monthly outlay		$270
Less: Equity buildup	$ 10	
Tax savings (20% bracket)	37	
		-47
Condominium payments comparable to rent		$223

In this example, principal payments are shown as an average over the first 5 years of ownership. The after-tax monthly cost of ownership ($223) compares favorably with the monthly rent ($220). Thus the prospect may realize the advantages of ownership at a cost competitive with apartment rents.

Tenant Relations

The displacement of tenants by condominium ownership has led to local legislation governing tenant rights in conversion projects. If a project is proposed for conversion, care is taken in preventing rumors that lead to tenant turnover in anticipation of conversion. In this respect owners try to postpone tenant moves and maintain tenant goodwill for later condominium marketing.

Some developers postpone announcing conversion until the condominium has been established. One successful converter decorated a model beautifully and showed it to tenants at a cocktail party 60 days before the conversion began. Appointments were then made with individual tenants to explain how the conversion would affect their tenancy. It was explained how management would assist tenants to move and relocate. Information was provided on planned improvements, the refurbishing in individual units, and the tax benefits of owning as compared to renting. The tenants were given the right to buy units 30 days before the units were offered on the market. Some developers give tenants discounts and grant allowances for tenant self-improvements.[1]

In adapting the conversion to tenant ownership, surveys have shown, some problems may be anticipated before initial closings of the condominium and other problems develop after initial closings. In the first instance, project failures have been traced to misrepresentation of condominiums to new purchasers. Developers have "oversold" the condominium concept. In unrealistically raising tenant-purchasers' expectations, among persons who have not previously owned property, buyers misunderstand promises made by salespersons. Others have reported problems caused by poor-quality construction. The more successful projects have offered warranties against structural defects.

Dissatisfaction has been expressed for still other reasons, including delayed closings that can be traced to permanent lenders, the lengthy time necessary to prepare for condominium documents, and delays in processing mortgage applications. Some managers have reported that purchasers who were formerly tenants expect the same services, like interior maintenance, that they received as tenants. It is not uncommon to find owners on the first floor objecting to maintenance fees that include elevator operating expenses. Likewise, nonswimmers sometimes complain about maintenance fees that include swimming pool expenses.

After the developer has closed condominium sales, some purchasers have reported that developers have exercised excessive control over condominium operations before all units are sold. For example, developers have not always paid monthly condominium fees on unsold units, which means that early purchasers have either received less in the way of services or shouldered the burden of extra financing for association expenses. Slow sales have encouraged developers to rent unsold units, which leads to conflicts between renters and owners.

Marketing Converted Units

Unlike the case of single-family dwellings or even new condominiums, the marketing program for converted units must start with the initial organization of the condominium. While the management firm begins detailed plans for conversion, a separate marketing organization begins by sending letters to tenants, explaining that conversion is underway and that tenants will be given sufficient time to relocate (preferably 60 or more days). Each tenant is given a 30-day right of first refusal on all units. Some developers offer (1) a discount effective only before the unit is offered to the public and (2) a lump sum deduction from the listed price if they purchase the unit as is, that is, before recarpeting, repainting, and other renovation.

The marketing budget may be arranged so that tenants who elect not to purchase are offered moving and relocation assistance. The marketing program delays renovation of units in which nonbuying tenants elect to remain until their leases expire.

---

[1] See Herbert L. Aist, "Preparation for Marketing," in *How to Convert Apartments to Condominiums*, Los Angeles: California Real Estate Association, 1973, pp. 58–59.

For exposure to the public, the renovated unit serves as the professionally decorated model. Salespersons making the initial contact with visitors attempt to learn early in the interview:

1 Is this a return visit?
2 What attracted the prospect—newspaper want ads or referrals from friends?
3 Does the prospect live in the area (local prospects may purchase and stay in the area with the same friends, churches, and schools)?
4 How soon does the prospect want to move?

Advertisements are directed toward apartment dwellers in key areas; they concentrate on the 25- to 35-year-olds, the young marrieds, bachelors, and career persons. In explaining the advantages of purchasing a converted unit, salespersons emphasize these points:

1 Apartment conversions cost less than newly constructed condominiums.
2 Converted apartments capitalize on prime locations unavailable for new condominium construction.
3 Rising rent levels place tenants at a disadvantage in relation to condominium owners.

Because the marketing of conversion units requires a canvass of local apartment dwellers, direct mail is widely used to reach tenants in neighboring apartment buildings. Local papers circulated within the neighborhood are also effective in reaching nearby tenants. Outdoor advertising and display advertising in the daily newspapers supplement these efforts.

SUMMARY

In analyzing apartment operations, managers deal with the *gross possible rental income*, which includes rents from apartments, garages, stores, and offices. *Gross possible total income* consists of rents and miscellaneous income. *Total actual collections* are defined as gross possible total income, less vacancies and rental delinquencies. To make valid comparisons with like properties, these data are reduced to (1) a percent of gross possible total income, (2) dollars per square foot, and (3) dollars per rentable square foot.

Because of the difficulty involved in comparing rents directly, managers employ the *competitive apartment evaluation form*, which itemizes and rates comparable apartment buildings. For some purposes, these details are secured by shoppers who report on telephone techniques, appearance, initial rapport, and showing and closing techniques. The same type of rating system helps measure the efficiency of resident managers. With these comparisons, rents are established for the property managed on a competitive level.

Operating expenses, while reviewed on an individual item-by-item basis, are grouped in larger categories and reduced to expenses (1) per room, (2) per gross square foot, and (3) as a percentage of gross possible income. When expenses are converted to per unit values, valid comparisons may be made with competitive and fairly similar buildings. Just as total actual collections are analyzed by comparisons with other buildings, managers go into detail in reviewing expenses of operation.

Property managers convert income and operating expense data to a cash flow format, particularly for buildings that may undergo renovations. *Cash flow* shows the amount of income remaining after income taxes and mortgage payments. To make these calculations, property managers must make assumptions with respect to income tax rates, mortgage financing, and the depreciation schedule. With computer analysis, cash flow may be calculated over several years, showing the return on equity after taxes.

To give greater insight into the investment feasibility, apartment investments are judged with respect to certain financial ratios; for example, *debt service coverage* shows net operating income as a percentage of the total mortgage payment. That is, net operating income must be at least 125 percent greater than the total mortgage payment. Similarly, the *operating expense ratio* indicates operating expenses as a percentage of total actual collections. The *breakeven ratio* suggests the maximum vacancy and rental delinquencies that will still permit the project to pay operating expenses and mortgage payments.

Property tax assessments, which are ordinarily the single largest operating expense, are judged according to several ratios that show assessment uniformity. Property managers, in dealing with numerous properties, establish typical property taxes per unit, per room, and per square foot, and they judge property taxes as a ratio to market value and annual gross income. There is also, typically, a common ratio of the assessed value to market value.

Because apartment conversions to condominiums have certain advantages over new construction, they will continue in popularity. Apartment conversions are recommended because the location of existing apartment buildings is frequently superior to available locations for new construction. Investors favor apartment conversions because tenants may be expected to purchase a significant proportion of converted apartments. In addition, the income from leases helps finance apartment conversions.

Not all apartments are suitable for conversion; projects selected must have the highest degree of amenities common to new condominium projects. The purchase price and financing should be such that after-tax mortgage payments are competitive with prevailing rents.

Ordinarily, conversion calls for substantial rehabilitation of the common area and modernization of each apartment. Furthermore, under conversion, good tenant relations become critical. To promote goodwill, tenants are given 60 days or more to relocate, and if they elect to purchase they are usually granted price concessions that are not available to the general public. The marketing program concentrates on tenants in neighboring apartment buildings. Direct mail and neighborhood newspapers are ideally suited to reach these prospects.

DISCUSSION QUESTIONS

1 Define the technical terms used to analyze gross income.
2 Show how total actual collections are reduced to per unit values.
3 What information would be obtained in a competitive apartment evaluation?
4 Explain how you would undertake a rental market comparison.
5 What are the main functional apartment operating expenses?
6 Show how you would compare average operating expenses; give an example showing how operating expenses are reduced to per unit values.
7 What items would be shown in a cash flow analysis?
8 Give an example of how you would calculate a cash flow statement.
9 Explain debt service coverage. Give an example in illustration of your answer.
10 Define the operating expense ratio.
11 Show with an example how you would calculate the breakeven ratio.
12 How would you judge the fairness of property taxes?
13 Explain why apartment conversions appeal to investors and apartment tenants.
14 What criteria would you recommend in selecting an apartment for condominium conversion?
15 What costs would typically be encountered in apartment conversion?
16 Explain common methods of marketing condominium units.

KEY TERMS AND CONCEPTS

Gross possible rental income
Gross possible total income
Total actual collections
Competitive apartment evaluation
Cash flow analysis
Declining-balance depreciation

Straight-line depreciation
Debt service coverage
Operating expense ratio
The breakeven ratio
Assessment ratios

SELF-QUIZ

Multiple-Choice Questions

_____ 1 Total actual collections are defined as: (a) Rental income from all sources; (b) Gross possible rental income and miscellaneous income; (c) Gross possible total income, less vacancies and rental delinquencies; (d) Gross possible rental income, less vacancies and rental delinquencies.

_____ 2 Apartment rent comparisons are made with the assistance of: (a) An apartment shopper's report; (b) Apartment rent comparisons shown as a percent of gross possible income; (c) Apartment rent comparisons shown per room or per square foot; (d) All of the above.

_____ 3 Cash flow analysis requires assumptions with respect to: (a) The age of the apartment building, mortgage financing, and income taxes; (b) The depreciation schedule, corporate net income taxes, and capital gains taxes; (c) Income tax rates, first mortgage financing, and the depreciation schedule; (d) The depreciation schedule, utility costs, and capitalization rates.

_____ 4 Cash flow analysis shows the amount of income remaining after: (a) Income tax and mortgage payments; (b) Deducting operating expenses from total actual collections; (c) Deducting operating expenses, costs of vacancies, and costs of delinquent rents; (d) Mortgage payments and property taxes.

_____ 5 Debt service coverage is calculated by showing: (a) Total actual collections as a percentage of total mortgage payments; (b) Gross possible rental income as a percentage of depreciation allowances; (c) Net operating income as a percentage of total possible rental income; (d) Net operating income as a percentage of total mortgage payments.

_____ 6 The operating expense ratio shows operating expenses as a percentage of: (a) Total actual collections, less vacancies and delinquent rents; (b) Total actual collections; (c) Gross possible rental income and miscellaneous income; (d) Gross possible rental income, less vacancy and delinquent rents.

_____ 7 The breakeven ratio is equal to: (a) Operating expenses and mortgage payments as a percentage of gross possible income; (b) Operating expenses and mortgage payments as a percentage of total actual collections; (c) Mortgage payments as a percentage of gross possible income; (d) Operating expenses as a percentage of total actual collections.

_____ 8 Cash flow refers to: (a) Net operating income and depreciation allowances; (b) Income remaining after income taxes and mortgage payments; (c) Total actual collections, less operating expenses and mortgage payments; (d) Total actual collections, less mortgage payments and income taxes.

_____ 9 Which of the following statements is correct? In apartment conversions: (a) Developers expect a substantial number of current tenants to purchase units; (b) Available financing and unit price should make mortgage payments competitive with the prevailing rent; (c) The floor plan should be dominated by two- and three-bedroom apartments; (d) All of the above.

_____ 10 Marketing of converted apartment units focuses on: (a) Out-of-town buyers; (b) Owners of single-family dwellings; (c) Tenants of neighboring apartment buildings; (d) Low-income groups.

Answer Key

1 (c), 2 (d), 3 (c), 4 (a), 5 (d), 6 (b), 7 (a), 8 (b), 9 (d), 10 (c).

Fill-In Questions

1 _____ are equal to the gross possible total income, less vacancies and rental delinquencies.

2 The_____ itemizes the more important apartment features that affect apartment rents.

3 For apartments, _____ usually represent the largest single expense.

4 For analytical purposes it is common to analyze operating income and expenses by the amount per_____ , _____ , and _____ .

5 Property owners subject to income tax rates of 40 percent or more are often concerned with _____ rather than with net operating income.

6 The_____ shows whether net operating income is sufficient to cover mortgage payments in addition to providing a suitable reserve.

7 The_____ indicates the minimum occupancy rate required to meet expenses and mortgage payments.

8 The feasibility of apartment conversions to condominiums increases if_____ _____ are competitive with the prevailing rent.

9 Newly constructed condominiums usually cost more than _____ _____ .

10 Conversion to condominiums requires that each apartment be placed in _____ _____ .

Answer Key

1	Total actual collections	6	debt service coverage
2	competitive apartment evaluation	7	breakeven ratio
3	property taxes	8	mortgage payments
4	apartment, square foot, room	9	apartment conversions
5	cash flow	10	like-new condition

SELECTED REFERENCES

"Apartment Management: Four Keys to Lower Costs," *House and Home*, **47**(9): 52–61 (1975).

Blazar, Sheldon M., and Hugh G. Hilton: "Investment Opportunities in Existing Apartment Buildings," *Real Estate Review*, **6**(2):47–52 (1976).

Carless, Daniel G.: "More than Rents and Repairs," *Real Estate Today*, **11**(5):22–29 (1978).

Downs, James C., Jr.: *Principles of Real Estate Management*, Chicago: Institute of Real Estate Management, 1975, chaps. 10, 20, and 22.

How to Convert Apartments to Condominiums, Los Angeles: California Real Estate Association, 1973.

How to Manage an Apartment House, Los Angeles: California Real Estate Association, 1974.

Kelley, Edward N.: *Practical Apartment Management*, Chicago: Institute of Real Estate Management, 1976.

Chapter 13

Condominium Management

After studying this chapter, you should be familiar with:
1 Condominium terms and documents
2 Functions of the condominium association
3 Provisions for condominium insurance
4 Specialized condominiums: time sharing and business

Property managers face two added problems in managing condominiums: (1) condominium ownership, which many owners misunderstand, and (2) multiple ownership, which substitutes for the more common single ownership (ownership in severalty). The ownership interest requires an understanding of new legal entities associated with condominiums. Multiple ownership requires that managers deal with the condominium association, its board of directors, and individual owners.

In part, the manager's task is made more difficult because of certain abusive practices by less responsible developers. Developers of new condominiums have often understated maintenance fees to encourage sales. Among projects where units have sold slowly, buyers have complained that their maintenance fees pay for the maintenance costs of the unsold units. Then there are the disillusioned purchasers who have been led to believe that the maintenance fee covers all maintenance, when in fact the maintenance charge covers only the exterior. Faulty construction and poor materials with a lack of builder warranties on construction have led to still additional complaints.

The frequency of these problems has encouraged a wave of state legislation governing condominium sales and management. Typical of these laws are requirements that deposits be placed in escrow, that purchasers be given copies of the master deed or declaration and bylaws, and that developers fully disclose all relevant facts. Some states allow purchasers a stated period of time to cancel their purchase contract.

Such a provision is incorporated in the 1974 Horizontal Property Act (Chapter 4.1) in Virginia. Article 4 requires that the developer give purchasers a public statement at least 10 days before the date of sales. After signing the purchase contract, the purchaser has 10 days in which to cancel without penalty on written notice. The law also provides that the developer warrant condominium units against structural defects for 1 year after the sale.

Similarly, the Florida Condominium Act enacted in 1976 (Chapter 76-222) requires that condominium developers warrant each unit for 3 years after building completion. The same act allows purchasers to cancel purchase contracts and have their deposit refunded 15 days after the required documents have been delivered to the buyer.

CONDOMINIUM OWNERSHIP

To communicate effectively, managers must help clients understand the legal terms associated with condominium ownership. The legal documents necessary to condominiums are also unique and specialized.

Condominium Terms

Condominium terms apply to many property types. For residential buildings, management may deal with high-rise elevator condominiums, with construction comparable to that of a high-rise apartment building. Residential condominiums parallel other apartment projects; one example would be garden court condominiums, which are generally no more than three stories and which generally consist of several buildings placed around a landscaped court. Other condominium projects consist of townhouses with units sharing party walls and forming row houses that have separate entrances and private patios. Even single detached units have been developed as condominiums.

Business condominiums are yet another form. Office buildings, medical dental facilities, industrial parks, and retail structures have been constructed under condominium ownership. While more popular for residential projects, condominium ownership and the terms employed cover a wide variety of commercial and industrial properties.

Condominium A condominium is a multiunit project with individual ownership with an unrestricted right to one or more units; land and all other parts of the project are held in common with owners in other units.

Condominium Unit   As defined in state statutes, the ordinary meaning of condominium unit is the cubic space in which a unit owner holds a fee-simple title.

Common Elements   Common elements are the components of a condominium project, less individual units. Alternatively, the term refers to land, buildings, lobbies, corridors, roofs, and other construction. Defined in detail in the declaration, common elements include parking, storage areas, and other facilities.

Limited Common Elements   Limited common elements are facilities used exclusively by unit owners, but not by all unit owners, for example, parking stalls, patios, balconies, and assigned storage, which may be outside the unit. Common elements, which are not limited, refer to the lobby, swimming pool, and other areas for use of all unit owners.

Condominium Association   Referred to also as the homeowners' association (HOA), the condominium association is an unincorporated association of unit owners who automatically become members as owners.

Condominium Declaration   In some states called the condominium conditions and restrictions (CC & R's), the condominium declaration refers to the legal document provided by state statute that creates the condominium entity.

Fixtures   Important to insurance coverage, the term "fixtures" refers to everything contained within the four perimeter walls, floor, and ceiling of units. Fixtures may include paint and wall coverings, carpets, floor coverings, drapes, cabinets, appliances, non-load-bearing interior walls, doors, plumbing, and electrical fixtures.

Articles of Incorporation   The articles of incorporation is a document filed with state authorities which establishes the existence of a corporation, and lists its founders, purposes, powers, membership procedures, and like details.

Corporate Bylaws   Corporate bylaws set forth the rules and regulations of a corporation, define powers and duties of officers and directors, and define the members' voting rights and procedures.

Architectural Use Restrictions   With respect to unit owners, architectural controls affect the appearance of interior areas or limited common areas, such as porches and patios. Exterior walls and services are maintained by the association, subject to maintenance by the homeowners' association as common elements.

The Management Agreement   The management agreement is an employment contract that spells out the terms and conditions of employment; the services to be performed, including remuneration for those services; and terms for cancellation of the agreement.

Condominium Assessments Assessments refer to the pro rata share of condominium operating expenses assessed to each individual unit.

The definition of a condominium, as defined by state statute, usually describes unit ownership in terms of cubic air space. While the owner has exclusive use of the unit and an undivided interest in common elements, the fixtures, attachments, floor coverings, wall coverings, cabinets, and appliances are considered part of the common elements.

The terms of the condominium interest usually make individual owners responsible for the repair and maintenance of everything within their cubic air space. A typical clause that defines this responsibility reads ". . . each owner shall, at his [her] sole cost and expense, maintain and repair his [her] unit, keeping the same in good condition." In most cases, if an owner does not maintain his or her particular unit, the association has the right to do so and charge the expense as a lien against the unit. In turn, the condominium association maintains the exterior of units and common areas. Other rights and duties are described by other condominium documents.

Condominium Documents

Documents that create the condominium interest, establish property rights, and provide for their administration include the declaration, articles of incorporation, the bylaws, the unit deed, and rules and regulations. Before condominiums could be formed it was necessary for each state to enact legislation: (1) describing property in three dimensions rather than in a flat plane common to fee ownership; and (2) permitting property taxes to be divided among unit ownerships, with an undivided share in common elements. All 50 states have enacted the necessary legislation.

The Declaration The *declaration* dedicates land to condominium ownership. It has all the legality of a certificate of incorporation or the constitution of a government. It is recorded, and it must contain information required by state statute. The declaration identifies the land committed to the project and includes the legal description of each unit.

In addition, the declaration allocates the undivided interest in the common elements to each unit. The condominium act of Virginia allows for the allocation of the undivided interest in the common elements to be proportionate to the size or "par value" of each unit. If square foot area is used, the Virginia statute states "the undivided interests in the common element . . . shall add up to one stated as fractions or 100 percentum as stated as percentages."

For example, suppose that a 105-unit condominium were to provide three floor plans of one-, two-, and three-bedroom units. The total floor area would be found by multiplying the number of units by floor area.

Number of units	Floor plan	Floor area per unit	Total floor area
15	1-bedroom	794	11,910
30	2-bedroom	950	28,500
60	3-bedroom	1,075	64,500
105		—	104,910

With a total of 104,910 square feet, the pro rata share assumed by each unit would be the proportion of floor area of each unit to the total of 104,910.

Pro Rata Share of Common Elements

1-bedroom
794/104,910   = .007568 or .7568%

2-bedroom
950/104,910   = .009055 or .9055%

3-bedroom
1,075/104,910 = .010246 or 1.0246%

Under this arrangement, the owner of a one-bedroom unit would own .7568 percent of the common elements. This proportion would also control the share of operating expenses assumed by the owner of a one-bedroom unit. With an annual operating expense of $100,000, each owner of a one-bedroom unit would pay an annual share of $756.80, or $63.07 monthly. In assessing the value of common elements to each unit owner, the local property tax assessor would apportion the assessment of common elements to the unit owners on the basis of the same pro rata share.

In addition the declaration, to qualify the building as a condominium, must include a diagram of each condominium unit, a survey, and a plat of the land; furthermore, the declaration describes the ownership and the common elements, and lists the legal responsibilities of unit owners.

Articles of Incorporation Some states require that detail outlining the rights and duties of unit owners be included in the declaration. Others require that such condominium regulations be included in the articles of incorporation. In either case, the *articles of incorporation* establish the governing organization as a nonprofit corporation. The articles duplicate provisions of the declaration in giving the legal description and in describing association membership and voting rights.

The more critical articles of incorporation refer to the powers granted to the condominium association and to the method of conducting its affairs through the board of directors. The articles will grant the association the right (1) to perform duties and obligations outlined in the declaration, including the enforcement of covenants, conditions, and restrictions; (2) to establish and collect assessments; and (3) to own and maintain common property. The articles further provide for a board of directors, specify the method of election, and describe the terms of office.

Bylaws The *bylaws* of the homeowners' association control the administrative procedures. Flexibility is provided by allowing amendments to the bylaws by majority vote. Like the traditional bylaws of other organizations, they cover:

1 Membership meetings
2 Election procedures
3 Powers and duties of the board and officers
4 Board meeting procedures

5 Provision for committees
6 Insurance requirements

Membership meetings, usually required annually, and board elections with staggered terms of office agree with conditions in comparable organizations. Similarly, board meetings and committee appointments divide board responsibility; in this case, recommended committees include various maintenance, budget, and social committees.

Bylaws assign legal responsibilities to the board for purchasing insurance, contracting, or providing for maintenance by hiring staff. The bylaws place responsibility for taxes, for member assessment, and for security measures with the board. The board must prepare the annual operating budget, and must levy and collect assessment fees. It must keep necessary records and perform other duties essential to condominium operation.

The Unit Deed The *unit deed* conveys title to the condominium unit and to a stated share in the undivided common elements. Conforming to requirements of an enforceable contract, the deed will include the price, description, reservations, purchase terms, and other details. In some states such as Florida, a prospective buyer will be given a purchase agreement and deposit receipt, which acknowledges that the buyer has received copies of:

the declaration of condominium and exhibit
articles of incorporation
bylaws
rules and regulations
estimated operating budget for the first year
estimated closing costs
the insurance agreement
a construction warranty
a sales brochure
floor plan of the condominium unit purchased

Rules and Regulations Condominium members, since they share common facilities, must have rules governing the conduct and personal behavior of each member. Initially the house rules originate with the developer. As the units are sold, members may desire changes in rules and regulations. The bylaws should provide means of changing house rules on majority vote. House rules will affect members' rights to keep pets, the hours in which the swimming pool may be used, and the regulation of outside storage; generally, they also prohibit nonresidential use and offensive acts such as playing radios or musical instruments loudly after stated hours.

Contrast with Cooperatives

Unlike condominium owners, the cooperative owner owns no real estate. The title, the land, and the building are owned by a nonprofit cooperative corporation. The price of an apartment unit is established by the cooperative, with each cooperative owner buying stock that corresponds to the value of each unit. Purchasers take possession under a proprietary lease from the cooperative. Similar to a condominium owner, the cooperative occupant pays a monthly assessment to cover expenses, taxes, and mortgage payments.

A cooperative owner pays a pro rata share toward a single mortgage on the whole project. Therefore, the cooperative does not offer the financing flexibility of a condominium. Because of this feature, cooperative members are liable for members who default on their pro rata share of mortgage payments. In addition, the liability of the condominium owner is limited to the pro rata share interest; the cooperative owner has unlimited liability for obligations of the cooperative. Because of this potential liability, prospective purchasers of cooperatives are carefully screened.

THE CONDOMINIUM ASSOCIATION

A nonprofit organization, the condominium association represents the governing organization, functions like a business, and operates exclusively for the benefit of residents. Originally organized by the condominium developer, it seeks to preserve the design and character of the condominium project. Its operation is established by the declaration of covenants, conditions, and restrictions and by corporate bylaws.

The Board of Directors

Usually the bylaws provide for voting rights according to the pro rata share of common interest. One of the principal duties of the board is to arrange for management and maintenance tasks. Their duties cover a long list of responsibilities.

Board Duties   As the governing organizations of the condominium, boards must:

1   Provide physical maintenance of common areas and facilities
2   Keep proper accounting records
3   Prepare the operating budget
4   Take legal action against owners who are delinquent in paying assessments
5   Enforce house rules and regulations
6   Select accountants, auditors, and legal counsel
7   Supervise management through an agent, independent contractors, or employees
8   Enforce architectural controls
9   Appoint committees
10   Develop recreational and social programs
11   Contract for insurance
12   Comply with notices of assessments and meetings
13   Arrange for bonding of officers or employees handling condominium funds
14   Arbitrate between the developer and condominium unit owners[1]

---

[1] *Managing a Successful Community Association*, 2d ed., Washington, D.C.: Urban Land Institute and the Community Associations Institute, 1977, p. 14.

In reviewing this list, note the differences between condominium operation and apartment operation. In illustration, item one gives the board control over the level of physical maintenance. Although certain duties may be delegated to the property manager, note that the board takes legal action against delinquent owners (item 4). The manager may send out delinquent notices, but final action to collect delinquencies is handled by the governing board.

Probably the most important work of the board is preparation of the operating budget (item 3). To illustrate the necessary detail, note Table 13-1, which shows the operating budget and common expenses for a 70-unit condominium in Fort Walton Beach, Florida. In this case the budget includes management fees, repair and maintenance allowances, utilities, taxes, and insurance. The 70-unit owners, according to this budget, would be assessed for a monthly maintenance of $3,949.73.

Committee Organization The board must appoint operating committees, which ideally consist of three to not more than nine members. Appointed committees cooperate with the board of directors, and function through an appointed committee chairman. The successful operation of the board depends largely on the work of selected committees.

The *architecture committee* continually surveys units and advises unit owners that all visible changes to their property, including painting, must be approved in advance by the committee. Committee members distribute guidelines and standards to unit owners, and investigate complaints of problems affecting the architectural integrity of the project. The committee is assigned the responsibility of reviewing and approving or disapproving plans for exterior alterations. It may be charged with making recommendations to the board for architectural improvements to the common area.

Table 13-1 Estimated Operating Budget and Common Expenses: 70 Units

Common expenses	Monthly	Annual
Management fee		
Clerical	$ 450.00	$ 5,400.00
Management fee	560.00	6,720.00
Repair and maintenance		
Grounds	400.00	4,800.00
Swimming pool	165.00	1,980.00
Exterminator	30.00	360.00
Tennis court	15.00	180.00
Miscellaneous supplies and equipment	175.00	2,100.00
Utilities		
Sanitation, water, and sewerage	980.00	11,760.00
Electricity	484.73	5,816.72
Taxes on association property	15.00	180.00
Reserves	100.00	1,200.00
Insurance	500.00	6,000.00
Audit and legal expenses	75.00	900.00
Total	$3,949.73	$47,396.72

The *budget committee* advises the board on the final annual budget. Before the budget is adopted, the committee holds open hearings on expenditures recommended by the various committees advising on snow removal, the swimming pool, the clubhouse, and other recreational facilities. As a result of these hearings, the budget committee recommends additions or deletions to the preliminary budget and advises the board on budget procedures, insurance programs, and the budget audit.

The *maintenance committee* works to preserve and enhance the physical environment. The committee advises the board on methods of developing a maintenance program to meet needs of the owners. It also advises the board or managing agent on budget recommendations affecting maintenance, and it may suggest maintenance projects involving improvements to the common area. Contracts for landscaping or other maintenance are reviewed for final recommendations to the board.

Condominiums frequently include a *communications committee*, which prepares monthly newsletters and arranges for publicity about coming events. The *recreation committee* may have subcommittees dealing with the clubhouse, swimming pool, and social functions. Subcommittees on social events and educational programs fall into this category.

The board of directors makes the final decision on management policies. In fulfilling this function, the board is responsible for a management plan that should be understood by unit owners. The objective of the management plan is to implement accepted policies and operating procedures. These policies vary according to the type of management selected: self-management, employment of a resident manager, or professional management.

Management Policies

Self-management requires that the board utilize a combination of volunteer services, contract services, and part-time employees. It is the least costly method of management, and is probably more popular among condominiums of less than 50 units. It requires careful supervision so that unit owners are not directing contractors, part-time employees, and volunteers. A successful self-management plan requires central direction by a designated person who agrees to supervise custodial operations.

Service contracts enable the association to employ qualified persons for specific tasks such as grounds maintenance, keeping accounts and records, and janitorial services. This system, while relieving the board of day-to-day operations, involves the board in numerous contracts with responsibilities for negotiation, supervision and monitoring of contract performance. The board is placed in an untenable position if contractors fail to perform.

Employment of a *resident manager* gives the board maximum control of condominium operations. The board delegates responsibilities to the manager, assigning duties such as correspondence, maintenance, and supervision over unit owner activities. Under this plan of operation, the board is highly dependent on a single individual who is subject to termination, illness, absences, and varying degrees of competence.

The *professional management* firm is more economical for condominiums of 100 or more units. The services delegated to the management agent may range from selected duties to performance of all management functions. Some condominium units combine professional management with self-help programs.

The more experienced management firms offer a full range of services for condominium operations. While the expense increases with the responsibilities assumed, the complexity of the larger units, say 500 or more, makes it preferable for services to be performed by third party management. The majority of services offered fall into one of the following categories:

    maintaining accounting records
    collecting assessments and delinquencies
    supervising maintenance
    supervising repairs
    attending board or committee meetings
    negotiating service contracts
    making emergency repairs
    supervising contractors and staff
    preparing annual, capital, and interim budgets
    representing the association before public agencies
    other services as required

While these services are fairly broad, each condominium must decide on the particular duties which will be delegated to professional management.

Delegating Management Responsibilities

Since board members decide policy, they must agree on functions assigned to the management firm. Duties delegated to the firm deal with fiscal, maintenance and administrative functions. Committees formed by the board of directors usually assist in determining those responsibilities assigned to outside management.

Fiscal Duties Though the managing agent acts in an advisory capacity, his or her advice normally would be based on close familiarity with supplies and their prices, job performance standards, wage rates, and preferred maintenance procedures. In assuming fiscal responsibilities a managing agent may suggest an operating budget that meets service requirements of the association. Final decisions on budget matters and the level of services will be made by the board of directors.

In assuming fiscal responsibilities, which include meeting payrolls, tax payments, utility bills, and the like, the agent will have responsibility for association funds. And because certain expenses are unpredictable, the management agreement places limits on the amount the agent is authorized to spend without seeking board approval. Usually the management will be given authority to act in emergencies that affect personal safety or property value. The management agreement recommended by the Institute of Real Estate Management covers this point by stating:

    the agent shall not make any expenditures nor incur any nonrecurring tax obligation exceeding $_____without the prior consent of the board. . . . Notwithstanding these limitations, the agent may, on behalf of the board without prior consent, extend any amount required to deal with emergency conditions which may involve the danger of life or property or may threaten the safety of the condominium or the owners and occupants or may threaten the suspension of any necessary service to the condominium.

The accounts maintained by the manager are subject to an audit and, by agreement, the agent reports annual operating income and expenses to the board.

Maintenance Duties As part of the management plan, the board may direct the agent to submit an operating plan covering the maintenance of common areas, the staff required, and recommended contract services. Under supervision of the board of directors, the manager is given the authority to invite bids from contractors for ground maintenance, swimming pool maintenance, window washing, painting, and other services. The typical management agreement will state:

> The agent will do everything reasonably necessary for the proper management of the property, including periodic inspections, the supervision of maintenance and arranging for such improvements, alterations and repairs as may be required of owners. No improvements, alterations or repair work costing more than $_____shall be made by an agent without owner's prior authorization. However, in case of an emergency which requires immediate repairs or alterations, if owner is not readily available for consultation, agent shall use his own discretion regarding same.[2]

Details of maintenance and repair duties assigned to the manager will be listed in the management agreement. For greater efficiency, some management firms insist that maintenance employees work directly for the management firm. The firm can maintain greater control over its own employees than it would if employees were hired by the board. Supervised training and incentive plans are administered by recognized management firms. Even if the association hires maintenance employees and a management firm acts as a coemployer, the management agent operates as the personnel supervisor.

Administrative Duties In the larger associations, recordkeeping requires professional services. Responsibility for records of title transfers, insurance policies, government reports, and local property taxes is generally assigned to a professional management firm. The duties may be expanded to include communications among unit members, the board and their committees; preparing newsletters and meeting notices; distributing rules and regulations; and even planning the agenda for scheduled meetings.

It should be noted that the manager, while assuming certain limited authorities of the board, must observe certain exclusions to his or her authority. The management agent performs no legal services. The preparation of documents such as deeds, contracts, and conveyances requires the services of an attorney. Similarly, the manager

---

[2]*Source:* Benjamin J. Henley, Jr., vice president, Coldwell Banker Property Management Company, San Francisco, California.

performs no audit function and gives no personal income tax advice. Architectural and engineering matters are also tasks assigned to others. In undertaking their duties, managers avoid negotiations and disputes between unit owners and the developer and assume no responsibility for maintenance of unit interiors or other legal responsibilities of owners or of the association.

The Transition Period

Up to this point it has been assumed that the condominium is a functioning organization. However, all condominiums start with a developer who assumes the authority that is later delegated to the association. The initial management agreement gives the developer rights and duties and responsibilities of the association until a certain number of units, ranging from 50 to 80 percent, have been sold. In other cases, a time limit is specified in addition to a number of units sold.

At the start, the developer assigns duties and functions of the association to a manager, who must initiate maintenance programs that provide efficient operation at the least cost. Some developers prepare a management policy manual to guide maintenance personnel. The initial management drafts rules and regulations consistent with corporation bylaws.

The Organization Meeting

As required by the bylaws and the declaration, the developer must issue a notice of the first meeting of owners to elect the board of directors and set the date of the first annual meeting. To these ends, the developer prepares an agenda to explain the following items:

> the election procedure provided by the bylaws
> cumulative voting rights
> duties of officers and of the board of directors
> the financial report submitted by the developer
> a progress report on condominium sales
> a report on special events sponsored by the condominium
> insurance coverage
> procedures in handling complaints

Some states allow unit owners to vote for the board of directors under a cumulative voting plan. If each owner has one vote, the cumulative plan allows unit owners to cast a vote for each director or allocate votes to other directors as desired. For example, with a nine-member board, a unit owner could cast nine votes for a single director or one vote for each director or any combination of nine votes.

The first annual meeting is established for a date 1 year from the organizational meeting. After the election of officers, the board of directors may set an organization meeting for the board, at which time the officers of the condominium will be elected and chairpersons of the various committees will be appointed.

The Acceptance Committee

The acceptance committee is a temporary committee consisting of unit owners and the newly elected board of directors. Members of this committee inspect common areas, recreational facilities, landscaping, and grounds. Deficiencies covered by written or implied warranties of the developer are noted and described. A written statement of deficiencies is sent to the developer for correction.

This procedure follows a negotiation process in which both parties must make compromises. The alternative, if the homeowners' association makes unreasonable demands, would be a costly lawsuit. In the end, the board of directors makes the final decision on acceptance of the common areas. If legal action is taken against an uncooperative developer, the board will usually require a majority vote of homeowners before seeking a special assessment to finance a lawsuit.

CONDOMINIUM INSURANCE

Standard coverages available to the homeowner are unsuitable for condominiums. While the declaration may specify insurance that the board of directors must arrange, all declarations are not so definite. Even if the declaration details the required insurance, unit owners are advised to seek special coverages for their individual property interests. Condominium ownership requires separate insurance policies for the homeowners' association and the unit owners.

Homeowners' Association Insurance

The homeowners' association in its responsibility for limited common areas, including personal property, requires coverage on *physical damage* as the named insured. Physical damage coverage should cover personal property owned by the association in the common areas. Preferably the coverage would relate to the full replacement cost on buildings rather than actual value. Since actual value is calculated on replacement cost less depreciation, the association, facing a loss, might not be able to replace buildings if the insurance applied only to the cash value.

Physical Damage Although the standard fire insurance policy protects against fire, lightning, and damage by "removal of premises endangered by perils insured against," condominium boards are advised to consider *extended coverage* that gives protection from certain additional perils: wind storms, hail, explosion, riots, civil commotion, aircraft, vehicles, and smoke.

Though coverage secured may represent "all-risk" coverage, typically, special coverage is required for water damage, sprinkler leakage insurance, vandalism insurance, boiler and machinery coverage, and, where appropriate, flood and earthquake insurance. Condominiums with a considerable amount of exterior glass buy plate glass insurance covering breakage to the full amount, less a deductible per pane.

If coinsurance is provided, say 80 or 90 percent, the board of directors must secure sufficient insurance to provide full recovery. Besides meeting initial coinsurance requirements, the board periodically reviews the stipulated amount of coverage in the light of current property inflation. An annual review of replacement cost guards against the danger of underinsurance.

The association may create conflicts if an insurance company pays a homeowners' association and then files suit for damages caused by a unit owner. To avoid this possibility, associations require a *waiver of subrogation*. The waiver protects the unit owner from being held personally liable for occurrences within his or her unit that damage other condominium property.

Liability Insurance Besides securing protection from physical damages, the associations are generally required to contract for *comprehensive general liability insurance*. While the board of directors may set the limits of liability, the association must be protected for *bodily injury liability*, *property damage liability*, and *medical payments*. Ordinarily the medical payment coverage covers guests of unit owners, since medical payments to unit owners are covered by their individual policies.

The board frequently purchases special types of liability insurance, for example, insurance that protects owners and guests for damages to automobiles parked in garages. Similar policies are available for liability arising from the operation of watercraft and automobiles, and, for construction contracted for by the homeowners' association, for contractual liability. In addition, personal injury liability protects the association against claims of libel, slander, invasion of privacy, or wrongful eviction.

As an employer, the association will be subject to workers' compensation payments. The board of directors, depending on its assumed liabilities, may also purchase errors and omissions coverage for acts of the association directors. A fidelity bond, protecting those handling association cash, is another common form of association insurance. Moreover, the board of directors normally negotiates for deductibles applied per occurrence rather than per building. For example, if a damage policy covering a project of 200 buildings has a $100 deductible per building, damage to each building would result in a total deductible of $20,000.

Property Insurance of the Unit Owner

Unit owners have an insurable interest in (1) personal property; (2) additions and alterations in their units; (3) that portion of the condominium unit under exclusive possession and use; (4) continued use of the unit; (5) rights to limited common areas such as balconies, patios, garages, and carports; and (6) special condominium assessments.

Usually personal property insurance will provide coverage on a named peril basis, with a stated maximum coverage. Some insurance will provide special limits of liability on certain property such as jewelry, securities, watercraft, and trailers. Additions and alterations refer to permanent attachments to the unit, namely, carpets, built-in cabinets, appliances, light fixtures, and the like. Some policies include provision for additional living expense coverage, which protects the owner against relocating expenses while repairs are made to a damaged condominium.

Loss assessment coverage protects owners from unusual expenses of the association that are not otherwise insured. An association subject to a liability judgment for more than the association insurance must cover the judgment by special assessments against members. The loss assessment endorsement covers the proportion of excessive losses shifted to unit owners by special assessments.

Unit owners are responsible for personal liability with respect to their units. Special endorsements are available to cover personal property of unit owners in hobby shops, storage sheds, and poolside areas.

SPECIALIZED CONDOMINIUMS

For the present purpose, *specialized condominiums* refer to time-sharing interests and business condominiums. The former represents an interval ownership interest, usually a week or more, in a vacation residential unit. Business condominiums include offices, retail stores, and industrial space. The success of these more specialized condominiums depends largely on competent management.

Time-sharing Management

Though time-sharing plans cover different types of ownership, one popular form provides for fee ownership: the buyer acquires fee ownership in a particular unit and a corresponding exclusive right of use for a specified period annually. The period may extend from one week to several months. Under this plan the buyer acquires access according to a specified calendar date. Weeks are numbered on a calendar basis, beginning at noon on the first Saturday and ending at noon on the following Saturday. The time-sharing periods begin and end on weekends to agree with vacation plans.

At the end of 1977, of the 140 known time-sharing programs, about 75 percent of the projects belonged to an exchange program. Under an exchange program, members may trade occupancy among other time-sharing owners in other national and even international resorts.[3]

Time-sharing management has grown to a highly specialized discipline. Managers specializing in this property type must communicate more frequently with unit owners. Since owners hold only a small fraction of the project, they are highly dependent on competent management. Competence requires close observance of certain basic management rules:

There must be an efficient and courteous staff.
There must be efficient check-in and check-out procedure.
Units must be kept clean and provided with new furniture and appliances.
The project must have attractive, well-maintained amenities.

[3] Carl H. Burlingame, "An Introduction to Timesharing" in *Timesharing*, Washington, D. C.: The Urban Land Institute, 1977, pp. 1–8.

Management must help with resales.

Management must be familiar with time-sharing exchanges.

It will be appreciated that these rules combine certain aspects of hotel and resort operation with management practices common to residential apartments.

Efficient managers closely supervise maid service, require a 24-hour period between users for a major cleaning, replace furniture every 5 years, and provide two annual maintenance and renovation periods. Since theoretically the time-sharing unit could have as many as 52 owners, communication with so many owners assumes unusual importance.

Communication starts by writing time-share owners a month before their expected arrival. If no answer is received a week before occupancy, a phone call verifies the arrival time. Soon after arrival each owner is reminded of available facilities and given a copy of house rules and a list of current attractions. Some managements host a weekly cocktail party to acquaint share owners with supervisory staff.[4]

In short, management focuses on satisfying two markets: (1) the market for luxury resorts in distant locations, such as Hawaii and the Caribbean; and, even more significantly, (2) the time-sharing market for middle-income groups. Time sharing appeals to middle-income families who substitute maintenance fees for daily hotel rates. They are purchased by families who face the alternative of two or three hotel rooms during each vacation for growing children or other relatives. Such families take 2- or 3-week vacations, and they prefer a time-sharing unit within reasonable commuting distance. Time sharing will probably continue in popularity for these families.

Business Condominiums

The Urban Land Institute has identified 40 office condominiums and 11 industrial condominiums. Though some shopping centers provide for unit ownership of leading department stores, most condominium shopping center developments conform to Plaza 70 East, a 51,000 square-foot shopping center in Marlton, New Jersey. Other known shopping center condominiums are relatively small.[5] In these commercial condominiums, management procedures vary considerably from those of residential management.

Commercial Condominium Management

One of the first issues facing management is board representation. In residential condominiums, the board may function under an elected board of directors. In the commercial business condominiums, unit owners lack a common unity of interest. Frequently their demands for facilities and condominium services vary widely. Because of the diverse interest of unit owners, management frequently recommends that key management decisions require the approval of all members.

[4] See Robert Edwin Lee, "Timesharing Management: Possibilities and Pitfalls," and Carl G. Berry, "Timesharing Management: One Project's Experience," in *Timesharing,* op. cit, pp. 89–98.

[5] See John C. Melaniphy, Jr., *Commercial & Industrial Condominiums,* Washington, D.C.: Urban Land Institute, 1976, p. 45.

Moreover, the management process may be degraded by appointment of subordinate employees to the condominium board. Employee members who must seek approval of higher authority for final decisions delay board action. To circumvent this problem, management limits membership on the board to executives who have decision-making authority.

Another characteristic common to business condominiums is the preselection of unit owners. Ordinarily it is difficult to finance a business condominium without commitments from prospective purchasers. Furthermore, in a medical-dental office condominium, prospective unit owners would purchase units only if other owners were compatible. A pediatrician would be unlikely to buy into a condominium if another pediatrician, as a unit owner, would offer professional competition. Prospects for a business condominium may be expected to review the credit rating and business history of other unit owners.

The demands of commercial condominium unit owners require special attention to certain other aspects of condominium management. Condominium management must consider that:

1 Commercial unit owners must plan to relocate according to definite planned dates. Time of occupancy is critically important for business enterprises.

2 Special attention must be given to bylaws that regulate the design and placement of signs. Commercial signs must be compatible with building architecture.

3 Businesses make different demands on parking and truck-loading facilities. Some unit owners require restricted common areas for their exclusive parking and truck-loading needs.

4 Commercial tenants must agree to restrictions on interior decorating, exterior lighting, and sound emission. The building must be designed and property uses must be such that tenants do not create nuisances or abuse property rights of unit owners.

Security requirements are more critical for commercial owners. The building should be designed with the latest security devices, which frequently require 24-hour surveillance.

The provisions for off-hour utility and other building services must be anticipated for some unit owners. Others have no need for heat, light, and air conditioning beyond office hours.

Providing these issues are resolved, the condominium has the following special incentives for commercial businesses:

1 The price of a condominium unit is probably less than the price of purchasing an individual building, because of common walls, building equipment, parking maintenance, and other facilities and services.

2 With continued property appreciation, the condominium unit owner, like the homeowner, anticipates capital appreciation.

3 The condominium owner gains from the deductibility of property taxes and interest on mortgage payments.

4 There are some advantages in participating in property management as an owner.

5 As in other condominiums, the unit owner delegates management duties to the owners' association, namely, exterior maintenance, and landscaping and maintenance of common areas.

Against these recognized advantages are certain limitations of the commercial condominium. With respect to office space, the owner faces a limited resale market. For this reason, business condominiums are more popular for medical office buildings. Because of the questionable resale value, condominium office space commits the unit owner to a fixed location; the unit owner loses the flexibility available to office tenants.

Similar problems are found in the industrial condominium. While owning an industrial condominium unit is more financially advantageous than renting, the unit owner has less flexibility in adding space as the business expands. As a consequence, industrial condominiums are largely limited to buildings of less than 10,000 square feet. For these reasons, most observers project limited use of condominium ownership for commercial purposes.[6]

SUMMARY

Condominium ownership introduces unique terms: though statutory definitions differ by state, ordinarily a *condominium unit* refers to cubic space in which a unit owner holds fee-simple title. Accordingly, the *common elements* refer to a condominium project less its individual units. The term refers to that portion of the condominium available for the use of all unit owners. *Limited common elements* refer to common facilities used exclusively by unit owners, such as parking stalls, patios, balconies, and assigned storage space.

Condominium documents define the ownership interest and property rights. The *declaration*, which is recorded, dedicates the property to condominium ownership. The declaration document conforms to state statutes and identifies the land committed to the project, including a legal description of each unit. The declaration allocates the undivided interest in common elements to each unit. The most common allocation plan allocates the undivided interest according to the proportion of the unit area to the total project area. This proportion controls property taxes on the common interest share and the pro rata share of operating expenses. The *articles of incorporation*, the *bylaws* (which provide administrative procedures), the *unit deed*, and *rules and regulations* further define property rights and duties of unit owners.

Condominiums are governed by the condominium association. Unit owners are automatically members of the condominium association. The bylaws or articles of incorporation determine how the homeowners' association elects the board of directors, who manage through appointed committees that advise the board on architecture, budgets, maintenance, communication, and other matters.

[6] Ibid.

Condominium owners may elect to manage according to *self-management*, which combines volunteer services, contract services, and the services of part-time employees. Alternatively, *resident managers* may be appointed to give the board maximum control of condominium operations. For the larger condominiums of 100 units or more, *professional management* firms undertake management responsibility under direction of the board.

Management firms assume fiscal duties, take responsibility for maintenance, and perform certain delegated administrative functions. Management must give the transition period special attention.

The *transition period* refers to the transfer of control from a developer to the homeowners' association. For new condominiums, the bylaws and the declaration provide for the first organizational meeting. In this meeting, the initial board of directors is elected, which subsequently holds a board meeting to appoint operating committees.

One of the prime responsibilities of new unit owners and the board is to appoint the acceptance committee—a committee that reviews written and applied warranties of the developers for deficiencies in construction, landscaping, or equipment. Usually final acceptance requires compromises by the board, which has the final responsibility for acceptance.

Condominium insurance involves insurance for the homeowners' association and for unit owners individually. The homeowners' association requires insurance against physical damage to personal property and other property owned by the association in the common areas. The association may be required to contract for comprehensive general liability insurance to protect the association from bodily injury, property damage, and medical liabilities. Special endorsements may be advised to protect the association against other claims.

Property insurance of the owner offers: (1) reimbursement for personal property losses; (2) reimbursement for damage to permanent attachments to the units. such as carpets, built-in cabinets, appliances, and the like; (3) additional living expense coverage, which protects the owner from relocation expenses during the repair of damaged units; and (4) loss assessment coverage, which protects unit owners from those liabilities against which the association is not insured. These latter liabilities must be paid by special assessments against members.

Specialized condominiums, for the present purpose, cover time-share condominiums and business condominiums. The time-share condominiums combine aspects of resort hotel management with aspects of condominium management. Services of management are critically important to time-share owners who have purchased exclusive rights of use for a limited time over the calendar year. Time-sharing interests may be exchanged for other national and international time-share interests.

Business condominiums are specialized ownerships that concentrate in offices, shopping centers, and industrial properties. The more successful office condominiums concentrate on medical and dental facilities in the suburbs located near hospitals. The few shopping centers developed as condominiums cover relatively small community shopping centers. In the same way, industrial condominiums appeal to unit owners who purchase relatively small units of 10,000 square feet or so. Though the condominium ownership provides all the advantages of ownership and its tax deductions, the limited market for condominium commercial space has prevented its general acceptance.

DISCUSSION QUESTIONS

1 Define the common terms associated with condominium ownership.
2 Explain the purpose and content of five condominium documents.
3 Explain the calculation of the pro rata share of common elements allocated according to square footage. Give an example in illustration of your answer.
4 Contrast condominium ownership with cooperative ownership.
5 What committees would you recommend to advise the board of directors (a) for a condominium serving elderly persons, and (b) for a luxury resort condominium?
6 Evaluate three types of management available to condominiums.
7 What three main duties are delegated to professional management firms? Explain fully.
8 What is meant by the transition period?
9 What is the function of the organization meeting?
10 What type of insurance would you recommend for the homeowners' association?
11 Explain the purpose of the acceptance committee.
12 What type of property insurance is advised for unit owners?
13 Contrast the management of time-sharing condominiums with that of residential condominiums.
14 Explain the special problems encountered in managing business condominiums that are not found in managing residential condominiums.

KEY TERMS AND CONCEPTS

Condominium unit	Resident manager
Common element	Transition period
Limited common elements	Organization meeting
Homeowners' association	Cumulative voting rights
Declaration	Acceptance committee
Fixtures	Actual value
Articles of incorporation	Coinsurance
Corporate bylaws	Waiver of subrogation
Condominium assessment	Comprehensive general liability
Management agreement	insurance
Unit deed	Loss assessment coverage
Self-management	Time-sharing management

SELF-QUIZ

Multiple-Choice Questions

_____ 1 Which of the following describes a condominium unit? (a) A condominium project less its individual units; (b) Facilities that are used exclusively by unit owners but not by all unit owners; (c) Cubic space in which the unit owner holds a fee-simple title; (d) Land and all other parts of the project held in common with owners in other units.

_____ 2 Which of the following refer(s) to everything contained within the four perimeter walls, floor, and ceiling of units: (a) Fixtures; (b) Personal property; (c) Common elements; (d) Limited common elements.

_____ 3 The declaration: (a) Dedicates land to condominium ownership; (b) Allocates the undivided interest in the common elements to each unit; (c) Describes the ownership and the common elements, and lists the legal responsibilities of unit owners; (d) All of the above.

_____ 4 Which of the following statements is correct? (a) Cooperative owners buy a share of real estate initially owned by the cooperative; (b) Cooperative purchasers take possession under a fee-simple title; (c) Cooperative owners are responsible for their individual mortgages; (d) The cooperative owner owns no real estate.

_____ 5 In a condominium, the budget committee: (a) Reserves the final right to approve the budget; (b) Advises the board on the final annual budget; (c) Prepares the final budget with the advice of the board of directors; (d) Operates independently of other committees.

_____ 6 Condominiums operating under self-management: (a) Are usually larger condominiums of 100 units or more; (b) Delegate management responsibilities to resident managers; (c) Utilize a combination of volunteer services and part-time employees; (d) Represent the most costly method of management for condominiums of less than 50 units.

_____ 7 Duties delegated to professional management firms include: (a) Fiscal, maintenance, and administrative functions; (b) Only maintenance duties; (c) Only administrative functions; (d) None of the above.

_____ 8 The purpose of the organizational meeting is to: (a) Elect the board of directors and set the date of the first annual meeting; (b) Encourage the sale of remaining condominium units; (c) Draft rules and regulations consistent with corporation bylaws; (d) Prepare a management policy manual.

_____ 9 Loss assessment coverage protects unit owners from: (a) Personal liability occurring within condominium units; (b) Physical damages to condominium units; (c) Physical damages to common elements; (d) Unusual expenses of the association that are not otherwise insured.

_____ 10 Business condominiums seem more successful for: (a) Regional shopping centers; (b) Industrial parks of more than 250 acres; (c) Medical and dental office buildings in suburbs, near hospitals; (d) Downtown office buildings.

Answer Key

1 (c), **2** (a), **3** (d), **4** (d), **5** (b), **6** (c), **7** (a), **8** (a), **9** (d), **10** (c).

Fill-In Questions

1 _____ refer to facilities used exclusively by unit owners but not by all unit owners.

2 The _____ of the homeowners' association control administrative procedures.

3 The _____ conveys title to the condominium unit and to a stated share in the undivided common elements.

4 The _____ is more economical for condominiums of 100 or more units.

5 The _____ is a temporary committee consisting of unit owners and the newly elected board of directors.

6 The _____ protects unit owners from personal liability for any occurrences within their individual units that damage other condominium property.

7 _____ refers to fee ownership in a particular unit and a corresponding exclusive right of use for a specified period of time annually.

8 Time-sharing owners, since they own only a small fraction of the project, are highly dependent on _____ .

9 _____ is a common characteristic of business condominiums.

10 _____ appeal to unit owners who purchase relatively small units of 10,000 square feet or so.

Answer Key

1 Limited common elements
2 bylaws
3 unit deed
4 professional management firm
5 acceptance committee
6 waiver of subrogation
7 Time sharing
8 competent management
9 Preselection of unit owners
10 Industrial condominiums

SELECTED REFERENCES

Clurman, David: *The Business Condominium*, New York: Wiley, 1973.

The Condominium Community, Chicago: Institute of Real Estate Management, 1978.

Creating a Community Association, Washington, D.C.: Urban Land Institute and Community Associations Institute, 1976.

How to Manage Condominiums, Los Angeles: California Association of Realtors, 1976.

The Insuring of Condominiums and Cooperatives, Indianapolis: The Rough Notes, 1977.

Managing a Successful Community Association, 2d ed., Washington, D.C.: Urban Land Institute and Community Associations Institute, 1976.

Chapter.14

Managing
Low-Income Housing

After studying this chapter, you should be familiar with:
1 Critical management issues in managing low-income housing
2 Management operations appropriate for low-income housing
3 Special management leasing techniques
4 Principles of managing housing for the elderly

In low-income housing, management is the most critical factor in determining project success. Management is judged according to *maintenance*, the time taken for making repairs; *management fairness*, and how the management staff treats tenants; *management responsiveness*, the concern of management in answering tenant complaints; and, above all, *firmness in enforcing rules*. Management, in fulfilling these roles, largely determines the financial viability of the project.[1]

Clearly, for low-income rental projects, management techniques deserve special attention. A professional manager faces different issues and must give more personal

[1] See, for example, Roger S. Ahlbrandt, Jr., Paul C. Brophy, and Katherine C. Burman, "Key to Satisfied Tenants: Good Management," *Journal of Property Management*, 39(3):213–215, 1974.

attention to tenants who face unique problems not found with moderate- and upper-income tenants. A discussion of the more critical management issues precedes the equally important points of management operations, leasing techniques, management performance, and housing management for the elderly.

CRITICAL MANAGEMENT ISSUES

Low-income units are often available to low-income groups in federally subsidized housing projects. This means that the property manager must observe regulations of federal agencies. And since many of the programs are undertaken by nonprofit sponsors, management deals with groups who are socially oriented rather than profit motivated.

Moreover, low-income tenants typically have great economic and social problems not faced by the more affluent. This means that the property manager must deal with a broad range of individual and family problems. And further, low-income rental housing is often racially integrated, giving the manager an added reason for developing the best possible administration. Elderly persons constitute another important segment of the low-income—and specialized—tenant market.

In working with low-income residents, management finds its resources fairly limited. This means that management expenses, which tend to be budgeted relatively low, require even greater emphasis on management efficiency. Rents are kept at the lowest possible level and most of the operating expenses are relatively fixed, namely, principal, interest, taxes, insurance, and other fixed costs such as heat, water, gas, and electricity. Thus, management has little operational flexibility; utility expenses, accounting, bookkeeping, and a minimum maintenance budget typically absorb most of the management resources.

In the face of these unique difficulties, the industry depends heavily on individuals with specialized management skills. In a report prepared for the Department of Housing and Urban Development by the National Corporation for Housing Partnerships, it was stated:

> *A new approach to the management of assisted housing must be defined and introduced.* To keep our housing livable we must design a new doctrine of housing function which recognizes that the rights and duties of owners, managers, and residents are all based on the authority which each retains, delegates or shares. *The duty of management must be to achieve the harmonious balance of the interest and needs of sponsors who own dwellings and residents who live in them.*[2]

The same report explained that high operating costs, security problems, and resident apathy, as well as the critical shortage of trained or experienced personnel, adversely affect new, rehabilitated, and existing assisted units. Predicting that 4.5 million units of assisted low-income housing will be occupied by 1980, officials

---

[2]National Corporation for Housing Partnerships, *Needed: A Strategy for Housing Management Training*, Washington, D.C.: Department of Housing and Urban Development, 1971, p. 6.

believed that the gaps between housing production and management should be closed. It was reported that more concern must be given to how housing functions, with the creation of accredited and responsive management personnel in sufficient numbers. Providing management that assured tenants in federally assisted housing a safe, sanitary, and satisfying place to live was considered of equal importance to the production of new housing units.

The Changing Concept of Management

In conventional practice, management works to protect the owner's investment. Such management activities, therefore, focus on the physical property, its daily maintenance, normal repair, and upkeep. In this role, the manager selects residents, collects rent, and supervises maintenance. The project manager assumes final responsibility for smooth functioning of the management process. This conventional practice is suitable for moderate- and upper-income housing, but low-income housing requires added duties.

To be sure, operational problems remain the same for low-income rental housing, but here management deals with the social environment common to low-income tenants. Management seeks a closer relationship between management operations and residents by establishing a sense of community within the housing project.

Compared to those of conventional rental housing, communications between residents and management are much closer. Communications can develop a feeling of pride among new tenants about their apartment and can provide assurance of adequate service. In sum, management gives added emphasis to the needs of residents.

Characteristics of Low-Income Families

For housing purposes, it is traditional to divide families by income—high, moderate, and low. While important for financial purposes, segregation of families by income alone does not focus on the critical management problems of low-income housing. For the present purpose, it seems more useful to classify low-income groups by three additional categories: (1) the upwardly mobile families, (2) the potentially mobile families, and (3) the nonmobile families.

Upwardly Mobile Families Families in the upwardly mobile group include a wage earner who will move up the economic scale as a result of education and motivation. The household head will convey the same motivation to children. Being proud and highly self-respecting, these families are typically reluctant to seek charity. They prefer housing without subsidies, but if subsidies are granted, they are needed for a relatively short time. These families give stability and character to a neighborhood. The central problem is to arrange housing services to help the family move up the economic scale.

The Potentially Mobile Families In some instances, families, through children, develop mobility over two generations. This group will also have some parents with earning capacity, so that economic mobility covers both parents and children.

In other groups, no parent is capable of earning income. And though the present generation is nonmobile, economic mobility may be secured through the children.

Consider the first group in which the household head, because of lack of education, experience, skills, or motivation, will not reach economic independence, that is, seasonal workers, handicapped persons, and those with social problems that leave them little sense of responsibility. The main problem in housing these families is to provide an environment whereby, if the household head does not achieve upward mobility, the children will have better opportunity. For if the children adopt the parent's attitude toward work, they become dropouts or gang members, or otherwise assume a sense of defeat. Suitable housing for the parents consequently represents an investment in the children.

Consider next the family that can never have a wage earner. The household remains nonmobile until the children reach working age. Included in this group are the single parents and households with disabled or otherwise handicapped wage earners. These households are the most disorganized, with many school dropouts, drug problems, and the like. This group will need housing subsidies for relatively long periods. The housing environment should provide incentives, assistance, and examples that increase the possibility of mobility—social, educational, and economic.

The Nonmobile Families Members of the nonmobile group will need housing subsidies indefinitely. They have no hope of increasing income; they have no children who can benefit from incentive programs. The group includes the elderly, the disabled, and the socially or physically handicapped. Housing managers must treat these families so that they may live with a sense of belonging. At the same time they need a maximum number of social services.[3]

MANAGEMENT OPERATIONS

Since housing for low-income groups usually requires some form of subsidy, management organization must be supplemented by a tenant organization, social services, and, to a limited degree, medical services. Such a scheme is shown in Figure 14-1, which shows the relationship between management that works under a nonprofit board of directors and the tenant organization. The board of directors acts like a property owner, establishes long-range policies, and assumes final responsibility for personnel, management, financing and tenant selection.

In addition to the common duties of management, namely, maintenance, emergency repairs, and administrative services, management services cover a broad range of social services not found in the privately owned luxury apartments. Figure 14-1 shows that the staff directs residents to various family, consumer, education, and financial planning agencies or private services. Even medical services come under the supervision of the project manager. Though not directly servicing medical needs, the project manager is responsible for seeing that residents know where to get the required assistance.

[3]Quoted from a government publication by Bernard A. Gray, Sr., "Some Thoughts on Managing Low-Income Housing," *Journal of Property Management*, 38(2):88–89, 1973.

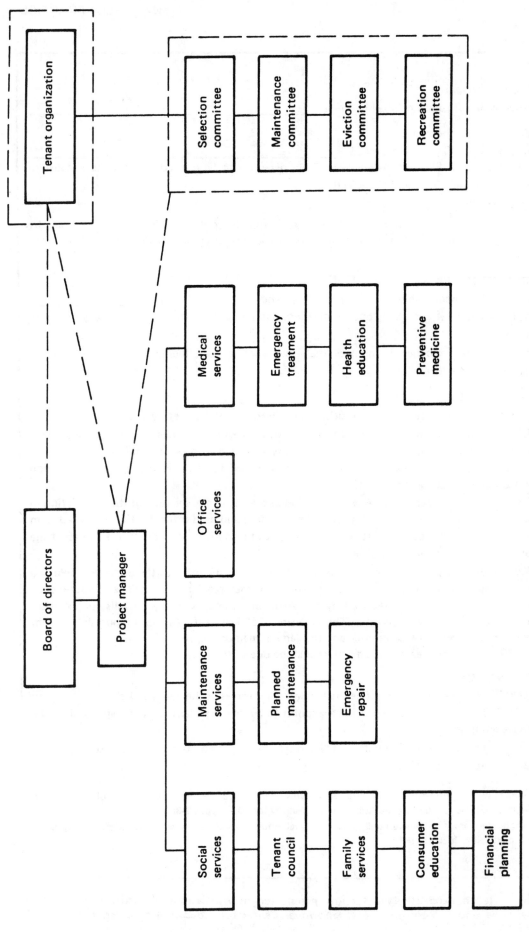

Figure 14-1 Recommended management organization for subsidized housing. (*Source: Adapted from Bernard A. Gray, Sr., "Some Thoughts on Managing Low-Income Housing," Journal of Property Management, 38(2):9, March/April 1973.*)

ARTICLE I   (Name)
The name of this organization shall be the _____

ARTICLE II   (Membership)
All adult residents 18 years and over of _____
are members of the Resident Association.** No person is to be refused membership because of
race, color, religion, sex, or national origin.

ARTICLE III   (Purpose)
The purpose of this association is to provide for expanded opportunities for participation by
residents in the management of housing development affairs and in programs designed to improve
community life.

ARTICLE IV   (Meetings)
SECTION 1   The membership shall meet regularly. The meetings will be held _____
(day, time, location if constant). Special meetings can be called with _____ days notice to
the membership.
SECTION 2   The Executive Committee shall meet before each membership meeting and as
requested by the President.

ARTICLE V   (Officers)
The elected officers shall consist of: President, Vice President and Secretary-Treasurer.
SECTION 1   The President—The President shall preside at all general meetings of the Association
and of the Executive Committee. In his absence, any officer may preside in the following order:
Vice President, Secretary-Treasurer. The President may call special meetings of the association
after appropriate notice to all residents.
SECTION 2   Vice President—The Vice President shall preside at any meeting of the Association in
the absence of the President. He shall succeed the President and hold office for the unexpired term
in the event that the President shall resign or is unable to finish his term of office. He will assist the
President in the program of the association.
SECTION 3   Secretary-Treasurer—The Secretary shall write a summary of the discussion held at a
general meeting. Minutes shall be read at the beginning of each regular meeting. The Treasurer shall
be responsible for any income received by the Association and shall pay all bills for expenses
approved by the Executive Committee. The Treasurer shall keep a full financial report and present
such report to the Executive Committee and the general membership.
SECTION 4   The term of each elected officer shall be one year.

ARTICLE VI   (Committees)
SECTION 1   The Executive Committee shall create committees as they are needed.
SECTION 2   Committee chairmen will be appointed by the President with the approval of the
Executive Committee.
SECTION 3   The Executive Committee shall consist of the elected officers of the Association and
the Chairman of each committee.

*These sample by-laws are adapted from "Resident Involvement Guide," National Association of Housing and
Redevelopment Officials, 2600 Virginia Avenue, N.W., Washington, D.C., pp. 25–36.
**All lease holders or all immediate family members or all adults over 21 years can be specified as long as the
membership eligibility is clearly defined.

Figure 14-2 Recommended bylaws for low-income tenant associations. *(Source: Housing Manager's Resource Book, Washington, D.C.: National Center for Housing Management, 1976, pp. 286–287.)*

ARTICLE VII (Finances)

The financial accounts of the Association shall be reviewed by the Executive Committee every three months. No membership dues shall be charged.

ARTICLE VIII (Nominating and Election of Officers)

SECTION 1 The Nominating Committee shall prepare a list of at least two candidates for each office. This list shall be presented at the July meeting of the general membership.

SECTION 2 At that time, members may nominate additional candidates for any office.

SECTION 3 The names of any additional nominees shall be added to the ballot after these nominations have been "seconded" and the person so nominated has agreed to have his or her name put on the ballot.

SECTION 4 Election of officers for the following year shall be held at the July meeting of the general membership. Officers shall be elected by a majority vote of the membership.

SECTION 5 The retiring President shall serve ex-officio on the Executive Committee for one year.

ARTICLE IX (Amendments)

SECTION 1 These by-laws may be changed by a two-thirds vote of the members present at a meeting of the general membership.

SECTION 2 Members shall be notified of proposed amendments by special announcements delivered to their units at least two weeks before the meeting.

Figure 14-2 *(continued)*

Tenant Organizations

The tenant organization helps to implement management policies. A selection committee helps orient new residents, while the maintenance, eviction, and recreation committees assist in other management duties. Surely, management organization for subsidized housing goes beyond maintaining physical aspects of the project.

Tenant associations serve as a means of communicating with residents. Prospective policy changes may institute feedback from residents, which makes implementation of policies much easier. Tenant associations make management more accessible. And when tenants know that management is willing to work with resident representatives, there is likely to be a more workable relationship between manager and residents.

While tenant organizations may be instituted by residents, occasionally management takes the initiative. In taking these first steps, management would set a date and location for an organizational meeting, present the benefits of the tenant association, and provide assistance in selecting a temporary chairperson. From this point, management reverts to an "invitation only" basis. It is advised that no management should sit in on future meetings unless specifically requested to do so. No comments on group opinions should be offered unless they have been directly solicited. In suggesting a tenant organization, project managers introduce the articles of the organization shown in Figure 14-2.

In dealing with tenant organizations, it is realized that groups take more time to make a decision, but the advantage lies in commitment by a group in gaining overall cooperation from residents. With tenant groups, managers are advised to develop trust by following through on decisions, keeping promises, and carrying out promises as quickly as possible. In responding to formal or verbal requests, resident managers let residents know of actions based on their request, or if the request has been denied.

Above all, managers explain decisions to help avoid misunderstandings and to avoid appearing arbitrary. Managers show that they care enough about residents to tell them why a decision was made. Finally, managers observe certain other recommended rules: they do not control or dominate the meeting, they do not schedule meetings, they do not attend all the meetings or sit through entire meetings unless requested, and they do not act as chairpersons.

Tenant Selection

It would be difficult to overemphasize the importance of tenant selection. Even the Department of Housing and Urban Development endorses and supports screening of applicants to eliminate individuals or families that will be a threat to the peaceful enjoyment of the homes of other residents. According to this source:

> We endorse and support screening of applicants to identify those with demonstrable, continuing patterns of nonpayment of rent, destructive use of the premises, or other substantial lease violations. Good managers still admit many such applicants but subject to special agreements designed to zero in on the problems. Good managers focus services on such tenants, where indicated. Good managers rule such families ineligible, if the family is unwilling to accept special lease provisions and services.[4]

To observe these warnings, more than ever, the manager must make value judgments that relate human housing requirements to monthly payments and housing operations.

Regretfully, the manager must often make decisions within stringent limits of these financial systems that may not generate sufficient net income to meet required services. Consequently the manager operates in a state of frustration created by demands to pay property expenses and demands of tenants. Hence, these pressures make tenant selection critically important, for it is not unusual to have ten applicants for every available unit. The major issue here is to avoid a tenant selection by irrational and emotional judgments about good tenants.

Management Attitudes Stereotypes are demonstrated by the manager who accepts only persons with excellent credit rating, and in this way rejects unmarried women and divorced or separated women with children. The selection policy leads the manager "to accept very nice people who will pay their rent, keep the place clean, and behave themselves...."[5]

It is quite clear that this statement reveals certain erroneous assumptions about what constitutes a good tenant. Assumptions about marital status and behavior have little correlation. Questions over housekeeping, tenant behavior, and life-style are of

[4] Orville E. Freeman, "What Is a Good Public Housing Manager?" in *Public Management in the Seventies: Readings*, Washington, D.C.: National Association of Housing and Redevelopment Officials, 1974, p. 14.
[5] Edwin D. Abrams and Edward B. Blackman, *Managing Low and Moderate Income Housing*, New York: Praeger, 1973, p. 57.

no concern to management except as they affect the condition of the property or other tenants.

It should be noted also that low-income tenants frequently have distorted views of management. Tenants often see the owner or managing agent as someone more interested in the physical property and income than in persons. Some tenants believe that the tenant selection process is inconsistent, irrational, and less than fair.

In contrast, in selecting tenants the manager should be primarily concerned with whether tenants have the financial means to pay rent promptly and whether they are willing to meet that responsibility. In addition, managers look for cooperative and understanding tenants—tenants who realize that management has certain limitations and that managers attempt to deal effectively with their problems.

Tenant Selection Criteria To be sure, not all eligible residents can be selected. Managers must establish certain priorities, remembering that it is easier to keep out a potentially unsatisfactory resident than to remove an existing one. Selection of elderly residents must take into account that their physical and mental capabilities to live independently must be compatible with the available services of the project. With these qualifications, applicants will be selected by certain guidelines:

1 Selection criteria should be based on sound business criteria.
2 There should be an objective plan for selecting residents.
3 Each applicant should be judged according to the accepted selection criteria. The selection system should be based on good records.
4 Selection should follow an acceptable marketing strategy. Selection policy should be known and explained to applicants and to residents.

Managers with a policy of selection then tend to judge acceptable tenants according to (1) employment stability, (2) credit ratings, (3) past rent-paying history, (4) family stability, and (5) history of vandalism or other indications of trouble.[6] A form for rental applicants is shown in Figure 14-3. From information on this form, the manager may review applicants' past rent history, employment and income, credit and banking references, and personal references. If prospects apply for federally assisted housing, special forms to establish eligibility must be used.[7]

While the manager wants to select the ideal tenant, some tenants look merely for shelter at a cost within their financial means. Most tenants, however, look for more than mere shelter they look to the total environment and atmosphere created by the neighbors and management policy. Tenants hope to find a housing project in which management will be responsive to tenant needs, will be sympathetic to their life-style, will answer questions honestly, and administer the project in a fair and just manner. Prospective tenants see the potential success or failure of their housing according to their judgment of the manager.

---

[6] *The Housing Manager's Resource Book*, Washington, D.C.: The National Center for Housing Management, 1976, pp. 62-63.
[7] For instance, see ibid., pp. 45-61.

(Please Print)

NAME _____ AGE ____ SOCIAL SECURITY NO. _____

PRESENT ADDRESS _____ HOW LONG _____

                                        HOME PHONE _____

LANDLORD'S NAME _____ HIS PHONE _____

AND ADDRESS _____

REASON FOR MOVING _____

EMPLOYED BY _____ HOW LONG _____

_____ BUS. PHONE _____

POSITION _____ GROSS INCOME _____ ☐ WK. ☐ MO. ☐ YR.

OTHER INCOME SOURCE _____ AMOUNT _____ ☐ WK. ☐ MO. ☐ YR.

CAR(S) _____ MAKE _____ YEAR _____ LICENSE & STATE _____

_____

REFERENCES:

BANK _____ CHECKING ACCT. NO. _____

_____ SAVINGS ACCT. NO. _____

CREDIT _____

_____

PERSONAL _____

_____

ARE YOU SUBJECT TO TRANSFER ____ REASON _____

WHEN DO YOU WISH TO MOVE IN _____ HOW MANY WILL LIVE IN APT. _____

HOW DID YOU LEARN ABOUT THESE APARTMENTS?

          NEWSPAPER ____ RADIO ____ DRIVING BY ____ ROAD SIGN _____

          RESIDENT ____ OTHER _____

I CERTIFY THAT THE FOREGOING INFORMATION IS TRUE AND COMPLETE TO THE BEST OF MY KNOWLEDGE. I AUTHORIZE INQUIRIES TO BE MADE TO VERIFY THE STATEMENTS ABOVE.

NCHM FORM 101
      (6/76)

_____

_____

Figure 14-3 Application for apartment rental. *(Source: Housing Manager's Resource Book, Washington, D.C.: National Center for Housing Management, 1976, p. 44.)*

On-Site Resident Managers Shannon and Luchs of Washington, D.C., after researching low-income housing management for the Department of Housing and Urban Development, concluded that "on-site resident managers are essential to operation of properties for low-income families. Particularly when there are heavy concentrations of large families in a relatively small area, such a staff person can make or break a project."[8]

In making this recommendation, the researchers stated further that resident managers should be selected for their sensitivity to the needs of residents, even to the point of answering emergency calls at night. Consistent with other authorities, property maintenance should follow a planned schedule; requests from tenants should be answered within 24 hours and major repairs should be made within one week. It was advised further that staff employees be residents of managed properties.

Statutory Requirements Federal law prohibits the exclusion of tenants on the basis of race, color, creed, sex, religion, or national origin. Similarly, many state laws forbid discrimination on additional grounds—discrimination on the basis of children, welfare assistance, or personal handicaps. Some communities may require that housing agencies give priority to certain groups. For instance, some state housing finance agencies require a specified percentage of low-income units to be available to welfare recipients.

Managers tend to be guided by certain financial rules in selecting tenants. That is, there is some relationship between the desired income and the rent payment, usually considered to be 25 percent, though some programs suggest a maximum ratio of rent to income of 35 percent. However, the rental agency must consider the total fixed debt of a family. If time payments absorb a considerable portion of family income, the rent may be beyond their means, even if the rent-to-income ratio falls within accepted limits. Generally, the higher the percentage of debt payments, the greater the incidence of delinquency.

Sources of Referrals Some programs may require that the local manager pursue an affirmative action program. In other instances, managers are dependent on referrals to gain a proper tenant balance. If welfare agencies refer a tenant, they appreciate learning the outcome of their referrals. If the agency is advised that the tenant has been accepted, the agency is likely to refer other qualified tenants. In the same manner, if the tenant does not qualify, and the agency is given reasons for the disqualification, the agency is likely to send better-qualified people.

Churches are another source of qualified tenants. The church staff often knows families who require low-and moderate-income housing. In addition to these sources, the usual channels of communication such as newspapers, direct mail, and other mass media are utilized by low-income property managers. These channels are particularly effective in following affirmative action programs, which usually require a positive means to reach selected tenant groups.

[8] Linda Kuzmack, "Private Realtors, Public Housing Tenants Work Together to Manage Public Housing," in *Public Housing Management in the Seventies: Readings*, Washington, D.C.: National Association of Housing and Redevelopment Officials, 1974, p. 139.

Social Services

By knowing about available social services, the manager may correct problems that affect rights of quiet enjoyment. For example, marital quarrels in late hours that disturb other families would require that the manager refer the family to marriage counselors or legal aid societies. Alcoholism that disturbs others requires that the manager direct the family to Alcoholics Anonymous or other medical, social, or legal community agencies.

Managers must give special attention to children, and must respond to needs of the children with respect and with positive expectations. Frequently managers must invest personal time in developing healthy and wholesome relationships with children and their families—but there is no quick and easy solution. Children should learn to respect house rules and regulations.

In brief, low-income rental housing emphasizes social management. A family with financial problems must be quickly referred to local agencies that are equipped to deal with unemployment or prolonged illness. Managers must discover these problems at an early stage; the problem of rent that is 2 or 3 months delinquent is virtually without solution. Familiarity with church and nonprofit sponsors who may help distressed families may alleviate financial problems.

MANAGEMENT LEASING TECHNIQUES

For low-income housing, the lease is treated as a contract between landlord and residents and as a conveyance of a property right: the leasehold estate. While subject to statutory and common law, leases for low-income property tend to be more specific about certain duties of the tenant. In addition, for subsidized projects, project managers may be required to follow the model FHA lease form. Figure 14-4 illustrates a short-form lease. Though this lease may not agree with local statutory and common law, attention is directed to the duties listed for the landlord and tenant.

Lease Terms

The first part of the lease dedicates the premises to the lease, establishes the rent terms, and identifies the landlord and tenant. In the first part of the lease, the landlord conveys the leasehold interest to the tenant.

The contractual rights start with paragraph one, which requires that the landlord maintain the grounds. In addition, the landlord promises to maintain the real estate and supply utility services in a reasonable and customary manner.

The tenant in return promises to keep premises in a clean and sanitary condition, that is, in the same condition of repair and improvement as received and without any alteration. The tenant agrees to occupy premises with only the immediate family—for residential and no other purpose—and with no other persons, and promises not to permit unlawful or immoral practices or to disturb other tenants in any way. An additional clause requires payment of the monthly rent as long as the tenant remains in possession of the premises.

LEASE, made this_____day of _____, 1969.

Landlord: _____

_____

Tenant: _____

_____

Premises: _____

_____

TERM: Commencing at 12:01 A.M. on _____, 19_
and ending at midnight on the last day of _____, 19_
and from month to month thereafter.

Rent: $_____ per month, payable monthly in
advance on the first day of each calendar month from the date of
this lease to April 30, 19__. Thereafter the monthly rental may
be adjusted by Landlord once each year on the first day of May.

Landlord hereby leases to Tenant and Tenant takes and hires
from Landlord the said Premises for said Term and at said Rent
and Tenant agrees to pay said Rent in the manner and at the time
above set forth. It is further agreed as follows:

1. Landlord shall:

a. Keep the sidewalks and lawns free of litter and
rubbish, and the sidewalks free from snow; keep the lawns properly watered and cut, and any flowers, shrubs, or trees in a
proper state of care and maintenance; all on the real estate of
which said premises are a part;

b. Maintain said real estate in accordance with all
applicable laws and ordinances; and

c. Supply at his expense those of the following
utilities and services which are indicated, in reasonable amounts
and at such times as customarily furnished:

Garbage collection	____	Vermin Control	____
Cold Water	____	Hot Water	____
Cooking Gas	____	Electricity	____
Heating	____	_____	____

2. Tenant shall:

a. Keep said Premises in a clean and sanitary condition, in good state of repair and maintenance, in the same condition of repair and improvement as when received, without any
alteration, and in accordance with applicable laws and ordinances;

b. Keep said Premises as the private dwelling of only
Tenants and his immediate family, as shown on his application to
Landlord, and for no other purpose or persons;

c. Not permit unlawful or immoral practices on the
Premises, nor allow the Premises to be so used that the reputation of said real estate may be injured or the insurance thereon
cancelled or the rate therefor increased, nor deface or injure
said real estate in any way, or disturb the other tenants in any
way;

Figure 14-4 Short-form lease for low-income families.

d. Pay (1) the monthly rental as long as he remains in possession of the Premises, regardless of the filing of a suit against him, or the recovery of judgment thereon, (2) all costs and expenses incurred by Landlord in enforcing this Lease or in securing possession after its termination, (3) the expense incurred by Landlord in making repairs, alterations, and replacements occasioned by Tenant's breach of this Lease. The costs and expenses set forth in (2) and (3) shall constitute additional rent due and payable on the 1st day of the month following that in which they were so incurred.

3. And:

a. This Lease may be cancelled by the cancelling party giving the other party five days written notice when said other party has breached or violated the provisions of this Lease; or

b. This Lease may be cancelled without cause by either party giving the other party at least 15 days' written notice of such cancellation.

c. This Lease shall terminate if the Premises are rendered untenantable by fire or other casualty.

4. Further:

a. Rent shall be paid at _____ _____, or at such other place as Landlord may designate in writing. Notices shall be served on Landlord at said address or at such other place, and on Tenant at the Premises.

b. Tenant's interest in the Premises may not be sublet or assigned nor may his interest in this Lease be assigned, voluntarily or by operation of law.

c. Landlord shall have reasonable access to the Premises for the purpose of determining whether Tenant's agreements are being performed, and for the purpose of doing necessary repairs and maintenance.

d. Landlord reserves the right to subordinate the Lease at all times to the lien of any mortgage now or hereafter placed upon the Premises, and Tenant agrees to execute and deliver on demand all instruments so subordinating this Lease to any such lien, and for this purpose hereby irrevocably appoints Landlord his attorney in fact to execute and deliver any such instrument for and in the name of Tenant.

WITNESS the hands and seals of the parties hereto in duplicate this day and year first above written.

Seal	Tenant

Seal	Tenant

Seal	Landlord

Figure 14-4 *(continued)*

The final paragraph states the manner in which rent will be paid, prohibits the tenant from subletting or assigning his or her interest, gives the landlord reasonable access, and allows the landlord to subordinate his or her interest.

Management Performance

There are relationships among rent delinquencies, collection losses, tenant turnover, and management performance. Yet it will be recognized that certain factors are not under control of management. Neighborhood conditions, social services, and physical characteristics such as the number of units, age of buildings, and construction quality are part of the environment that must be accepted by management and residents alike.

On other issues under control of management, research has shown that management performance is critical in three main areas: (1) strict rule enforcement, (2) management responsiveness to tenant needs, and (3) occupant concern for their unit and the project. More successfully managed projects illustrate these three operational practices.[9]

Strict Rule Enforcement Benefits of strict rule enforcement have been well documented. Tenants tend to be more satisfied, operating expenses tend to be lower, and delinquent payments tend to decrease.

This suggests that incoming tenants should be given a copy of the house rules and instructed in their importance. While house rules may be included in the lease form, the special importance of house rules may be emphasized by giving each tenant a readable copy. The assistance of a tenant association in enforcing house rules is highly recommended.

Management Responsiveness to Tenant Needs Management responsiveness may be measured by the reaction time given requests for repairs. Management concern over adequate recreational space and courteous treatment by staff also assumes major importance. Again, the rate of rent delinquencies tends to be lower where management response is the highest.

Experienced managers make sure that tenants know who to contact for repairs. In part, responsiveness of management follows from the competence of the project manager and the staff.

Occupant Concern Tenant concern for the project depends on the extent to which tenants actively participate in social and recreational programs. In part, occupant concern is shown by the number of residents willing to volunteer services in various project programs. Again the record shows that operating costs are lower, that tenants take better care of their apartments, and that they express more satisfaction in projects where they show a high degree of concern for their units. Moreover, vandalism, burglaries, and violence tend to occur less often in these cases.

[9] Robert Sadacca, Morton Isler, and David Carlson, "Effective Subsidized Housing Management Practices," *Journal of Property Management*, 41(5):210–215, 1976.

MANAGING HOUSING FOR THE ELDERLY

At the outset it is worthwhile to recognize certain myths about the elderly that bear on housing management. The more relevant myths may be summarized in seven points:

1 Most old people are feeble.
2 Most old people live in institutions.
3 Most old people are childish.
4 A person declines in intellectual ability as he or she becomes older.
5 Most old people cannot learn new things.
6 Old people do not need education.
7 Older people do not care about their appearance.

In truth, the only similarity among elderly people is their age. Otherwise, the elderly are individuals with differences like the rest of the population. While their physical strength declines with age, there is a wide variation in individual strength and physical agility.

Only a minority of the elderly live in institutions, which indicates that only a few want institutional supervision. Unless affected by disease, old people are not childish, they behave maturely; they perform better than young people in tests on vocabulary, verbal comprehension, and arithmetic; and, though learning may take more time, their ability to learn remains. There is no evidence showing that motivation to learn disappears in the aging process, especially if learning is stimulated and rewarded. It is equally true that the elderly maintain the same interests, clothing, and appearance as they had in the past.

The Tenant Mix

It is fairly certain that managers must be increasingly responsible for administering to elderly tenants. In the next 30 years, the number of elderly is expected to increase to 30 million people of an estimated population of 310 million persons. According to the 1970 census, there were 138 elderly women to every 100 elderly men. Further, most elderly men are married while most elderly women are widows—there are more than four times as many widows as widowers.[10]

In view of these trends, the manager guards against forming an unbalanced development, and hopes to avoid housing overwhelmed with women. Ideally, the manager balances the number of elderly single men, single women, and couples. The mixture of tenants ensures that no group is such a minority that its members' needs are neglected. The management staff provides opportunities for numerous social contacts among the tenants.

A further complication is that the elderly are often on fixed incomes and subject to continuing inflation. Subsequently, housing represents not only a major living cost but a growing proportion of family expenses. Consequently, managers must keep informed about assistance and services available to the elderly.

---

[10] *Managing Houses and Services for the Elderly*, Washington, D.C.: The National Center for Housing Management, 1977, p. 2.

Housing Design

Housing for the elderly should meet physical and social needs of the aging. Special attention should be given to:

1 The conservation of energy; minimize the need to reach, lift, bend, pull, or climb
2 Special safety features, such as rails and easy-to-open windows
3 Adequate temperature controls
4 Natural and artificial light
5 Protection from disturbing noises
6 Space for group activity
7 Aesthetic construction qualities[11]

The recommended list of design features is shown in Figure 14-5.

These design criteria show a relationship between type of project, resident selection, services to tenants, and the financial feasibility of the project. With a balance among these four variables, the type of residents served controls the level of nonshelter services; the physical project design should meet the needs of proposed tenants.

Nonshelter Services

The services provided for tenants depend on the resident profile, which should identify the age groups, sex distribution, family status, income groups, special health problems, educational levels, and hobbies of residents. The cost and services supplied will center on

social services
transportation services
security
housekeeping services
meal service
health services

The higher the degree of tenant independence, the lower the service level. With increasing dependence, more services must be provided. The service package will be minimal for residents who live in independent housing facilities. For individual apartments, the services are primarily nonessential or merely a convenience. Most nonshelter services are directly controlled by residents.

Congregate housing refers to housing for tenants who need special services intermittently. For example, they may need occasional health or transportation services. Facilities for the highly dependent, at the extreme, cater to those who require long-term nursing care and hospitalization.

In some developments, transportation for independent housing will take the form of car pools or volunteers from community organizations, such as churches that provide recreation or special transportation needs.

[11] *Managing Houses & Services for the Elderly*, Washington, D.C.: National Center for Housing Management, 1977, p. 18.

HOUSING DESIGN FOR THE ELDERLY

Needs of Elderly	Design Features	Does your property have these?
Touch Sensation	Temperature and climate controls	_____
	Heat lamps in the bathrooms	_____
	Hot-cold water temperature controls	_____
	Regulated air flow	_____
	Front range controls	_____
	Lever door handles	_____
Mobility-Agility	Hand rails along halls and stairs	_____
	Benches in shower stalls	_____
	Grab bars in bathroom areas	_____
	Kitchen shelves less than 63" high	_____
	Electrical outlets at least 24" high	_____
	Non-skid floors	_____
	Automatic front doors	_____
	Benches in elevators and elevator lobbies	_____
	Sturdy, comfortable furniture	_____
	Easy-to-open windows	_____
	On grade entrances	_____
	Automatic elevators	_____
	Public laundry facilities	_____
	Easy-to-use garbage disposal system	_____
	Wall hung light fixtures	_____
	Self-defrosting refrigerators	_____
	Easy-to-use fire extinguishers	_____
Smell Sensation	Electric stoves instead of gas	_____
	Smoke detectors	_____
	Adequate ventilation	_____
	Sanitary garbage disposal system	_____
Sight	Well lighted apartments, halls, parking areas	_____
	Use of color contrasts	_____
	Highly visible risers	_____
	Large print readable signs, papers, controls	_____
	Front door peep holes	_____
	Height of windows	_____
	Fluorescent lighting in kitchens	_____
Hearing	Adequate sound insulation	_____
	Specially tuned door bells	_____
	Good fire alarm systems	_____
Social Needs	Outdoor recreation areas	_____
	Adequate indoor community space	_____
	Lobby areas with furniture	_____
	Benches in mailbox areas	_____
	Chairs or benches near building entrances	_____
	Health care facilities	_____
	Furniture for sitting in laundry rooms	_____
Security	Emergency alarm system in apartments	_____
	Strong secure locks	_____
	Two-way communication in elevators	_____
	Entrance-exit monitoring system	_____

Figure 14-5 Judging housing design for the elderly. (*Source: Managing Housing & Services for the Elderly, Washington, D.C., National Center for Housing Management, 1977, p. 18.*)

Security is particularly critical with housing for the elderly. Security may be provided through use of the proper *hardware*—locks on windows and doors. Security is also advanced by designing the project in small components so that it creates defensible space (fenced-off public areas, or use confined to residents of individual buildings. In addition, security personnel educate tenants to develop their own security, emphasizing elementary precautions such as keeping doors locked, carrying entrance keys to storage areas, using closed-circuit intercoms and television monitoring, locking personal property, and advising tenants on free neighborhood services and self-protection advice.

In brief, nonshelter services combine tenant fees and monthly charges with financing services from state, local, and federal sources and the assistance of local social and community groups.

SUMMARY

Low-income rental housing requires familiarity with regulations of federal agencies. Moreover, low-income tenants have greater economic and social problems than the more affluent. At the same time, management resources are fairly limited, which places a premium on specialized management skills. Skills focus not only on the physical property but on the social environment common to low-income tenants.

In this respect property managers deal with the *upwardly mobile* families, the *potentially mobile* families, and the *nonmobile* families. In the first group, low-income housing is a temporary arrangement pending movement of the individual family to higher economic, social, and housing status. Potentially mobile families are usually those whose mobility can be gained through children. The housing environment must provide the potential for upward mobility in this second group. The nonmobile families require housing that gives the occupant a sense of belonging; they require the maximum number of social services.

Management operations must adapt to federal and state regulations, and, frequently, a nonprofit board of directors—a board that administers a broad range of social services in addition to providing shelter. Tenant organizations are another aspect of housing management that is not always faced in higher-income rental housing. Both the board and tenant organization help select compatible tenants who have been screened for adaptation to rental housing. The critical importance of tenant selection requires on-site resident managers.

Management leasing techniques start with leases that are more specific with respect to the duties of the landlord and tenants. For subsidized housing, rental leases follow model forms recommended by federal agencies. In the properly executed lease, professional management strictly enforces rules, maintains a high degree of responsiveness to tenant needs, and develops occupants' concern for their units by encouraging tenant participation in volunteer work and participation in tenant organizations.

Management for the elderly calls for specialized management that provides a balance between single men, women, and couples. The housing design must meet the physical and social needs of the aging. The degree to which housing design is adapted to each of the elderly depends on resident selection and services offered to tenants.

Like low-income housing, nonshelter services meet the needs of particular age groups, sex distribution, family status, income groups, and special health problems. The range of nonshelter services depends partly on residents' widely diversified education and interest levels. Security measures, in particular, are examples of nonshelter services designed specifically for housing for the elderly.

DISCUSSION QUESTIONS

1   Discuss the more critical management issues encountered in managing low-income-level housing.
2   Discuss how the management of low-income rental housing differs from the management of moderate- or upper-income housing. Explain thoroughly.
3   Explain how you would classify low-income housing with regard to social, economic, and occupational mobility. How do these groups affect housing management administration?
4   In what way do tenant organizations help implement housing policies?
5   Explain how you would establish a policy for tenant selection in a low-income housing project.
6   Why are social services part of the management task in low-income rental housing?
7   Explain the typical social services provided by low-income rental housing managers.
8   Describe in your own words the landlord duties commonly listed in low-income residential leases.
9   Describe in your own words the tenant duties commonly listed in low-income rental housing leases.
10 Explain three main ways in which management may improve performance.
11 Discuss common myths that relate to the elderly. How do these myths affect housing management policy?
12 In what special ways is housing adapted to needs of the elderly?
13 What nonshelter services do the elderly generally require?

KEY TERMS AND CONCEPTS

Upwardly mobile families	Strict rule enforcement
Potentially mobile families	Management responsiveness
Nonmobile families	Occupant concern
Tenant selection	Tenant mix
Management attitudes	Nonshelter services
Resident managers	Congregate housing
Social services	Resident profile

SELF-QUIZ

Multiple-Choice Questions

_____ 1 Which of the following applies to the management of low-income rental property? (a) The property manager must often observe regulations of federal agencies; (b) Low-income tenants typically have greater economic and social problems than the more affluent; (c) Management resources are fairly limited; (d) All of the above.

_____ 2 In dealing with low-income rental property, property managers: (a) Concentrate on physical property; (b) Deal with the social environment that is common to low-income tenants; (c) Have less need for communications with tenants; (d) Do not require on-site representation.

_____ 3 Low-income tenants: (a) Are treated as nonmobile individuals or families; (b) As a group, require permanent housing subsidies; (c) Include upwardly mobile families who require housing assistance for a relatively short time; (d) None of the above.

_____ 4 Which of the following statements is *not* correct? (a) Tenant organizations help implement management policy; (b) Tenant associations serve as a means of communicating with residents; (c) Tenant associations make management more accessible; (d) Management is advised to attend all tenant meetings, and often serves as chairperson.

_____ 5 In selecting tenants for low-income housing, property managers: (a) Must accept applicants in the order that they appear on a waiting list; (b) Follow procedures dictated by federal regulation; (c) Reject single, divorced, or separated women with children as poor credit risks; (d) None of the above.

_____ 6 Research has shown that: (a) On-site resident managers are unnecessary for low-income housing; (b) On-site resident managers are essential to the operation of properties for low-income families; (c) On-site resident managers are required for every 25 units; (d) Volunteers may assume on-site resident manager responsibilities.

_____ 7 While subject to statutory and common law, leases for low-income rental property tend to be more: (a) Specific about certain duties of the tenant; (b) Detailed with respect to responsibilities of the landlord; (c) Specific on occupancy by only the immediate family as shown on the lease; (d) All of the above.

_____ 8 Management performance tends to improve with: (a) Relatively low rents and strict rule enforcement; (b) Management responsiveness to tenant needs and the highest possible rent; (c) Rental projects in central-city areas; (d) Strict rule enforcement, management responsiveness to tenant needs, and occupant concern for the unit and project.

_____ 9 Which of the following statements is correct? (a) Most old people are in institutions; (b) Most old people cannot learn new things; (c) The only similarity among elderly people is their age; (d) Most old people are childish.

10 Primary considerations in housing for the elderly are the: (a) Relationships among the type of project, resident selection, service to tenants, and financial feasability; (b) Age of the elderly and their income; (c) Physical design and nonshelter services; (d) Resident profile and family expenses.

Answer Key

1 (d), **2** (b), **3** (c), **4** (d), **5** (d), **6** (b), **7** (d), **8** (d), **9** (c), **10** (a).

Fill-In Questions

1 The _____ emphasizes the added efficiency required for low-income housing management.

2 Conventional management practice focuses on the _____.

3 Property managers deal with the _____ common to low-income tenants.

4 In the case of potentially mobile families, families develop mobility over two generations_____.

5 _____ help implement management policy.

6 In selecting low-income tenants, the major issue is to avoid tenant selection by _____ judgments about good tenants.

7 For low-income residents, generally, the higher the percentage of _____ _____ , the greater the incidence of delinquency.

8 For low-income housing, the lease is treated as a _____ between landlord and residents and as a _____ of a property right.

9 Under _____ , tenants tend to be more satisfied, operating expenses tend to be lower, and delinquent payments tend to decrease.

10 Nonshelter services provided for elderly tenants depend on the _____ _____ .

Answer Key

1 below-average management expense
2 physical property
3 social environment
4 through children
5 Tenant organizations

6 irrational and emotional
7 debt payments
8 contract, conveyance
9 strict rule enforcement
10 resident profile

SELECTED REFERENCES

Abrams, Edwin B., and Edward B. Blackman: *Managing Low and Moderate Income Housing*, New York: Praeger, 1973, p. 167.

Managing Housing Services for the Elderly, Washington, D.C.: National Center for Housing Management, 1977, p. 64.

Needed: A Strategy for Housing Management, Washington, D.C.: National Corporation for Housing Partnerships, 1971, v.p.

Polikoff, Alexander, *Housing the Poor*, Cambridge, Mass.: Ballinger Publishing, 1978, p. 216.

Public Housing Management in the Seventies: Readings, Washington, D.C.: National Association of Housing and Redevelopment Officials, 1974.

Chapter 15

Shopping Center Management

After studying this chapter, you should be familiar with:
1 Characteristics of shopping centers
2 Management's responsibilities to the owner and to the tenants
3 Shopping center maintenance policies
4 The function of the merchant association
5 Environmental and zoning issues facing shopping center owners

Management is especially critical to the success of shopping centers. A shopping center is more than simply the cluster of individual stores on separate lots that is typical of a shopping district. On the contrary, a preplanned layout and a unified operation give shopping centers added appeal. They create a favorable image through single ownership and joint owner-tenant promotion under one management.

A review of physical characteristics precedes the discussion of relevant management topics. With this background, shopping center management is explained in terms of the management role, maintenance practices, the merchant associations, and special environmental problems. Leasing practices are discussed in Chapter 16.

SHOPPING CENTER CHARACTERISTICS

At this writing, shopping centers number over 18,000, with an estimated 800 new centers opening each year. A shopping center is defined as:

> A group of retail stores and related businesses, developed and managed as a unit with adequate on-site parking; the center size and stores depend on the trade area.[1]

In conformity with this definition, shopping centers are identified by size and their trade market area.

Size is measured by the *gross leasable area*, which refers to the floor area designed for tenant occupancy and exclusive use. It includes basements, mezzanines, and upper floors, measured from the center line of joint partitions and from outside wall surfaces. It is the area under exclusive tenant control and use for which tenants pay rent. Because some shopping centers have individually owned stores, gross leasable area may describe only part of the shopping space. In these cases, *total area* refers to the area owned by the center and by individual stores, but physically part of the center.

Table 15-1 identifies the more common types of shopping centers. Though only typical gross leasable areas are shown, their square feet and site areas extend over a broad range. There is much overlapping of size among groups.

Shopping Center Types

Usually the smallest of the seven centers listed in Table 15-1, neighborhood centers typically have 50,000 square feet of gross leasable area. They concentrate on convenience-good sales, and they are dominated by supermarkets, which represent principal tenants. Drugstores, variety stores, and certain personal services such as laundries, dry cleaning, barber shops, and shoe repair shops complete the neighborhood center. Figure 15-1 illustrates a neighborhood shopping center layout in the form of an L-shaped building.

The next most common center is the *community center*, organized around a junior department store as the key tenant. While the community center typically has a supermarket, it does not have sufficient sales volume to support a full-line department store. Compared to the neighborhood center, it has a wide range of goods and services available to suit family needs, such as clothing, shoes, and variety store items. Though usually built with 100,000 square feet of gross leasable area, their area may range from 100,000 to 300,000 square feet on 10 to 30 acres. Such a site layout is shown in Figure 15-2.

The *regional center*, beginning with the Northgate Regional Center in Seattle, Washington (1950), successfully competes with the downtown merchants. Constructed around at least one full-line department store of 100,000 square feet or more, it

---

[1] Adapted from Horace Carpenter, Jr., *Shopping Center Management*, New York: International Council on Shopping Centers, 1978, p. 5.

Table 15-1 Shopping Center Classification

Center type	Leading tenant	Typical gross leasable area (in square feet)	Usual minimum site area (acres)	Minimum required population
Neighborhood	Supermarket or drug-store	50,000	3	2,500–40,000
Community	Variety, discount, or junior department store	150,000	10 or more	40,000–150,000
Regional	One or more full-line department stores of at least 100,000 square feet GLA	400,000	30–50 or more	150,000 or more
Superregional	Three or more department stores	750,000		750,000–1,000,000
Vertical	Full-line department store	Variable	Variable	Variable
Specialty	No leading tenant	Variable	Variable	
Mini-malls	Junior department, food, drug, or variety store	80,000–150,000	8–15	Variable

Source: Shopping Center Development Handbook, Washington, D.C.: Urban Land Institute, 1977, p. 7.

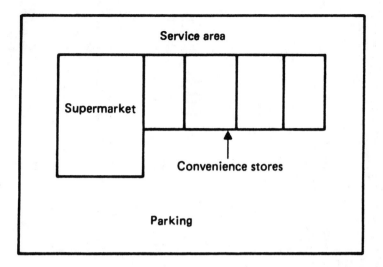

Figure 15-1 Site plan layout of a neighborhood store. Neighborhood centers tend to form a U- or L-shaped rectangle, with key tenants at the ends of the building.

offers shopping goods, general merchandise, apparel, furniture, and home furnishings. Figure 15-3 illustrates the modern concept of a regional center that incorporates offices and multiple-family dwellings as part of the shopping center plan.

The *superregional center* extends the concept of the regional center by offering more facilities and extending the trade market area to 10 or 15 or more miles, and may even include three or more full-line department stores. Note that with 1,000,000 square feet of gross leasable area, there would be almost 23 acres under tenant lease.

Other, more specialized shopping centers include the multilevel enclosed regional mall referred to as the *vertical center*. Customers move from floor to floor on ramps, escalators, and stairways. Here shoppers reduce horizontal walking distances; the shopping center site is more intensively used. A multilevel regional center is shown in Figure 15-4.

Figure 15-2 Community center with a junior department store and two other key tenants.

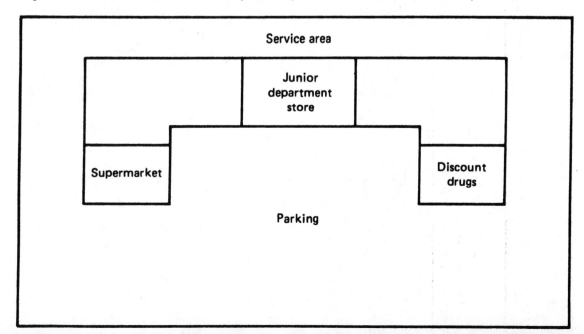

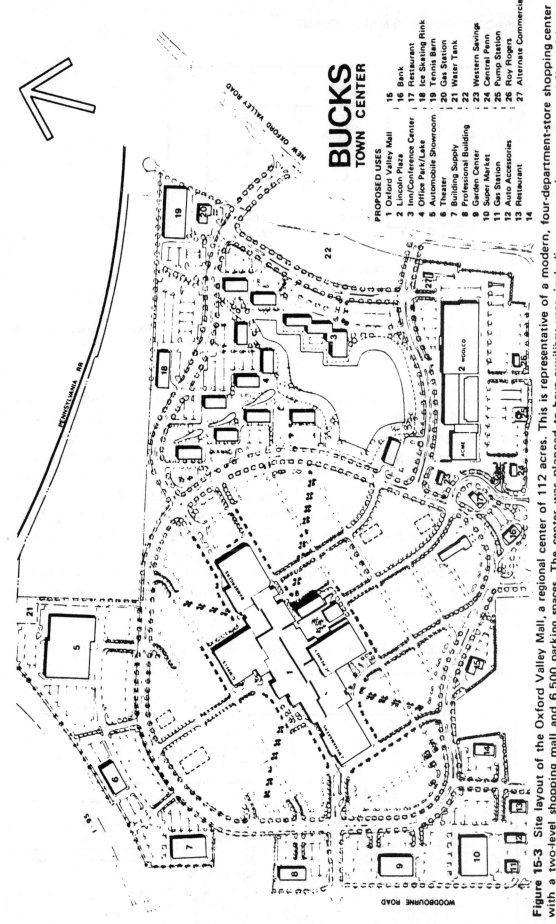

BUCKS
TOWN CENTER

PROPOSED USES

1	Oxford Valley Mall	15	Bank
2	Lincoln Plaza	16	Restaurant
3	Inn/Conference Center	17	Ice Skating Rink
4	Office Park/Lake	18	Tennis Barn
5	Automobile Showroom	19	Gas Station
6	Theater	20	Water Tank
7	Building Supply	21	
8	Professional Building	22	Western Savings
9	Garden Center	23	Central Penn
10	Super Market	24	Pump Station
11	Gas Station	25	Roy Rogers
12	Auto Accessories	26	Alternate Commercial
13	Restaurant	27	
14			

Figure 15-3 Site layout of the Oxford Valley Mall, a regional center of 112 acres. This is representative of a modern, four-department-store shopping center with a two-level shopping mall and 6,500 parking spaces. The center was planned to have auxiliary uses, including a convenience center, and financial and restaurant facilities on the fringe. The four department stores total 760,000 square feet of gross leasable area with other tenants absorbing another 450,000 square feet. (*Source: James O. York, President, R. H. Macy Properties.*)

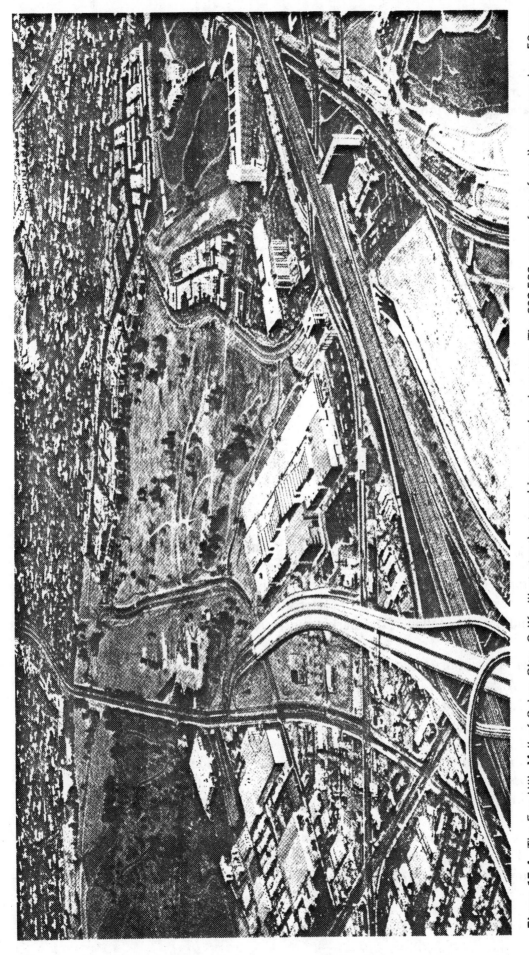

Figure 15-4 The Fox Hills Mall of Culver City, Calif., illustrates the trend in new regional centers. The 902,566 square feet of retail space occupies a 50-acre site at the intersection of the Marina Freeway and the San Diego Freeway. The three-level mall and the four levels of parking save 50 acres, as compared to a one-story construction. *(Photo courtesy of Gruen Associates, project architects, and Earnest W. Hahn, Inc., and Carter Hawley Hale Projects, Inc., project developers.)*

The trend seems to favor construction of the vertical center in place of the large expanse of the one-story center. The need to conserve land, to take maximum advantage of the location, and to protect the environment encourages vertical construction.

The disadvantages lie in:

the additional cost of escalators, stairways and freight elevators

more expensive heating and air-conditioning systems

lost merchandising space in areas required for stairways, escalators, elevators, service corridors, and utility ducts.

Besides these problems, management faces the difficult task of adapting tenants to a multiple-level layout. More care must be taken in encouraging maximum pedestrian traffic for the smaller stores.

The *specialty centers* have no leading tenant. They form a group of stores that sell a narrow category of goods. Centers may cater to interior decorating needs, sporting equipment, fashion apparel, and other specialties. They draw business by offering a wide selection of goods within a given specialty.

The *mini-mall centers* started a trend in the early 1970s. Enclosed and air-conditioned, they serve a community with a convenient, selected group of goods and services. Shoppers attracted to the key stores benefit from the smaller businesses offering retail services and specialty goods. Such businesses shorten driving time and help customers reduce transportation cost.[2]

Market Characteristics

Since the sales volume must be sufficient to support rentals that justify the investment, site characteristics are especially critical. Shopping center development proceeds only after a comprehensive market analysis. The analysis projects the potential sales volume expected at a particular location. The final site selection, key tenant commitments, zoning, and financing follow if the market study proves project feasibility.

Key Tenants The ultimate success of a center depends on the strength of the principal tenant. A shopping center development will not proceed unless a key tenant makes a definite lease commitment.

With a commitment by one or more key tenants, the size of the center and the value of the land will be largely determined by the expected market potential. For the main object is to match the potential purchasing power of the trade market area with the optimum gross leasable area. The analytical process for estimating the sales potential is illustrated in Figure 15-5.

Trade Market Area Figure 15-5 shows the interrelationship between the trade area analysis and purchasing power analysis. The trade area analysis starts with an estimate of driving time to the proposed center. Not only driving time access, but

[2] See *Shopping Center Development Handbook*, Washington, D.C.: Urban Land Institute, 1977, pp. 3–10.

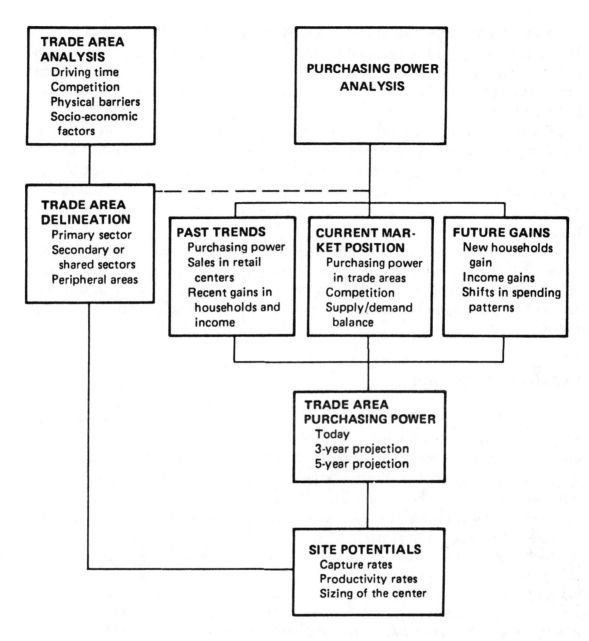

Figure 15-5 The analytical process in estimating shopping center sales potential. *(Source: Shopping Center Development Handbook, Washington, D.C.: Urban Land Institute, 1977, p. 23.)*

distance to and the nature of competing shopping facilities partly determine the total market area. Physical and socioeconomic factors such as the employment base, stability of employment, and seasonal factors further affect shopping center feasibility.

In delineating the trade market area, analysts divide the market into three areas: *primary*, *secondary*, and *fringe*. For the regional center, the primary area extends out to a 10-minute driving time and accounts for 70 percent of the sales volume. The secondary area extends further to 15 or 20 minutes' driving time and accounts for 20 percent of estimated sales. The fringe area goes out to 30 minutes' driving time, accounting for the balance of the sales volume.[3]

[3] *Shopping Center Development Handbook*, op. cit., p. 25.

To a large degree, the trade market area is controlled by competitive retail stores. For instance, the record shows that the average person travels not more than 1.5 miles to a supermarket or not more than 5 miles for clothing and household items. Shoppers appear willing to drive 10 miles for more expensive goods in which variety, selection, and price seem more important.

Given the trade market area, the site must meet the highest standards of access; the shape must be usable—a site divided by a highway, or a highly triangular or odd shape, limits the shopping center potential. At the same time, topography, drainage, and the subsoil should be suitable for building construction. Moreover, the surrounding land use, available utilities, and zoning must be compatible with an architecturally attractive center.

With the trade area defined, note the detail followed in analyzing purchasing power. Past purchasing power, the current market, and projected gains besides household income are considered in making current and up to 5-year projections. With this data in hand, the optimum size and the probable net operating income may be estimated.

THE MANAGEMENT ROLE

The outstanding feature of shopping center management is the dual role assumed by the property manager; in the first place, the manager serves the interest of the owner, which, for shopping centers, requires operations common to running a business and operations common to managing real estate. In the second place, the manager has obligations to tenants, who, in turn, have a large community interest in the welfare of other tenants. In this latter role, the manager must observe contractual obligations of the lease and enforce tenant responsibilities.

Some centers are owner managed. Typically the owner-manager operates a business or service on the premises, such as a real estate or attorney's office or another business. Under this arrangement, there are no payrolls; housekeeping and maintenance will be contracted to outside firms. For the larger centers, the owner may actually be a leading tenant who employs a salaried manager. Such an arrangement is typical for the larger regional and superregional centers.

Add to this list investor-owned, intermediate-size centers that employ a professional management firm. Their compensation ranges from 2 percent to 6 percent of rent collections, depending on size of the center and the degree of delegated responsibility. In addition, managers earn commissions for negotiating leases. Compensation for this service is paid under a separate agreement.

Management Responsibilities to the Owner

Most centers are managed according to the tax status of the owner. Usually the shopping center will be incidental to other sources of owner income. Consequently, managers make decisions in the light of tax factors affected by operations. While the manager works to maintain the integrity of invested capital through prudent maintenance and repair policies, managers must be aware of the owner's interest in "reportable income." Reportable income refers to income on which income tax is payable.

Reportable Income The reportable income figure varies from the cash flow that is the concern of private owners, partnerships, and privately held corporations. Reportable income is based on the equation:

$$RI = NOI - MP - D + P$$

where RI = reportable income
NOI = net operating income
MP = mortgage payments
D = depreciation
P = mortgage principal payments

Starting with net operating income and subtracting mortgage payments produces spendable income sometimes referred to as "cash flow." Deducting depreciation and adding mortgage principal gives the amount of income subject to income taxes. Alternatively, reportable income (for income tax purposes) is net operating income, less depreciation and mortgage interest.

Because of the tax consequences of operating decisions, management keeps accounts that (1) control and account for cash and physical property, (2) conform to income tax regulations, and (3) show operating income and expenses for decision-making purposes. In the latter instance, accounts are formed to help maximize tenant sales. These records are particularly significant for tenants who are subject to percentage rents. A historical review of tenant sales helps in negotiating leases and in selecting more qualified tenants.

Expense Decisions Managers have limited flexibility in minimizing operating expenses. Even a cursory review of the operating expense budget shows the dominance of mortgage payments, real estate taxes, and insurance costs. These items are not subject to short-term variation. Expenses that remain rarely exceed 20 percent of the total, and frequently may amount to only 10 percent. Assuming that 20 percent of total expenses are subject to short-term control, a saving of 5 percent in this proportion constitutes only 1 percent of the total budget.

Hence, although managers work toward greater efficiency, they have less flexibility in minimizing expenses than they do in the management of apartments. Therefore managers concentrate on selecting the best tenant mix and managing to gain the largest possible sales volume. Most of their attention is occupied by their promotional programs.

This does not mean, however, that managers do not weigh the importance of each individual expense. Yet in planning the budget, decisions must account for the tax consequences of each expenditure. For instance, faced with the decision whether to acquire a $20,000 maintenance machine, management may consider alternative financing plans. If the owner is subject to a 50 percent net income tax, a cash purchase would give full advantages of the depreciation deduction. On the other hand, the equipment could be leased with the full deduction of the rental cost. Again, equipment might be purchased under an installment plan, giving the owner the advantage of less capital outlay and the deductibility of interest payments and depreciation. In short, each capital expenditure must be analyzed according to the after-tax advantages of different methods of acquisition.[4]

Responsibility to Tenants

Since most shopping center leases provide for percentage rents, the manager has a direct interest in promoting successful tenants. While the shopping center is arranged to maximize sales volume, tenants must take advantage of the shopping center facility by their individual merchandising skill. In exercising the management function, therefore, the manager enforces the lease provisions governing tenant operations and operates the shopping center as an ongoing business with all of its promotional, advertising, public relations, and daily tasks. In performing this role, the manager confronts two main issues: (1) enforcing uniform store hours, and (2) enforcing lease terms.

Enforcing Uniform Store Hours Consider the divergent interests of the owner and the individual tenants: First, it will be recognized that shopping center income depends on the gross sales volume. But the center's operating expense is largely unrelated to daily hours of operation. Secondly, the tenant faces the opposite result. Store operating expenses increase almost in direct proportion to hours of operation. Yet the daily sales volume will not increase in direct proportion to the number of store hours. For example, suppose a tenant remains open for an additional 3 hours until 9:00 p.m., and increases operating expenses by one-third. It is unlikely that sales will increase by one-third. Therefore, as the sales per hour decrease with additional store hours, the tenant may earn less net income by staying open for more hours.

However, these results are not common to all tenants. A supermarket with a low payroll expense in terms of sales volume may employ idle cashiers for restocking and other housekeeping chores. In contrast, an apparel store with a relatively high payroll has limited ways to use salespersons during off-peak hours.

Add to these differences the variations in shopping habits. In some communities, shoppers patronize convenience stores in the evening while higher-priced apparel shops, jewelry stores, and other stores dealing with luxury goods do less business during late hours and weekend nights.

Because of the different ways that store operating hours affect the owner and the individual tenants, enforcing hours of operation is a source of continual conflict. As part of an organized shopping center community, generally tenants do not have the freedom to maintain store hours based upon the economics of their own individual store as, for example, a downtown merchant does. If store hour operation is not governed by specific lease terms, the manager faces uncooperative tenants who establish operating hours according to their individual circumstances.

[4] See Horace Carpenter, Jr., op. cit., pp. 38–52.

Enforcing Lease Terms Certain nonfinancial terms of the lease control the shopping center environment. The manager, remembering that the shopping center is an integrated community sharing store hours with limitations on the kind of merchandise carried, works toward establishing a good real estate operation. Accordingly, employees as provided by the lease, are restricted as to where they can park.

Moreover, the nonfinancial lease terms help preserve the property. Typical tenant operations that require attention deal with improper placement of garbage, encroachment on public space by tenants, the wrongful use of exterior loudspeakers, and other details such as cleanliness. Even the acceptance of delivery by public entrances rather than by the rear door affects the center's attractiveness.

Because managers select tenants for their merchandising ability, there is a question as to whether the managers should inquire into the internal management of tenant stores. If store fixtures or store layout are unsuitable, if the tenant's method of selecting merchandise and displaying it is unsatisfactory, if the level of housekeeping is below standards or if employee relations tend to lower sales, then what is the proper duty of shopping center management?

On this issue, most authorities advise that the manager counsel tenants who demonstrate below-average sales volume. By accepting helpful counsel, often with the cooperation of the merchants' association, tenants benefit by increasing profits, and at the same time increase shopping center rent. Some shopping center managements even arrange educational conferences with experts in marketing, newspaper advertising, and display methods to increase tenant sales.

MAINTENANCE POLICIES

In large measure, management determines the shopping center image by its maintenance policy. While managers are responsible for the long-term maintenance of the center and the parking lot, it is the day-to-day maintenance that creates the proper image. Some experienced managers refer to the day-to-day operations as housekeeping—the process of keeping buildings and grounds clear of litter and of performing other duties such as window washing, cleaning floors, and garbage removal.

Technically speaking, maintenance preserves the existing center. Maintenance tasks may be either *restorative* in the sense that worn out parts and equipment are restored to their original operating condition, or *preventive*. Preventive maintenance is based on regularly scheduled inspections and parts replacement. In establishing a maintenance policy, management must establish certain decisions regarding the economic life of the center.

For instance, shopping center investments are determined largely by external economic forces and not by the physical lives of the structure. Because of changing consumer preferences and competitive shopping facilities, property managers must frequently adapt a maintenance program to the modernization and renovation of existing facilities. In illustration, there is little point in resurfacing the pedestrian mall if market forces indicate the feasibility of expanding stores over the mall. Thus, the maintenance policy hinges on the analysis of forces that affect future operations. Leading questions that deserve continual review cover such topics as:

1 *What are the trends in surrounding land uses?* Surrounding land uses may enhance the attraction of the center as a place to shop. Here expansion and modernization may be advised. Conversely, land-use trends that show deteriorating or static conditions would indicate a more conservative renovation policy.

2 *What are the demographic trends in the trade area*—the unemployment rate, changes in household income, or changes in population characteristics? These trends, which affect retail sales, largely determine promotional, maintenance, and renovation plans.

3 *What transportation changes might affect future sales volume?* New road construction, mass transportation availability, or other related factors might change customer accessibility.

4 *What are the expected changes in competitive stores?* Downtown revitalization programs, new shopping centers, and expansion of existing centers may change the trade market area and affect future investment policy and operations.

Above all, what are the interpretations of the shopping trends by principal tenants? A review of tenant sales volume helps in interpreting a tenant's probable plans for lease renewal. In short, besides being responsible for daily and long-run maintenance, managers must continually review the economic status of the shopping center.

Maintenance Procedures

Maintenance procedures may be classified under three plans: (1) contract for maintenance services, (2) combined contract services with a full time on-site custodian, and (3) maintenance performed under the supervision of the manager, who employs a full-time staff.

For neighborhood and community centers probably most owners rely on contractors. Under this system, supervision is minimized; administration is reduced to making a single monthly payment, with occasional field checks on services performed.

If the independent contractor method is used, usually competitive bids are obtained after the manager has prepared a detailed list of maintenance duties. The physical differences among shopping centers requires that the contract for services be adapted to each shopping center, with specifications negotiated in writing. An effective means of reviewing performance is an integral part of contract administration.

Maintenance Schedules

For programs that depend on staff maintenance, managers rely on checklists and maintenance schedules. Checklists are adapted to tenants who assume responsibility for certain repairs and maintenance. In some instances management may complete repairs and charge the lessee. A checklist for this purpose is shown in Table 15-2.

Note that a maintenance repair record is provided for each tenant. Space is provided to charge the lessee for repairs that are made by management on behalf of the tenant.

Besides the daily maintenance schedule, managers prepare a checklist covering weekly, monthly, and yearly duties. The *weekly* schedule would provide for landscaping maintenance; minor parking lot repairs; and preventive maintenance con-

Table 15-2   A Shopping Center Maintenance Checklist

	Checklist				
	Maintenance and repair record				

Date of issue:
Revision no.:
Revision date:
 	
Shopping center:
Store
  Name:
  Number:
  Tel. no.:
 	
Tenant
  Name:
  Address: } (emergency)
  Tel. no.:					

	Maintenance		Repairs		
Item	Lessee	Lessor	Lessee	Lessor	Remarks
Storefront					
Show windows					
Floors					
Walls					
Ceilings					
Lights					
Electrical wiring					
Plumbing					
Hot water tank					
Heating					
Ventilation					
Air conditioning					
Sprinklers					
Elevators					
Escalators					
Roof					
Structure					
Rear doors					
Interior signs					
Exterior signs					
Garbage					
Cleaning store					
Cleaning glass					
Other					
Prepared by: Approved by: Date:	Distribution:				

Source: Edgar Lion, *Shopping Centers: Planning, Development, and Administration*, New York: John Wiley, 1976, p. 155.

sisting of checking, cleaning, and lubricating equipment as recommended. *Monthly* checklists require an examination of building exteriors, for example, the roof, walls, curbs, copings, and canopies. Preventive maintenance on a monthly schedule would include the inspection of mechanical equipment and provision for such preventive maintenance as cleaning filters, changing belts, and checking boilers. The *yearly* maintenance would consist of more complex assignments, such as repainting parking grids, conducting the major overhaul of cleaning equipment, repainting exteriors, and undertaking major building repairs.

THE MERCHANTS' ASSOCIATION

Merchants' association membership is usually compulsory. Each tenant member pays dues and is entitled to one vote. Commonly the bylaws provide that shopping center management should be represented on the board of directors.

The purpose of the organization is to promote the shopping center:

through the sponsorship of commercial, cultural, educational, community and other programs; and, in furtherance of such purpose, to engage in and conduct promotional programs and publicity, special events, decorations, cooperative advertising in the general interest and for the benefit of the shopping center.[5]

Acting in this capacity, the association serves as a forum for suggestions, ideas, and the programming of merchandising events. In this respect the merchants' association is the single most important device for improving community relations.

The manager organizes the association even before construction is completed. Special assessments are levied against tenants for preopening events. In the early meetings the main task is to develop a spirit of teamwork among merchants, resolving their conflicting interests, and bringing about cooperation between large and small businesses, national chains and local independents.

Association Operation

In practice, managers follow one of two plans. In the first case, the owner acts as agent. The member organization operates the association through an executive secretary or professional promotions director. In the other case, the owner actively directs the association through the board of directors and committees, who cooperate in advertising and promotional programs. Under either plan, a part-time or full-time executive secretary administers correspondence, prepares newsletters, and helps coordinate promotional activities.

While the association functions under a board of directors with part- or full-time staff, management usually absorbs 25 percent of the annual budget. Failure of the tenant to pay association dues is a violation of the lease, which may serve as grounds for terminating the leasehold interest.

[5] "Sample Merchant's Association Bylaws," Appendix D in *Shopping Center Development Handbook*, op. cit., p. 282.

Experience shows that an effective merchants' association benefits management and tenants alike. Promotional activities increase sales; tenants realize more profit; and the center earns more percentage rents. This relationship gives management sufficient incentive to provide leadership and other organizational skills for the promotion of sales events, public events, and community services.

For example, it is reported that full-time salaried promotion directors are quite common for shopping centers of 600,000 square feet or more. Few full-time directors are found in centers with less than 400,000 square feet. For centers of 200,000 to 400,000 square feet, promotional programs are usually jointly administered by owners and tenants through the merchants' association. For the convenience-dominated center of less than 200,000 square feet, promotional programs are usually confined to holidays, back-to-school, and Chirstmas functions. A year-round promotional program is not common in these smaller centers, though spot attractions are often financed at a nominal cost with a special assessment budget.[6]

Financing the Association

The merchants' association budget varies by type of center. The superregional centers spend, on the average, $.23 per square foot of gross leasable area. This amount decreases to $.10 and $.09 for the community and neighborhood center as shown below.

Type of center	Total assessment per square foot of gross leasable area*
Superregional	$.23
Regional	.18
Community	.10
Neighborhood	.09

*Dollars & Cents of Shopping Centers, 1978, Washington, D.C.: Urban Land Institute, 1978, p. 286.

Among the superregional centers, the principal tenants pay approximately 25 percent of the total budget. The key tenants in the community and neighborhood centers pay slightly smaller proportions, 16 percent and 22 percent of the total association budget. The balance is divided between the other tenants and the shopping center owner.

Most centers levy association assessments according to the gross leasable area, including sales and storage space. It is also common to grant percentage discounts, say 50 percent, for basements or balcony space. Alternatively, a few centers levy association expenses according to the number of front feet or gross sales.

To counter the argument that small businesses do not carry their fair share or that large businesses gain a lower assessment rate, some authorities recommend a graduated scale. One reference graduates merchants' association dues from $.15 per square foot

6 See Horace Carpenter, Jr., op. cit., p. 103.

Table 15-3 A Graduated Scale for Levying Merchants' Association Expenses

Square-foot area	Cumulative dues	Cumulative total
0–1,000	$.15	$150
1,000–2,000	.14	140
2,000–4,000	.13	260
4,000–7,000	.12	360
7,000–10,000	.11	330
10,000–15,000	.10	500
15,000–20,000	.09	450
Over 20,000	.06	—

Source: Adapted from Robert S. Nyburg, *Shopping Center Merchants Association*, New York: International Council of Shopping Centers, 1978, p. 14.

for an area of 1,000 square feet to $.06 per square foot for tenants leasing over 20,000 square feet. The square footage and cumulative dues follow the schedule in Table 15-3. Under this suggested formula, a store that leases 2,000 square feet would pay annual dues of $290; at the other extreme, a 20,000-square-foot area would require dues of $2,190 per year.

The amount raised depends on the proposed budget. Shopping center managers recommend an opening or preopening budget and an annual budget. A budget for the first 8 months of operation and the first year thereafter for a 500,000-square-foot center with 60 stores and one department store is shown in Table 15-4. The first 8 months of operation, including the preopening publicity, totals $45,345, of which one-third is paid by the owner. The next 12 months of promotional programs totals $54,950, or approximately $.18 per square foot.

The itemized budget proposed for the first year of operation shows how the proposed expenditure of $54,950 will be spent (see Table 15-5). Notice that the largest single expenditure of $17,000 is allocated to special events and decorations for the main holidays. Newspaper and outdoor advertising are next in importance, with $5,450 and $6,900 allocated to these expenditures. Other significant amounts cover radio, administrative, and advertising agency fees.

The merchants' association will sponsor special promotions planned over the calendar year. The larger centers organize special events such as carnivals, the good old days, the gay nineties, western days, presummer, summer, spring, and fall fashion parades. In addition, various anniversary sales, renovation sales, and sidewalk sales complete these special promotion calendars. Their variety is extensive, depending on

Table 15-4 A Proposed Promotional Budget for a New Shopping Center

Budget period	Total	Square foot	Merchants total	Square foot	Owner total
Preopening and first 8 months	$ 45,345	$.12	$30,000	$.06	$15,345
Next 12 months	54,950	.18	45,000	.06	15,950
Total	$100,295		$75,000		$31,295

the type of center and geographic area involved. Besides these special events, certain other promotions are common to each month.

January January clearance sales	**July** 4th of July Mid-year clearance
February Valentine's Day, February 14 Washington's Birthday	**August** Back-to-school day
March St. Patrick's Day, March 17 First day of spring, March 20	**September** Labor Day First day of Autumn, September 22
April Easter	**October** Halloween
May Mother's Day	**November** Thanksgiving
June Father's Day First day of summer	**December** Christmas

Table 15-5 Proposed Annual Budget: Merchants' Association

First Year of Operation	
Proposed expenditures	**Amount**
1 Newspaper Twelve sections, monthly dates subject to events schedule. Association share, including additional 10,000 reprints mailed, art, front page ad, one page, make good space.	$ 5,450
2 Outdoor 24 sheets or painted board for 12 months, including 6 changes.	6,900
3 Radio Saturation to back up four events on two stations.	2,500
4 Events, promotion, decor a For Spring, Christmas, July 4th, anniversary.	17,000
b Additional events, concerts, automobile and boat show, Mother's and Father's Day, Washington's Birthday, back-to-school, basis—8 events, average $650.	5,200
5 Donations and small publications	2,000
6 Administration a Association secretary and association payroll taxes.	3,500
b Hall expenses.	4,000
c Communications, insurance, stationery, multigraphing, postage audit, etc.	2,100
7 Contingent	1,500
8 Agency fee, 12 months @ $400 per month.	4,800
Total	$54,950

Source: Robert S. Nyburg, *Shopping Center Merchants Association*, New York: International Council of Shopping Centers, 1978, p. 73.

The main effort in these promotions is not to attract crowds but to bring customers into the stores. In these efforts, shopping centers have sponsored most types of public entertainment: symphony concerts, boat shows, horse shows, foreign car shows, station wagon shows, art shows, flower shows, sport shows, beauty contests, and many like events. To advance these activities, the larger centers have provided community halls for various community and entertainment purposes. Some associations budget as much as 50 percent of their funds for entertainment purposes.

ENVIRONMENTAL PROBLEMS

Developers of shopping centers, like other property owners, cope with environmental laws and, unlike other property owners, face unique zoning problems. Although shopping centers may be affected by higher gasoline prices, most developers believe that customers will not curtail their use of automobiles for shopping. Nevertheless, public transportation will probably assume greater importance in providing access to shopping centers.

Environmental Laws

Several federal laws complicate shopping center development and operation. The Clean Air Act of 1970 indirectly affects developments with large parking areas. The Federal Water Pollution Control Act Amendments of 1972 and the Coastal Zone Management Act and other state and local restrictions add further regulations to shopping center operations. New centers face delays in project approval and increased costs of construction. For example, solar energy collectors may become popular in shopping centers because of the large roof areas with unlimited direct access to solar energy.

Developers have expressed concern over the opposition to converting open fields and wooded areas, which destroy vegetation. It is also true that shopping centers alter natural drainage patterns—even parking lot drains add to local sewer loads. Many of these issues have attracted attention to shopping center zoning regulations.

Zoning Issues

Traditionally, zoning has controlled the use of individual parcels. It is presumed that individuals purchase and develop their own sites, which are controlled with respect to land coverage, setback lines, building height, and land use. Shopping centers have characteristics that make this form of zoning obsolete.

The main elements of shopping center land use may be listed in four points:

1 Shopping centers are developed under a unified plan that provides buildings managed as a unit for the benefit of individual tenants. The unified land use follows only after a favorable market feasibility study.

2 Shopping centers are located for easy access according to market need, and they provide for planned parking space utilization.

3 On-site parking separates walking customers, customer parking, and service traffic.

4 Tenants are grouped according to their mutual attraction in agreeable surroundings that provide safe and comfortable shopping.[7]

Besides these points, it will be appreciated that shopping centers are managed as a community. Management controls operations by lease terms that govern tenant operation. In practice, tenant leases are comparable to performance standards that ensure the best possible operation for the benefit of the shopping center and customers.

In sum, tenants acting together in a community of stores advance their own interests. Under these conditions, zoning and planning officials have less need to rigidly control land use practices. The essential elements of control are inherent in the enforcement of rules governing tenant operations. As a result, only general guidelines are recommended for shopping center zoning.

Prerequisites to Shopping Center Zoning Recommended guidelines for shopping center zoning assume that the shopping center is justified as an economic community. The guidelines deal with *floating zones*, *parking*, *landscaping*, *signs*, and *lighting control*. The decision to approve shopping center zoning is based on the documentation listed in Figure 15-6.

Floating Zones Floating zones adapt easily to planned shopping centers. The zone applies to a land area which, in effect, remains unzoned until the area is planned for shopping facilities. Specific zoning does not take place until the developer submits the shopping center plan for rezoning for shopping center use. Under this plan, the land remains unzoned until a specific project is proposed for a specific location.

Parking Zoning requirements in excess of the required parking waste land. Zoning density controls that set maximum building coverage, moreover, may not agree with the recommended parking. At the present time, recommended parking for shop-

[7] See, for example, *Shopping Center Zoning*, Technical Bulletin 69, Washington, D.C.: The Urban Land Institute, 1973, p. 14.

Figure 15-6 Prerequisites to shopping center zoning approval.

1 Documentation of a need based on market analysis.
2 A site area suitable in shape and size for the type of center and building area.
3 A location with access, entrances and exits compatible with traffic flow without introducing traffic hazards.
4 On-site parking that conforms to accepted industry standards.
5 An architectural plan suited to the site which avoids depreciating surrounding property.

ping centers is 5.5 parking spaces per thousand square feet of gross leasable area. This is equivalent to a parking ratio of 2.2 square feet of parking for 1 square foot of gross leasable area. This standard has been provided by allowing 350 square feet for each car stall.

While this standard assumes a stall width of 9 by 18.5 feet, foreign cars adapt easily to smaller parking areas, that is, 7.5 by 15 feet. Smaller cars, reported to be 51 percent of all cars registered in the state of California, have caused shopping center authorities to predict that parking areas may be reduced by 10 percent from the present standard.[8]

Landscaping While general in nature, the zoning ordinance preferably would require landscaping in open space, area borders, and landscaping of buffer areas.

Signs Signs are part of the graphic controls administered by shopping center management. Local ordinances for shopping centers should prohibit moving or flashing sign parts. Practice also prohibits paste-on window stickers and garish pylon illuminated signs. Developers go further in providing signs of the same scale and style by lease terms. Compromises may be granted for individual trade market signs owned by national chain merchants.

Lighting Control Zoning provisions should specify only that night lighting must be directed downward with a height that does not create nuisances to adjacent property. With this general requirement, managers recommend downward-directed lighting that provides 1.5 foot candles at street grade. Lighting should be sufficient for public protection and safety.

SUMMARY

Shopping centers may be classified into one of seven types, depending on the gross leasable area and the leading tenant. Besides the neighborhood, community, and regional centers, four other centers represent highly specialized shopping: (1) the superregional center of 750,000 or more gross leasable square feet, (2) the vertical center, (3) the specialty centers with no leading tenants, and (4) the mini-malls that are enclosed with a junior department or other leading tenant. In each instance, the shopping center depends on a trade area's division into the primary, secondary, and fringe market areas.

In representing the owner, the manager makes decisions on capital expenditures according to tax consequences. In other respects, expenses under the control of the manager represent a small proportion of the total expense budget. In working with tenants, managers enforce uniform store hours and develop the shopping center as a

[8]*Shopping Center Zoning*, op. cit., pp. 25–26.

community of stores that have a mutual attraction. By enforcing lease terms, managers preserve shopping centers as pleasing, attractive shopping environments.

Maintenance may be either *restorative* (replacing worn-out parts and equipment) or *preventive*. In organizing the maintenance program, management reviews economic trends affecting the shopping center. For the center to remain competitive, renovation and expansion may be required.

Merchants' associations deserve special attention, for they benefit management and tenants alike. Their promotional activities lead to increased sales, more profits, and higher rent. The owner ordinarily pays 25 percent of the total association budget; the remainder is allocated among tenants, usually according to their gross leasable area.

The larger centers sponsor special promotions over the calendar year. The proposed association budget includes preopening expenses and an annual budget that provides for institutional advertising and sponsorship of entertainment, promotion days, and holiday decorations.

Shopping centers are sensitive to environmental controls, including clean air, regulation of water pollution, and other laws that require approval in advance of construction. Preferred practice favors floating zones that allow shopping center developers to prepare a proposal for rezoning, given documentation of the need for a shopping center. Parking currently requires 5.5 spaces per 1,000 square feet of gross leasable area. Shopping center zoning codes provide guidelines on landscaping, signs, and lighting controls. Specific industry standards are left to the developer to arrange for maximum shopping utility.

DISCUSSION QUESTIONS

1 Define the term "shopping center."
2 What areas are included in the gross leasable area?
3 Give the main characteristics of neighborhood, community, and regional centers.
4 Describe the main features of four other shopping center classifications.
5 What is the importance of key tenants?
6 How would you determine the trade market area? Explain fully.
7 What are the main management responsibilities to the owner?
8 In what way does management serve tenant interests?
9 How do questions about future operations affect maintenance policy?
10 What is the purpose of the merchants' association?
11 What are the recommended ways to finance the merchants' association?
12 What items are included in the association budget?
13 What main elements of shopping center land use make scattered-lot zoning obsolete for shopping centers?
14 What is the advantage of floating zones for shopping centers?
15 What are the normal parking standards for shopping centers?
16 What other issues are usually covered in shopping center zoning ordinances?

KEY TERMS AND CONCEPTS

Gross leasable area   Trade market area
Neighborhood center   Primary area
Convenience goods   Secondary area
Community centers   Fringe area
Regional centers   Reportable income
Superregional centers   Uniform store hours
Vertical centers   Restorative maintenance
Specialty centers   Preventive maintenance
Mini-malls   Merchants' association
Key tenants   Floating zone

SELF-QUIZ

Multiple-Choice Questions

_____ 1 A shopping center may be defined as: (a) A group of stores in a business district; (b) Individually owned stores in a commercially zoned retail district; (c) A group of retail stores and related businesses developed and managed as a unit with adequate on-site parking; (d) A group of stores sponsored by a national department store chain.

_____ 2 A community center typically has: (a) 150,000 square feet of gross leasable area; (b) A junior department store as a leading tenant; (c) A minimum site area of 10 acres; (d) All of the above.

_____ 3 A shopping center with three or more department stores of at least 750,000 square feet, with a minimum required population of 750,000 to 1,000,000, describes a: (a) Vertical center; (b) Regional center; (c) Community center; (d) Superregional center.

_____ 4 The ultimate success of a center depends on: (a) The strength of the principal tenant; (b) The type of merchandise sold; (c) A location in a suburban community; (d) The availability of mass transportation.

_____ 5 For a regional center the primary trade market area: (a) Covers an area within 20 minutes' driving time and accounts for 20 percent of estimated sales; (b) Extends to an area reached by 10 minutes' driving time and accounts for 70 percent of the sales volume; (c) Covers an area within 30 minutes' driving time and accounts for 10 percent of sales; (d) Accounts for 95 percent of the total sales volume.

_____ 6 Reportable income for shopping center management purposes is: (a) Net operating income, less mortgage payments and depreciation; (b) Net operating income less mortgage payments, plus depreciation; (c) Net operating income, less depreciation and mortgage principal payments; (d) Net operating income, less depreciation and mortgage interest.

_____ 7 In managing shopping centers, capital expenditures: (a) Must be analyzed according to the after-tax advantages of different methods of acquisitions; (b) Are treated like annual operating expenses; (c) Are unrelated to income taxes; (d) Are increased by leasing equipment.

_____ 8 Which of the following statements is correct? (a) For the shopping center owner, operating expenses are largely unrelated to daily hours of operation; (b) For tenants, store operating expenses increase almost in direct proportion to hours of operation; (c) Tenants vary in their ability to use salespersons during off-peak hours; (d) All of the above.

_____ 9 Shopping center maintenance policy: (a) Is unrelated to forces that affect future operation; (b) Should shift maintenance expenses to tenants; (c) Hinges on the analysis of forces that affect future operations; (d) Is unrelated to programs of modernization or renovation of existing facilities.

_____ 10 Which of the following statements is correct? (a) The principal tenant in superregional centers pays approximately 25 percent of the association budget; (b) Customarily the owner pays 25 percent of the association budget; (c) Most centers levy association assessments according to the gross leasable area; (d) All of the above.

Answer Key

1 (c), 2 (d), 3 (d), 4 (a), 5 (b), 6 (d), 7 (a), 8 (d), 9 (c), 10 (d).

Fill-In Questions

1 The_____ refers to the floor area designed for tenant occupancy and exclusive use.

2 The community center is organized around a_____ _____ as the key tenant.

3 The_____ have no leading tenant.

4 To a large degree the trade market area is controlled by_____ _____.

5 Managers have limited flexibility in _____ operating expenses.

6 Store operating expenses_____almost in direct proportion to hours of operation.

7 Most authorities advise that the manager_____tenants who demonstrate below-average sales volume.

8 For neighborhood and community centers, probably most owners rely on_____ _____ maintenance.

9 Recommended parking for shopping centers is based on_____ _____ per 1,000 square feet of gross leasable area.

10 In practice, tenant leases are comparable to _____ _____ that ensure the best possible operation for the benefit of the shopping center and customers.

Answer Key

1 gross leasable area
2 junior department store
3 specialty centers
4 competitive retail stores
5 minimizing

6 increase
7 counsel
8 contractor
9 5.5 parking spaces
10 performance standards

SELECTED REFERENCES

Applebaum, William, and S. O. Kaylin: *Case Studies in Shopping Center Development and Operation*, New York: International Association of Shopping Centers, 1974.

Carpenter, Horace, Jr.: *Shopping Center Management*, New York: International Council of Shopping Centers, 1974.

Corbin, Lee D.: "Golden Age of Shopping Centers," *Journal of Property Management*, **41**(6):263–266 (1976).

Drachman, Roy P.: "Shopping Center Update: A View from the Mall," *Real Estate Today*, **11**(5):16–19 (1978).

Lion, Edgar: *Shopping Centers*, New York: John Wiley, 1976.

Shopping Center Development Handbook, Washington, D.C.: Urban Land Institute, 1977.

Shopping Center Leasing

Leasing practices in shopping center management are sufficiently complex to deserve separate discussion. In this task *tenant selection* constitutes the most important single issue. Furthermore, it is also true that certain *lease terms* are unique to shopping centers. Likewise, the *rental terms* are not duplicated in other types of property. Finally, shopping center *investment analysis*, which is so closely related to leases, warrants additional explanation.

TENANT SELECTION

Shopping center managers concentrate on selecting tenants to secure (1) the appropriate range of merchandise, and (2) the best mixture of national and independent merchants. In both instances, not only does the selection of key tenants vary, but the general mix of tenants shows considerable variation by type of center. Before discussing these points, it is helpful to make certain preliminary observations.

Tenant Classification

Key tenants, also known as anchor tenants or principal tenants, actually "make" the shopping center. Key and other kinds of tenants for different types of centers may be classified as:

    1 *National chain stores*—Businesses operating in four or more metropolitan areas in three or more states.
    2 *Independent stores*—Businesses operating in not more than two outlets in only one metropolitan area.
    3 *Local chain stores*—Businesses that do not fall into either of the preceding categories.

    Tenants are also differentiated by their credit rating. A store with a Dun and Bradstreet AAA-1 rating will have net assets of over $1 million and a good composite tenant rating. In other cases, tenants will be identified as local businesses, and in still other instances tenants will be shown by their standard industrial classification codes—a listing found in the *Standard Industrial Classification Manual*, published by the Government Printing Office.

Tenant Placement

Key tenants, which are central to neighborhood, community, and regional centers, are arranged to maximize shopping convenience. It is unlikely that key tenants will be placed in contiguous stores. Rather, key tenants are sited at each end of a strip or mall to create pedestrian traffic for minor tenants. The main idea is to make key tenants accessible from parking areas and expose customers to the maximum number of complementary businesses.

    Tenants are therefore grouped in logical clusters. A common arrangement is to group variety, hardware, appliance, and home furnishings stores in close proximity. Good merchandising practices recommend a grouping of service and repair shops. Group also food and food services, providing that stores which offer convenience goods, such as drug and variety stores, have easy access to parking areas. Supermarkets, dry cleaners, laundries, and take-out stores should also avoid long walks for customers from parking areas to stores. In short, tenants are grouped according to their compatibility and mutual attractiveness.

Tenant Composition

Selection of tenants varies considerably among centers classified as neighborhood, community, and regional. Key tenants and the mix of tenants vary by type of center. As a general rule, certain tenants show a high degree of mutual attractiveness: men's apparel stores, shoes, clothing, and sporting goods tend to group together. Similarly, women's clothing stores, women's shoes, millinery, and children's clothes and toys group together to maximize sales.

By the same token, supermarkets, meat and fish markets, delicatessens, bakeries, doughnut shops, and candy stores are generally grouped together. The more common grouping of tenants by neighborhood and regional centers is shown in Table 16-1.

Recommended Tenants In Table 16-1, tenants are shown according to the percentage of gross leasable area and the percentage of sales. General merchandise tenants are department, junior department, variety, discount department, and showroom/

Table 16-1 Tenant Composition and Sales: Regional and Neighborhood Centers

Tenant group	Regional		Neighborhood	
	Percentage of gross leasable area	Percentage of sales	Percentage of gross leasable area	Percentage of sales
General merchandise	19.3	14.8	11.2	4.7
Food	7.3	12.3	30.2	64.4
Food services	5.8	6.2	6.4	5.1
Clothing	23.0	28.3	3.7	2.4
Shoes	6.2	7.3	1.0	.5
Home furnishings	2.4	1.9	2.4	.6
Home appliances	3.2	4.5	1.7	1.0
Building materials	.8	.6	3.2	1.3
Automotive	1.2	.6	2.4	.7
Hobby/special interest	3.1	3.5	2.4	1.2
Gifts/specialty	4.0	4.1	1.5	1.0
Jewelry and cosmetics	2.1	4.2	.5	.3
Liquor	.3	.4	1.3	1.4
Drugs	3.6	4.3	9.9	11.6
Other retail	3.6	3.1	2.4	1.1
Personal services	2.1	1.5	5.0	1.8
Recreation/community	4.1	1.3	4.0	.7
Financial offices	2.6	.4	3.3	—
Other offices	1.6	.6	2.1	.1
Other	3.7	.1	5.4	.1
Total	100.0	100.0	100.0	100.0

Source: Dollars & Cents of Shopping Centers, published triennially, Urban Land Institute, 1200 13th Street N.W., Washington, D.C. 20036, 1978, pp. 275-276.

catalog stores. Turning first to regional centers, it may be observed that clothing stores account for the greatest share of gross leasable area, 23.0 percent. General merchandise stores follow next in importance. All other stores account for less than 7.3 percent of gross leasable area. Similar relationships are shown for the proportion of sales: clothing and general merchandise account for 28.3 percent and 14.8 percent of total sales. Note that food stores represent 12.3 percent of total sales. All their stores account for 7.3 percent or less of total sales.

Neighborhood centers show marked differences. Table 16-1 shows the clear dominance of food stores, representing 30.2 percent of the gross leasable area and 64.4 percent of total sales. In the case of neighborhood centers, general merchandise tenants, who lease 11.2 percent of the leasable area, report only 4.7 percent of total sales. In contrast, drugstores show a greater share of sales, 11.6 percent.

Certain minor qualifications deserve mention. Stores that are an integral part of the shopping center but are owned by the store operator and not by the shopping center are not shown in this report. The most common exclusions cover service stations, banks, and free-standing restaurants.

But the main point is fairly plain: tenants are selected for their appropriate balance; the manager combines the many individual retail and other tenants to form a complex in which tenants are more successful operating as part of the center than as self-owned stores in separate locations. The central plan is directed to tenant selection, so that each tenant satisfies maximum shopping needs and contributes to the business of other tenants.

Tenant Operational Types The next most important issue is to select tenants according to one of three operational types: national chain store, local chain store, or independent tenant. The importance of selecting tenants by operational type varies within each shopping center classification. This point is demonstrated in Table 16-2. National chains dominate the superregional shopping center in terms of total gross leasable area and its percentage of sales—showing 78.4 percent and 72.6 percent in both cases. Their importance decreases with the size of the center; neighborhood shopping centers, on the average, rent 42.3 percent of gross leasable area to national tenants, though national tenants account for 58.3 percent of total sales. The local chains record 30.2 percent of total sales in the neighborhood center; independents absorb a slightly larger share of the gross leasable area: 32.1 percent.

There is one added point. Tenants are also judged according to the ratio of percentage of sales to the percentage of gross leasable area. For example, in Table 16-1, jewelry and cosmetics stores leased 2.1 percent of gross leasable area of regional shopping centers, but had sales equal to 4.2 percent of total sales. A ratio of the percentage of sales to percentage of gross leasable area, 2.03, means that jewelry and cosmetics stores contribute to sales more than double their proportion of gross leasable area. At the other extreme, building materials in Table 16-1 have an average ratio of percentage of sales to percentage of gross leasable area of .51.[1]

---

[1] For additional detail consult *Shopping Center Development Handbook*, Washington, D.C.: Urban Land Institute, 1977, chap. 3.

Table 16-2 Tenant Variation by Operation Type within Each Shopping Center Classification

Classification	Percentage of total gross leasable area	Percentage of total sales
Superregional shopping centers		
National	78.4	72.6
Local	14.3	18.2
Independent	7.3	9.2
Total	100.0	100.0
Regional shopping centers		
National	68.4	64.6
Local	19.8	24.2
Independent	11.8	11.2
Total	100.0	100.0
Community shopping centers		
National	54.6	60.7
Local	21.9	25.5
Independent	23.5	13.8
Total	100.0	100.0
Neighborhood shopping centers		
National	42.3	58.3
Local	25.6	30.2
Independent	32.1	11.5
Total	100.0	100.0

Source: *Dollars & Cents of Shopping Centers*, op. cit., p. 279.

Another way of judging the importance of tenant selection is to compare the percentage of total charges paid by national, local, and independent merchants. For superregional centers, national tenants dominate all shopping center categories, paying 80.7 percent of total charges in regional shopping centers to 65.6 percent in community shopping centers. Though national tenants lease only 42.3 percent of the gross leasable area in the neighborhood centers, they pay 74.7 percent of total charges. Total charges refer to (1) common area charges for maintenance of public areas, and (2) total rent (minimum, percentage, and additional rent).

It should be added that managers try to stagger lease expiration dates. The object is to avoid a situation where all leases expire at the same time. In such a situation the manager might face tenant collusion and might encounter a sudden and unusually large vacancy rate if tenants did not renew leases.

RENTAL TERMS

Some shopping center leases extend to 20 years for the principal department store tenants. Commonly, other major tenants lease space for 10 to 15 years. Smaller chains and local tenants seldom lease for longer than 7 to 10 years. Because of these long-term arrangements, management shifts increases in operating expenses to tenants. Hence center management negotiates various forms of "escalator clauses," in addition to charging *minimum* rents and providing rent based, in part, on a percentage of gross sales. *Common area charges* are other costs levied against tenants for the maintenance of parking and other public areas.

Because of the various sources of rental income, it is common to refer to total receipts as being made up of the sources shown in Table 16-3. The data apply to 83 regional centers. Note that most of the income is derived from the minimum rent. Common area charges are levied for maintenance of public areas, while the rent escalation charges are made on the basis of the share of increased taxes, insurance, and other added costs paid by the tenant. Since some centers purchase utilities directly and resell to tenants on a metered basis, total charges include this source of income.

Minimum Rents

Minimum rents are related to the cost of development. To illustrate, suppose that the land and its improvement cost $8 per square foot of gross leasable area. A 100,000-square-foot center would have a developed land cost of $800,000. If the building costs $30 per square foot of gross leasable area, the shopping center developer must earn a return on investment of $38 per square foot of gross leasable area. Assume further that a 15 percent return would be required on the total investment. In this case the center must earn an average rent of $5.70 per square foot of gross leasable area ($38 × .15).

Because the average minimum rent of $5.70 must be divided among major tenants, who absorb two-thirds of the gross leasable area, a higher-than-average minimum rent would be required from the local and independent stores. If the market rent and expenses of operation did not provide the required rate of return, the project would not be feasible.

Percentage Rent

Percentage rents usually apply after stores have made a stated volume of sales. Shopping center managers typically negotiate the minimum rent (per square foot of gross

Table 16-3 Total Receipts of Regional Shopping Centers Classified by Source

Operating receipts	Median dollars per square foot of gross leasable area	Median percentage of total receipts
Rental income—minimum	$3.52	61.9
Rental income—overage	.89	13.0
Total Rent	4.39	79.8
Common area charges	.40	10.3
Income from sales of utilities	.92	12.5
Miscellaneous income	.05	.9
Total other charges	.40	9.5
Total operating receipts	$5.25	100.0

Source: Dollars and Cents of Shopping Centers, op. cit., p. 270.

leasable area) to at least equal mortgage principal and interest, real estate taxes, and management fees, though this generalization is subject to much qualification.

To attract the necessary principal tenants, developers may offer minimum rents below industry standards, or, alternatively, they may provide high allowances for tenant construction to finish the building shell. Other developers offer land for an owner-operated store at a relatively low price. Subsidies granted to principal tenants will be compensated for by higher rents for other tenants.

Income derived from percentage rents is also referred to as *overage rents*. Initially, lenders may give no weight to overage rents because they are not payable until sales rise above some given point known as the gross sales break point—which, in the beginning, is highly uncertain.

To illustrate, assume that a department store in a regional center leases 100,000 square feet of gross leasable area. With a minimum rent of $500,000 ($5 per square foot), the break point is found by dividing the minimum rent by the percentage rent. Assuming a percentage rent of 2 percent, overage rent would be paid after sales reached $25 million ($500,000 ÷ .02). The $25 million point would be called the *gross sales break point*. The typical lease clause would read:

> The percentage rent for each lease year shall be an amount equal to the percentage rent times the amount of gross sales made in such lease year in excess of the gross sales break point.

Percentage rents are accompanied by a statement of the tenant's monthly gross sales.

For this purpose, the lease form developed by Federated Department Stores, Inc., defines gross sales as total gross sales of all goods, wares, and merchandise sold, and charges for services performed for cash or credit, including mail, telephone, catalog, and vending machine sales. The exclusions are confined to:

1 Exchanges of merchandise between other stores owned by the tenant
2 Returns to manufacturers
3 Cash refunds to customers
4 Sales of fixtures, machinery, and equipment not held for trade
5 Sales or excise taxes
6 Discount sales to employees not in excess of 1 percent of total gross sales

To enforce provisions of percentage rent terms, leases give owners the right to review books and accounts, and furthermore, the tenant will be required to keep copies of contracts, inventory records, and sales receipts for at least 3 years.

The importance of overage rent is indicated by the latest survey of 105 regional shopping centers by the Urban Land Institute. With a total rent of $4.10 per square foot of gross leasable area, regional centers report an overage rent of $.86 per square foot.

Additional Rent

Because leases provide for a fixed minimum rent with no guarantee of percentage rent, shopping center owners shift certain costs to tenants as part of the rental agreement.

The tenant may be required to pay a proportionate share of real estate taxes. Leases that provide for additional rent to cover a proportionate share of taxes might state:

> Tenant's proportionate share of the taxes shall be in the amount equal to the product obtained by multiplying the taxes, and landlord's expenses in obtaining or attempting to obtain any refund or reduction thereof, by the gross leasable area fraction.

Additional rents may be paid for the utilities supplied by shopping center owners. In other instances water, storm, and sewer charges will be subject to additional rent by multiplying the gross leasable area fraction leased by the tenant.

A variation of additional rent payments arises from escalator or tax stop clauses. These clauses require tenants to pay real estate taxes over a specified dollar amount or a pro rata share of an increase in real estate taxes after the first year's assessment. Because property taxes are the largest single expense of operating a shopping center, these clauses protect owners from property taxes that increase more rapidly than percentage rents.

Common Area Charges

Common area charges finance the maintenance of public areas: the shopping center site, less the total gross leasable area.

In levying this charge, owners include the real estate taxes on the common areas and provide for a pro rata share of heating and air-conditioning expenses for the enclosed mall. Daily costs of maintaining this space including security costs, insurance, wages for the maintenance crew, and a reasonable charge for administration. The lease will detail items to be included in common area charges.

Excluded from common area charges would be the cost of repairs or replacements, depreciation, and the salary of the mall manager and his or her secretary. With the common area charges identified, the lease may state:

> Tenant's pro rata share of the common area maintenance cost for each rent year shall be an amount equal to the common area maintenance cost incurred by the landlord during the rent year multiplied by the gross leasable area fraction.

OTHER LEASE TERMS

Table 16-4 reproduces a topic outline of a shopping center lease. Such a lease, in a printed form of legal size, would usually cover at least 40 pages, not including exhibits. While following no set method of presentation, most leases, in the introductory section, define technical terms, anticipate changes to the shopping center, and provide for easements, restrictions, and operating agreements on space leased by tenants.

Adapted to a new shopping center, Article 2 assumes that new tenants will be granted an allowance for completion of unfinished store interiors. Other terms of the lease define owner and tenant responsibilities. For instance, tenant-sponsored construction work may incorporate the design and installation of the store fronts, signs,

**Table 16-4 Topic Outline of a Shopping
Center Lease**

Article number	Content
1	Introductory provisions
2	Premises and tenant's work
3	Term
4	Rent
5	Taxes and assessments
6	Utilities
7	Use of premises
8	Common areas
9	Promotion of shopping center
10	Construction work
11	Indemnity and insurance
12	Reconstruction
13	Maintenance of premises
14	Fixtures and personal property
15	Assignment and subletting
16	Defaults by tenant
17	Liability of landlord
18	Subordination and attachment
19	Estoppel certificates
20	Quiet enjoyment
21	Surrender and holding over
22	Condemnation
23	Miscellaneous

Source: Federated Stores Realty, Inc., Cincinnati.

entrance doors, interior partitions, ceilings, floors, wall coverings, electrical service, heating, ventilating, air conditioning, plumbing systems, and sprinklers. Before construction commences, the owner reserves the right to approve design drawings. The lease will require that the tenant complete work by the opening date.

Of particular importance is Article 7, which governs the use of the premises. On this point leases commonly state: "Tenants shall not use or permit the premises to be used for any other purpose or purposes or under any other trade name without the prior written consent of the landlord." Under this article would be the requirement that tenant will keep the store open for business to the public every day of the week from 9:30 a.m. until 9:30 p.m., and on Sunday from 10:00 a.m. until 8:00 p.m. The landlord may change the required business hours unless 50 percent of the tenants object. In this way, store operating hours may reflect local customer and seasonal shopping habits. In every instance, hours of operation must apply uniformly to the majority of retail mall tenants.

Tenants are prohibited from sponsoring going-out-of-business sales, auction sales, or bankruptcy sales. Objectionable loudspeakers, flashing lights and other noise, noxious fumes, odors, or accumulations of trash are prohibited by the terms in this article. The tenant will be required to maintain proper heating and ventilation during opening hours.

The article on common areas governs rights of both parties to the use and maintenance of common areas. Under the article covering promotion, the tenants are required to contribute to promotional services on the basis of the gross leasable area on a graduated scale. "Charges per square foot" refers to the gross leasable area.

Annual charge per square foot	Square feet
($600 minimum)	0–1,200
$.25	1,201–1,700
.20	1,701–2,000
.15	2,001–5,000
.10	5,001 and above

Changes in these promotional charges may be arranged by adjusting the percentage increase or decrease according to percentage increases or decreases in advertising rates.

Rules governing the merchants' association will be included as part of the lease. Insurance clauses require that tenants provide general public liability insurance, generally not less than $1 million for personal injury or death and $500,000 property damage. Insurance will be required for damages to tenant improvements and, in some cases, business interruption insurance will also be required. In the same manner, the landlord will be required to have similar coverages on the common area. Article 12 covers rights of parties in the event of building damages.

Other terms of the lease follow leasing practices for similar properties. For instance, the miscellaneous section will cover the relationship of the parties, broker commission schedules, recording requirements, and, typically, the lease will say that time is of the essence.

Exclusionary Clauses

Before 1974, principal tenants negotiated for certain exclusive merchandising practices. Some key tenants reserved the right to disapprove other tenant leases, limit floor space to other tenants, and control other business practices such as discouraging discount sales and pricing. According to a 1972 complaint filed by the Federal Trade Commission, Gimbel Brothers, Inc., a full-line department store, negotiated such lease agreements in 24 shopping centers.

Section 5 of the Federal Trade Commission Act (15 U.S.C. Section 45) makes it unlawful to practice unfair methods of competition and commerce. Later amendments made unfair or deceptive acts or practices equally illegal. The courts have interpreted this act to mean that it is now against public policy to hinder competition or to create monopoly.[2]

[2]John W. Stack, "Section 5, Federal Trade Commission Act," in *Antitrust Update: The Shopping Center Industry and Antitrust Laws*, New York: International Council of Shopping Centers, 1974, p. 24.

As a result of the 1972 complaint, the Federal Trade Commission issued a final decision and order prohibiting certain exclusionary agreements in shopping center leases. In conformity with this consent order, lease agreements may not:

1 Give tenants the right to approve or disapprove leases to other tenants
2 Give tenants the right to approve or disapprove floor space leased by any other tenant
3 Prohibit developers from leasing space to any particular retailer or class of retailers
4 Limit the types of merchandise, brands of merchandise, or service that any other retailer in the shopping center may offer for sale
5 Specify that any other retailer may or may not sell merchandise or services at any price or within a range of prices

In addition to these points, lease agreements may not give a particular tenant the right to approve or disapprove the location of any other retailer or control advertising within the center. For example, the lease agreement recommended by the Federated Stores, Inc., of Cincinnati, Ohio states that:

> The landlord reserves the absolute right to effect such other tenancy in the shopping center as the landlord shall determine in exercise of its sole business judgment. Tenant does not rely on the fact, nor does the landlord represent, that any specific tenant or occupant or number of tenants or occupants shall during the term occupy any space in the shopping center.

Other terms of the lease may not prevent expansion of a shopping center.

While these practices prohibit certain restrictions formerly imposed by key tenants, Gimbel Brothers, Inc., was allowed to negotiate with developers to establish reasonable categories of retailers that the developer could select as tenants in the area immediately approximate to Gimbels department stores.

However, key tenants may not specify price ranges, price lines, trade names, store names, or trademarks; or identify particular retailers. Tenants may require the developer to maintain reasonable standards of appearance and may prohibit occupancy of objectionable tenants such as retailers of pornographic materials. Accordingly, lease clauses that give a tenant exclusive right to a particular price line probably violate the Federal Trade Commission Act.

Graphics Control

As part of the lease agreement, the store design criteria will be defined and illustrated in exhibits. To enforce the design criteria, the lease requires tenants to observe graphic controls. Accordingly, shopping center leases require the approval of the landlord before tenants may erect signs. Not only are the placement, size, and color of signs restricted, but rooftop signs, paper window signs, posters, and sidewalk displays must be consistent with store design. Thus, any sign, advertising matter, figure, emblem, or descriptive material that is not in conformity with store design criteria will be prohibited. Furthermore, if the tenant does not maintain decorations, signs, and advertising matter in conformity with the store design criteria, the landlord reserves the right to maintain such signs at the tenant's expense.

Other clauses of the typical shopping center lease conform to those of commercial leases and are generally adapted to local jurisdiction. These clauses are quite technical and their interpretation requires the services of a local attorney.

Because of the complexity of leases, they are sometimes accompanied by a summary of the main lease provisions. Such a form is illustrated in Table 16-5. The form is adapted to new shopping centers in that the beginning and ending construction dates, rental terms, gross sales break point, lease beginning date, and other charges are noted.

Table 16-5 Shopping Center Lease Summary

a	Tenant's trade name:	_____	(See § 7.01)
b	Main term:	Expires July 31, 19_____	
		Approximately _____ years	(See § 3.03)
c	Tenant space number:	_____	(See Exh. B)
d	Estimated GLA in premises:	_____ square feet	(See § 1.04 and § 1.05)
e	Tenant's construction commencement date:	_____, _____, 19 ____	(See § 2.05)
f	Tenant's construction period:	_____ days	(See § 2.06)
g	Minimum rent	$ _____ per year	
		$ _____ per month	(See § 4.03)
h	Percentage rent:	_____ percent on gross sales in excess of gross sales break point of $ _____ per lease year	(See § 4.04 ff.)
i	Rent commencement date	_____	(See § 4.02)
j	Opening deposit:	$ _____	(See § 2.02)
k	Promotional charge and grand opening promotional charge:	$ _____ $ _____	(See § 9.01)
l	Other sums payable:	Taxes (including sales tax on rent)	(See § 5.01 ff.)
		Common area maintenance costs	(See § 8.02)
		Common area electrical energy costs	(See § 8.03)
		Common area equipment charge	(See § 8.05)
		Utility charges for premises	(See § 6.01 ff.)
m	Use:	_____ _____ _____	(See Article 7)

Source: Federated Stores Realty, Inc., Cincinnati, Ohio.

INVESTMENT ANALYSIS

Investment analysis demonstrates the key role played by property managers. The documentation of the investment through a review of the tenant's gross income and expenses precedes investment calculations. After they have made investment calculations, shopping center analysts examine certain investment ratios common to shopping centers. Each of these three steps requires the services of a shopping center specialist.

Investment Documentation

The scope of documentation increases with the size of the center. For regional centers, investment analysis starts with an economic study that reports per capita income of population within the trading area. For in-depth studies, analysts include the value of houses, the number of house sales, foreclosure rates, the age of the present housing, and new housing sites. Both census data and surveys by local utility companies require review to identify trade area trends and projections.

To measure accessibility, economic and demographic data in the trade market area are supplemented by traffic counts, data about planned highways, and analysis of the impact of other expected changes in that area. The analysis concludes with a study of the effect of competitive stores—planned or existing—under expansion.

Tenant Analysis Recall that shopping center profitability hinges mostly on steps taken to maximize income rather than steps taken to reduce expenses. Moreover, the source of income is equally important. A large proportion of the minimum rent should be secured from national tenants with good credit rating. Leases to major tenants preferably should be negotiated for 15 or 20 years. And since percentage rent is speculative, it is reported separately from minimum rent.

A form providing this information is shown in Figure 16-1. Note that the form identifies each tenant, the tenant's credit, net worth, minimum rent, and remaining lease term. The amount of gross leasable area, sales per square foot, gross sales, and percentage rent are also listed for each lease.

Shopping center experts expect the key tenants to account for 70 to 80 percent of the gross leasable area and 65 to 75 percent of the gross rent. A good percentage or overage rent amounts to 10 percent or more of minimum rent. Investors look toward major tenants that have a Dun and Bradstreet rating of Triple A-1, indicating a high composite credit rating and net assets of over $1 million.

Moreover, in judging tenants, analysts make sure that nonretailing businesses such as movie theaters, bowling alleys, health clubs, medical centers, and office buildings are justified by the shopping center layout and size. These tenants frequently create parking and traffic problems that may lower retail sales.

Expense Analysis While shopping center operators have less flexibility in reducing expenses, they may anticipate rising expenses by requiring escalator clauses. For

				MINIMUM RENT		ESTIMATED RENT	
GROSS INCOME 46,320 square feet @ $3.24 per square foot			$	149	878	$	
LESS VACANCY (9.1 %) of Locals				4	195		
EFFECTIVE GROSS INCOME 46,320 square feet @ $3.15 per square foot				145	683		
EXPENSES:							
TAXES · · $46,320 sq.ft. @ $25.0¢ per square foot	$	11 580					
INSURANCE $46,320 sq.ft. @ 5.0¢ per square foot	$	2 316					
OPERATING $46,320 sq.ft. S.F. @ 27.7¢	$	12 827					
LESS TENANT CONTRIBUTIONS 46,320 sq.ft. @ 10.2¢ per sq.ft.	$	4 732					
NET OPERATING 46,320 per sq.ft. @ 17.5¢ per sq.ft.	$	8 095					
TOTAL EXPENSES 46,320 per sq.ft. @ 47.5¢ per square foot				21	991		
NET INCOME 46,320 per square foot @ $2.67 per square foot			$	123	692	$ 123	692
TIMES INT. 1ST. YEAR. (87,188) 930,000 @ 9.375%				1.42	x	98,952	x
TIMES ANNUAL LOAN REQUIREMENT ($ 98,952) $930,000 @ 10.64 (9⅜ - 22.83 yr)				1.25	x	24,740	x
MINIMUM NET INCOME ($123,692) CAP. @ 9.8 % EQUALS $ 1,240,000							
ESTIMATED NET INCOME $ 123,692							
VALUATION: LAND 264,400 S.F. @ 68.1¢ per square foot						$ 180,000	
BUILDING 46,320 S.F. @ $22.88						$1,060,000	
SITE IMPROVEMENT PAVING, WALKS, ETC. S.F. @ ¢						$	
TOTAL						$1,240,000	
RATIO OF LOAN ($ 930,000) TO VALUATION ($1,240,000) = 75.0 %							

BUILDING AREA - GROSS			S.F.	LOAN PER S.F. $		
BUILDING AREA - GROSS LEASABLE	46	320	S.F.	LOAN PER S.F. $		
BUILDING AREA - MERCHANDISING (EST.)			S.F.	LOAN PER S.F. $		
BREAKPOINT:						
TOTAL EXPENSES	23	151	Add back estimated annual maintenance of locals			
DEBT SERVICE	98	952	$21,991 + $1,160 = $23,151			
TOTAL	122	103	÷ (46,320) EQUALS $ 2.64			PER S.F.

RENTABLE SPACE			MINIMUM RENT		ESTIMATED RENT		
KEY TENANTS 35,720	S.F. 77.1 %		$ 107,176	69.3 %	$		%
OTHER TENANTS 10,600	S.F. 22.9 %		$ 47,434	30.7 %	$		%
TOTAL 46,320	S.F. 100.0 %		$ 154,610	100.0 %	$		%
BUILDING GROUND FLOOR AREA S.F.		LOAN YEAR	LOAN BALANCE			LOAN PER S.F.	
PARKING, WALKS, DRIVES, ACCESS, MALLS, ETC. S.F.		5	855,557			18.47	
TOTAL (EQUALS LAND AREA) 245,290 S.F.		10	736,814			15.91	
RATIO, PARKING, ETC. TO BUILDING RENTABLE		15	547,408			11.82	
ESTIMATED PARKING CAPACITY 267 CARS		20	245,290 (92.8¢per sq. ft. land)			5.30	
RATIO: NO. OF CAR SPACES PER 1,000 S.F. MERCHANDISING AREA 5.76							

Figure 16-1 Shopping center analysis form.

example, tax escalator clauses, referred to also as tax stop provisions, shift increased taxes from the base year, usually the first lease year, to the tenant. Other solutions provide a tax stop that uses a specific base rate per square foot, which shifts increased taxes per square foot to tenants if taxes exceed the base rate per square foot.

Operating expenses may be compared to those in the latest issue of *Dollars and Cents of Shopping Centers*, which is prepared by the Urban Land Institute. While local experience may vary, this report gives a range of expenses that serves as a guide to expense evaluation. For existing centers, expense statements for the most recent 5 years of operating history help to measure management efficiency.

Any substantial deviations from published average expenses deserve explanation. Other analysts provide cost comparables—experience of similar shopping center operations.

Typically, operating expenses, both fixed and variable, should approximate 30 percent of gross income. The most recent report of the Urban Land Institute shows a median percentage of operating expense (regional centers) ranging from 26.0 percent to 51.8 percent of total receipts. Operating expenses per square foot of gross leasable area and as a median percentage of total receipts are shown in Table 16-6.

Note that total maintenance and housekeeping dominates other operating expenses, with a median value of $.88 per square foot or 18.7 percent of total receipts. The importance of tax escalator stop clauses is shown by property taxes that have a median expense of $.43 per square foot or 9.8 percent of total receipts. In this example, the total operating expense of $1.68 represents 38.7 percent of total operating receipts of $5.25 per square foot of gross leasable area.

Investment Calculations

Shopping center analysts must summarize gross income and expenses and yet show the distribution of rents among key tenants and other tenants with respect to minimum and overage rent. Such an analysis is shown in Figure 16-2. Covering a shopping center of 46,320 square feet of gross leasable area, the form indicates a net income from minimum rents of $123,692, which is 1.42 times interest or 1.25 times the annual mortgage payment.

In addition to providing this summary, the form shows the income capitalized at 9.8 percent, straight line, which produces an estimated market value of $1,240,000. Some 77.1 percent of the rentable space is absorbed by tenants who provide for 69.3 percent of the minimum rent. Note that parking is 5.76 spaces per 1,000 square feet of gross leasable area—well within the recommended limit.

With this type of analysis, property managers contribute to shopping center feasibility analysis by estimating minimum rent required for proposed construction. For instance, given the gross leasable area and the average rent, this type of analysis produces the capitalized value of the shopping center. Table 16-7 presents such an analysis, where percentage overage rents are omitted for this purpose. In a new shopping center, these overages are too uncertain. In this study gross income after bad debt allowances, estimated as 2 percent, gives a gross effective income of $4,187,500. A summary of the estimated expenses (23.3 percent of gross effective income) provides for stabilized net income, which, capitalized at 9.14 percent, produces a value of $35,150,000 (rounded).

Table 16-6 Total Operating Expenses of Regional Enclosed Mall Shopping Centers

Operating expenses	Dollars per square foot of gross leasable area			Median percentage of total receipts		
	Median	Lower decile	Upper decile	Median	Lower decile	Upper decile
Building maintenance	$ .04	$ .01	$ .15	0.9	0.1	3.1
Parking lot, mall, and other common areas	.54	.20	1.18	12.5	4.4	19.3
Central utility systems	.42	.09	1.03	9.7	3.5	17.5
Office area services	.07	.01	.16	1.0	0.6	2.0
Total maintenance and housekeeping	$ .88	$ .33	$2.02	18.7	9.2	30.9
Advertising and promotion	$ .06	$ .02	$ .14	1.0	0.6	2.0
Real estate taxes	.43	.23	1.10	9.8	5.2	16.9
Insurance	.06	.03	.10	1.1	0.5	2.9
General and administrative	.22	.08	.70	6.0	1.7	9.2
Total operating expenses	$1.68	$ .83	$3.38	38.7	26.0	51.8

Note: Because data are medians and deciles, detail amounts to not add to totals.
Source: *Dollars and Cents of Shopping Centers*, op. cit., p. 270.

STORE NUMBER	TENANT	CREDIT TENANT	NET WORTH $	REMAIN LEASE TERM YEARS	GROSS LEASABLE AREA	MINIMUM RENT $	TENANT EXPENSE CONTRIBUTION $	MIN. PER SQ. FT. G.L.A. $	MERCHANDISING AREA (EST.) (B-BASEMENT) S F	PERCENT ON SALES %	SALES PER SQ. FT. MDSE. TO PRODUCE MIN. $	ESTIMATED SALES $	ESTIMATED SALE PER SQ. FT. $	ESTIMATED PERCENTAGE RENTS $	MINIMUM PLUS PERCENTAGE RENTS TOTALS	STAB. RENT PER SQ. FT. RENT $	REMARKS
TOTALS EXCLUDING BASEMENTS																	
PLUS BASEMENTS																	
TOTALS AND AVERAGES																	

Figure 16-2 Shopping center analysis. *(Source: Data furnished by Provident Life and Accident Insurance Company.)*

353

Table 16-7   The Capitalized Value of a Proposed Regional Shopping Center

Gross income estimate		
Minimum rent, 1,094,115 of gross leasable area, @ $3.55		$ 3,886,300
Common area charges, @ $.35 per square foot		386,200
Total gross income estimate		$ 4,272,500
Less vacancy and bad debts, 2%		−85,000
Gross effective income		$ 4,187,500
Less expenses		
Real estate taxes	$300,000	
Insurance	50,000	
Common area parking	283,000	
Heating and ventilating	135,000	
Building repairs	22,000	
Merchants' association	40,000	
Management, promotion	145,000	
Total estimated expenses (23.3%)		975,000
		$ 3,212,500
Net operating income, capitalized, @ 9.14% (rounded)		$35,150,000

Data furnished by Reaves C. Lukens, Jr., MAI, Jackson-Cross Company, Philadelphia, Pa.

The valuation of a neighborhood center that produced a percentage overage rent of $10,000 was analyzed as shown in Table 16-8. In this example, minimum rents produced a value of $1,320,000 (capitalized at 10 percent, straight line). While the percentage rent added $65,000 to the minimum rent, it was capitalized at a higher rate (15 percent) because of its uncertainty.

This type of analysis is incomplete without a comparison of the proposed gross rent and development costs. A survey on this point by the Urban Land Institute summarized the experience of 36 neighborhood centers. The development cost and total receipts are summarized in Table 16-9. Because the centers were widely dispersed throughout the United States and included centers of different age, location, and quality, the range of receipts and costs among these centers was quite wide.

Note, however, that land and land improvements show a median cost per square foot of $4.97 and $3.64. Adding the building and equipment costs and overhead

Table 16-8   Capitalized Income of a Neighborhood Center

Estimated gross income		$ 165,699
Less vacancy and bad debts		−3,646
Effective gross income		$ 162,053
Less expenses		−30,226
Net operating income		$ 131,827
Net operating income, capitalized, @ 10% (rounded)		$1,320,000
Percentage income, $10,000, capitalized, @ 15% (rounded)		65,000
Indicated value		$1,385,000

Source: Stewart Wight, CRE and CPM, Landauer Associates, Atlanta, Ga.

Table 16-9   A Summary of Capital Costs of 36 Neighborhood Centers

Cost item	Dollars per square foot of gross leasable area		
	Median	Lower decile	Upper decile
Land and land improvements			
Land	$ 4.97	$ 1.70	$11.70
Off-site and on-site improvement	3.64	1.10	5.93
Buildings and equipment			
Shell and mall buildings	16.24	11.18	26.51
Tenant improvements by owner	1.42	.06	11.26
Overhead and development			
Architecture and engineering	.68	.24	1.48
Interest and financing	1.60	.44	3.87
Administrative overhead and construction supervision	1.02	.16	2.64
Leasing costs and legal fees	.46	.00	1.30
Other overhead and development prior to opening	.23	.07	1.08
Total capital cost	$31.06	$20.63	$53.80
Rent	$ 4.29	$ 2.95	$ 6.21
Common area charges	.20	.12	.82
Other charges	.12	.03	.61
Total operating receipts	$ 4.48	$ 3.01	$ 6.78

Note: Because data are medians and deciles, detail amounts do not add to totals.
Source: Dollars & Cents of Shopping Centers, op. cit., p. 254.

resulted in a median capital outlay for these centers of $31.06 per square foot of gross leasable area. These data compare with median total receipts of $4.48. With these preliminary data, property managers then review income, expenses, and cost data with certain accepted shopping center investment ratios.

Investment Ratios

There are certain common financial relationships that help analysts judge shopping center management and values. Though the relationships vary widely by type of center, age, and geographic area, significant departures from established financial ratios deserve explanation. For example, a new center may be feasible in a growth area even though financial ratios show short-term distortion. Similarly, established centers in declining areas, where job opportunities are limited, may show financial ratios that vary significantly from normal standards.

There is the further point that published financial ratios may be expected to change as energy costs assume greater importance. And as land values, building costs, and other operating expenses vary in importance, adjustments in acceptable ratios will probably occur. However, with these qualifications, certain financial ratios fall within fairly narrow limits.

Loan ratios

The loan per square foot of gross leasable area	$12–27
The loan as a multiple of gross income	$5–7
The loan as a multiple of net income	$8–9
The loan as a percentage of market value	75%

Leases and rent of principal tenants

Percentage of gross leasable area	70–80%
Percentage of gross rent	65–75%
Rents of principal tenants as a percentage of operating costs and debt service	90% or more
Minimum rents	$1.30 to 1.65 per square foot of gross leasable area
Average rent of minor and local tenants	$2–4 per square foot of gross leasable area

Income coverage

Net income as a multiple of debt service	$1.25–1.50
Gross income as a multiple of debt service	$1.50–1.75
Operating expenses as a percentage of gross income	30% (average)
Mortgage principal and interest and operating expenses as a percentage of gross income	75% or less
Percentage rent	9.5–10% of minimum rent[3]

To be sure, an individual center may justify ratios that depart from these standards. Yet, given a current allowance for inflation, rising expenses, and local market conditions, shopping centers should conform to common financial ratios typical of shopping center investments.

SUMMARY

Tenants, who are classified according to whether they are national, independent, or local chain stores; their industrial classification code; or credit, are placed in such a way as to maximize shopping convenience. For each type of shopping center, there is a logical grouping of tenants.

It is common to group variety, hardware, appliance, and home furnishings stores in close proximity. Similarly, managers group together service and repair shops. The food group, namely supermarkets, meat and fish markets, delicatessens, bakeries, doughnut shops and food stores—because they attract the same kind of customers—are grouped together. Convenience stores must be within easy access to parking areas.

In comparisons of shopping centers, it can be seen that certain groups and tenants tend to dominate particular kinds of centers. In the regional center, general merchandise and clothing stores account for the largest percentage of gross leasable area

[3]For further detail, consult Francis P. Gunning, "On Submitting Mortgage Applications," *Shopping Center Report*, New York: International Council of Shopping Centers, 1977.

and gross sales. In contrast, the neighborhood shopping centers are dominated by supermarkets that account for almost two-thirds of total gross sales.

As an aid in judging total operating receipts, it should be noted that most centers earn the largest share of income from minimum rents. Percentage rents, referred to also as overage rent, are unimportant in considering new shopping centers because they are uncertain. Shopping center leases provide for percentage rent after sales reach the gross sales break point. This point is found by dividing minimum rent by the percentage rent.

Percentage rent terms require a detailed definition of gross sales. Total receipts include additional rent, negotiated to compensate for increased property taxes, utility, or other expenses over the lease terms. Common area charges are pro rated to tenants according to a list of common area expenses.

Other common lease terms control store operation and tenant construction. Shopping center managers are careful not to violate terms of the Federal Trade Commission Act, which prohibits lease agreements from giving tenants the right to approve or disapprove leases to other tenants or to control competition in other ways.

Because shopping centers operate as a complex of compatible tenants, graphic controls are equally important and are carefully detailed in shopping center leases.

Investment analysis of a shopping center emphasizes the key role played by property managers. It starts with documentation of the trade market area and trends that affect anticipated gross sales. The analysis requires a review of individual tenants—their credit rating, gross sales, minimum rent, and percentage rent for operating shopping centers. Typically, key tenants must account for 65 to 75 percent of gross rent. Operating centers should show overage rent equal to 10 percent or more of minimum rent. Shopping center leases, which extend up to 20 years, should have appropriate escalator clauses covering property taxes, utilities, and insurance expenses.

Investment calculations summarize gross income and expenses, showing the distribution of rents between key tenants and other tenants with respect to minimum and overage rent. Expenses are compared to those of comparable shopping centers and published reports of operating expenses. As part of an investment analysis, shopping centers are judged according to the investment ratios that are common to shopping center operation.

DISCUSSION QUESTIONS

1 What are the common ways to classify tenants?
2 Give three examples of the preferred grouping of tenants.
3 Describe the more important tenants found in regional centers and in neighborhood centers.
4 What is the importance of classifying tenants by operational type?
5 What are the sources of total operating receipts in shopping centers?
6 Give an example of how you would estimate the minimum required rent for a proposed shopping center.
7 Give an example of how you would estimate the gross sales break point to calculate percentage rent.

8 Define gross sales for purposes of estimating percentage rent.

9 What is meant by additional rent; common area charges? Explain fully.

10 What usual provisions govern tenant use of the premises?

11 What is the current rule on exclusionary lease clauses?

12 What is the purpose of graphics control? Explain thoroughly.

13 How would you analyze shopping center expenses?

14 What investment calculations are common to shopping centers?

15 What are the more common investment ratios associated with shopping center management and operation?

KEY TERMS AND CONCEPTS

National chain store

Independent store

Local chain stores

Standard industrial
classification code

Key tenant

General merchandise tenants

Minimum rent

Common area charges

Overage rent

Percentage rent

Gross sales break point

Gross leasable area fraction

Exclusionary clauses

Graphics control

Tax escalator clauses

Income coverage

SELF-QUIZ

Multiple-Choice Questions

_____ **1** Which of the following defines a national chain store? (a) Businesses operating in not more than two outlets, and only one metropolitan area; (b) Stores with net assets of over $1,000,000 and a good composite credit rating; (c) Businesses operating in four or more metropolitan areas in three or more states; (d) General merchandise tenants.

_____ **2** Which of the following statements is correct? (a) In regional centers, clothing stores account for the greatest share of gross leasable area; (b) In regional centers, general merchandise stores account for the greatest share of the gross leasable area; (c) Food stores are more important among regional shopping centers; (d) General merchandise stores are the largest single source of sales for neighborhood centers.

_____ **3** Shopping center managers tend to group the following tenants: (a) Men's apparel stores, men's shoes, clothing, and sporting goods; (b) Women's clothing stores, women's shoes, millinery, and children's clothes and toys; (c) Supermarkets, meat and fish markets, delicatessens, bakeries, doughnut shops, and candy stores; (d) All of the above.

_____ **4** Which of the following statements is correct? (a) Percentage rents are usually not payable until sales rise above the gross sales break point;

(b) Minimum rent applies after gross sales exceed the break point; (c) The minimum rent never exceeds the sum of mortgage principal and interest, real estate taxes, and management fees; (d) Percentage rents apply to gross income from any source without exclusion.

_____ 5 Common area charges normally include: (a) Repairs and replacements; (b) Depreciation; (c) Salary of the mall manager and his or her secretary; (d) None of the above.

_____ 6 Shopping center leases prohibit tenants from sponsoring: (a) Anniversary sales; (b) Inventory sales; (c) Sales unauthorized by the merchants' association; (d) Going-out-of-business sales, auction sales, or bankruptcy sales.

_____ 7 Under the Federal Trade Commission Act, lease agreements may not: (a) Give tenants the right to approve or disapprove leases to other tenants; (b) Prohibit developers from leasing space to any particular retailer or class of retailer; (c) Specify that any retailers may or may not sell at any price or within a range of prices; (d) All of the above.

_____ 8 An operating shopping center should have percentage or overage rents equal to: (a) 10 percent or more of the minimum rent; (b) 50 percent or more of the minimum rent; (c) 10 percent of gross sales; (d) 5 percent or more of the minimum rent.

_____ 9 Shopping center analysts expect: (a) Rent collected from principal tenants to be 70 to 80 percent of gross leasable area; (b) Rent collected from principal tenants to be 65 to 75 percent of the gross rent; (c) Overage rent to be 10 percent or more of minimum rent; (d) All of the above.

_____ 10 The capital costs of shopping center development include: (a) Land and land improvements; (b) Buildings and equipment; (c) Overhead and development costs; (d) All of the above.

Answer Key

1 (c),   **2** (a),   **3** (d),   **4** (a),   **5** (d),   **6** (d),   **7** (d),   **8** (a),   **9** (d),   **10** (d).

Fill-In Questions

1 _____are businesses operating in not more than two outlets in only one metropolitan area.

2 _____are situated at each end of the mall to create pedestrian traffic for minor tenants.

3 Among regional centers,_____ account for the greatest share of the gross leasable area.

4 In superregional centers,_____dominate other tenants in sales and in the area leased.

5 Minimum rents are related to the _____ .

6 Percentage rents are not payable until sales rise above some given point known as the_____.

7 Generally, lease agreements may not give a particular tenant the right to _____the location of any other retailer.

8 Shopping center profitability hinges mostly on steps taken to _____ _____ rather than steps taken to reduce expenses.

9 Shopping center operators anticipate rising expenses by requiring_____ _____.

10 Typically, operating expenses, both fixed and variable, should approximate _____ of gross income.

Answer Key

1	Independent stores	6	gross sales break point
2	Key tenants	7	approve or disapprove
3	clothing stores	8	maximize income
4	national tenants	9	escalator clauses
5	cost of development	10	30 percent

SELECTED REFERENCES

Applebaum, William, and S. O. Kaylin: *Case Studies in Shopping Center Development and Operation*, New York: International Council of Shopping Centers, 1974.

Downs, James C., Jr.: *Principles of Real Estate Management*, Chicago: Institute of Real Estate Management, 1975, chap. 18.

Klein, Philip E.: "Feasibility of Shopping Center Development," *Shopping Center Report*, New York: International Council of Shopping Centers, 1976.

Redstone, Louis G.: *New Dimensions in Shopping Centers and Stores*, New York: McGraw-Hill, 1973.

Shopping Centers 1976, New York: Practicing Law Institute, 1976.

Chapter 17

Office Building Analysis

After studying this chapter, you should be familiar with:
1 The classification of office buildings
2 Locational preferences of office building tenants
3 Methods of estimating the office building rental market
4 Techniques of estimating the office building absorption rate
5 Evaluating office buildings: operating experience, management objectives, building inspection, and the recommended annual budget

Because the market for office space may be classified in different ways, the first part of this chapter identifies different types of office space that meet local demands. The next section of the chapter reviews methods of estimating the demand and supply of available space and its condition. An explanation of building analysis concludes the chapter.

THE MARKET FOR OFFICE SPACE

The Building Owners and Managers Association International (BOMA) classifies office buildings by their age, height, size, and within each category, by whether their location is downtown or suburban. For certain other purposes office buildings are classified as speculative or owner-built structures.

These various systems of classification indicate that there is no single market for office space; offices are highly diversified and represent many grades, classes, and locations. For example, some managers divide office space by listing offices as class A, B, or C—with the A category representing the prestige of new modern construction, while the C grade represents the older structures in the less desirable locations. For the present purpose, it is believed more useful to refer to a more functional classification system.

Functional Classification

The functional classification, which incorporates speculative and owner-built offices, consists of four groups:

1 Institutional buildings
2 General commercial buildings
3 Medical/dental buildings
4 Industrial office space

The first category, *institutional offices*, serves the banks and other companies that construct buildings mainly for their own use. If such offices are partially rented, the tenants will be selected for their compatibility with owner occupancy.

The *general commercial building* houses professional tenants and service industries that require convenient access to auto transportation and to customers. The prestige address is less important than the convenience to transportation facilities such as freeways, airports, and parking. Within this category will be found the downtown multiple-tenant office building and the suburban office park. Figure 17-1 illustrates the open appearance of a suburban office complex. A typical building floor plan is shown in Figure 17-2.

Medical/dental buildings represent special-purpose construction that combines space for medical services, supplies, pharmacies, laboratories, and the other medical professions. Because their needs are specialized and because their clients are incompatible with commercial clients, medical tenants prefer specially designed buildings in the suburbs, often in close proximity to hospitals. Parking for staff and customers is critical to offices developed for medical/dental tenants.

The *industrially oriented office building* is found in organized industrial parks, primarily occupied by printers, distributors, and manufacturers who combine manufacturing with office headquarters. Usually because of the associated industrial use, these offices require industrial zoning. Frequently, the office will be part of a larger industrial complex.

This chapter concentrates on the general commercial building adapted to multiple-tenant occupancy. In choosing these buildings, tenants show a wide range of locational preferences.

Figure 17-1 These photographs of the Lloyd Plaza Office Complex in Portland, Ore., show the open, attractive appeal of a suburban office complex. Note the first-level parking and second-floor office use. *(Source: Photos courtesy of Skidmore, Owings & Merrill, Portland, Ore.)*

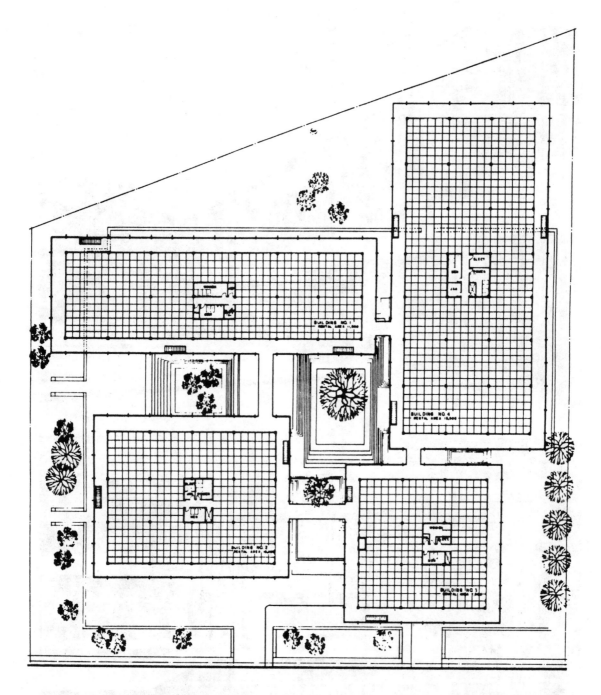

Figure 17-2 Floor plan layout of a typical building in the Lloyd Plaza Office Complex, Portland, Ore. The center plaza corresponds to the area shown in Figure 17-1. *(Source: Photos courtesy of Skidmore, Owings & Merrill, Portland, Ore.)*

Locational Preferences

Considerable emphasis is placed on the office location. Compromises are made in weighing advantages of location near financial centers, public buildings (including courthouses), customers, and transportation convenient to employees; others prefer the advantage of proximity to competitors or the advantage of the maximum possible prestige.

Table 17-1 Ranking of Location Factors Considered Very Important

Location factor	Percentage of companies rating very important
1 Cost	55.0
2 Bus, highway	27.9
3 Environment	27.3
4 Labor market	21.6
5 Location of allied industries	20.4
6 Banks and financial institutions	17.2
7 Location of competitors	8.9
8 Proximity to airports	4.8
9 Recreation facilities	0.5

These preferences were surveyed among 1,500 corporate officers responsible for office location in the Southwest.[1] Of the 30 percent who replied, 55 percent considered the *cost of space* to be the most important of nine factors considered in selecting office space. All nine items are ranked in Table 17-1. Note that bus and highway facilities, the environment, and the labor market were next in importance. In this area, recreational facilities were judged the least important to office site selection.

Officials responsible for office selection also indicated factors considered *not important* to office selection. In this list, recreational facilities, location of competitors, and proximity to airports were judged the least important. Again the results of this list showed the dominance of such factors as cost, the environment, and highway transportation facilities (see Table 17-2).

Apparently the degree of importance attached to locational factors varies by the size of the firm. The larger firms gave more weight to the importance of the local

[1] See Charles H. Wurtzebach, "Major Factors Affecting Selection of Office Facilities," *Journal of Property Management*, 41(5):22-23 (1976).

Table 17-2 Ranking of Location Factors Considered Not Important

Location factor	Percentage of companies rating not important
1 Recreation facilities	85.8
2 Location of competitors	76.2
3 Proximity to airports	57.6
4 Location of allied industries	52.6
5 Banks and financial institutions	50.5
6 Labor market	46.9
7 Bus, highway	33.9
8 Environment	21.1
9 Cost	8.4

labor market and the cost of space than did the smaller firms. Regardless of the size of the firm, however, cost leads all other factors in the choice of an office site, which indicates a highly competitive market for office space.

ESTIMATING THE MARKET

Two factors control office building profitability; one of these is market feasibility. The concept of *market feasibility* hinges on the demand for office space in relation to the supply available. Because of the lead time necessary to develop new office space or to rehabilitate older buildings, supply and demand projections must be made for future years. The second factor important to profitable office operation relates to the *financial feasibility*—the analysis of gross income and operating expenses.

The Employment Base

The demand for office space is closely related to the employment mix of the local community. In this respect, unlike the demand for apartment space and shopping centers, population only indirectly increases demand for office space. For each type of employment, there tends to be a given ratio of employees who need office space. For instance, studies by Coldwell, Banker & Company of San Francisco have shown that 83 percent of the jobs in finance, insurance, and real estate require office space. These studies suggest further, for example, that even for mining employment, 44 percent of the employees require office space. In general, 15 to 25 percent of all new employment requires office space.

Because of differences in the employment base, cities vary in their number of square feet of office space per person. For example, it is estimated that in Philadelphia there are approximately 6 square feet of office space per person. In New York City, which is more of a financial and corporate center, existing office space approximates 16 square feet per person.

There is also a need for replacement of obsolete office space by new construction. Some authorities claim that office space that is more than 50 years old will be replaced within the next decade. Furthermore, as companies move to new offices they generally require 10 to 20 percent more additional space.

Finally, the demand for office space is indicated by multiplying office space per employee by 200 square feet, which is the average office area required per office employee. Accordingly, Coldwell, Banker & Company (1) projects employment by standard industrial classifications, (2) multiplies the "office employee coefficient" by the projected employment by industry, and (3) allows 200 square feet per office employee to estimate the demand for office space. Along with these data other determinants of office space must be considered.

The Demand for Office Space

While the demand for office space is related to population and the employment base, the final demand for space arises from five sources:

1 Existing tenants
2 New tenants who are relocating from other communities
3 Newly organized businesses
4 Tenants who upgrade their space requirements
5 Tenants who are vacating abandoned space

The first three categories of tenants absorb the demand for new space, a demand faced by growth communities. The demand for space in this category is estimated from population and employment projections. Generally speaking, tenants who relocate require 20 to 25 percent more space. The last two categories are not major determinants of office demand, though tenants in the last two groups affect the demand for lower-quality space. Local surveys determine the number of tenants who plan to upgrade or abandon their present offices.

Estimating the Supply of Office Space

While supply is a function of five main factors, the reasons for change in supply of office space tend to fall within the first two categories listed here:

1 New office construction (including remodeled space)
2 Unrented office space held over from preceding years (termed the "space overhang")
3 Tenants who are going out of business
4 Tenants who reduce their office space
5 Tenants who move to other cities

The first two supply factors result from favorable changes in community economic growth. The last three groups are more prominent in declining or more stable communities. Tenants who withdraw from the office space market usually are found in communities that have a declining rate of employment.

The Absorption Rate

The annual rate of absorption of office space may be calculated by comparing the demand for space with the office supply as indicated by the five supply factors. If demand equals supply, the absorption rate is zero. It may be noted that even among communities experiencing no economic growth, a demand for office space may arise if tenants plan to upgrade their present office space. In contrast, new office space may not be feasible in a high-growth community because new office construction completed in former years may still be vacant.

The anticipated absorption rate may be calculated by comparing demand factors with projected changes in supply:

$$\text{Absorption rate} = \begin{bmatrix} \text{space required by new employment} + \text{space required by tenants' upgrading} + \text{new space removed} \end{bmatrix} - \begin{bmatrix} \text{space added} + \text{space overhang} \end{bmatrix}$$

$$R = [G + U + O_r] - [O_a + O_v]$$

To apply this model, field surveys are required to determine the space lost from the local inventory as a result of condemnation, change in use, demolition, and the like. The amount of available space remaining from preceding years (the space overhang) must be determined by field review. Building permit data indicate newly added space.

Demand Projections   The most critical part of estimating the absorption rate concerns the projection of (1) new tenants resulting from economic growth and (2) office space required by tenants who are upgrading their present offices. The former is based on employment projections undertaken by local planning agencies, regional planning offices, state development offices, local chambers of commerce, and similar agencies.

The demand for space from tenants upgrading offices is estimated from a detailed building-by-building survey. The more professional offices conduct office surveys, by building, to determine when office leases expire and what the need for future office space will be.

Managers rely on a prospect file that identifies the building, the company, and the present occupants. In addition, space is provided for prospect follow-up and for lease negotiations. A form to update this file annually is shown in Figure 17-3.

A summary of the office prospect file lists the number of square feet and the rent per square foot by industry groups, such as insurance, finance, and real estate. Another approach is to list the total square footage of leases that expire each year by industry groups. It will be observed that in the more established cities, the demand for office space from tenants upgrading their space is often greater than the demand for space from new tenants. In cities such as Houston, Texas, or Seattle, Washington and other growth areas, very little second class space exists; the demand arises primarily from new tenants.

Absorption Rate Illustrated   To apply the absorption rate estimate, it is recommended that allowances be made for a normal vacancy level to allow for tenant and owner adjustment to the current market for rental space. In illustration, suppose you project a demand for 500,000 square feet and you allow for a 6 percent vacancy factor. With V_a representing the vacancy rate, the space required would then equal

$$\text{Office space demand} = \frac{1}{1 - V_a} \ (500,000)$$
$$= \frac{1}{1 - .06} \ (500,000)$$
$$= 1.0638 \ (500,000)$$
$$= 531,900$$

If 531,900 square feet were available with a 6 percent vacancy factor, 500,000 square feet would be occupied and 31,900 square feet would be vacant (500,000 $\times$ .0638). With this qualification, the absorption rate formula assumes the following form:

$$\text{Absorption rate} = \frac{1}{1 - V_a} \ (G + U + O_r) - (O_a + O_v)$$

Date_____

Name of contact_____

Company name_____

Type of business_____

Address_____ Telephone_____

Presently occupy space in_____ building

Building address_____

Number of square feet_____ Floor number_____

Number of office employees_____ Professional_____

Secretarial_____ Office space needed _____

Locational preference_____

Special requirements_____

Source of information_____Telephone_____

Cooperating agent_____Telephone_____

Date of initial contact_____ Personal_____Telephone_____

Date of first call_____

Results_____

Date of second call_____

Results_____

Office space offered_____ Square feet_____Floor number____

Date offer submitted_____

Date of counteroffer_____

Date final offer accepted_____

Date lease submitted_____Date lease executed_____

Date lease begins_____Date lease terminates_____

Date of occupancy_____

Special Stipulations_____

_____

Figure 17-3 Office prospect sheet.

Suppose that a survey of office space results in the following estimates:

Normal vacancy (V_a) $\qquad\qquad$ = .06

Space for new tenants (G) $\qquad$ = 750,000 square feet

Upgraded demand for new space (U) = 1,000,000 square feet

Inventory of vacant space (O_v) $\qquad$ = 250,000

Space added to market (O_a) $\qquad$ = 200,000

Space removed (O_r) $\qquad\qquad$ = 0

$$
\begin{aligned}
\text{Absorption rate} &= \frac{1}{1 - V_a}\,(G + U + O_r) - (O_a + O_v) \\[2mm]
&= \frac{1}{1 - .06}\,(750{,}000 + 1{,}000{,}000) - (200{,}000 + 250{,}000) \\[2mm]
&= 1.0638\,(1{,}750{,}000) - (450{,}000) \\[2mm]
&= 1{,}861{,}650 - 450{,}000 \\[2mm]
&= 1{,}411{,}650
\end{aligned}
$$

The allowance for vacancy expands the demand to account for added space plus 6 percent vacancy. The data reveal a demand for approximately 1,400,000 square feet of additional space. If space is removed from the market because of demolition or eminent domain, the demand for additional space will be increased accordingly.

BUILDING EVALUATION

Given the potential demand for space, the next issue is to relate the gross income expected to the expenses of operation. When added to the cost of construction, these data would indicate the feasibility of proposed office building construction. The same analysis is used to maximize net operating income from an existing building. Property managers regularly undertake this type of analysis. Before analyzing income and expense detail, it is worthwhile to define certain technical terms.

Technical Definitions

BOMA and IREM employ standard terms in reporting office income and expense data. The following standard definitions are widely accepted.

Gross Area of Entire Building Gross square feet refers to the sum of the areas of all floor levels, including cellars, basements, mezzanines, penthouses, corridors, lobbies, doors, offices, garages within the building or within the outside faces of the exterior walls, not including architectural setbacks or projections. Areas include floor surfaces with a minimum of 6-foot, 6-inch ceiling height, and exclude unroofed and unenclosed roofed over space.

Gross Rentable Area Gross rentable area is computed by measuring the inside finish of permanent outer building walls, or by measuring from the glass line where at least 50 percent of the outer building wall is glass. The area includes outside walls, but excludes stairs, elevator shafts, flues, pipes, shafts, vertical ducts, and balconies.

Net Rentable Area: Multiple-Tenancy Floor Net rentable area of a multiple-tenancy floor is the sum of all rentable areas on that floor. Net rentable area is measured from the inside finish of permanent outer building walls, or from the glass line if at least 50 percent of the outer building wall is glass, to the office side of corridors, to other permanent partitions, and to the center of partitions that separate premises from adjoining rentable areas. No deductions are made for columns or projections supporting the building.

Net Rentable Area: Single-Tenancy Floor Net rentable area of a single-tenancy floor is measured to the inside finish of permanent outer building walls, or from the glass line where at least 50 percent of the outer building wall is glass. Rentable area includes the area within outside walls, excluding stairs, elevator shafts, flues, pipe shafts, vertical ducts, air-conditioning rooms, fan rooms, janitor closets, electrical closets, and other rooms not actually available to the tenants. Lavatories within and exclusively serving only the floor involved are included in the rentable area. No deductions are made for columns or projections necessary to the building.

Retail Store Space Retail space is measured from the building line; in the case of street frontages, it is measured from the inner surfaces of other outer building walls and from the inner surface of the corridor and from other permanent partitions to the center of partitions that separate premises from adjoining areas.

Income and Expense Analysis

Property managers have developed a standard set of accounts for office building management. An example of an accounting worksheet recommended by BOMA is shown in Figure 17-4. Note that rental income provides for separate listing of office storage and other sources of income. Expenses are classified by several groups: operating; fixed charges; and a separate category that includes expenses of alterations, decorating, and repairs. Note that fixed charges include the expenses of tenant alterations, which are sometimes paid by the owners and amortized over the lease. From net operating profit the statement provides for the deduction of ground rent, organizational expenses, interest, corporate taxes, and other financial expenses. Each summary account is supported by a more detailed set of accounts that corresponds to the entries listed in Table 17-3.

Given the technical terms and standard accounting statements, managers evaluate office buildings under a four part program:

operating experience
management objectives
building inspection
recommended annual budget

NAME OF BUILDING _____

YEAR ____

	Average Figures all Reporting Buildings	Averages in the Age Group of your Building	Averages in Same Size Group as your Building	Averages in your Region	Averages in Your City or City near You	Your Computation of Adjusted & Weighted Averages to Compare with your Bldg.	Actual Figures of your Building
A1 Cleaning							
A2 Electrical Systems							
A3a Heating							
A3b Air Conditioning-Ventilating							
A3c Combined Heating/Air Conditioning							
A5 Elevators							
A6a General Building Costs							
A6b Administrative Costs							
A7 Energy Expenses							
TOTAL OPERATING 'A'							
B1 Alterations—Tenant Area							
B3 Decorating—Tenant Area							
TOTAL CONSTRUCTION 'B'							
TOTAL A and B							
C1 Insurance							
C2a Property Taxes—Land							
Property Taxes—Building							
C2b Personal Property Assessment							
TOTAL FIXED CHARGES 'C'							
TOTAL EXPENSE A, B and C							
NET (Before Cap. Charges)—GAIN —LOSS							
Lease Expense							
Amortized Tenant Alterations							
C3 Depreciation							
NET (Before Cap. Charges)—GAIN —LOSS							
OFFICE RENTAL INCOME							
STORE RENT							
BASEMENT RENT							
SPECIAL AREA RENT							
Total Rental Income							
Miscellaneous Income							
Electricity Income							
TOTAL INCOME							

Figure 17-4 A data comparison worksheet using standard accounts for office buildings. (Source: 1978 Downtown and Suburban Office Building Experience Exchange Report, Washington, D.C.: Building Owners and Managers Association International, 1978, p. 159.)

Operating Experience Operating experience is judged by verifying past income and expense statements. The analysis rests not on the most recent statement but on income and expense reports over the past 3 to 5 years. There are two reasons for the analysis of past operating experience; first, usually an owner's latest statement will cover only out-of-pocket expenses. If no expenditures have been made for replacing carpets, lobby furniture, or exterior or interior painting, income statements will be distorted. A review of past income statements will show the degree of maintenance and number of replacements authorized by the owner. Furthermore, the analysis of past operating expenses reveals historical trends in expenses, which are usually increasing.

For instance, the annual report published by BOMA records operating expenses for 226 identical buildings from year to year. A four-year comparison of changes in these buildings suggests the degree to which expenses and operating incomes have changed over the most recent year. These results are reported for calendar year 1974 to 1977 in Table 17-3. Note that over 4 years, office rental income increased from $6.24 to $7.22 per rentable area—a 15.7 percent increase. Over the same period, total operating expenses increased 21.1 percent from the $3.99 experienced in 1974.

More specific data on suburban office buildings may be obtained by studying the annual suburban office report issued by the Institute of Real Estate Management. This report covers office projects within a 30-mile radius of a metropolitan area and outside central business districts. The latest report covered income and expenses of 302 suburban office buildings of over 5,000 square feet in which 80 percent or more of the rentable area was occupied by office tenants.

The report summarizes income and operating expenses for office buildings, which are classified by metropolitan areas; by regional areas; and if the sample is sufficiently large, by building size, building type, age groups, and rental range. Table 17-4 shows the median income and expenses per net rentable office area, with low and high limits, for seventeen buildings in the Houston, Texas area. Each table gives the average occupancy level and the expense/income ratio, including the expense of tenant alterations amortized over 3 or 5 years.

Table 17-3 Selected Operating Expenses of 226 Office Buildings: 1974–1977

Operating item	Year (cents per square foot)		Percentage of change
	1974	1977	
Cleaning cost	80.8	96.3	19.2
Energy cost	70.1	107.7	53.6
Labor cost	102.6	121.3	18.2
Real estate taxes	128.2	133.5	4.1
Total operating expenses	399.0	479.1	21.1
Office rental income	623.9	721.6	15.7
Total operating income	606.0	723.3	19.4
Average gain	149.2	165.0	10.6
Average loss	127.9	107.0	-19.5
Average vacancy	4.4%	6.3%	43.2

Source: Adapted from *1978 Downtown and Suburban Office Building Experience Exchange Report,* Washington, D.C.: Building Owners and Managers Association International, 1978, pp. 12–13.

Table 17-4   Annual Income and Operating Expenses of 17 Suburban Office Buildings, Houston, Texas

Building Age: 6 Yrs. or Less

Income and expenses	Amount per net rentable office rent		
	Median	Low	High
Gross income			
Offices	$6.07	$6.03	$7.35
Retail	—	—	—
Parking	.39	.33	.50
Escalation	.16	.14	.24
Miscellaneous income	.03	.01	.03
Vacancy	.25	.08	.56
Utilities			
Electricity	.50	.48	.57
Water	.03	.02	.04
Sewer	.02	.02	.02
Heating fuel	—	—	—
Gas	.05	.05	.09
Fuel oil	—	—	—
Electricity	.07	.07	.07
Steam	—	—	—
Other	.38	.38	.38
Combination electric	.89	.73	.89
Total energy plant	—	—	—
Janitorial			
Payroll/contract	.41	.39	.45
Cleaning supplies	.04	.04	.06
Miscellaneous	.05	.01	.06
Maintenance and repairs			
Payroll	.09	.08	.13
Supplies	.03	.01	.06
Heating/ventilation and air-conditioning repairs	.03	.02	.06
Electrical repairs	.02	.01	.02
Plumbing repairs	.01	.00	.01
Elevator repair/maintenance	.04	.04	.06
Exterior repairs	.00	.00	.01
Roof repairs	.00	.00	.00
Parking lot repairs	.00	.00	.00
Decorating—tenant	.06	.02	.07
Decorating—public	.02	.01	.02
Miscellaneous repairs	.03	.02	.03
Administrative			
Payroll—administrative	.09	.08	.23
Advertising	.03	.00	.03
Management fee	.25	.17	.27
Other administrative	.04	.04	.06

Table 17-4 *(Continued)*

Income and expenses	Amount per net rentable office rent		
	Median	Low	High
Other payroll costs			
Payroll taxes	.00	.00	.01
Employee benefits	.01	.00	.01
Insurance	.04	.03	.08
Services			
Landscape	.03	.01	.05
Trash removal	.01	.01	.01
Security—payroll	.05	.04	.07
Window washing	.00	.00	.00
Snow removal	—	—	—
Miscellaneous	.02	.01	.02
Net operating costs	1.82	1.81	2.15
Real estate taxes	.56	.47	.73
Other tax/fee/permit	.12	.08	.12
Total operating costs	2.58	2.27	2.75

Source: Adapted from *1977 Income/Expense Analysis: Suburban Office Buildings*, Chicago: Institute of Real Estate Management, 1977, p. 39.

On a national basis, the IREM summarizes the median annual income and operating cost for offices in their report. These results are shown in Figure 17-5. On an average basis, dollars per net rentable office area for the last year reported totaled $2.78 compared to total actual collections of $5.66, a net operating income of 49.1 percent of total actual collections.

Figure 17-5 Median annual income and operating costs: suburban office buildings. *(Source: 1977 Income/Expense Analysis: Suburban Office Buildings, Chicago: Institute of Real Estate Management, 1977, p. 124.)*

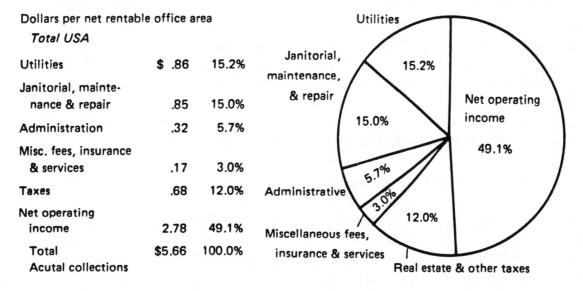

Dollars per net rentable office area
Total USA

Utilities	$ .86	15.2%
Janitorial, maintenance & repair	.85	15.0%
Administration	.32	5.7%
Misc. fees, insurance & services	.17	3.0%
Taxes	.68	12.0%
Net operating income	2.78	49.1%
Total Acutal collections	$5.66	100.0%

While published annual reports provide an invaluable guide for judging vacancies, expenses, and gross rents, the best reference is a comparison with operating results of similar and competing buildings. Published reports are usually at least 1 year old; they cover a wide variety of buildings that may differ from the buildings studied; and they may not be comparable with respect to location, office services, and quality of space. If vacancies, expenses, and gross income do not compare closely with those of comparable buildings, questions are raised with respect to wasteful practices, poor management, or below-market rents.

An intensive review of expenses covers three main categories: the service contract, operating expenses, and expenses omitted from operating statements.

1 *Service Contracts* Service contracts may be easily verified by utility bills and by contractual agreement for services rendered. The property manager will determine the date contracts may be terminated and the extent of services covered. Rental income would be verified by rent records and by records of income from miscellaneous services such as vending machines, garage rents, and coin-operated equipment. Taxes would be reviewed with city, county, township, or school officials.

2 *Operating Expenses* Operating expenses must be verified during the building inspection. They cover lamp replacements, cleaning supplies, payrolls, building maintenance, tenant alterations, decorating expense, mechanical equipment, repairs, and past management practices. In each instance the expenses and services rendered are compared with data for similar buildings locally and with published reports.

3 *Expenses Omitted from Operating Statements* It is not unusual to find certain accrued expenses deferred and not reported in earlier years, such as the replacement of carpets, exterior painting, roof repairs, advertising, legal fees, court costs, and the like. An evaluation of the condition of personal property such as lobby furniture is made during the checking of the inventory. During the course of this inspection retail merchants and their rental will be verified by securing credit reports of tenants and competing merchants in the area.

Lease income will be judged by a review of the rent roll. Leases will be reviewed to determine when each lease expires, including the tenant's name, type of business, office number, and space rented (including storage). Leases will be listed according to whether options for renewal are available and according to the way charges for heat, lights, and power services are billed or supplied to tenants.

Particularly important are lease stipulations that control the operation of elevator service, air conditioning, lights and heat, and hot water during nights, holidays, and weekends. In sum, expenses are closely related to the condition of the building and the level of services provided. Property managers interpret expenses and make future projections on the basis of a detailed interior and exterior inspection.

Management Objectives Management objectives determine operating policy. Some owners want tax shelters; others prefer to maximize current income; still others invest for capital appreciation. Within this framework, it is management to a large extent that determines the desirability of the building and the efficiency of tenant services. Management may compare operating policy with how operations promote or handicap the realization of stated objectives.

Figure 17-6 The 100-story John Hancock Center in Chicago is the tallest combined office-residential building in the world. In addition to serving institutional advertising objectives, the building has considerable rentable space. The complex includes 812,000-square feet of office space, 705 condominiums, and five restaurants. Retail stores are leased through the twelfth floor. *(Source: Photo courtesy of John Hancock Mutual Life Insurance Company.)*

For one thing, the policy toward maintenance and replacements is particularly vital; it affects the increase or decrease of expenses. That is, for a limited time maintenance such as replacement of carpets and interior and exterior painting may be deferred. But at some point, continued profits require that these maintenance deficiencies be remedied. On the other hand, maintenance expenditures cannot be lavish. The point is that the building should be somewhere between poor and exceptionally good condition. Ideally, operations would be well balanced and result in a proper physical and acceptable operating condition.[2]

Building Inspection   Preferably, the building inspection is documented by a form covering the exterior, interior, and building equipment. In each instance, the condition, recommended repair or maintenance, and estimated expense would be shown for each item. For example, the exterior walls would be inspected by reviewing the condition of:

    type
    base
    top
    tuck pointing
    stone sills
    coping
    parapet walls
    terra cotta
    metal strip
    glass
    other

The building interior deserves considerably more detail. Items judged according to their character or condition, needed repair or maintenance, and their expense would include the following general categories:[3]

    lobby
    interior doors
    stairways
    corridors
    office interiors
    windows
    public restrooms
    basement area

In each case the item would be judged according to added detail. For instance, office interiors would include an inspection of:

[2] For additional discussion consult John D. Azzara, "Building Analysis Points to Profitability as New Account," *Journal of Property Management*, 35(3):129–135 (1970).
[3] Forms to itemize building condition are available from the Institute of Real Estate Management, National Association of Realtors®.

ceilings
walls
floors
lighting
fixtures
switches
electrical outlets
radiators
air conditioning
doors
transoms
hardware
baseboard

The review of equipment is more technical. Frequently mechanical engineers with specialized experience may be necessary. The items reviewed would include:

elevators, passenger and freight
boiler equipment
water softeners
compressors
vacuum pump cleaning system
hot water heaters
vacuum pumps
insulation
air conditioning
electrical equipment

The technical nature of this inspection can be seen by the amount of detail needed to cover hot water heaters, which are judged according to inside lining, steam coils, insulation, gaskets, thermostats, steam traps, safety valves, fire box, fuel burners, and the like. Besides noting the present condition, the inspection would indicate the (probable) remaining economic life.

Furthermore, these estimates would be supplemented by judgments about the quality of service rendered—for example, about the average waiting time for elevators. More specifically, each item of equipment would be viewed according to three questions:

1   Is the equipment adequate at present and is it well maintained?
2   Is it of high or poor quality?
3   What is its probable economic life?

For instance, are the number and quality of restrooms (and their maintenance) adequate for the public and tenants? Are offices serviced with sufficient electrical outlets and wall switches? And is the electrical system of sufficient capacity to carry tenant loads?

In brief, the inspection of equipment identifies the degree of past maintenance and the replacement policy of past management. The inspection might indicate that while services, equipment, and facilities were adequate for the early years of the building, they may be inadequate in terms of current tenant requirements. Today, the general appearance, layout, lighting, type of electrical fixtures, floor coverings, sound proofing, insulation, and current tenant usage may justify considerable repair, updated maintenance, and remodeling.

Recommended Annual Budget At this point, the property manager judges the office building from the point of view of tenants: the building, its utility for office purposes, and its operation. From a review of competing buildings, recommendations for the appropriate tenant occupancy may be made. Property managers recommend a maintenance program and remodeling of exteriors, interiors, lobbies, elevators, and corridors.

Given the program of physical improvement, maintenance, and management policy, the manager prepares a pro forma operating budget. The budget includes: (1) recommended expenditures to adapt the building to the current tenant market, (2) recommended expenses of operation, and (3) estimated rent roll that will take effect after the management plan has been executed. In short, the management budget represents a forecast of income, expenses, and capital expenditures to place the building in its optimum condition for the purpose of maximizing net operating income.

SUMMARY

It is convenient to classify office buildings by age of building, height, size, and whether its location is downtown or suburban. Buildings may also be classified as speculative or owner built. Some property managers divide office space into class A, B, or C divisions: The A group represents prestige and new modern construction, while C buildings represent older structures in less suitable locations.

A functional classification includes (1) institutional, (2) general commercial, (3) medical/dental, and (4) industrial office space. The first group services financial institutions and other companies that construct buildings for their own use. Similarly, the medical/dental buildings and industrially oriented office buildings are special structures that require unique facilities. For the most part, managers deal with the general commercial building suited to multiple-tenant occupancy.

Depending on the tenant market, office buildings seek to locate near financial centers, near public buildings such as courthouses, near customers and transportation, and near parking convenient to employees and customers. Surveys show that the cost of space leads all other considerations in the selection of office space. Transportation and highway facilities, the environment, and the labor market are next in importance. The least important locational factors relative to the first four items and the location of allied industry are recreation, proximity to airports, and location of competitors.

Office buildings tend to be profitable to the degree that they meet *market feasibility standards* and to the degree that they exhibit *financial feasibility*—the analysis of gross income operating expenses in relation to cost. Market feasibility starts with associating the demand for office space with the local employment mix. For each community and for each industry, there tends to be a relationship between the number of employees who need office space and the total employment. In general, 15 to 20 percent of new employment requires office space, though the percentage varies widely from city to city.

Accordingly, the demand for office space depends partly on a projection of employment by industrial classification and the office-employee coefficient—the number of employees requiring office space in proportion to total employment. Allowing 200 square feet per office employee provides a basis for projecting the office space demand as employment increases.

The total demand for office space, while it is related to total population and to the employment base, arises from (1) the demand for additional space by existing tenants, (2) new tenants who relocate from other communities, (3) newly organized businesses, (4) tenants who upgrade their space requirements, and (5) tenants who vacate abandoned space.

The demand is then related to changes in the supply, which are determined by: (1) new office construction (including remodeled space), (2) unrented space held over from preceding years, (3) tenants who reduce office space, and (4) tenants who move to other cities.

The comparison of these factors gives the *absorption rate*, which is defined as the demand for office space, less the supply available and supply projected. These projections are made from a building-by-building survey and a review of employment and population projections.

Building evaluation requires common agreement on certain technical definitions: namely, the gross area of the entire building, gross rentable area, net rentable area (multiple-tenancy floor), net rentable area (single-tenancy floor), and retail space. Buildings are judged according to a standard set of accounts that record gross income and operating expenses. A comparison may be made with annual published operating experience, which is summarized annually in publications by the Building Owners and Managers Association International and the Institute of Real Estate Management. In addition, property managers compare operating experience with that of nearby comparable buildings.

A specific building will be reviewed according to *operating experience, managing objectives*, the *building inspection*, and the *recommended annual budget*. Expenses are judged according to outstanding service contracts, past operating expenses, and operating expenses not covered in past operating statements. Suburban office buildings, according to the Institute of Real Estate Management, typically operate under a net operating income of 49.1 percent of dollars per net rentable office area.

Considerable technical expertise is exercised in making building inspections. An inspection will intensively review the *exterior*, the *interior*, and the *building equipment*. The inspection will identify the type of construction, its present condition, and the cost of needed repairs, maintenance, or remodeling. Equipment, because of its complexity, may require an evaluation by a trained engineer who records the present condition and the remaining probable life. Furthermore, the inspection will evaluate the adequacy of tenant services in relation to management objectives.

It is largely management objectives that determine future operating expenses. Past management policies control the level of past repairs, maintenance, and replacements, and partly dictate the proposed annual budget. The property manager completes a building analysis by preparing a pro forma operating expense statement and proposed budget that leads to maximization of net operating income.

DISCUSSION QUESTIONS

1 Explain the different methods of classifying office buildings.
2 Describe the main locational preferences of office building occupants.
3 Explain how the employment base relates to the potential demand for office space.
4 What are the five sources of demand for office space? Give examples to illustrate your answer.
5 What determines the supply of office space and its projection? Give your answer in terms of five main supply factors.
6 Explain and give an example of how to estimate the office absorption rate.
7 What technical definitions are important to evaluating office income and expense data?
8 Explain how you would judge the operating experience of an office building; what three categories are important to evaluating operating expenses?
9 What is the importance of management policy?
10 Review the items and steps you would take in making a building inspection. Explain fully.
11 What factors would you include in recommending an annual office building budget?

KEY TERMS AND CONCEPTS

Institutional building
General commercial building
Medical/dental building
Industrial office space
Locational preferences
Employment base
Demand for office space
Supply of office space
Absorption rate
Demand projections
Space overhang
Service contracts

Gross area of entire building
Gross rentable area
Net rentable area: multiple-
   tenancy floor
Net rentable area: single-
   tenancy floor
Retail store space
Operating experience
Management objectives
Building inspection
Recommended annual budget

SELF-QUIZ

Multiple-Choice Questions

_____ 1 The functional classification of office buildings consists of: (a) Institutional buildings, speculative, and owner-built structures; (b) Industrially oriented office buildings, medical/dental buildings, and downtown and suburban buildings; (c) Institutional, general commercial, medical/dental, and industrial buildings; (d) Old and new buildings, and speculative or owner-built structures.

_____ 2 Which of the following statements is correct? (a) Surveys have shown that the cost of space is the single most important consideration in selecting office space; (b) Recreational facilities, according to survey, are the least important to office site selection; (c) Larger offices give greater weight than smaller offices do to the importance of the local labor market; (d) All of the above.

_____ 3 Which of the following statements is *not* correct? (a) The demand for office space is unrelated to the employment base; (b) Cities reveal varying relationships in the number of square feet of office space per person; (c) It is more likely that office space now over 50 years old will be replaced within the next decade; (d) Office employees generally require an area of 200 square feet per person.

_____ 4 Which of the following (is, are) included as part of the demand for office space? (a) The demand for additional space by existing tenants; (b) Newly organized businesses and new tenants relocating from other communities; (c) Tenants who upgrade their space requirements; (d) All of the above.

_____ 5 In estimating the supply of space, which of the following would *not* be considered? (a) New office construction; (b) Unrented office space held over from preceding years; (c) Abandoned buildings that may be converted to new office space; (d) Tenants who are going out of business.

_____ 6 Which of the following defines the absorption rate? (a) The demand for office space, less the office supply; (b) The demand for office space in high-growth communities; (c) Office space needed in communities experiencing no economic growth; (d) None of the above.

_____ 7 The net rentable area, multiple-tenancy floor, may be defined as: (a) The gross rentable area, including outside walls, stairs, elevator shafts, flues, pipe shafts, vertical ducts, and balconies; (b) The area measured from the inside finish of permanent outer walls, or from the glass line if at least 50 percent of the outer wall is glass, to the office side of corridors, other permanent partitions, and the center partitions that separate premises from adjoining rentable area; (c) The rentable area within outside walls, plus stairs, elevator shafts, flues, pipe shafts, vertical ducts, air-conditioning rooms, and other rooms not actually available to tenants; (d) Space measured from the exterior building line.

_____ 8 An evaluation of operating expenses of preceding years would concentrate on: (a) Service contracts, operating expenses, and expenses not covered in the operating statement; (b) Property taxes, service contracts, and insurance premiums; (c) Expenses not covered in the operating statement, utility costs, and the depreciation allowances; (d) Annual operating expenses, service contracts, and income taxes.

_____ 9 An office building inspection will include an evaluation of the present condition and needed expenses of repair, maintenance, or remodeling on: (a) Interior walls, floors, and exterior; (b) Building equipment, tenant alterations, and utilities; (c) Building exterior, interior, and equipment; (d) None of the above.

_____ 10 Which of the following would be relevant to an evaluation of building equipment? (a) Is the equipment presently adequate and well maintained? (b) Is it of high or poor quality? (c) What is its probable economic life? (d) All of the above.

Answer Key

1 (c), 2 (d), 3 (a), 4 (d), 5 (c), 6 (a), 7 (b), 8 (a), 9 (c), 10 (d).

Fill-In Questions

1 _____ serve banks and other companies that construct buildings mainly for their own use.

2 Surveys have suggested that the most important locational factor is the_____ _____ .

3 The demand for office space in relation to the supply available is referred to as _____ .

4 The average office area required per office employee is approximately_____ _____ .

5 Supply factors resulting from favorable changes in community economic growth include_____and the_____ _____ .

6 If the demand for office space equals the available supply, the absorption rate is _____ .

7 Net rentable area of single-tenancy floors includes areas within outside walls, _____ stairs, elevator shafts, flues, pipe shafts, vertical ducts, and other space not actually available to tenants.

8 An intensive review of office expenses covers three main categories:_____ _____, _____, and _____ _____ .

9 Management objectives determine ———————————— ———————————— .

10 The building inspection covers the exterior, the interior, and ————————————

———————————— .

Answer Key

1 Institutional offices
2 cost of space
3 market feasibility
4 200 square feet
5 new office construction, "space overhang"

6 zero
7 less
8 service contracts, operating expenses, expenses omitted from operating
9 operating policy
10 building equipment

SELECTED REFERENCES

Downtown and Suburban Office Building Experience Exchange Report, Washington, D.C.: Building Owners and Managers Association, annual issues.

Gonczy, Stephen I.: "The Office Building Manager: A Jack of All Trades!" *Journal of Property Management*, **41**(6):267–271 (1976).

Income/Expense Analysis: Suburban Office Buildings, Chicago: Institute of Real Estate Management, annual issues.

Kilroy, John B.: "Owner/Developer Decisions Determine Marketibility," *Buildings*, **64**(8):49–52 (1970).

Lex, Richard A.: "Marketing Studies for Office Buildings," *Real Estate Review*, **5**(2):101–103 (1975).

Chapter 18

Office Building Management Techniques

After studying this chapter, you should be familiar with:
1 The marketing of office space
2 Techniques of making a competitive market analysis
3 Office leasing practices: the building standard and work letter
4 Management operations
5 Office remodeling
6 Common energy conservation techniques for office buildings

The key issues in building management concern the marketing of office space, management operations, and leasing practices. In addition, today's managers must devote time to the analysis of energy conservation techniques. In serving these ends, managers develop files on competing offices; they refine their selling skills, and they assume all the problems of an administrator who is responsible for a going concern. Moreover, office leasing requires a certain specialization not found in other property types. Even energy conservation requires special applications for office buildings.

MARKETING OFFICE SPACE

Property managers assume a dual role: they must operate the building to maximize income, and they must make sure that the building is continually occupied. In this latter role, success at marketing space hinges on a study of competitive office buildings, as well as a knowledge of available space and special techniques to attract new tenants. While some of these procedures are more significant for new buildings, the points mentioned apply equally to existing buildings.

The Competitive Market Analysis

For an established metropolitan center, most tenants move from older to newer buildings; this is historically true, for instance, in the downtown Chicago loop. To lease new space, property managers undertake a personal canvass of prospects within the immediate area of the new building. This means that managers must determine how much space each user in the immediate vicinity occupies, how many people work in the available space, and more importantly, who are the decision-making executives. Records are maintained on dates when leases expire and on the corresponding square foot rental. To secure these data, property managers make a door-to-door canvass.

The canvass starts with a survey of buildings within the immediate area. The canvass extends to more distant space—in a widening circle—until the building is leased. A record is kept of every call, with a summary of telephone calls, personal visits, and "follow-up" mailings. This last is recommended because not more than 10 or 15 percent of prospects will say yes at the first proposal. The visits are arranged by telephone canvassers who average 50 calls per day, including 25 conversations with decision-making executives. Prospects who show interest are provided with an analysis of space needs.

Analysis of Space Needs While certain tenants may take additional space at a higher cost as they move to new space, a financial analysis may show that new space costs less than the existing space.

This result follows for several reasons: first, the interior designer may suggest a more efficient use of office space. A more efficient office layout may reduce space requirements typically by 10 to 15 percent. More than likely, if tenants have expanded and occupied the same building for 3 or more years, they have probably added space as needed without planning for an integrated, functional layout for their current operation.

Secondly, by placing a dollar value on tenant-supplied services, the existing space may cost considerably more than the cost indicated by rent per square foot. For instance, the tenant who has paid 50 percent of the cost of partitioning, lighting, telephone, and electrical outlets should prorate the cost over the life of the lease. Tenant alterations that cost $500,000 over a 10-year lease represent a cost of $50,000 per year, and for 100,000 square feet of space represent an annual cost of $.50 per square foot.

Thirdly, office employees who work in obsolete, poorly designed, and poorly equipped offices show higher rates of turnover. Old-style construction and inadequate heating and air-conditioning facilities, among other deficiencies, increase employee turnover at a substantial net cost to the tenant. This cost, in effect, represents an addition to the actual cost of rented space. In other cases tenants have been known to lease 75,000 square feet of space when a more efficient layout would reduce their requirement to 45,000 square feet. After adjustments for these deficiencies, the actual rental costs of existing space could be as much as 75 percent above the cost of new space.

Common Deficiencies Office buildings completed in the late 1920s or early 1930s reveal certain functional inefficiencies in the form of poorly heated interior offices, the lack of central air conditioning, inconvenient elevators, and massive interior columns. These deficienices commonly result in a 10 to 20 percent loss of space compared to recently constructed buildings. In contrast, new construction adds certain amenities, namely, sound insulation, superior lighting, air-conditioning, elevator capacity and speed, movable partitions with new ceiling systems, light controls, and thermostatic controls. Even buildings of the 1940s and 1950s may be challenged by the more efficient construction of today.

Moreover, tenants make new demands because of sophisticated office equipment that requires the latest air conditioning, humidity controls, floor loading capacity, ceiling height, power requirements, and specialized electrical wiring. As a result, new buildings show more efficient utilization of space so that tenants who move may need less space in new buildings (with added utility) in comparison with their existing space. A professional office planner will work toward this goal.

Knowledge of Available Space

Like the salesperson selling a house, the agent must know building details. Among the leading questions that may be anticipated are the following:

1 What are the rules and hours for unloading supplies at the loading dock?
2 What is the history of tax and other escalation clauses?
3 What procedures are followed in gaining access to the building during non-business hours?
4 What services are provided during office business hours and holidays (heating, cooling, water services, and elevator service)?
5 How many footcandles of lighting do you provide?
6 What are your cleaning and trash removal practices, including window washing?
7 What provisions do you have for fire protection?
8 What security measures have been provided?

Building managers should be prepared to emphasize unique features: cafeterias, public restrooms, conference rooms, vending machines, and services that appeal to tenants and their employees.

In their presentation, managers are advised to quote rent according to the per square foot cost per month rather than in annual dollars per square foot. Also, managers express additional charges for electricity, other utilities, property taxes, or insurance in terms of dollars per square foot per month. In other words, property managers not only know the building details but they point out building prestige, locational value, convenience, and efficiency, remembering all the while that they will be asked a series of questions about building operation and services.

Office Space Promotion

In the process of making contact with prospects, the general rules of good selling prevail. Attitude, appearance, and planning of the presentation must be of the highest order. Managers follow the usual sales procedures in evaluating successes and in reviewing failures.

While telephone and direct mail techniques are used, the most effective approach is personal contact. With each contact, the agent completes an office building survey questionnaire for each tenant. Such a form is shown in Table 18-1, which provides information on the existing tenancy. If the tenant shows interest, a record of each contact will be made leading, hopefully, to lease negotiation.

In negotiating the lease, the agent reviews management rental policy. For instance, the square foot rental may include heat, electricity, water, janitorial service, and elevator service (described in terms of frequency and quality). Tenants may be allowed a maximum dollar allotment for office partitions. Some managers allow 1 linear foot of standard partitioning for each square foot of rental space. Conversely, management may furnish one telephone and one electrical outlet for a certain minimum area of rented space. Agreement must be reached on the floor covering; generally, tenants pay for carpets or special floors beyond the standard floor tile. Usually management provides for fluorescent lights and a suspended ceiling.

In considering tenant alterations, most managers recommend that tenants pay for special construction since alterations for a specific tenant will be unlikely to suit other tenants. In negotiating space, it is recommended further that tenants with fewer employees be situated next to larger businesses. With the longer-term leases typical of the larger businesses (say 10 years), and with smaller businesses limited to 1 to 3 years, the larger businesses are provided with the possibility of space for later expansion.

In promoting office space, most managers find newspaper advertising to be fairly ineffective. Direct mail, telephone canvass, and personal canvassing are preferred. Some managers concentrate on specific groups such as insurance companies, accountants, employment agencies, and the like. In each company the property manager contacts the key person.

OFFICE LEASING PRACTICES

The lease of a new building requires agreement on leasing policy. The rental schedule must be established according to the office rental market and competitive space.

Table 18-1 Office Building Survey Questionnaire

I   Tenant _____ classification _____

II   Bldg. _____ suite no. _____

III Sq. ft. occupied _____

IV   Rent per month $ _____

V   Rate per sq. ft. $ _____

VI   Date of original occupancy _____

VII Date lease expires _____

VIII Renewal options _____If yes, terms _____

     _____

IX   Services provided: (check)

     A Air conditioning _____

        1 Central _____

        2 Window _____

        Ownership of unit: owner _____ tenant _____

     B Janitorial _____

        1 At what interval?_____

        2 Includes washing and waxing of tenants' floors? _____

     C Electricity _____

        1 Who pays for abnormal use? _____

        2 Fluorescent tubes by: landlord_____ tenant _____

     D Heat _____

     E Parking _____

        1 Free _____

        2 Monthly charge $ _____

     F Hours of operation of building _____

     G Security _____

     H Other _____

X   Would tenant be interested in move?   Yes _____ No _____

     A If yes, what is anticipated requirement? _____

     B If no, why? _____

IX   Remarks: _____

     _____

     _____

Source: Developed from a form recommended by C. R. Griffith, Jr., CPM.
See "Office Building Feasibility Study: For Medium-Size Metropolitan Areas,"
Journal of Property Management, 34(6):246–250 (1969).

A lease form must be developed with special clauses common to standard form leases. Preferably the printed form will include special stipulations that avoid the long riders and amendments to printed clauses. Rental adjustment clauses would be developed to keep the tenant from making a searching inquiry into building owner accounts.

In this task a leasing plan would be followed that typically reserves the top floors for premium tenants. The next lower floors would be held for tenants that appreciate the prestige of higher office space. Some floors will be reserved for full-floor tenants. The lower floors typically would be developed for multiple-tenant occupancy. Such a plan avoids a situation where tenants select floors in a random pattern that places one or two tenants on every floor. If this pattern develops, the owner cannot satisfy prospects for full-floor or multifloor space.

An office lease that covers about 95 percent of office leases in Chicago provides for special terms necessary to the office lease. Before the lease is prepared, certain issues must be negotiated. George R. Bailey of Turner, Bailey & Zoll (Chicago) recommends that 10 leading questions be resolved before the lease is signed:

1 Does the lessor pay taxes?
2 Does the lessee pay property taxes in part or entirely?
3 Does the lessor or lessee maintain the building?
4 If the lessor maintains the building, is the obligation on the structure only?
5 Who has the obligation of placing and paying insurance?
6 What are the provisions for rent escalation or for reappraisal of rent?
7 What are the provisions for subletting?
8 Who pays special assessments?
9 Who pays for unanticipated improvements required by law over the lease term?
10 What are the provisions for restoration of premises when the lease terminates?

For instance, an agreement on janitorial services would typically state:

The lessor shall provide: (a) janitor service in and about the premises on Saturdays and Sundays, holidays excepted. The lessee shall not provide any janitorial service without the lessor's written consent. If the lessor's consent be given, such janitorial service shall be subject to the lessor's supervision but at the lessee's total responsibility. The lessee shall not provide any janitorial service in the premises except through a janitor contract or employees who are, and shall continuously be, in each and every instance satisfactory to the lessor.

The lease agreement, in further illustration, would normally require the owner to supply heat from 8 a.m. to 5 p.m. and on Saturdays until 1 p.m., Sundays and holidays excepted. The office lease will normally require elevator service during business hours and Saturdays until 1 p.m., Sundays and holidays excepted. Similar provisions relate to air conditioning, electricity, water service, and other utilities.

Alterations usually require the owner's advance written consent. The agreement might require that the tenant pay the cost of all such alterations and additions and also the cost of decorating occasioned by such alterations and additions. Leases provide that alterations become the property of the lessor upon termination of the lease. Furthermore, the lessor may request that the lessee remove additions and other alterations, and failure to do so gives the lessor the right to remove tenant improvements and charge the tenant for the cost.

Special attention will be given to the use of premises. For example:

The lessee shall not display, inscribe, paint, maintain, or affix on any place in or about the building any signs, notice, legend, direction, figure or advertisement except on the doors of the premises and on the directory board and then only such name or names that matter in such color, size, style, place, material that shall first have been approved by the lessor in writing.

The critical importance of the "use clause" requires considerably more language than space allows here. While fairly restrictive, agreement on tenant use and enforcement of these provisions ensures that each tenant will be protected from encroachments by other tenants.

The complex detail of an office lease is suggested by Table 18-2. It should be noted that leases are unique to each transaction. Negotiations usually lead to riders attached to the lease that cover special needs of the tenant. A clause in the miscellaneous section of the lease provides for variation in standard lease terms by stating: "Provisions typed on the back of this lease and signed by the lessor and the lessee and all riders attached to this lease and signed by the lessor and the lessee are hereby made a part of this lease as though inserted at length in this lease."

The Building Standard

The *building standard* is an itemized account of the construction that the owner agrees to supply and install for each tenant. The building standard lists construction work agreed upon during lease negotiations, and covers interior items of construction provided by the owner at the owner's cost, for example, partitioning, lighting, ceilings, floors, doors, telephone, electrical outlets, hardware, painting, venetian blinds, or drapes. The building standard will be defined by the work letter.

The Work Letter

A fairly detailed document, the *work letter* supplements the lease agreement. It defines the agreement between tenant and owner concerning work the landlord agrees to furnish as part of the rent. A typical work letter would cover:

tenant's plans and specifications
landlord's plans and specifications
landlord's work
tenant requirements in excess of the building standard
scheduled delivery of tenant's plans
delays in landlord's work
tenant's entry prior to commencement date
entry after substantial completion

On the first point, tenant's plans or specifications, agreement will be reached on who prepares architectural and mechanical working drawings. A delivery schedule for the plans, provisions for landlord approval, and processing of tenant changes in plans

Table 18-2 Subject Outline of an Office Lease

I	Granting clause and rent schedule
II	Service
	A Janitor service
	B Heat
	C Water
	D Passenger elevator service and freight elevator service
	E Electricity
III	Lessor's title
IV	Certain rights reserved to the lessor
V	Default under other lease
VI	Liability for acts or neglect
VII	Holding over
VIII	Assignment and subletting
IX	Condition of premises
X	Alterations
XI	Use of premises
XII	Repairs
XIII	Untenantability
XIV	Eminent domain
XV	Lessor's remedies
XVI	Subordination of lease
XVII	Notices
XVIII	Miscellaneous

Source: Building Manager's Association of Chicago.

are among the more important items covered in a work letter. In the section dealing with landlord's plans and specifications, other significant items will be covered, namely, electrical, plumbing, heating, ventilating, and air conditioning—and the degree to which the landlord may make substitutions and changes in the shell, core, and tenant areas. The owner will detail items to be furnished as part of the building standard.

More significantly, tenant requirements to be made beyond the standard of the building will be identified in considerable detail. Substitutions, limitations on substitutions, and construction delays are among the key issues. Rules will be established for tenant construction and the method of estimating and pricing work. Time of payment for extra work on the part of the owner for the tenant and circumstances controlling the issuance of a certificate of completion are among other topics found in the work letter.

Because tenants may have special computer and other office equipment, details on floor loading, air conditioning, plumbing, electrical loads, and telephone equipment must be acceptable to both parties. Here the location of partitions, doors, ceilings, outlets, and other equipment required by the tenant will be identified. Decorating plans, ceiling heights and materials, and failure to meet the schedules represent other matters for negotiation. These last three items deal with the timing in the flow of work undertaken by both tenant and landlord. In short, the agreement anticipates problems encountered during construction. In this sense it may be the most crucial element of the lease.

MANAGEMENT OPERATIONS

Few laypersons recognize the complexity of building operations. A high-rise building of 600,000 square feet or more may require 50 to 100 persons directly working full time on building operations. The final number depends on the number of service contracts arranged to perform certain operations such as office cleaning, window washing, and repainting or redecorating. The larger high-rise office buildings will have an organization similar to the one shown in Figure 18-1.

Management Staff

The smaller office building will usually be headed by a building manager who supervises (1) the *mechanical superintendent*, who is responsible for electrical service, redecorating, plumbing and heating, and air conditioning; and (2) the *service manager*, who assumes responsibility for janitorial service, cleaning, window washing, and other tenant services.

While the organizational chart of Figure 18-1 provides for functional operations, considerable supporting staff would generally be required. For instance, the 50-story Seattle First National Bank building, with a gross area of 622,476 square feet, employs four executives, the operations manager, assistant manager, night superintendent, and night supervisor. One clerk-typist serves the management staff.

Besides these supervisory personnel, two day janitors and a day maid and night worker supplement other personnel. Cleaning is undertaken by a staff of 30, in addition to three wall washers and four toilet cleaners. Floor finishers, window washers,

Figure 18-1 Organizational chart for office building management.

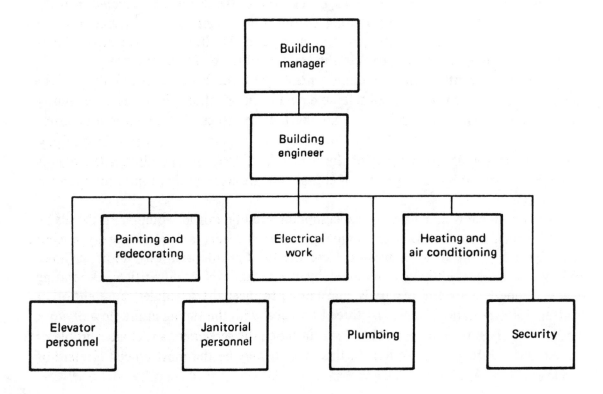

three night security workers, and three others service the electrical, heating, and air-conditioning systems. The building employs three building receptionists and three staff painters.

Depending on the building design and the lease agreement, management bases staff needs on functions performed for the tenant. Typically these functions would support:

cleaning
electrical system
heating
air conditioning/ventilating
plumbing
elevators
tenant alterations
repairs-maintenance
decorating
personnel hiring and training

For instance, office cleaners may be expected to service an area of 2,000 to 2,500 square feet per hour. Given the square foot area, this ratio indicates the number required to staff the nightly cleaning staff.

The same analysis holds for other operations. Each function is allocated a unit of time. For example, one person may be able to clean and service 18 washrooms a day. If a building has 72 washrooms, four persons would be required daily. Similar ratios may be calculated for floor cleaning, window cleaning, and even changing fluorescent lights and washing light fixtures.

Office Remodeling

In adapting older office space to new tenants, a property manager has two main options, and possibly a third. Depending on tenant needs, the office may be laid out according to either an *integrated* or a *compartmented* plan. The former calls for open general office space with a minimum of partitioning. This plan gives more flexibility, is more economical, and results in better worker supervision. Under this plan, office workers share equal facilities. See Figure 18-2 for an example of an integrated layout covering the four floor plans of the Sears Tower in Chicago.

Integrated office space must be uniformly lighted and must have modules for under-floor ducts for telephones and electrical outlets. Air conditioning and sound conditioning should be suitable for office use. As a compromise, movable partial-height partitions may be used in open general areas, giving maximum flexibility in desk arrangement. The movable partition adapts to continuous strip overhead lighting layouts, with structural modules for telephone, lighting, and air conditioning.

Under the compartmented layout, offices are partitioned, providing space for the exclusive use of executives, their assistants, secretaries, and other office personnel. For example, suppose that the office employed 150 professional people who served eight functions. The 150 personnel then would be partitioned so that space would be

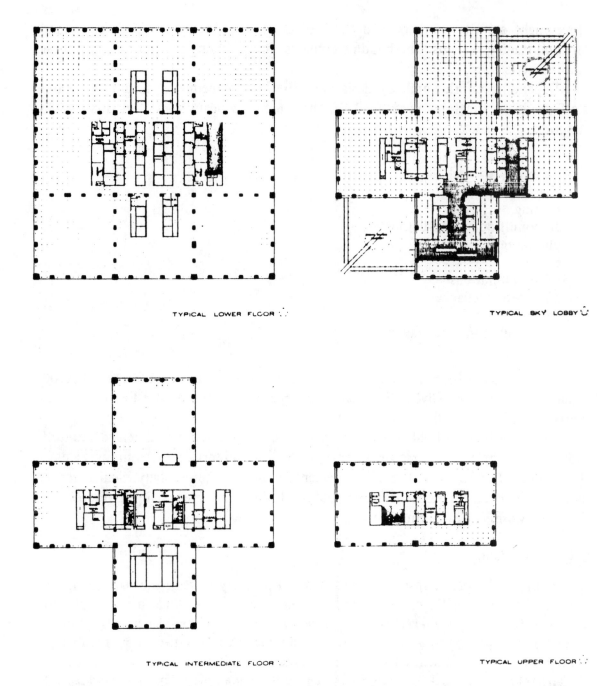

TYPICAL LOWER FLOOR

TYPICAL SKY LOBBY

TYPICAL INTERMEDIATE FLOOR

TYPICAL UPPER FLOOR

Figure 18-2 An integrated floor plan layout. The diagrams show the available floor space in modular form for the 110-story Sears Tower in Chicago. *(Diagrams supplied by Sears, Roebuck and Company.)*

available for supervisory staff and units of eight sections with their separate secretarial and service staffs. Usually, executives and professional personnel prefer a compartmented layout. The detail of a compartmented layout is shown in Figure 18-3.

A variation that departs from the more common regimented office layout is the *landscaped office*, which maximizes available space. It avoids fixed partitions or completely open space. In contrast, office space is functionally divided with plants and low screens in place of fixed partitions. Screens are usually 55 or 72 inches high. Plants are placed according to work flow patterns.

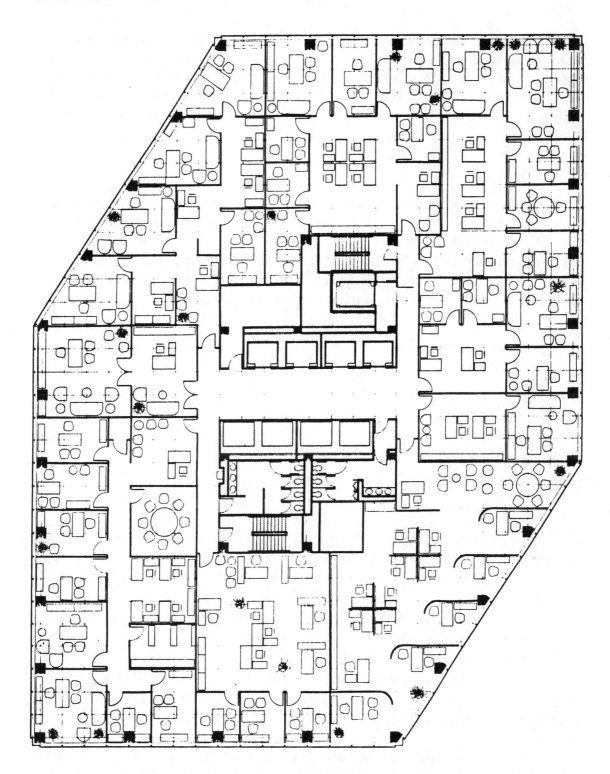

Figure 18-3 A compartmental floor plan for a typical floor of the Orbanco Building in Portland, Ore. *(Courtesy of Edward Petersen, Skidmore, Owings & Merrill, Portland, Ore.)*

While maintaining the integrated plan, landscaped offices give a higher measure of individual privacy. Proponents claim a saving in work efficiency and greater flexibility in space planning. Major attention is given to uniform air conditioning, heating, and soundproofed ceilings. The main problems lie in the heating, ventilating, air-conditioning, lighting, power, and telephone distribution systems, with special attention given to the acoustical design.

Remodeling Procedures

Given preliminary decisions on the preferred layout, the first step requires preparation of the architecturally designed office layout. The architect will lay out the building according to preferred placement of interior partitioning with a floor plan drawn to scale (without dimensions) and with furniture scaled in place; door swings will be noted with the placement of partitions and windows. The layout scheme is purposely kept simple for the tenant. The cost of remodeling will incorporate:

> demolition of existing partitions
> wall construction
> doors
> electrical construction
> lighting
> heating
> ceiling
> air conditioning
> decorating

The architect will attempt to salvage existing walls, but in some instances demolition will be required. Ordinarily the largest single expense is wall construction, which would typically consist of galvanized metal studs, with sheet rock on each side, fastened to the floor and to a false ceiling. Less privacy prevails if space dividers are used, such as "bank partitions," which extend 5 or 6 feet in height. Their cost is usually measured according to the number of linear feet.

Preferably doors are remodeled by rehanging, by revarnishing, and by adding new hardware—an operation generally less expensive than new doors. To some extent the type of doors installed will be controlled by local building codes. Some areas require interior doors that have a stated fire rating, which makes hollow-core doors obsolete.

Remodeling will usually entail expensive electrical, lighting, ceiling, and new heating, ventilating, and air-conditioning construction. Depending on the space utilization, electrical outlets will extend from the floors or ceilings or along the wall. Wiring may involve new fluorescent light fixtures recessed in new ceilings. The design will meet standard footcandle requirements.

Similarly, engineering advice will be required for ceilings, not only because of their appearance but because of the desired sound insulation. Building engineers will suggest necessary duct work to adequately serve newly partitioned space.

Professional advice is recommended for decorating. Interior decorators often suggest vinyl covering as a less expensive alternative to painting. A combination of wood paneling, mirrored walls, imitation brick or stone, and wall-to-wall carpeting completes the design.

In some respects decorating is one of the more critical issues. Most tenants may not be able to judge the quality of other building services and equipment, yet the quality of decorating will be more apparent to the tenant and to clients. Final cost estimates of redecoration will be based on per unit values:

Remodeling item	Cost basis
Architectural fees	Per square foot
Demolition costs	Square feet of wall space
Wall construction	Linear feet
Electrical	Per square foot
Duct work for heating and air conditioning	Lump sum
Redecorating	Lump sum
Carpets	Per square foot

The financing for remodeling depends on the rental market. If the competition for tenants is keen, the owner probably pays for remodeling. If the converse holds, the tenant pays for remodeling costs. Often there will be a compromise. Tenants may be asked to amortize a certain share of the construction cost over the lease with interest, which is added to the monthly rent. While this increases the cost per square foot, it allows the tenant to remodel space to suit current needs.

ENERGY CONSERVATION: OFFICE BUILDINGS

Like residential buildings, office buildings are subject to intensive energy conservation measures. *Relamping*—the replacement of high-wattage light bulbs with lower-wattage or fluorescent fixtures—timing devices that lower hot water availability during off-peak hours, and specially installed thermostats that have maximum and minimum limits for heat and cooling are representative of energy retrofitting measures.

The innovations for offices are more common among new buildings. Recommendations for new construction concern the selection of the site, orientation of the building on the site, construction for energy efficiency, and new heating and air-conditioning systems. A brief summary of recommendations grouped according to these subject areas seems worthwhile.

Site
1 Use deciduous trees for summer shading and windbreak for up to three stories.
2 Use evergreen trees for summer and winter sunshading and windbreaks.
3 Reduce paved areas; use grass and other vegetation to lower outdoor temperatures.

4 Use ponds and water fountains to reduce outdoor air temperature around buildings.

5 Locate buildings where they will minimize wind effects on exterior surfaces.

6 Select sites that allow optimum orientation to minimize yearly energy consumption.

The Building

1 To reduce heat loss, construct buildings to minimize the north exposure.

2 In other areas construct buildings to minimize the southern exposure to lower temperatures.

3 Reduce infiltration by avoiding cracks and joints in the building.

4 Provide solar control for walls and rooms in areas in which solar heat proves feasible.

5 Reduce infiltration by reducing cracks around doors and windows.

    a Provide external doors with weather stripping.

    b Seal windows.

    c Provide entrances with vestibules or revolving doors.

    d Reduce the ratio of window area to wall area: use double or triple glazing.

    e Provide exterior shade that reduces direct sunlight but reflects light into occupied spaces.

    f Use permanently sealed windows to reduce infiltration.

Heating, Ventilation, and Air Conditioning

1 Provide controls to shut down all air systems at night and weekends except when used for economizing the cooling cycle.

2 Lower indoor air temperatures in winter and increase temperatures in summer.[1]

While this list does not exhaust all possibilities, these points demonstrate the trend toward new construction that saves energy. Typical of buildings constructed for energy conservation is the headquarters building of IBM General Systems Division in Atlanta, Georgia. The main innovation of this 375,000-square-foot, 11-story office building is the recycling of heat generated by ten computers for building space heat. This one innovation alone saves enough electricity annually to meet the power needs of 700 average homes.

The building owners report that approximately 3.4 million BTUs per hour may be recovered, which is enough to heat the building until temperatures drop to 11°F, at which time the boilers supplement recycled heat.

The building is located on a hillside providing summer shade and air cooling from a 5-acre lake 15 feet deep. The lake was planted with some 5,000 fish to help with insect control and to restore the ecological balance. The temperature system is controlled by computer from a weather station that measures the dew point, wind velocity, and temperature changes, allowing the system's computer to compensate for building needs.

[1] For additional recommendations consult "New Guidelines for Energy Savings in Office Buildings," *Journal of American Institute of Architects*, 61(5):32–38 ff (1974).

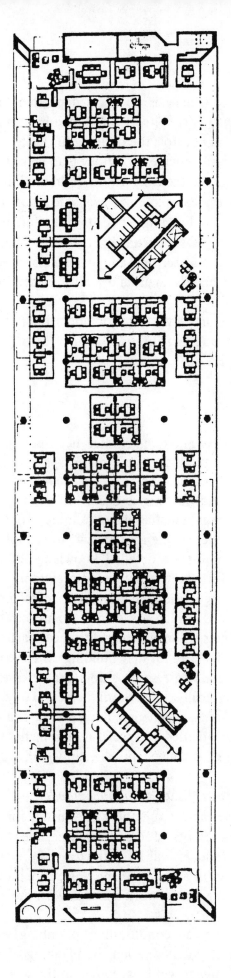

PLAN - TYPICAL FLOOR

Figure 18-4 Typical floor plan layout in the energy-efficient IBM Systems Division Building in Atlanta. Heat from computers is recycled for space heating. Note the uniform size of partitioned offices.

Because the computer facility is critically dependent on a continuous, uninterrupted power source, power is supplied from two substations supplemented by emergency power generation that controls the building life system.

Other design innovations provide for a floor plan layout that gives every executive equal office space. Interior landscaping and a combination of compartmentalization and open space for service areas maximize available floor space. The secretarial staff occupies the periphery of the building while the files and storage are centered in the interior space. The building is supported by columns. Maximum space flexibility is provided by movable partitions, screens, and an all-glass exterior wall. Trash chutes on each floor, a conveyor system for mail, and janitor closets on each floor help reduce elevator use.

The security system starts with exterior doors operating with coded cards; ten video cameras survey the building interior, with three outside cameras that monitor entrances and the parking lot.

SUMMARY

Though property managers work to maximize net operating income, they must be skilled in marketing space. In leasing new office space, managers rely heavily on a door-to-door canvass. The canvass constitutes a survey of buildings over an increasingly widening area until the building is leased. In dealing with prospective tenants, managers analyze space needs, emphasizing the more efficient use of new space and possibly the lower *real cost* per square foot relative to occupied older space.

Leasing office space requires a detailed knowledge of the buildings, their operation, services, and facilities. Rent is expressed preferably on a cost per square foot per month basis, and in negotiation, management rental policies are reviewed with prospects. Tenant alterations, which are subject to negotiation, are usually assumed by the tenant if special construction is required to meet particular needs.

Leasing practices, particularly for new buildings, reserve upper floors for premium tenants. In multitenant buildings, some floors are reserved for full-floor tenants. Larger businesses, with typically longer-term leases (10 years), are preferably surrounded by short-term tenants, which gives longer-term tenants opportunities for later expansion. Leases must be adapted to special requirements of office tenants. Special attention is given the use of premises and the supply of utilities during normal business hours.

Every office building establishes a *building standard*—an itemized account of the construction that the owner agrees to supply and install for each tenant, that is, partitioning, lighting, ceilings, floors, doors, telephone, electrical outlets, and interior decorating. The building standard will be defined by the work letter, which is a fairly detailed document executed in advance of the lease. It defines the agreement between tenant and owner concerning tenant work and the work the owner furnishes as part of the rent.

Details on floor loading, air conditioning, plumbing, electrical loads, and telephone equipment may be negotiated. Even the planning of the flow of work undertaken by both tenant and owner will be specified in the work letter. In sum, the work letter anticipates problems encountered during the preparation of premises for tenants. And to this extent, the work letter constitutes one of the more critical elements of lease negotiations.

The management of a high-rise office building may require 50 to 100 persons who directly work full-time on building operations. Smaller buildings will be headed by a building manager who supervises the mechanical superintendent and service manager responsible for janitorial, cleaning, window washing, and other tenant services. Management and its staff depend on a survey of per unit labor time required to perform essential building services.

In planning an office remodeling, managers decide on an *integrated* or *compartmented* layout plan. The integrated plan refers to open general office space with a minimum of partitioning, which is more economical and more flexible, and provides better work supervision. The compartmented plan requires partitioned offices providing for exclusive space for executives and other office personnel.

A variation in these plans is illustrated by the *landscaped* layout that maximizes available space, avoids fixed partitions, and provides for an open space appearance. Under this plan the office is functionally divided with plants and low screens, which are portable and usually limited to 55 or 72 inches in height. Screens and plants are arranged to satisfy work flow patterns.

Office remodeling, which minimizes new wall construction and new door replacement, usually requires some demolition of existing partitions, new wall construction, remodeling of doors, electrical lighting, heating, ceilings, air conditioning, and interior decorating.

Energy conservation, which is more efficient for new construction, may require retrofitting common to other properties, primarily the replacement of inefficient lighting fixtures, new limiting thermostats, and similar measures. Other energy efficiencies are gained by adapting a building to the site with appropriate tree shading and slope exposures and with special building design to reduce heat loss. Heating and ventilation equipment, in the same manner, follow new designs for a more efficient energy-saving system.

DISCUSSION QUESTIONS

1 Explain how you would undertake a competitive market analysis.
2 What points would you emphasize in analyzing tenant space needs?
3 What are the common deficiencies of office buildings constructed before the 1960s?
4 What questions may be anticipated in canvassing for new tenants?
5 What factors are considered in establishing a management rental policy?
6 What features would you recommend in developing a leasing plan for a high-rise office building?
7 What questions must be resolved before a lease is signed?
8 What points are covered in the building standard?
9 What is the usual content of a work letter?
10 Explain the typical organization for managing an office building.

11 What layout plans are available for remodeling office space?
12 What are the principal costs in remodeling office space?
13 Discuss six energy conservation measures for office buildings. Explain thoroughly.

KEY TERMS AND CONCEPTS

Competitive market analysis	The work letter
Office layout	Integrated office layout
Tenant alterations	Compartmented office layout
The building standard	Landscaped office layout

SELF-QUIZ

Multiple-Choice Questions

_____ 1 For an established metropolitan center, most new tenants come from: (a) The formation of new businesses; (b) Tenants' moving from older space to newer space; (c) Tenants who abandon unusable space; (d) Tenants' moving from suburban to downtown locations.

_____ 2 Financial analysis may show that new office space costs less than existing space because: (a) Tenants who move need fewer employees; (b) The higher rent per square foot of new space forces tenants to lease less space; (c) More efficient office layout may reduce space requirements by 10 to 15 percent; (d) Tenants who move usually experience a decrease in business volume.

_____ 3 Which of the following (is, are) common functional inefficiencies in 40- or 50-year-old office buildings? (a) Lack of central air conditioning; (b) Inconvenient elevators; (c) Massive interior columns; (d) All of the above.

_____ 4 Which of the following questions typically is *not* anticipated by agents leasing space? (a) What are the rules and hours for unloading supplies in the loading dock? (b) What is the history of tax and other escalation clauses? (c) What are the prevailing wage rates for window washers? (d) What are the cleaning and trash removal practices including window washing?

_____ 5 Which of the following (is, are) leading questions to be resolved before an office lease is signed? (a) Does the lessor or the lessee pay taxes and maintain the buildings? (d) What are the provisions for rent escalation and the right to sublet? (c) What are the provisions for restoration of premises when the lease terminates? (d) All of the above.

_____ 6 Which of the following statements is correct? (a) A work letter is prepared after the lease is signed; (b) The work letter defines the agreement between tenant and owner concerning work the landlord agrees to furnish as part of the rent; (c) The work letter covers all points essential to lease negotiations; (d) The work letter is a statement showing only the work performed by the owner for the tenant.

7 Which of the following statements is correct? (a) The building manager is responsible for supervision of the mechanical superintendent and the service manager; (b) The building manager supervises functional operations; (c) The manager bases personnel needs on an allocation of a unit of time for each building operation; (d) All of the above.

8 The integrated office layout: (a) Gives more flexibility, is more economical, and results in better work supervision; (b) Requires partitioning of office space used exclusively for executives and supporting personnel; (c) Is preferred by executives and professional personnel; (d) Provides office space that is functionally divided with plants and low screens.

9 Energy conservation measures for new office building construction: (a) Covers selection of the site, orientation of the building, and construction for energy efficiency; (b) Concentrates only on superior insulation; (c) Deals solely with the heating, ventilation, and air-conditioning systems; (d) Are not very effective in new office building construction.

10 Which of the following represents an energy conservation measure for office buildings? (a) Lower indoor temperatures in winter and increased indoor temperatures in summer; (b) Providing entrances with vestibules or revolving doors; (c) Reduction of exterior paved areas; (d) All of the above.

Answer Key

1 (b), 2 (c), 3 (d), 4 (c), 5 (d), 6 (b), 7 (d), 8 (a), 9 (a), 10 (d).

Fill-In Questions

1 The canvass of office space starts with a survey of buildings within the_____ _____.

2 Office employees who work in obsolete, poorly designed, and poorly equipped offices show higher rates of_____.

3 The most effective approach in marketing office space is the_____ _____.

4 In promoting office space, most managers find_____ _____to be fairly ineffective.

5 Office leases usually stipulate that_____require the owner's advance written consent.

6 The_____is an itemized account of the construction the owner agrees to supply and install for each tenant.

7 The_____defines the agreement between tenant and owner concerning work the landlord agrees to furnish as part of the rent.

8 The_____ provides for open general office space with a minimum of partitioning.

9 The_____ maximizes space by avoiding fixed partitions and completely open space.

10 In remodeling office space, it is advisable to prepare an _____ _____office layout.

Answer Key

1 immediate area

2 turnover

3 personal contact

4 newspaper advertising

5 tenant alterations

6 building standard

7 work letter

8 integrated office layout

9 landscaped office layout

10 architecturally designed

SELECTED REFERENCES

Collins, William J., Jr.: "What You Can Do to Save Energy in Your Offices and Plants," *Management Review*, 65(1):8–14 (1976).

Locke, W. W.: "Landscaping the Office Interior," *Journal of Property Management*, 38(2):70–74 (1973).

"New Guidelines for Energy Savings in Office Buildings," *Journal of American Institute of Architects*, 61(5):32–38 ff (1974).

Prior, Robert E.: "Remodeling Office Space," *Journal of Property Management*, 41(3):101–104 (1976).

Rubenstein, Albert I.: "Secrets of the Office Building Developer," *Real Estate Review*, 4(1):43–50 (1974).

Chapter 19

Managing Special Purpose Properties

After studying this chapter, you should be familiar with:
1. The management role in neighborhood rehabilitation
2. Techniques of managing single-family dwellings
3. Management recommendations for downtown redevelopment
4. General principles for managing industrial property
5. Techniques of managing industrial parks
6. Recommended management practices for "miniwarehouses"

For the present purpose, it seems worthwhile to review three management issues: the management of single-family dwellings, of downtown buildings, and of industrial property. Some managers work with numerous other properties such as marinas, golf courses, hotels and motels, and farms. Yet because these have a specialized nature, managers of these properties operate businesses rather than manage real estate. Consequently their management calls for special training in a particular business, which is beyond the present purpose. Single-family dwellings, downtown real estate, and industrial property, however, call for specialized real estate knowledge.

MANAGEMENT OF SINGLE-FAMILY DWELLINGS

In the last census, 37.1 percent of all occupied housing units were rented. There appears to be a continuing demand to manage single-family dwellings, for several reasons. Absentee owners, who find it more economical to rent than to sell, require professional management services. Managers work with small investors who purchase rental houses for their tax advantages and capital appreciation.

Furthermore, families with pets or children often prefer dwelling rentals to apartment rentals. Some firms specialize in managing vacation homes in resort areas. Usually these houses are rented by the day or by the week. And because of limited assets or income, some families have little choice but to rent residential houses.

Residential property management has certain advantages over the management of other properties: for one thing, residential houses that are rented are likely to be sold during the management contract, and the management firm is in the best position to secure an exclusive listing.

To take full advantage of the management business, Jack Carter Realty, Inc., of San Diego manages 180 dwellings and condominiums, which provide enough volume to employ full-time managers. Though salespersons account for most referrals to the management department, it is reported that 75 percent of the dwellings under management are sold through the company.[1]

Though the management does not require the technical knowledge and record systems of office buildings, shopping centers, and apartments, simple forms and routine procedures make this source of management a profitable undertaking. And because of the responsibilities assumed, property managers may charge fees of 10 or 15 percent of gross rentals. In many cases, duties of the property manager supplement the main office activities in listing and selling houses. To demonstrate these techniques, property managers assume two roles; they are frequently active in neighborhood rehabilitation as well as in managing the single-family dwelling.

Neighborhood Rehabilitation: The Management Role

The expertise of the professional manager seems suited to neighborhoods that show (1) declining trends in housing quality, (2) a rising level of rental occupancy, and (3) nonconformity with housing and other codes. If lenders are reluctant to finance houses in neighborhoods showing declining values, the services of management are even more highly recommended.

Neighborhood Conservation Corporations The problem is even more serious, since homeowners (or tenants) individually have little impact on neighborhood trends. In fact, if future neighborhood quality is questionable, property owners postpone improvements and defer maintenance, which results in even more rapid decline. In

[1] Al Watson, "Single-Family Rentals: A Goldmine or Loss Leader?" *Journal of Property Management*, 43(1):16 (1978).

this respect, the central role of the property manager is to develop a favorable attitude toward the neighborhood among owners and tenants. A favorable attitude encourages residents to maintain houses in good condition.

Joint action is best achieved through a housing association operating as a conservation corporation. The Southeast Organization of Kansas City, Inc., illustrates such a nonprofit neighborhood conservation corporation.[2] The neighborhood conservation corporation provides common services to improve the neighborhood. The emphasis is on private, not government, relief. Their goal is directed to:

1 Providing maintenance at lower prices
2 Minimizing crime and developing a greater sense of neighborhood security
3 Encouraging the sale or rent of dwellings by promoting the neighborhood

Given these goals, managers cooperate with community organizations that have a continuing interest in neighborhood preservation. Like the salesperson who concentrates on a neighborhood for listings, the property manager works with organizations to improve the neighborhood and gain additional management contracts. Representative organizations in this group include community councils, block clubs, model city neighborhoods, housing committees, and similar community groups.

The neighborhood selected should have at least 600 homeowners to provide a suitable inventory of houses for professional attention. With a neighborhood defined, the manager determines local policy with respect to municipal services, housing and building code enforcement, proposed public improvements, and available government assistance—local, state, or federal.

Neighborhood Management Program With these preliminary facts, managers propose a neighborhood management program. The program outlines the neighborhood services of the management organization; that is, the manager (1) negotiates maintenance contracts with local building contractors, (2) acts as the agent of the conservation corporation in dealing with government agencies and private contractors, (3) makes inspections to determine compliance with maintenance contracts, (4) recommends a public relations program to advertise the neighborhood, and (5) organizes a maintenance training program.

The management fee becomes a part of the conservation corporation operation budget. It may be based on the number of houses or it may be a membership fee based on a monthly charge.

Some managers go further and help draft a constitution, elect officers, and appoint committees. Preferably the management fee would be sufficient to support a project manager, with an inspection officer, bookkeeper, and two area maintenance workers for a 600-member neighborhood.

[2]Joe L. Mattox, "Neighborhood Management: Its Time Has Come," *Journal of Property Management*, 39(4):154 (1974).

In illustration, the typical inspection officer would develop programs to:

1 Correct conditions that encourage crime and vandalism
2 Eliminate vacant properties through rehabilitation or removal (including removal of abandoned cars)
3 Provide play space if children have no play space other than the streets
4 Repair gutters, downspouts, and broken windows, and repaint houses
5 Maintain lawns and repair fences
6 Organize the community to negotiate for the repair of sidewalks, curbs, and streets
7 Remove outside storage of garbage and junk
8 Correct conditions or circumstances that distract from the beauty and harmony of the neighborhood[3]

Thus the neighborhood manager coordinates a neighborhood management program with the management of individual houses. An increase in management contracts for individual dwellings not only provides new business but adds to the company reputation.

Managing Single-Family Dwellings

The management of single-family dwellings tends to be more profitable in neighborhoods adjacent to military or government facilities that have a high proportion of transient families. In these areas, management firms may pay management agents 50 percent of the gross leasing commission, a commission rate similar to sales commissions on dwelling sales. The management staff spends most of its time inspecting vacated property and handling tenant requests for repairs and maintenance. It will be appreciated that servicing 100 detached single-family dwellings is much more time consuming and costly than serving 100 units in a single apartment complex. Part of the compensation for these added costs lies in management agreements that give the management agent the right to an exclusive listing during the management agreement and 90 days thereafter.

Management Services In other instances, property managers experience economies of scale by providing an in-house maintenance service. Maintenance fees charged to the owner for these services tend to be lower than comparable contract rates. The property management of single-family dwellings, then, not only concentrates on the management task but includes maintenance and repair services for a fee, and listing rights if the property is placed on the market.

In arranging for the management of single-family dwellings, Jack Carter Realty, Inc., of San Diego provides management services that relieve the owner of common management responsibilities. As part of their services they perform the following duties:

[3] Ibid.

1 Advertise for tenants and supervise move-in procedures

2 Collect rents and deposits

3 Complete move-out procedures by professionally cleaning the premises after each occupancy

4 Provide 24-hour emergency repair service

5 With owner approval, pay operating expenses

6 Administer utility charges and other liabilities assumed during tenant occupancy

7 Administer monthly collections and disbursements during the management contract[4]

Because tenants are carefully screened with a credit application, the company reports that a substantial number of tenants become buyers; with a management inventory of 180 houses, they report gaining 3 listings per month as a result of this program.

In sum, the management of single-family dwellings is rewarding, providing that the property manager acquires a large inventory of dwellings under management. The larger inventory leads to certain economies of scale: in-house maintenance and repair services, listings and sales, and specialized full-time management.

Furthermore, the area served must be within reasonable commuting distance of management personnel. Finally, routines must be established to perform the main management tasks: rental collection, maintenance repairs, and recordkeeping. With these initial qualifications, single-family-dwelling management provides a source of income that does not have the seasonal variations common to real estate sales commissions.

Single-Family Dwellings as Investments In managing single-family dwellings, it is appropriate to recognize investment advantages. Because they require relatively small equity, they appeal to the small investor with $10,000 or less equity. They are relatively easy to finance under long-term mortgages. In the better neighborhoods, they will require relatively little maintenance. Their popular demand lowers vacancy losses. Compared to other income property, they are relatively easy to market; their liquidity adds to their attractiveness as an investment.

In fact, most investors look toward the tax shelter arising from the income tax deductibility of mortgage interest and property taxes. Usually, the relationships among mortgage payments, expenses of operation, and rent do not provide much cash flow. Consequently owner compensation, in contrast to the situation with other income properties, must be found in tax shelter and capital appreciation.

With rising housing values (assuming a stable or growing neighborhood), persons in the higher-income tax brackets (over 40 percent) may convert relatively high marginal income tax rates to lower marginal capital gain taxes. This point is demonstrated by a house that was originally purchased for $47,500, held for 5 years, and financed with a $42,500, 9 percent, 25-year mortgage. In this example, a depreciation basis of $37,500 and 125 percent declining balance depreciation over 40 years

[4] Al Watson, op. cit., p. 17.

Table 19-1   Estimating Tax Shelter Benefits

Annual gross income		$5,160
Less: vacancy (1 month)	$430	
expenses	750	-1,180
Annual net operating income		$3,980
Less annual mortgage payments		-4,284
Gross spendable income		$ -304
Add tax shelter benefits		352
Spendable income		$ 48

provided annual tax shelter. Suppose that the property were held for 5 years and sold for $70,000 (an annual compounded price increase of approximately 8 percent).

With a monthly rental of $430, annual net operating income was projected at $3,980. With annual mortgage payments of $4,284, it would appear that the owner is subject to a negative return of $304 after mortgage payments. After considering tax shelter benefits, spendable income is increased to $48. These data are shown in Table 19-1.

Tax shelter benefits arise from the mortgage interest and depreciation deduction. For the first year these taxable deductions equal $4,987, resulting in a tax shelter of $1,007. Assuming a 35 percent income tax rate, this provides a benefit of $352 (see Table 19-2).

Table 19-2   Tax Shelter Calculations*

Annual net operating income		$3,980
Less: mortgage interest	$3,816	
depreciation		
($.03125 \times \$37,500$)	1,171	-4,987
Tax shelter		($1,007)
Tax shelter benefit (35% tax rate)		$ 352

*Mortgage interest may be derived from published mortgage tables or by using capitalization tables:

Monthly mortgage payment	$ 357.00
Less first month's interest	
($.09/12 \times \$42,500$)	-318.75
	$ 38.25
Principal payments, first year	
$38.25 × 12.507508 (amount	
of one per period, 12 periods, 9%)	$ 478.00
Annual mortgage payments	$4,284.00
Less principal payments	-478.00
	$3,806.00
Add rounding error	10.00
	$3,816.00

Nominal differences between two methods result because of rounding errors. The newer calculators also make these calculations. For a fuller explanation, consult William M. Shenkel, *Modern Real Estate Appriasal*, New York: McGraw-Hill, 1978, p. 282.

Table 19-3   The Calculation of Capital Gains

Gross sales price	$70,000.00
Less sales costs (10%)	-7,000.00
Net sales price	63,000.00
Original cost	37,500.00
Less accumulative depreciation 125%, 40-year life	-5,505.00
Adjusted basis	31,995.00
Net sales price	63,000.00
Less adjusted basis	-31,995.00
Taxable amount	31,005.00
Less depreciation recapture	-817.50
Capital gain	$30,187.50

The tax shelter benefit of $352 results in an estimated spendable income of $48. This result follows because of the tax deductibility of the mortgage interest, $3,816, and depreciation of $1,171. It will be observed that these data apply only to the first year.

Next suppose that the property owner sells the dwelling for $70,000, representing an annual price increase of approximately 8 percent compounded. Under the assumptions given, the sale would result in a capital gain of $30,187.50. These data are summarized in Table 19-3. In this example, a sales cost of 10 percent provides for a net sales price of $63,000. To calculate capital gain, the original depreciation basis of $37,500 is reduced by the amount of depreciation declared over the 5 years. The adjusted basis is then $31,995.

The next step is to calculate the depreciation recapture. The 125 percent declining balance depreciation exceeds the straight line rates. The depreciation recapture under this assumption would be given by:

$$\$37,500 \times .1468 = \$5,505.00$$
$$\$37,500 \times .125 \;\; = \underline{4,687.50}$$
$$\$\;\;817.50$$

Straight line depreciation is found by multiplying the annual rate, 2.5 percent, times five years to give $4,687.50. Reference to depreciation tables shows that 125 percent declining balance depreciation approximates 14.68 percent over the first five years or $5,505.00, resulting in recaptured depreciation of $817.50.[5]

Under the Revenue Act of 1978, capital gains are eligible for a 60 percent deduction. For individuals, the balance is taxed at ordinary rates. Sale proceeds after tax, under the assumptions as given, are shown in Table 19-4. After the 60 percent deduction, the owner would be liable for taxable gain of $12,075. Since a tax rate of 35

[5] Alternatively, declining balance depreciation may be calculated arithmetically by multiplying $37,500 by 3.125 percent, which is equal to $1,171.87. Second-year depreciation would be found by multiplying ($37,500 - $1,171.87) × .03125. The rate of depreciation would be applied each year to the declining balance.

Table 19-4   Sales Proceeds after Tax

Capital gain	$30,187.50
Less 60% exemption	-18,112.50
Taxable gain	$12,075.00
Less income tax (ordinary rate, 35%)	-4,226.25
	$ 7,848.75
Tax on depreciation recapture	
($817.50 × .35)	-286.13
After-tax gain	$ 7,562.62
Add exemption	18,112.50
Sales proceeds after tax	$25,675.12

percent is assumed, the sale is subject to a $4,226.25 tax liability. Deducting the tax on the depreciation recapture of $286.13 gives an after-tax gain of $7,562.62. Adding the exemption gives the final sales proceeds after tax of $25,675.12.

This example does not imply that all dwellings increase in value. Poorly maintained dwellings, declining neighborhoods, and local unemployment may decrease the value of a given house. Tax shelter benefits with corresponding property appreciation depend on (1) favorable financing, (2) relatively high marginal income tax rates, and (3) property appreciation over the investment period. Indeed, tax shelter benefits may be regarded as compensation for assuming investment risks.

Rehabilitation of Rental Housing Some investors profitably purchase rental houses that are in poor condition. The risk here is that the cost of rehabilitation may not be economical because of extensive necessary repairs. Investors attracted to this program require careful estimates of needed repairs, an anticipated rental over 2 or 3 years, and an eventual sale for capital appreciation.

Houses suitable for this program must meet certain minimum standards. First there is the location. Such houses should be in a desirable location, convenient to neighborhood shopping and not adversely affected by surrounding properties. In these circumstances it is more likely that houses will increase in value above the improvement cost. Conversely, the cost of repairs may not be economically justified for a house in poor condition and in a poor neighborhood.

In these latter circumstances, only if other owners undertake rehabilitation would the project be feasible. Investors are not attracted to a $50,000 house that needs improvements costing an additional $10,000 if the improved house would only have a value of $53,000.

Then there is the condition of the home—a second minimum standard. Major structural repairs to heating, air conditioning, and plumbing should be avoided. To be sure, it may be worthwhile repairing a $100,000 structure with a new air-conditioning and heating system, but the same cost may not be justified for a more modest home. Some experts prefer that repairs and maintenance should be limited to 3 percent of the dwelling's value.[6]

[6]Kenneth R. Kuhn, "The Art of Cosmetic Improvements," *Real Estate Today*, 11(4):30 (1978).

The key to rental housing rehabilitation is that it requires correction of observed deficiencies in the exterior: the repair of exterior cracks in brick veneer, repainting, and inexpensive but adequate landscaping to make the outside more appealing. Landscaping should be limited to clearing weeds, removing overgrown shrubs, and trimming hedges. The interior may justify refinishing interior walls; replacing carpets; refinishing floors; and in some instances, adding curtains, blinds, drapes, bathroom vanities, and new kitchen cabinets. Some management firms specializing in single-family dwellings would arrange for rehabilitation with an in-house maintenance staff.

DOWNTOWN REDEVELOPMENT

Property managers are heavily committed to downtown redevelopment. While cities continue to lose manufacturing jobs, many show gains in government, finance, and service employment. Since 1967, some 80 percent of the 34 million square feet of office space constructed in the Chicago area has been situated downtown. The added 133,000 new jobs have resulted in total downtown office employment equal to 90 percent of total office employment in the Chicago area.[7] These developments suggest that downtowns will typically develop as service, educational, and cultural centers.

Mixed-Use Developments

A recent survey of 2,000 persons in the real estate industry by the Building Owners and Managers Association International confirms these trends. Data indicated that 86 percent of those surveyed were undertaking or planning building modernization. The building manager and owner developer were found to be the most heavily involved in modernization as compared to other groups. Most modernization plans covered commercial structures, that is, apartment buildings, retail stores, and shopping centers.[8]

A review of these trends suggests mixed-use development concentrated in retail, office, hotel, and motel projects. Major redevelopments calling for management of mixed-use developments are demonstrated by the Broadway Plaza and Century City (a 260-acre development) in Los Angeles, California. Likewise, Detroit's Renaissance Center and Atlanta, Georgia's Peachtree Center, or the Houston Center in Texas and Chicago's Water Tower Place, a 74-story multiuse project, are representative of multiuse projects.

Public-Private Cooperation

For the most part, successful downtown revitalization follows from joint public and private initiative. Under numerous local, state, and federal programs, cities offer investors redevelopment sites for new multiuse projects. Downtown redevelopment for multiuse projects tends to be feasible if:

[7] Harold S. Jensen, "The Future of the Cities," *Urban Land*, 37(2):3 (1978).
[8] "Modernization Increases," *Buildings*, 71(6):66–67 (1977).

1 The proposed use is appropriate for the site

2 The site available for proposed downtown development is ready for use

3 Sites are planned and vacant (sites covered with buildings and easements either raise costs of development or prohibit the best land use)

4 The local public agency provides investment incentives (frequently the community must provide assistance in the form of land value right-downs, special public improvements such as parking or improved street access, and property tax concessions)

5 The governing organization supports the project. This means that public agencies must help in gaining cooperation from local business and labor[9]

These are the main points that ensure multiuse project feasibility. Clearly these projects replace construction of single downtown buildings, which formerly were subject only to local zoning and building codes. In the past, downtown space was parceled into single lots for individual improvement by proprietary businesses that usually followed no set planning scheme. The result was inadequate parking, poorly integrated development, and in many cases, positioning of incompatible businesses. In short, the downtown lacked the planning and land-use controls common to the integrated shopping center.

INDUSTRIAL PROPERTY

The central concern of property managers in dealing with industrial property hinges mostly on managing industrial parks, and more recently, on the "miniwarehouse." The miniwarehouse is a specially designed facility that provides self-storage units structured in several buildings with doors providing access to each unit. Before covering these points, one must first consider certain general principles that are common to industrial property management.

General Management Principles

Though managing industrial property represents a specialized service, industrial properties show wide variation. Property managers deal with buildings leased to a single firm for manufacturing purposes; they also manage warehouses, distribution facilities, and industrial buildings for multiple occupancy. Add to this list certain specialized structures constructed for a particular manufacturing operation.

In the latter case, buildings tend to be constructed for *assembly lines*—buildings adapted to production of a single product. The contrasting industrial building adapts to production organized in *process centers*. Multiple-product firms such as prefabricated metal production will have process centers for such things as metal finishing, dye casting, metal lathes, or drill presses. These buildings require space for storage and flexible machine layouts.

Because of the differences among industrial processes, the manager must know industrial requirements with respect to ceiling height; floor load capacity; electric service requirements; loading dock design; and special utility requirements for heat,

[9] Harold S. Jensen, "Cities, How Well Are Your Sites Set?" *Urban Land*, 37(8):12-13 (1978).

steam, and waste water. Leasing industrial space, therefore, requires that managers match special tenant requirements with available buildings.

In leasing industrial space, moreover, managers qualify prospective tenants. Before approving tenants, their credit, business history, and financial status will be determined. In addition, the manager must review operations proposed by the tenant. Depending on the property in question, tenants may be rejected on grounds of noise generation, noxious smells, unsightly outside storage, or other operations that may increase insurance rates or disturb neighboring tenants. Tenants are supervised to prevent overloading of floors or operating premises in a way that was unanticipated during lease negotiations, such as the use of flammable materials in manufacturing operations.

Property managers preserve property values by maintaining exterior appearance, much the same way as they do with apartment or shopping center buildings. Industrial buildings require the same attention to exterior maintenance and landscaping. Buildings constructed for a tenant under a long-term lease, say 20 or 25 years, would be leased at a rental sufficient (1) to retire the mortgage during the lease term, (2) to provide building maintenance and repairs, and (3) to provide an acceptable investment. To gain mortgage financing, credit of the tenant must satisfy requirements of the mortgage lender. Property tax, insurance, and utility escalator clauses are common to these leases.

Industrial Park Management

Industrial parks may be defined as land developed according to a comprehensive plan for a community of industries under proprietary control. Proprietary controls refer to land-use controls that preserve industrial park attractiveness, besides controlling the selection of industry and its operations. The plan incorporates space for employee and customer parking, truck loading, and maneuvering; rail, truck, and employee traffic are separated. Frequently the industrial park plan requires landscaping and architectural approval before tenant or owner occupant construction.

Specialists in industrial park management concentrate efforts over a three-phase operation: (1) The implementation phase requires much coordination to establish the industrial park reputation. (2) After the park has been established, managers move to the second phase—emphasizing sales, leasing, and a marketing strategy. (3) The final phase largely constitutes a monitoring task of reviewing industrial operations and property maintenance. Hence, in large measure, industrial park management stresses sales, leases, and public relations.

The Initial Development Phase The importance of the initial phase is highlighted by a study that indicates that communities with less than 30,000 population *with* industrial parks had twice the number of jobs per 1,000 population as communities *without* industrial parks. In these communities there were fewer low-wage jobs and a higher percentage of high-paying jobs inside the industrial park than among firms locating outside the industrial park. Furthermore, manufacturers expressed preferences for locating in communities with organized industrial parks.[10]

---

[10] Mike McGuire, Chander Kanal, and Paula Lovett, "Land Has to Be Kept Ready for Site-Seeking Industry," *Industrial Development*, 146(3):16 (1977).

A model to estimate industrial land required for a given time, say 5 years, takes the form:[11]

$$ILR = \frac{(\Delta ME^t - LE - LC)}{EA - CS^{uc, es}}$$

where ILR = industrial land requirement
ΔME = change in manufacturing employment
    t = time (i.e., 1980–1984)
   LE = latent employment (unemployed returned to work)
   LC = latent capacity (plant expansion on site)
   EA = employees per acre
   CS = competitive surplus
   uc = unused industrial capacity (vacant buildings)
   es = existing industrial sites

To make effective use of this model, certain estimates are required for each of the items.

Industrial Land Requirements (ILR) ILR refers to the estimated land requiring development over a selected time, say 5 years.

Change in Manufacturing Employment (ΔME) The ΔME estimate is derived from a study of past changes and the most probable estimate of number of manufacturing employees anticipated over the study period.

Time (t) Time refers to the number of years for which the model applies, such as 1980 to the end of 1984.

Latent Employment (LE) LE are local employees formerly employed in manufacturing and presently unemployed. Since they return to former jobs, their reemployment will not require new industrial development.

Latent Capacity (LC) Because industrial firms purchase land for expansion, some expected growth in manufacturing employment will be absorbed by industries that expand present facilities. Again, this is a trend that will require no additional land.

Employees per Acre (EA) For each type of industry, there is generally a fairly common ratio between the number of employees and industrial acreage. Chemical plants and refineries tend to have a low number of employees per acre (8.7), while apparel firms, for example, have a larger number of employees per acre (19.0). With an estimated increase in employment, there will be a given number of acres required for new employees. The model may include separate estimates for several industries.

Competitive Surplus (CS) Competitive surplus refers to either unused industrial buildings (uc) or existing industrial sites ready for industrial development (es). Hence, industrial expansion may take place using the competitive surplus rather than on additional industrial land.

To implement a 5-year model, the manager must subtract the present employment from the projected employment at the end of 5 years. Then subtract the latent em-

---

[11] Adapted from ibid.

ployment and the growth of manufacturing expected to take place on vacant industrial land owned by present industry. Finally divide by the average number of employees per acre. The result will be the estimated acreage required for manufacturing over the next 5 years.

The Second Phase In the next operation, tenants with compatible goals are carefully selected to provide a community of interest. The marketing program seeks prospects who conform to permitted uses and who operate according to industrial park covenents.

The covenants go beyond the usual zoning code. The general purpose of industrial park covenants is stated by restrictions enforced in the Irvine Industrial Complex of Irvine, California:

> It is the intent and purpose of these covenants and restrictions to allow the location on the Property of general manufacturing activities, provided that such activities are confined within a building or buildings and do not contribute excessive noise, dust, smoke or vibration to the surrounding environment nor contain a high hazard potential due to the nature of the products, material or processes involved.[12]

These purposes are accomplished by permitted uses and development standards. The permitted uses, which are listed in broad categories, generally are confined to tenants or owner-occupants engaged in research activities, developmental laboratories, and like manufacturing. Permitted users must conform to development standards that control the placement of buildings, restrict land coverage (a 50 percent ratio is common), and provide standards for parking and landscaping. For example:

> The Front Yard Set Back Area of each site shall be landscaped with an effective combination of street trees, ground cover and shrubbery. All unpaved areas not utilized for parking shall be landscaped in a similar manner.

Generally, outside storage is prohibited, loading docks typically must be at the rear of the building, and signs and building construction must meet management approval.

The Third Phase In the final management phase, managers work closely with the industrial park occupant association. This group enforces standards of industrial park restrictions and covenants. Managers make semiannual inspections, gradually delegating enforcement of standards to industrial park occupants and municipalities. In short, professional management benefits tenants, the community, and the project profitability.

The Miniwarehouse

Started in Corpus Christi, Texas, the miniwarehouse typically consists of a complex of one-story buildings on 2-acre sites near residential and business neighborhoods. Tenants

[12] *Industrial Development Handbook*, Washington, D.C.: Urban Land Institute, 1975, p. 248.

may ordinarily select storage from 30 to 400 square feet. Individual buildings range from 20 to 40 feet wide and 100 to 400 feet long. Flexibility is provided by dividing space into hundreds of compartments with steel partitions that may be moved according to individual needs.

Some developers provide parking space with water and electricity for the outside storage space of recreational vehicles, mobile homes, and boats. On-site managers, who live on the site, provide 24-hour security and access. Surrounded by 6-foot-high chain-link fences, the grounds are locked at night; outside areas are well lighted.

The Demand for Miniwarehouses   The demand for miniwarehouse space falls into fairly narrow categories.

1 Apartment residents who need additional space for personal property
2 Homeowners who desire additional garage space for hobbies, storage, and workshops
3 Businesspeople who have limited storage in shopping centers or arterially located retail sites; they may lease additional storage space in the miniwarehouse at cheaper rates than the cost of comparable retail space
4 Salespersons who store samples for inventory
5 Contractors who prefer to store goods under secure conditions while constructing local buildings
6 Business offices that need additional and inexpensive storage space for files

Add to these groups military personnel, boat owners, and apartment operators who need space for storage of supplies and maintenance equipment.

Some managers report that three out of eight users of miniwarehouse facilities are apartment residents. It is claimed that approximately 23 out of every 1,000 apartment units need additional storage for household goods. Another 5 of 1,000 apartment dwellers require space for recreational vehicles.

Miniwarehouse Operations   To satisfy these demands, miniwarehouse location becomes fairly critical. Miniwarehouses tend to be more successful in densely populated areas. Preferably they are located in the direction of growth in areas that are more than 80 percent built-up with middle-income housing. The site selected should be within 2 to 5 acres and should be protected from excessive noise, odors, or other uses incompatible with industrial and commercial property. Access should be convenient to the local freeway system, with good visibility from well-traveled highways.

According to one authority, for a 2-acre site, it is recommended that five buildings (40 by 200 feet) with 40,000 total square feet provide for 250 rental units in the following proportions:[13]

[13]Edward L. Locke, "The Mini-Warehouse: A New Dimension in Industrial Property," *Urban Land*, 33(10):3–9 (1974).

Unit sizes (ft)	Mix (in percentages)
6 x 5/6 x 6	10
5 x 10/6 x 10	15
10 x 10	15
10 x 15	10
10 x 20	30
10 x 30	20
	100

Costs of operation include the salary for the resident manager, who typically lives in the resident manager's apartment, and his or her office; electricity; water; maintenance; security; insurance; and property taxes. These expenses are reported to range from 15 to 20 percent of gross income.

Other successful warehouses lease to machine shops, foundries, craftspeople, welding shops, light manufacturers, and private individuals. A typical 1,000-square-foot unit leases for $205 per month (1977), with an additional $39.50 for overhead lights, water, sewer, gas, and maintenance services, including garbage pick-up. Usually on a month-to-month tenancy, tenants are charged a $25 key deposit and the first and last months' rent. For the rental of multiple units, managers negotiate 12-month leases with a separate charge for clean up at the end of the lease.

In miniwarehouses, tenants are prohibited from keeping pets or using warehouse space as living quarters. Signs are prohibited, and no dangerous or hazardous materials may be stored on premises. While parking is provided for each 1,000-square-foot unit, cars are not allowed to park for more than 24 hours. Subleases are prohibited and tenants are required to carry public liability and property damage insurance.[14]

The main management duties consist of collecting rent and enforcing delinquent rent payments. Recordkeeping duties require monthly accounts that show receipts and disbursements. Resident managers are responsible for maintenance and marketing space to new tenants. The main marketing techniques employ billboards, brochures, and door-to-door canvassing of local businesses. Managers report success in renting space from referrals by other satisfied tenants.[15]

SUMMARY

For several reasons, the demand for professional managers of single-family dwellings will continue. Managers specializing in dwellings serve absentee owners who prefer renting to selling. Moreover, rental housing appeals to the smaller investor who gains from tax shelter and from capital appreciation. Families with children and pets frequently prefer the independence of dwelling rentals to apartment rentals. Furthermore,

[14] Stephen Dorcich, "Miniwarehouse/Maxiuse," *Real Estate Today*, 10(9):20–21 (1977).
[15] For additional detail, consult Richard E. Cornwell, *Miniwarehouse: A Guide for Investors and Managers*, Chicago: Institute of Real Estate Management, 1975.

managers have a ready source of clients among owners of "vacation" houses and occupants with questionable credit who favor the dwelling rental market.

In the rental of single-family dwellings, some managers participate in neighborhood rehabilitation. They negotiate management contracts with neighborhood housing associations organized as nonprofit conservation corporations. In this assignment, managers negotiate contracts for maintenance services, act as agent of the corporation in dealing with government agencies and private contractors, make inspections to determine compliance with maintenance contracts, and participate in neighborhood promotional programs. They also organize maintenance service and training programs.

Management fees are based on a monthly assessment against owner-members. The neighborhood management program leads to management contracts for individually rented dwellings.

Managing single-family dwellings requires a fairly large volume of houses that increase management efficiencies. The larger portfolio allows the manager to offer "in-house" maintenance repairs at less expensive rates than contract services. The management function contributes to sales commissions in that management agreements usually provide exclusive rights of listing during the management agreement and for 90 days thereafter. Management fees range from 10 to 15 percent of actual rent collected. Duties of the manager start with advertising for tenants, supervising the tenant move-in, operating the property during occupancy, and taking responsibility for move-out procedures.

Managers specialize in managing single-family dwellings purchased for investment purposes. Owners gain from tax shelter and capital gain tax advantages. In the better neighborhoods, rented houses have relatively little maintenance, are easily sold, and appeal to the smaller investor.

The rehabilitation of rental housing is usually confined to cosmetic treatment: repainting the exterior; refurbishing floors, interior walls, carpets, and the like.

With respect to downtown redevelopment, managers participate in mixed-use development: retail, office, and residential use (hotels, motels, and apartments). These projects require close working relationships with public agencies and private investors. Public and private cooperation overcomes deficiencies of downtown buildings that were formerly subject only to local zoning and building codes. The practice of developing single lots for individual improvement by proprietary business has been replaced by mixed-use development following downtown area development plans.

Managers of industrial property must learn industrial requirements with respect to ceiling height, floor load capacity, electric service requirements, loading dock design, and special utility requirements. Preferences range from buildings adapted to assembly line production to buildings arranged for a series of processes.

In leasing industrial space, managers qualify prospective tenants according to their industrial operation, their credit rating, and business history. And as with managing apartments or shopping centers, industrial property managers work to preserve property values. Some managers specialize in industrial park management that divides into a three-phase operation: The implementation phase, which establishes the industrial park reputation; the second phase, which emphasizes sales, leasing, and marketing strategy; and the final phase, which involves monitoring industrial operations and property maintenance.

Miniwarehouses are found in high-density areas providing space for apartment tenants and businesses and even homeowners who require additional storage and at relatively low space rates. To serve this market, the typical miniwarehouse occupies a 2-acre site improved with five buildings with a total of 40,000 square feet. The interior will be arranged in cubicles with removable partitions for maximum adaptability. On-site managers provide security, 24-hour access, and assistance in collecting rents. They keep monthly records, provide maintenance, and help market space to new tenants.

DISCUSSION QUESTIONS

1 Why will there be a continuing demand for the management of single-family dwellings? Explain thoroughly.
2 Explain how managers participate in neighborhood rehabilitation by working through a housing association; what are the goals of a neighborhood conservation corporation?
3 What services are provided by the management firms for neighborhood conservation programs?
4 What conditions are necessary for the profitable management of single-family dwellings?
5 Why are single-family dwellings managed as investment property? Explain thoroughly.
6 Under what conditions would you recommend rehabilitation of rental housing?
7 Under what circumstances would downtown redevelopment for multiuse projects tend to be feasible?
8 What general management principles would you associate with industrial property?
9 Describe the main duties of industrial park management under a three-phase operation.
10 Explain how you would estimate the demand for industrial land over 5 years.
11 What are the main characteristics of a miniwarehouse?
12 What groups are served by the miniwarehouse?
13 What are some of the restrictions imposed on tenants by miniwarehouse managers?

KEY TERMS AND CONCEPTS

Neighborhood rehabilitation
Neighborhood conservation
  program

Mixed-use development
Organized industrial park
Miniwarehouses

SELF-QUIZ

Multiple-Choice Questions

_____ 1 There will be a continuing demand for professional management of single-family dwellings largely because: (a) Single-family dwellings are built for their net operating income; (b) Rental housing appeals to the small investor who gains from tax advantages of ownership and from capital appreciation; (c) Single-family dwellings are exempt from rent controls; (d) Single-family dwelling rent is less than apartment rent.

_____ 2 Which of the following is associated with a neighborhood conservation corporation? (a) Providing maintenance at lower prices; (b) Minimizing crime and developing a greater sense of neighborhood security; (c) Encouraging the sale and rent of dwellings by promoting the neighborhood; (d) All of the above.

_____ 3 Which of the following is *not* a neighborhood service of the management organization? (a) Negotiating contracts for maintenance services; (b) Acting as agent of the conservation corporation in dealing with government agencies and contractors; (c) Appraising neighborhood houses for condemnation; (d) Recommending promotional steps to advertise the neighborhood.

_____ 4 In managing single-family dwellings, the management staff spends most of their time: (a) Collecting delinquent rents; (b) Inspecting vacated property and handling tenant requests for repairs and maintenance; (c) Soliciting new accounts; (d) Listing houses for sale.

_____ 5 Management fees for single-family dwellings typically are: (a) Less than 5 percent of actual rents collected; (b) 10 percent or more of net operating income; (c) 20 percent or more of gross possible income; (d) 10 to 15 percent of actual rent collected.

_____ 6 To rehabilitate potential rental housing, houses should: (a) Be in a desirable location convenient to neighborhood shopping; (b) Not be adversely affected by surrounding properties; (c) Not require major structural repairs to heating, air conditioning, and plumbing; (d) All of the above.

_____ 7 Downtown redevelopment tends to be feasible if: (a) The site available is ready for use and the use is appropriate to the site; (b) The site is suitable for major full-line department stores; (c) The site is developed exclusively for high-rise office buildings; (d) Retail use dominates the redevelopment plan.

_____ 8 Managers qualify prospective industrial tenants by reviewing: (a) Their credit, business history, and financial status; (b) Operations proposed by the tenant; (c) Operations that may increase insurance rates or disturb neighboring tenants; (d) All of the above.

_____ 9 In the second phase of managing industrial parks, the manager: (a) Emphasizes programs that establish the industrial park reputation; (b) Concentrates on industrial operations and property maintenance; (c) Emphasizes sales, leasing, and marketing strategy; (d) None of the above.

_____ 10 Which of the following represents operations permitted by tenants in a miniwarehouse? (a) Keeping pets or using warehouse space as living quarters; (b) Storing dangerous or hazardous materials if the fire department is notified; (c) Operation of hobbies and storage of personal effects; (d) Unlimited parking privileges.

Answer Key

1 (b), 2 (d), 3 (c), 4 (b), 5 (d), 6 (d), 7 (a), 8 (d), 9 (c), 10 (c).

Fill-In Questions

1 Joint action among neighborhood residents is best achieved through a housing association operating as a _____.

2 The management of single-family dwellings is rewarding providing the property manager requires _____ of dwellings under management.

3 Because rental dwellings require relatively _____, they appeal to the small investor.

4 Downtown revitalization results from combined _____ _____.

5 _____ refer to land developed according to a comprehensive plan for a community of industries under proprietary control.

6 The _____ refers to the estimated land requiring development over a selected time.

7 _____ go beyond the usual zoning code.

8 _____ refer to a complex of one-story buildings on 2-acre sites near residential and business neighborhoods.

9 Some managers report that three out of eight users of miniwarehouse facilities are _____.

10 Miniwarehouse expenses are reported to range from _____ _____ of gross income.

Answer Key

1 conservation corporation
2 a large inventory
3 small equity
4 public and private enterprise
5 Industrial parks
6 industrial land requirement
7 industrial park covenants
8 Miniwarehouses
9 apartment residents
10 15 to 20 percent

SELECTED REFERENCES

Cornwell, Richard E.: *The Miniwarehouse: A Guide for Investors and Managers*, Chicago: Institute of Real Estate Management, 1975.

Industrial Development Handbook, Washington, D.C.: Urban Land Institute, 1975.

"The New Downtown Complex," *National Real Estate Investor*, 18(8):24–30 (1976).

Kuhn, Kenneth R.: "The Art of Cosmetic Improvements," *Real Estate Today*, 11(4): 28–32 (1978).

Watson, Al: "Single-Family Rentals: A Gold Mine or Loss Lender?" *Journal of Property Management*, 43(1):16–20 (1978).

Index

432

  supervision, 178–183
    management policy book, 182–183
    responsive, 180–182
    routine, 180
Management:
  concept of, 291
  duties of, 126–127
  establishing policy for, 168–178
    resident manager, 169–177
      training of, 177–178
  general principles, 416–417
  leasing techniques, 300–303
    lease terms, 300–303
    performance, 303
  objectives, 376–378
  operations, 167, 292–300, 394–399
    office remodeling, 395–398
    remodeling procedures, 398–399
    social services, 300
    staff, 394–395
    tenant organizations, 295–296
    tenant selection, 296–299
  organization, 166–168
    and budget preparation, 167–168
    operations of, 167
    and record keeping, 168
  performance, 303
    occupant concern, 303
    responsiveness to tenant needs, 303
    strict rule enforcement, 303
  personnel policy, 183–187
    employee training, 185–186
    employment contracts, 187
    job performance standards, 186
    recruiting personnel, 184–185
  policies, 275–276
  policy book, 182–183
  responsibilities, 50–51, 158–160
    for problem tenants, 159
    and tenant guidebooks, 159–160
    to the owner, 320–322
  services, 410–411
  single-family dwellings, 408–415
    as investment, 411–414
    management services, 410–411

Management, single-family dwellings:
    neighborhood rehabilitation, 408–410
    rehabilitation of, 414–415
Management agreements:
  elements of, 126–138, 269
  general terms, 126
  management duties, 126–127
  management fees, 137–138
    compensation on income, 138
    cost of management, 137
    percent of gross income, 137
  responsibilities of owner, 127–128
  specialized, 128–137
    for condominiums, 131–132
    for consulting, 136–137
    for motels, 133–136
    for shopping centers, 128–130
    for vacation homes, 132–133
Management attitudes, 296–297
Management staff, 349–395
Management survey, 138–141
  economics of alternatives, 140–141
  income analysis, 139–140
  market analysis, 139
  neighborhood analysis, 139
  objectives, 138
  operating expense analysis, 140
  physical real property inventory,
    138–139
Managing, 9–11, 136–137, 304–307
  community of tenants, 9–11
  consulting agreements, 136–137
  housing for the elderly, 304–307
    design of, 305
    nonshelter services, 305–307
    tenant mix, 304
Market analysis, 139
Market for apartments, 221–225
  supply, 222–223
    floor area, 223
    other, 223
    room size, 223
  tenant demand, 223–225
    by groups, 224
    for units, 224–225
    localized, 224